Christopher Wordsworth

Theophilus Anglicanus

Manual of Instruction on the Church and the Anglican Branch of It

Christopher Wordsworth

Theophilus Anglicanus
Manual of Instruction on the Church and the Anglican Branch of It

ISBN/EAN: 9783337162122

Printed in Europe, USA, Canada, Australia, Japan

Cover: Foto ©Lupo / pixelio.de

More available books at **www.hansebooks.com**

THEOPHILUS ANGLICANUS;

OR,

MANUAL OF INSTRUCTION

ON

The Church,

AND

THE ANGLICAN BRANCH OF IT

BY

CHR. WORDSWORTH, D.D.

SOMETIME BISHOP OF LINCOLN.

FIFTEENTH EDITION.

LONDON:
LONGMANS, GREEN, AND CO.
AND NEW YORK: 15, EAST 16th STREET
1890.

TO THE RIGHT HON. AND RIGHT REV.

CHARLES JAMES BLOMFIELD, D.D.

FOR MORE THAN A QUARTER OF A CENTURY

BISHOP OF LONDON;

IN WHOM ENGLAND HAS SEEN A BRIGHT EXAMPLE

OF PIETY, LEARNING, MUNIFICENCE, AND ZEAL;

AND TO WHOM SHE IS MAINLY INDEBTED,

UNDER THE DIVINE BLESSING,

FOR AN EXTENSION OF THE EPISCOPATE

IN HER VAST COLONIAL POSSESSIONS,

AND FOR A QUICKENING OF SPIRITUAL LIFE

IN HER DENSE POPULATION AT HOME;

This Volume

IS, BY HIS LORDSHIP'S PERMISSION, DEDICATED,

WITH DUTIFUL VENERATION AND AFFECTIONATE GRATITUDE,

BY

THE AUTHOR.

PREFACE

TO THE NINTH EDITION.

In putting forth this revision, probably the last, of THEOPHILUS ANGLICANUS, the Author cannot forego the pleasure of recording, with feelings of devout thankfulness to the Giver of all good, that in its first passing through the Press, about a quarter of a century ago, the sheets were revised by two mutual friends, whose memory will be ever most dear to the Writer, the late JOSHUA WATSON, Esq., and his own revered father, the late Master of Trinity College, Cambridge; and that, on its first appearance, it was honoured with the written sanction of the Archbishop in whose Province it was published, ARCHBISHOP HOWLEY, and with that of the Bishop of the Diocese, BISHOP BLOMFIELD. It has been reprinted in America, with modifications suitable to the circumstances of the case, under the title of THEOPHILUS AMERICANUS, by a learned American lawyer, Mr. H. DAVEY EVANS, of Baltimore. The work has been translated into Modern Greek, 1847; and has been published in French, with a valuable preface, by the Rev. Dr. F. GODFRAY, at Paris, 1861; and it has also been printed in Italy, under the title of IL TEOFILO CATTOLICO, at Turin, in 1863.

Cloisters, Westminster Abbey,
  July, 1865.

CONTENTS.

PART I.

ON THE CHURCH.

CHAP.		PAGE
I.	On the Name and Attributes of the Church	1
II.	On the Attributes of the Church as visible and militant, and as invisible and triumphant	8
III.	On the Dignity and Glory of the Church	20
IV.	On Salvation in the Church	22
V.	On Errors in the Church	32
VI.	On Privileges in the Church: *Word of God.—The Church its Witness and Keeper*	43
VII.	On Privileges in the Church: *Right Interpretation of the Word of God*	52
VIII.	On Privileges in the Church: *Due Administration of the Sacraments by a lawful Ministry*	66
IX.	On the Three Orders of Ministers in the Church	75
X.	Bishops; Divine Institution of Episcopacy	79
XI.	Functions of Bishops	90
XII.	Of Bishops as Diocesans, Metropolitans, and Patriarchs	95
XIII.	Privileges in the Church: *Discipline.—Power of the Keys*	106
XIV.	Privileges in the Church: *Absolution*	112

CONTENTS.

CHAP. PAGE
XV. Privileges in the Church: *Sacerdotal Intercession and Benediction* 120
XVI. Privileges in the Church: *Set Forms of Public Prayer* 132

PART II.

ON THE ANGLICAN BRANCH OF THE CATHOLIC CHURCH.

I. Church of England: its Origin 134
II. Church of England independent of Rome: *Period before the Arrival of S. Augustin* 138
III. Church of England independent of Rome: *Mission of S. Augustin* 146
IV. Church of England independent of Rome: *Period between the Mission of S. Augustin and the Reformation* 157
V. The Reformation in England a removal of what was new, and a restoration of what was old . . 170
VI. Uninterrupted Succession of Holy Orders in the Church of England 187
VII. The Church of Rome is guilty of the Schism between herself and the Church of England . . . 196
VIII. The Church of England has never separated from the Catholic Church 208
IX. The Bishop of Rome has no supremacy, spiritual or temporal, in these Realms 214

PART III.

THE CHURCH OF ENGLAND IN ITS CIVIL RELATIONS.

I. Definition of Church and State 234
II. On the Duty of Kingdoms and States to profess and to promote the True Faith 239

CHAP.	PAGE
III. On the Church of England as the Spiritual Mother of Christians in this Country	254
IV. On the Ecclesiastical Supremacy of Christian Rulers	264
V. The Royal Supremacy in the Church of England	272
VI. On the Royal Supremacy in the Church of England. *In Ecclesiastical Synods*	287
VII. On the Royal Supremacy in the Church of England. *In Ecclesiastical Promotions and Judicature*	292

PART IV.

RITES AND CEREMONIES IN THE CHURCH OF ENGLAND.

I. On the Rites and Ceremonies of the Church of England	312
II. Objections considered	317

INDEXES.

INDEX I. Of Matters	325
INDEX II. Of Authors and Places cited	332

THEOPHILUS ANGLICANUS.

PART I.

On the Church.

CHAPTER I.

ON THE NAME AND ATTRIBUTES OF THE CHURCH.

Q. WHAT is the etymology and meaning of the English word CHURCH?

A. It is derived from the Greek word Κυριακὴ, a feminine adjective, from Κύριος, the *Lord;* and it means Κυριακὴ οἰκία, or the *Lord's House* [1].

Chap. I.
1 Pet. ii. 5.
Heb. iii. 6.
x. 21.
1 Tim. iii. 15.

---

[1] CASAUBON, Exercit. Baron. xiii. § xvii. Ecclesias primi Christiani vocabant *Dominica* et Κυριακὰ, unde mansit apud Anglos appellatio *Church.*
HOOKER, Eccl. Pol. V. XIII. 1. VALES. ad Euseb. Laud. Const. xvii. Bp. PEARSON on the Creed, Art. ix. Bp. BEVERIDGE, ap. Routh, Reliq. Sacræ, iii. 448; and on XXXIX Articles, Art. xix. vol. ii. 98, ed. Oxf. 1840.
The word Κυριακὸς occurs twice in the N. Test. 1 Cor. xi. 20, and Rev. i. 10. Κυριακὴ in the Eastern Church, is the *Lord's* DAY, as *Dominica* and *Dimanche* in the Western. The German *Domkirche,* for the Basilica or Cathedral, seems to be a combination of both the Latin and Greek words for CHURCH, i. e. *Dominicum* (whence *il Duomo* in Italian, and Irish *Domnach*) and Κυριακόν. STAVELEY on Churches, pp. 21, 22, ed. Lond. 1712.

Part I.

Q. Is there not another word, the same both in Greek and Latin, by which CHURCH is expressed?

A. Yes, ECCLESIA.

Q. Whence is this word derived?

A. From the Greek ἐκ, *forth*, and καλέω, *to call*.

Q. How is this word modified in living European languages?

A. In Italian it has become *Chiesa*; in French, *Eglise*; and in Spanish, *Iglésia*.

Q. What did the word *Ecclesia* originally mean?

A. A Public Assembly; and it was specially applied to designate the Popular Assembly[1] at *Athens*, to which all free citizens were convoked, and which was summoned by Presidents (πρυτάνεις), each of whom (as ἐπιστάτης) held in rotation the keys[2] of the Civic Treasury and Archives and the State Seal.

[1] Bp. PEARSON on the Creed, Art. ix.
[2] JULIUS POLLUX, viii. 6. HERMANN's Manual of Polit. Antiq. of Greece, § 127.

Q. What do you infer from the two words Κυριακὴ and Ἐκκλησία, with respect to the character of the Church?

A. That it is the Lord's House, or Common Assembly of His People, presided over by Persons entrusted with certain powers, and to which men are convoked, as the Athenians were to their *Ecclesia*[1].

[1] FIELD on the Church, i. 5. Bp. PEARSON on the Creed, Art. ix. *note*. Ἐκκλησία is the same with the κλητοί, or the company called and gathered together.

Q. But is not the Christian Church something more than an *Assembly*?

A. Yes, the Church is indeed an *Assembly*, it being *convoked*; but it is a permanent *Society*[1] in that having been convoked it will *never* be dissolved:

[1] HOOKER, III. i. 14. The Church is *always* a Visible Society of men.

Q. And this Assembly or Society is presented to us in Holy Scripture under what form?

A. As consisting of believing and baptized persons, continuing " stedfastly in the Apostles' doctrine and fellowship, and in breaking of bread and in the prayers;" and who were thus reputed to be Members of the same Church, and to which were added (οἱ σωζόμενοι) such as were being saved [1]. {Acts ii. 41 —47. xx. 7} {Acts ii. 47. See below, p. 28.}

[1] Bp. PEARSON, Lectiones in Acta Apostolorum, pp. 34, 35, ed. 1688 (in Act. i. 13. ii. 48). Hæc nobis forma quasi atque imago primæ Ecclesiæ ab Apostolis congregatæ, formatæ, gubernatæ. Fide semel Apostolico sermoni habitâ per Baptismum in Ecclesiam admittebantur; in Ecclesiam admissi Cœtus Publicos frequentabant; in cœtu publico Doctrinæ Apostolorum sedulò attendebant; et Eucharistiæ participes fiebant (*fractione panis*, i. e. Eucharistiâ, p. 34); Publicis denique et Communibus Orationibus in eodem Cœtu factis Deum colebant. Atque ita *Ecclesiis omnibus* usque ad consummationem sæculi *Exemplum* præbebant.

Q. What are the designations by which the Church is described in the Apostles' Creed, and in the Nicene or Constantinopolitan Creed [1]?

A. It is called ONE, HOLY, CATHOLIC, and APOSTOLIC (μία, ἁγία, καθολικὴ, Ἀποστολική).

[1] The originals of these Creeds, and of the Athanasian, may be seen in Bp. BEVERIDGE on the XXXIX Articles, Art. viii. Voss. de Symbolis, 1662. WATERLAND, ii. 309 —331. iv. 130—314.

Q. How is the Church ONE, or United?

A. Inasmuch as all its members have one God and Father; and are united as sheep of one fold, under one Shepherd; and as Members, under Christ their Head, of one Body, into which they are all baptized in one Spirit; and all are partakers of one Bread and of one Cup in the Holy Eucharist; have all one Faith [1] and one Hope of their calling; are all of one heart and one soul, {Eph. iv. 6. John x. 16. Rom. xii. 5. 1 Cor. xii. 12. 20. 1 Cor. xi. 3. Eph. iv. 2—5. 1 Cor. x. 17. Jude 3.}

PART I.
Col. iii.
12—15.
Acts iv. 32.
1 Pet. iii. 8.
Eph. iv. 3.
Phil. iii. 19.
Acts ii.
41—47.
Rom. xv. 6.

loving each other as Brethren, and keeping the unity of the Spirit in the bond of peace; walking by the same rule, and minding the same thing; united by the same [2] Apostolic government, discipline, and worship; and all living with one aim, that they may with one mind and one mouth glorify God [3].

[1] S. IREN. adv. Hæreses, i. c. iii. p. 46, Grabe. τοῦτο τὸ κήρυγμα καὶ ταύτην τὴν πίστιν, ὡς προέφαμεν, ἡ Ἐκκλησία καίπερ ἐν ὅλῳ τῷ κόσμῳ διεσπαρμένη παρειλειφυῖα ἐπιμελῶς φυλάσσει, ὡς ἕνα οἶκον οἰκοῦσα, καὶ ὁμοίως πιστεύει τούτοις ὡς μίαν ψυχὴν καὶ τὴν αὐτὴν ἔχουσα καρδίαν, καὶ συμφώνως ταὐτὰ κηρύσσει καὶ διδάσκει καὶ παραδίδωσιν ὡς ἓν στόμα κεκτημένη.

S. CYPRIAN, Unit. Eccles. p. 108, Fell. Ecclesia una est, quæ in multitudinem latius incremento fœcunditatis extenditur, quomodo solis multi radii, sed lumen unum, et rami arboris multi, sed robur unum tenaci radice fundatum, et cum de fonte uno rivi plurimi defluunt, numerositas licet diffusa videatur exundantis copiæ largitate, unitas tamen servatur in origine.

[2] TERTULLIAN, Apol. 39. Corpus sumus de conscientiâ religionis, et disciplinæ unitate, et spei fœdere.

S. CYPRIAN, ad Antonian. p. 112, Fell. Cum sit a Christo una Ecclesia per totum mundum in multa membra divisa, item Episcopatus unus Episcoporum multorum concordi numerositate diffusus.—Ep. lxvi. Florentio, p. 168, Fell. Ecclesia a Christo non recedit, et illi sunt Ecclesia plebs sacerdoti adunata, et pastori suo grex adhærens, unde scire debes Episcopum in Ecclesiâ esse, et Ecclesiam in Episcopo; et si qui cum Episcopo non sint, in Ecclesiâ non esse, et frustrà sibi blandiri eos qui pacem cum sacerdotibus Dei non habentes obrepunt et latenter apud quosdam communicare se credunt; quando Ecclesia, quæ Catholica una est, scissa non sit neque divisa, sed sit utique connexa et cohærentium sibi invicem sacerdotum glutino copulata.

S. CYPRIAN, ad Cornel. Ep. 52. Nec remanere in Ecclesiâ possunt, qui Deificam et Ecclesiasticam Disciplinam nec actûs sui conversatione nec morum pace tenuerunt.

HOOKER, III. I. 4 and 14. See below, chaps. ix. and x. and Pt. ii. ch. vi.

[3] BARROW on the Unity of the Church, p. 297, ed. 1683.

PALMER on the Church, ch. iv. v.

Q. How is the Church HOLY?

A. In respect of its Head, Christ; of its Holy Calling; of its Holy Baptism, wherein we are created anew after God in righteousness and true holiness; of the Holy Offices performed in it; of the Holiness of Life required from its members; of the "Inheritance, Holy and undefiled," which God has promised to them.

Chap. I.
1 Pet. i. 15, 16.
2 Tim. i. 9.
Eph. iv. 24.
2 Tim. ii. 19.
1 Pet. i. 4.

Q. What is the derivation and meaning of the term CATHOLIC?

A. *Catholic* is from the Greek adjective καθολικὸς, *universal*, and is derived from the adverb καθόλου, *throughout*, which is from the preposition κατὰ, and ὅλος, *whole*; and *Catholic* means *diffused throughout the whole*, or *universal*[1].

[1] Bp. PEARSON ad S. Ignat. ad Smyrn. 8. "Prima *Catholicæ* Ecclesiæ mentio in Polycarpi Martyrio sub Marco Antonio, secunda in passione Pionii sub Decio," says Valesius; but, as Bp. PEARSON observes, the word had been previously used by S. Ignat. l. c. Cf. S. AUG. de Unit. Eccles. 2.

Q. How is the Church thus CATHOLIC or UNIVERSAL?

A. In respect of *Time*[1], as enduring throughout all ages, from the beginning till the end of the world. In respect of *Place*[2], as not limited, like the Jewish Church, to *one* People; but as comprehending those of *all* Nations who are in the main points of religion one and the same. In respect of *Faith*[3] and *Practice*, as teaching all truth, and as requiring holiness from all; and as ministering, by God's appointment, all His means of spiritual *Grace*[4].

Matt. xxviii. 20. xxiv. 31.
Mark xvi. 15.
Luke xxiv. 47.
Rev. v. 9.

[1] S. CYRIL. HIEROS. Catechesis xviii. p. 296, ed. Ven. 1763. Καθολικὴ καλεῖται διὰ τὸ κατὰ πάσης εἶναι τῆς οἰκουμένης ἀπὸ περάτων γῆς ἕως περάτων, καὶ διὰ τὸ διδάσκειν καθολικῶς καὶ ἀνελλιπῶς ἅπαντα τὰ εἰς γνῶσιν ἀνθρώπων ἐλθεῖν ὀφείλοντα δόγματα περί τε ὁρατῶν καὶ ἀοράτων πραγμάτων ἐπουρανίων τε καὶ ἐπιγείων, καὶ διὰ τὸ πᾶν γένος ἀνθρώπων εἰς εὐσέβειαν ὑποτάσσειν ἀρχόντων τε καὶ ἀρχομένων, λογίων τε καὶ ἰδιωτῶν, καὶ διὰ τὸ καθολικῶς ἰατρεύειν μὲν καὶ θεραπεύειν ἅπαν τὸ τῶν ἁμαρ-

PART I. τιῶν εἶδος, τῶν διὰ ψυχῆς καὶ σώματος ἐπιτελουμένων, κεκτῆσθαι δὲ ἐν αὐτῇ πᾶσαν ἰδέαν ὀνομαζομένης ἀρετῆς ἐν ἔργοις καὶ λόγοις καὶ πνευματικοῖς παντοίοις χαρίσμασιν.

² S. AUG. in Ps. lvi. (iv. p. 754, ed. Paris, 1835.) Corpus Christi est Ecclesia, non ista aut illa, sed toto orbe diffusa, nec ea quæ nunc est in hominibus qui præsentem vitam agunt, sed ad eam pertinentibus etiam his qui fuerunt *ante nos*, et his qui futuri sunt *post nos*, usque *ad finem sæculi*. Tota enim Ecclesia constans ex omnibus fidelibus, quia fideles omnes sunt membra Christi, habet illud Caput positum in cœlis, quod gubernat corpus suum. See also Serm. iv. 11.

³ S. IREN. V. xx. p. 430. Ecclesiæ quidem prædicatio vera et firma, apud quam una et eadem salutis via in universo mundo ostenditur. Huic enim creditum est lumen Dei.—Ubique enim Ecclesia prædicat veritatem.

⁴ Archbp. CRANMER, Works, iv. p. 278, ed. Jenkyns, *De Ecclesiâ*. Bp. BULL, Corruptions of the Church of Rome, in Answer to the Bp. of Meaux's (Bossuet's) Queries. Works, ii. p. 243, ed. Burton. Archbishop POTTER on Church Government, p. 29, ed. 1724.

See further below, chap. iv.

Q. Are the members of any *particular* or national Church (for example of Italy, Greece, France, England, &c.) rightly called *Catholics?*

A. Yes; being members of the Universal Church of Christ, they are Catholics [1], *generally;* or, more *particularly*, Italian Catholics, Greek Catholics, French Catholics, and English or Anglo-Catholics.

[1] S. PACIAN, Ep. 1, ad Sempronian. Christianus mihi nomen, *Catholicus* cognomen; illud me nuncupat, istud ostendit.

Q. And what thence do you conclude concerning the claim which is put forth by the Church of Rome to be called "*the* Catholic Church?"

A. The Church of Rome is a *part* of the Catholic Church, as the other Churches before mentioned are; but neither the Church of Rome [1], nor the Church of England, nor the Greek Church, nor any other *particular* Church, is *the* Catholic or Universal Church [2], any more than a *Branch* is a *Tree*, or a *Hand* is the *whole Body*.

[1] S. Hieron. ad Evag. lxxxv. Et Galliæ, et Britannia, et Africa, et Persis, et Oriens, et India, et omnes barbaræ nationes unum Christum adorant, unam observant regulam veritatis. Si auctoritas quæritur, Orbis major est Urbe.

Casaubon, ad Cardinal. Perron. Epistol. p. 493, ed. 1709. Romana, Græca, Antiochena, Ægyptia, Abyssina, Moscovitica, et plures aliæ *membra* sunt Ecclesiæ Catholicæ.— Mirandum igitur, Romanam Ecclesiam jus omne Universitatis ad se trahere, appellationem Ecclesiæ Catholicæ sibi propriam facere; et reliquas omnes, quæ in ullâ re a se dissentiant, excludere communione suâ, ac statim illas ad Catholicam nihil pertinere audacter affirmare.

Necessary Doctrine and Erudition for any Christian Man, Art. ix. A.D. 1543. And therefore the Church of Rome, being but a *several* Church, challenging that name of *Catholic above all other*, doeth great wrong *to all other Churches*, and doeth only by force support an unjust usurpation : for that Church hath no more right to that name than the Church of France, Spain, England, or Portugal, which be justly called Catholic Churches.

[2] S. Aug. de Civ. Dei, xiii. c. 12. Universa Ecclesia ex multis constat Ecclesiis. Theophylact ad 1 Cor. xii. 27, τὴν ἀπανταχοῦ τῆς οἰκουμενης καθολικὴν ἐκκλησίαν, ἧς τὸ σῶμα συνέστηκεν ἐκ τῶν ἀπανταχοῦ ἐκκλησιῶν.

See below, Pt. ii. ch. i. and Pt. ii. ch. viii.

Q. How is the Church Apostolical?

A. As built on the foundation of the Apostles Eph. ii. 20 **and Prophets, Jesus Christ Himself being the Chief Corner Stone; as continuing stedfastly in** Acts ii. 42. **the doctrine of the Apostles, and in communion with them and their lawful successors**[1].

[1] Rev. xxi. 14. The wall of the (heavenly) city had *twelve* foundations (foundation-stones, θεμελίους, sc. λίθους), and in them the names of the *Twelve Apostles* of the Lamb. This is the scriptural description of the Church in glory.

S. Ignat. ad Smyrn. 8. Ὅπου ἂν φανῇ ὁ ἐπίσκοπος, ἐκεῖ τὸ πλῆθος ἔστω . . . . οὐκ ἐξόν ἐστιν χωρὶς ἐπισκόπου οὔτε βαπτίζειν οὔτε ἀγάπην ποιεῖν.

Tertullian, de Bapt. c. 17. Dandi quidem (Baptismum) habet jus summus sacerdos, qui est Episcopus; dehinc Presbyteri et Diaconi, non tamen sine Episcopi auctoritate.

S. Optatus, II. 2 and 28. IV. 3. VI. 2.

See below, Pt. i. ch. ix. and x. Pt. ii. ch. vi. and ch. ix. and the Editor's note on Matt. x. 2 in his edition of the Greek Testament.

PART I.

CHAPTER II.

ON THE ATTRIBUTES OF THE CHURCH AS VISIBLE AND MILITANT, AND AS INVISIBLE AND TRIUMPHANT.

Q. How do we become Members of this One, Holy, Catholic, and Apostolic Church?

Acts viii. 36.
Matt. xxviii. 19.

A. By Baptism[1] with water, in the name of the Father, and of the Son, and of the Holy Ghost.

[1] HOOKER, III. I. 6. Entered we are not into the visible church before our admittance by the *door* of Baptism.

Bp. PEARSON in Acta Apostolorum, p. 33. (in Act. ii. 41.) Hi per Baptismum recipiebantur in Ecclesiam Christi; neque *alio modo unquam recipi potuerunt* aut *Christiani fieri;* quicquid in contrarium nuper deliravit Socinus.

Q. Are all, who have been duly baptized, to be considered as continuing thenceforward in a state of Grace, and in the way to Salvation?

Eph. iv. 30.
2 Tim. i. 6.
1 Thess. v. 19.
Luke vii. 30.

A. No. They were *placed* at Baptism in a state of Grace, and in the way to Salvation; but Baptism did not destroy their free will[1]. A man may grieve the Spirit, resist the Spirit, and quench the Spirit given him at Baptism, and reject the good counsel of God towards himself (εἰς ἑαυτόν). We were regenerate, or born anew, by Baptism. But Regeneration does not cancel the necessity, but strengthens the obligation, of daily renewal and growth in grace.

[1] S. AUGUSTIN, Tract. v. In Epist. Joannis, 6. Ecce accessit *Sacramentum nativitatis* homo baptizatus; Sacramentum habet, et magnum Sacramentum, divinum, sanctum, ineffabile. Considera quale, ut novum hominem faciat dimissione omnium peccatorum. Attendat tamen in cor, si perfectum est ibi, quod factum est in corpore: videat si habet charitatem, et tunc dicat, *Natus sum ex Deo.* See also contra Faustum, xix. xii.

HOOKER, V. LVII. 4. Sacraments are not physical but moral instruments of salvation; duties of service and worship, which unless we perform as the Author of grace requireth, they are unprofitable. Ibid. LIX. 2. LX. 2.

WATERLAND, Regeneration Stated and Explained, Works, vi. 361, and Bp. VAN MILDERT's Remarks, ibid. i. p. 179.

CHAP. II.

Q. You have before said (p. 5) that the Church is *Holy;* may there, then, be *evil* men in the Church of God?

A. Yes. " All are not Israel who are of Israel." Rom. ix. 6, and ii. 28.

Q. Will this state of things continue to the end of the world?

A. Yes. "[1] On *earth* the evil will ever be mingled with the good."

[1] XXXIX ARTICLES, Art. xxvi. HOOKER, III. i. 8.

Q. How do you show this?

A. From the figures and parables by which the Church is described in Holy Scripture.

Q. Mention some of these.

A. The Church was typified by the Ark[1], in which were clean and unclean animals; it is like the Holy City, in which Jebusites were with God's people; the Apostolic Company, in which was a Judas, as well as a Peter, James, and John.

Gen. vi. 19.
1 Pet. iii. 20.
Josh. xv. 63.
Judges i. 21.
Matt. x. 2—4.

[1] S. HIERON. adv. Lucifer. p. 428, ed. 1643. Ut in Arcâ Noë pardus et hædi, lupus et agni, sic in Ecclesiâ peccatores et justi.... Dies me deficiet si omnia Arcæ Sacramenta cum Ecclesiâ componens edisseram.

S. AUGUSTIN, Epist. CVIII. ii. p. 471. Agnoscamus Arcam quæ præfiguravit Ecclesiam; simul illuc munda animalia simus; nec in eâ nobiscum etiam immunda portari usque in finem diluvii recusemus. *Simul* in *arcâ* fuerunt, sed *non* simul in odorem *sacrificii* de immundis obtulit Noë. Nec ideò tamen a mundis aliquibus arca ante tempus propter immunda deserta est.—*Corvus* tantum *arcam deseruit*.

OFFICE of Public Baptism, in the Book of Common Prayer. Wash *him* and sanctify *him* with the Holy Ghost, that he being delivered from Thy wrath may be received into the *Ark* of Christ's Church.

See below, p. 11.

Q. You thence infer that a Church does not cease to be a Church by reason of the bad lives of some of its Members?

A. I do. St. Paul recognizes the Christian Society at Corinth as a *Church,* although it con-

PART I.

1 Cor. i. 2.
iii. 3. v. 1.
vi. 6. iv. 18.
xv. 12.
Gal. i. 6.
iv. 21.
Rev. ii. 15.
20. iii. 16.

tained within it, as he himself says, contentious persons, carnal, envious, schismatical, fornicators, litigious, insubordinate, and sceptics concerning the Resurrection; and he calls the Galatians a *Church*, though some of their number had relapsed into Judaistical opinions. So the Church of Pergamus contained Nicolaitans, that of Thyatira a Jezebel, even as a Teacher; and that of Laodicea was lukewarm; yet still they were *Churches*[1].

[1] S. HIERON. adv. Lucifer. i. 439. Galatas ad observationem legis traductos Apostolus iterum parturit; Corinthios resurrectionem carnis non credentes pluribus argumentis ad verum iter trahere conatur..... Angelo Ephesi deserta charitas imputatur. In Angelo Pergamenæ Ecclesiæ idolothytorum esus, et Nicolaitarum doctrina reprehenditur. Item apud Angelum Thyatirorum Hiezabel prophetissa et simulacrorum escæ et fornicationes increpantur. Et tamen *omnes hos* ad *Pœnitentiam* Dominus hortatur sub comminatione quoque futuræ pœnæ nisi convertantur.... Numquid dixit, *Rebaptizentur*, qui in Nicolaitarum fide baptizati sunt?
HOOKER, V. LXVIII. 6.

Q. You mentioned Scripture Parables; how does this *mixed* condition of the Church on *earth* appear from them?

Matt. xiii. 30.
Isa. v. 2.
See below, Pt. iii. ch. iii.
Matt. iii. 12.
Matt. xxv. 32.
Matt. iv. 19. xiii. 47.
Matt. xxii. 10.
John xv. 1.
Acts x. 11.
St. Aug. in John viii. 35.
2 Tim. ii. 20.
Catena in Act. Oxon. 1838, p. 175. 177.

A. Our Lord describes the Church on earth under the similitude of a Field in which Wheat and Tares (i. e. ζιζάνια, which are hardly distinguishable from the wheat) remain growing together until the Harvest. The Church is a Threshing-floor, in which lie Grain and Chaff together[1] (the chaff often parting and obscuring the grain); the Church is a Fold, with Sheep and Goats[1]; it is described as a Net, in which are enclosed Fish of every kind, good and bad; a Marriage Feast, with Guests bad and good; a Vine, with fruitful and unfruitful branches; St. Peter's Sheet[2] let down from heaven, containing clean and unclean beasts; a great House, in which are vessels not only of gold and silver, but also of wood; some to honour and some to dishonour[3].

[1] FULGENT. de Fide ad Petrum, c. 43. Firmissimè tene Aream Dei esse Catholicam Ecclesiam, et intra eam usque in finem seculi *frumento mixas paleas* contineri; hoc est bonis malos Sacramentorum communione misceri.

[2] S. AUGUST. contra Faust. lib. xii. 15. Quod cuncta animalium genera in *arcâ* claudantur: sicut omnes gentes quas etiam *Petro* demonstratus *discus* illo significat, Ecclesia continet. Quod et munda et immunda ibi sunt animalia: sicut in Ecclesiæ Sacramentis et boni et mali versantur.

[3] S. CYPRIAN, ad Antonian. Ep. lv. p. 112.

S. AUGUSTIN, in S. Joann. Evangel. 61. De Fide et Oper. c. v. et in Ps. viii. et lv. et in Tichonii Regulam de *permixtâ Ecclesiâ*, t. iii. p. 101, ed. Paris. Contra Faustum, viii. p. 386.

HOOKER, V. LXVIII. 6. Heresy and many other crimes, which wholly sever from God, do sever from the (Visible) Church of God in part only. To this, and no other purpose, are meant those *Parables* which our Saviour in the Gospel hath concerning mixture of vice with virtue, light with darkness, truth with error.

See below, p. 15, and Pt. iii. ch. iii.

Q. What are the moral and religious lessons to be learnt from this *mixed and imperfect* state of the Church on earth?

A. We are to consider it as an exercise of our Faith. The *present mixture* ought to make us look forward to the future time of *final separation*. The *Field* ought to remind us of the *Harvest*. We ought to carry our thoughts from the earthly *Threshing-floor* to the heavenly *Garner;* from the present *union* of the Sheep and Goats to their future *severance;* from the *Net*, we should look to the *Shore* to which it is to be drawn. This present state of things is also to teach us other lessons, with respect to our fellow-men, and to the Church at large.

Q. What are these?

A. We are to learn from it the duties of bearing and forbearing[1]; of remembering, that while there are many *bad* men in the Church, who *do appear*, there are many *good* who are *not* certainly known to man as such; of taking care, that while we communicate with *sinful men,* we do not com-

[1] Kings xix 18.
Rom. xi. 4.

municate with them in any *sin*[2]; of not disparaging an Apostolic Church, much less of *separating*[3] from it, on account of the errors or vices of some of its members or ministers; but of endeavouring to promote its welfare, and the repentance and amendment of our erring brethren, by our prayers and our example.

[1] S. AUG. iv. 497 (addressing the Donatists). *Tolera et zizania, si triticum es; tolera paleam, si triticum es; tolera pisces malos inter retia, si piscis bonus es. Quare ante tempus ventilationis avolasti? Quare ante tempus messis frumenta eradicâsti tecum? quare, antequam ad littus venires, retia disrupisti?* S. AUG. v. 129. *Geme* in *areâ,* ut *gaudeas* in *horreo.*

[2] S. AUGUST. Epist. cv. 16. Quos autem corrigere non valemus, etiamsi necessitas cogit pro salute cæterorum ut Dei Sacramenta nobiscum communicent, *peccatis* tamen eorum non communicemus, quod non fit nisi *consentiendo* et *favendo.* Sic enim eos in isto mundo, in quo Ecclesia catholica per omnes gentes diffunditur, quem *agrum suum* Dominus dicit, tanquam *zizania* inter *triticum*, vel in hâc unitatis areâ tanquam *paleam* permixtam *frumento*, vel intra *retia* verbi et sacramenti tanquam *malos pisces* cum *bonis* inclusos, usque ad tempus *messis* aut *ventilationis* aut *littoris* toleramus, ne propter illos eradicemus et triticum, aut grana nuda ante tempus de areâ separata, non in horreum mittenda purgemus, sed volatilibus colligenda projiciamus; aut disruptis per schismata retibus, dum quasi malos pisces cavemus, in mare perniciosæ libertatis exeamus.

[3] S. CYPRIAN, de Unit. Eccles. p. 111. Nemo existimet *bonos* Ecclesiâ posse discedere. Triticum non rapit ventus; *inanes paleæ tempestate jactantur.* S. CYPRIAN, Epist. LIV. p. 99. Nam etsi videntur in Ecclesiâ esse zizania, non tamen impediri debet aut fides aut caritas nostra, ut, quoniam *zizania* esse in Ecclesiâ cernimus, ipsi de Ecclesiâ recedamus. *Nobis* tantummodo laborandum est ut *frumentum* esse possimus; ut, cum cœperit frumentum Dominicis horreis condi, fructum pro opere nostro et labore capiamus. Apostolus in Epistolâ suâ dicit: *In domo autem magnâ non solum vasa sunt aurea, et argentea, sed et lignea, et fictilia, et quædam quidem honorata, quædam vero inhonorata. Nos* operam demus, et quantum possumus laboremus, ut vas *aureum* vel *argenteum simus:* ceterum fictilia vasa confringere Domino *soli* concessum est, Cui et *virga ferrea data* est.

2 Tim. ii. 20.

Rev. ii. 27.

IDEM, Ep. LIV. p. 99, and S. AUG. v. p. 131, on the duty of *prayer* for the erring.

Q. By what name is the Church called, in this *mixed* condition upon *earth?*

A. It is called the *Visible Church.*

Q. Why is it so called?

A. Because it is a Visible " Congregation of faithful" or believing persons, " in which the pure *Word* of God is openly preached, and the *Sacraments* are visibly administered[1] according to Christ's ordinance, in all those things that of necessity are requisite to the same," and which enjoys the right use of *Ecclesiastical Discipline*[2].

[1] S. Aug. Brev. Coll. 3. Ecclesia est corpus vivum in quâ est Anima et Corpus : Anima significat interna dona Spiritûs Sancti ; Corpus vero externam fidei professionem et sacramentorum communionem.

XXXIX Articles, Art. xix. Hooker, III. i. 14.

[2] Homilies, p. 428. (Homily on Whitsunday.) See the passage cited below, chap. xiii.

King Edward VIth's Catechism, 1553. The Marks of this Church are, first, pure preaching of the Gospel ; then, brotherly love ; thirdly, upright and uncorrupted use of the Lord's Sacraments ; last of all, brotherly correction and excommunication, or banishing those out of the Church that will not amend their lives. This mark the holy fathers termed *discipline.*—See also Certain Conferences between Ridley and Latimer, A.D. 1555, and Hooper's Fifth Sermon on Jonas.

Hence it appears, that although in her nineteenth Article cited above, the Church of England has specified only the two marks of Sacraments and the Word of God, yet she does not regard them as *sufficient* of themselves to constitute a visible Church, without the additional note of *discipline* and *government,* concerning which it may be well to cite the words of Cassander on the Augsburgh Confession, Art. vii. Quod autem subjicitur, ad veram Ecclesiæ unitatem satis esse consentire de *doctrinâ evangelii* et *administratione sacramentorum,* id *non satis* est ad schismaticos ab Ecclesiæ societate segregandos. Requiritur ad hanc unitatem Ecclesiæ præter *doctrinæ* et *morum* similitudinem etiam *unitas* animorum, in quâ potissimum spectanda est *obedientia* quæ debetur *Ecclesiarum Præfectis,* qui inde usque ab Apostolis per successionem Ecclesiam Dei gubernandam et verbo vitæ pascendam susceperunt, qui etsi non semper eâdem fide officium suum præstiterunt, in illis tamen quæ officii sunt obtemperari illis necessum est, *tum in auditu veræ doctrinæ,* tum in *legitimo usu sacramentorum,*

PART I. tum in *disciplinâ* et *correctione ecclesiasticâ*.—Hanc *tertiam* notam necessario requiri etiam hujus Confessionis (Augustanæ) auctor posteà agnovit, qui multis in locis, ubi de signis Ecclesiæ agit, tertio loco addit *obedientiam* debitam ministerio Evangelii seu Catholicæ Ecclesiæ.

GROTII Opera, iii. pp. 566-7. See also his own adhesion to Cassander's remarks on this subject, *ibid.* p. 617.

Q. Is it called *Visible* for any other reason?

A. Yes, as distinguished from the *Invisible*[1] *Church*.

[1] S. HIERON. ad Galat. i. p. 120. Noscendum Ecclesiam dupliciter dici posse, et eam quæ non habeat maculam et rugam, et vere corpus Christi sit, et eam quæ in Christi nomine absque plenis perfectisque virtutibus congregetur.

Archbishop CRANMER, Works, iv. p. 278.
Bp. TAYLOR, x. p. 333, ed. 1828.
BARROW on the Unity of the Church, p. 296.

Q. What do you mean by the *Invisible Church?*

Eph. ii. 19.
Heb. xii. 22, 23.
Rev. iii. 12.
John iii. 29.
Rev. xxi. 2.
xix. 7.
Eph. v. 27.
Rom. xii. 1.
Eph. iv. 11—16.
Col. ii. 19.
John x. 14.
2 Tim. ii. 19.
Luke x. 20.

A. I mean the family of God, not only in earth but heaven; the City of the living God; the Spouse of Christ, without spot or wrinkle; the mystical Body of Christ, whose members are known to God, and to *God alone*, and whose names are written in heaven[1].

[1] HOOKER, III. I. II. 4—8. That body consisteth only of *true* Israelites, true sons of Abraham, true servants and saints of God. VIII. I. 6.

Q. You speak of the Visible and Invisible Church; are there then *two* Churches?

A. No: these two terms do not describe *two* Churches, but the one Church considered in two different states. The Church is *visible*, in that it *contains* persons existing only on *earth*, and known to *men* by certain visible tokens: it is *invisible*, in that it *consists* of persons *both* in *heaven* and *earth*, *from the beginning to the end of the*

John x. 14. 27.
1 Cor. viii. 3.
2 Tim. ii. 19.
Matt. xx. 16.
Rev. xvii. 14.

world, known to God[1], but *not* clearly distinguishable by *men*. The Church is visible, as far only as it is seen by men; it is invisible, as it is known by God. The *Visible* Church contains both *bad* and *good;* the *Invisible* consists of *good only.* In the Visible, are *wheat* and *chaff, wheat* and *tares,* mixed together; in the Invisible, *wheat* alone. The one is the Church of the Called, the other of the Elect of God only ².

CHAP. II.

¹ S. AUGUSTIN in Evangel. Joannis Tract. xii. 12. *Novit enim Dominus qui sunt Ejus:* novit qui permaneant ad coronam, qui permaneant ad flammam; novit in areâ suâ triticum, novit paleam; novit segetem, novit zizania.
S. AUGUSTIN, Breviculus Collat. 3. 10. Eadem ipsa una et sancta Ecclesia nunc est aliter, tunc autem aliter futura; nunc habet malos mixtos, tunc non est habitura.
² HOOKER, III. 1. 9. For lack of diligent observing the difference, first, between the Church of God *Mystical* and the Church *Visible;* then, between the Visible (Church) sound, and (the same Visible Church) corrupted, sometimes more and sometimes less, the oversights are neither few nor light that have been committed.
Bp. PEARSON on the Creed, Art. ix. One and the same Church, in relation to different times, admitteth, or not admitteth, the permixtion of the wicked, or the imperfection of the godly.

Q. By what other name is the Visible Church on *earth* known?

A. It is sometimes called the Church *Militant,* as existing in a State of *Warfare* against evil; and as distinguished from what it will be in its future condition, as *Triumphant* or *Glorified.*

Eph. vi. 10, 11, 12.
Heb. xii. 22.
Rev. ii. 10.
26. vii. 9.

Q. Is there any *one Visible Head* of the Church on earth?

A. No. CHRIST is the Head of all Principality and Power; He is over all things to the Church, which is His spouse, and has no other Head or Husband but Christ. He only "that hath the Bride is the Bridegroom ¹." He is the Chief Pastor.

Col. ii. 10.
Eph. i. 22.
John iii. 29.
x. 11.
1 Pet. v. 4.
Matt. xxiii. 8.

¹ THEOPHYLACT in S. Joan. iii. Οὐδεὶς ἄλλος ἐστὶ νυμφίος εἰ μὴ μόνος ὁ Χριστὸς, πάντες δὲ οἱ διδάσκοντες νυμφαγωγοί εἰσιν ὥσπερ ὁ πρόδρομος· οὐδεὶς γὰρ ἄλλος δοτήρ ἐστι τῶν ἀγαθῶν εἰ μὴ ὁ Κύριος· οἱ δὲ ἄλλοι πάντες μεσῖται καὶ τῶν παρὰ τοῦ Κυρίου δεδομένων ἀγαθῶν διάκονοι.

Q. Can you show this further from Scripture?

A. Yes. *If* Christ had appointed any one Visible Head over His Church, we should certainly find directions in Scripture concerning our own duty to this Supreme Head, where so much *is* said of our duty to temporal governors, and to our spiritual Guides. But no such directions are found there. Jesus Christ never appointed any one Head of the Catholic Church on earth, any more than He appointed One Monarch of the whole world. Nor did the Christian Church ever hear of any such supremacy over itself for six hundred years from the birth of Christ [1]; and when that supremacy began to be asserted, it brought with it innumerable calamities [2].

---

[1] CRAKANTHORPE, Def. Eccl. Anglic. p. 167.
Bp. BULL, ii. 242. If a Visible Head were *necessary*, the Church did *not exist* for the *first six centuries after Christ* during which that title was never heard of.

[2] HOOKER, VIII. III. 6. See note, p. 19.
Bp. OVERALL's Convocation Book, pp. 285—306.
Abp. LAUD against Fisher, sect. 26. The Church of England does not believe there is any necessity to have one Pope or Bishop over the whole Christian world; which, were it possible, she cannot think fit.
LESLIE, Letter on an Universal Bishop, xi. Christ appointed no Universal Bishop over His Church, more than an Universal Monarch over the world.
See further below, Pt. ii. ch. ix.

Q. But since the Church is *always* a Visible Society of men, united by visible tokens, (above, p. 13,) and since every Society requires a governing power for its own preservation, what is the power which governs the Visible Church?

A. The Church, as a whole, is subject, under Christ, to the laws given her in Holy Scripture, and to those laws which (not contrary to Scripture) have been enacted by her for herself, and which have been generally received and put in use with the assent of the faithful in the Church.

Q. But laws require living Interpreters and

Executors: who then have this office in the Church?

A. Specially, the Bishops[1] and Pastors of the Church; particularly when convened in Councils or Synods, grounding their decrees on Holy Writ.

[1] Bp. OVERALL'S Convoc. Book, ed. Lond. 1690, p. 256. We have before laboured to make it manifest, that our Saviour Christ is the Creator of the world, and the Governour of it; that He hath redeemed and sanctified unto Himself His Church, whereof He is the sole Monarch; that He hath neither appointed any one Emperour under Him to govern the whole world, *nor any one* Priest or Archbishop to rule the whole *Catholic Church;* that, as in respect of Christ, the Creator, all the world is but one Kingdom, whereof He is the only King; so in respect of Christ our Redeemer, all that believe in His name, wheresoever they are dispersed, are but one *Catholic Church;* and that the said one *Catholic Church* is not otherwise visible in this world, than is the said one universal kingdom of Christ, the Creator of it, viz. by the several and distinct parts of them, as by this or that *National Church,* by this or that temporal kingdom. For our Saviour Christ having made the external government of His Catholic Church suitable to the government of His universal monarchy over all the world, hath, by the institution of the Holy Ghost, ordered to be placed in every kingdom, Archbishops, Bishops, and inferior Ministers, to govern the *particular Churches* therein planted .... as He hath in like manner appointed Kings and Sovereign Princes, with their inferior Magistrates of divers sorts, to rule and govern His people under Him, in every Kingdom, Country, and Sovereign Principality. See also MASON, De Ministerio Anglicano, pp. 278, 279. 419. 425. CASAUBON, de Lib. Eccl. c. 11. Epist. p. 179. BARROW, de Pot. Clavium, vol. iv. pp. 46—49.

Bp. STILLINGFLEET'S Rational Account of the Grounds of Protest. Relig. fol. 1665, pp. 301—303, on the words of S. Cyprian, "Episcopatus unus est, cujus a singulis *in solidum* pars tenetur." When Cyprian makes the universal government of the Church to be but one *Episcopal office,* and that committed in the several parts of it with *full power* to particular Bishops, can any one be so senseless to imagine that he should ever think the government of the Church in general to depend upon *any one particular Church, as chief over the rest?* And that the former words do really import such a full power in particular Bishops, over that part of the flock which is committed to them, appears from the true import of the phrase *in solidum;*

a phrase taken out of the civil law, where great difference is made between an obligation *in partem* and *in solidum*, and so proportionably between a tenure *in partem* and *in solidum*: those things were held *in solidum*, which were held in full right and power without payment or acknowledgment. And in this speech he compares the government of the Church to an estate held by *several freeholders*, in which *every one* hath a full right to that *share* which belongs to him. Whereas, according to the *Romish* principle, the government of the Church is like a manor or lordship, in which the several inhabitants hold at the best but by copy from the Lord, and they would fain have it *at the will of the Lord too*.

Q. And have Bishops and Pastors the power of putting these Laws in force?

A. Yes, *in foro conscientiæ*, by spiritual censures.

See note to next question, and below, ch. xiii. xiv. and Pt. iii. chaps. v. vi. vii.

Q. But since the Church, as such, has *no secular* power, how can these laws have any temporal effects?

A. Christ, as Creator, Redeemer, and Governor of the world, has delegated to every supreme Governing power, in a *Christian* State, an *external* superintending, directing, and controlling jurisdiction, with the exercise of which no *foreign* Prelate, Prince, or Potentate, can interfere. This jurisdiction is what the Emperor Constantine called that of an *Episcopus* ab *extra*[1]; and it consists, not only in maintaining and endowing the Church of Christ in its own dominions, but in regulating and governing it[2]; not however after any *new* code of Laws, but of those of God and of the Church. And where the State is not Christian, and where no particular form of Christianity is established by law, there the Church governs herself by the Laws derived from *Holy Scripture*, and from the usage of the *Ancient Catholic Church* of Christ, and *not* by the code of the *Roman Papacy*[3].

¹ GERHARD, Loci Communes, VI. p. 589. Distinguendum inter *potestatem Ecclesiasticam internam et externam*, quæ distinctio colligitur ex verbis Constantini apud Euseb. lib. iv. de vitâ Constant. c. 24. *Vos Episcopi in Ecclesiâ, ego extra Ecclesiam, seu templum, Episcopus a Deo constitutus sum;* illa ministris Ecclesiæ in solidum relinquitur, hæc vero magistratui Christiano communis est: Distinguendum *inter eorum, quæ ad divinum cultum pertinent, administrationem et externam eorundem dispositionem;* illa ministrorum Ecclesiæ est, hæc vero magistratûs. Minister prædicat verbum, utitur gladio Spiritûs, et ore pugnat adversus hostes et impios; Magistratus custodit verbi præcones et confessores, vibrat gladium contra hostes Christianæ Reipublicæ, et manu armatâ eosdem oppugnat. Ut ergò *oris* et *manuum* ministeria distincta manent, licet ad eundem finem, *corporis* scilicet incolumitatem, conspirent, sic Ministerii Ecclesiastici et Magistratûs politici officia distincta manent, licet ad *eundem finem* Reipubl. sc. Christianæ, quæ itidem mysticum aliquod *corpus* constituit, salutem, tutelam et incolumitatem utraque sint directa.

² Bp. OVERALL'S Convoc. Book, p. 262. Under such a form of Ecclesiastical Government the *Christian* Magistrate is become to be, as the chief member of the Church, so the chief Governour of it; to keep as well the said Archbishops within their bounds and limits, as all the rest of the Clergy, and Christians, Bishops, Ministers, and Parishioners, that every one, in their several places, may execute and discharge their distinct offices and duties which are committed unto them. See also Bp. Beveridge on XXXIX Articles, Art. xxxvii. and below, Pt. iii. ch. v. and vi.

³ HOOKER, VIII. III. 5. Dissimilitude in great things is such a thing which draweth great inconvenience after it. And the way to prevent it is, not as some do imagine, the yielding up of supreme power over all churches into *one only pastor's hands;* but the framing of their government, especially for matter of substance, every where according to the rule of one only law, to stand in no less force than the law of nations doth, to be received in all kingdoms. This shall cause uniformity even under several dominions, without those woeful inconveniences whereunto the state of Christendom was subject heretofore, through the tyranny and oppression of that one universal Nimrod (the Bishop of Rome) who alone ruled all.

And, till the Christian world be driven to enter into the peaceable and true consultation about some such kind of general law concerning those things of weight and moment wherein now we differ, if one Church hath not the same

PART I. order which another hath, let *every Church* keep *as near as may be the order it should have,* and *commend the just defence thereof* unto GOD, even as Judah did, when it differed in the exercise of religion from that form which Israel followed.

See further on this subject, below, Pt. ii. ch. ix. toward the end.

CHAPTER III.

ON THE DIGNITY AND GLORY OF THE CHURCH.

Q. By whom was the Church founded?

Matt. xvi. 18.
Acts xx. 28.
1 Cor. xi. 16.
Eph. iii. 10, 11. 21.

A. By JESUS CHRIST.

Q. For what purpose?

A. In order that by it might be known the manifold wisdom of God, and that in it, by the salvation of men, there might be glory to Him for ever.

Q. Whence appears the dignity and glory of the Christian Church?

A. From the titles before mentioned (chap. I.), which bespeak her Unity, Holiness, and Universality: from the promises made to her by God, that "all the Gentiles should come to her

Isa. lx. 3. 10. xlix. 23. liv. 17. lx. 12.

light;" that "Kings should be her nursing Fathers, and Queens her nursing Mothers;" that "no weapon formed against her should prosper;" that "the Nation and Kingdom which will not serve her, should perish and be utterly wasted;" and from other expressions by which she is described in Holy Writ, so that, therefore, as the

Ps. lxxxvii. 3.

Psalmist says, "Glorious things are spoken of thee, thou City of God."

LOWTH on Isaiah lxii. 1—12, and notes on Hosea ii. 19. S. AUG. de Civ. Dei, xvii. 28—35.

Q. Mention some of these expressions of Scripture.

Rom. xii. 1. 5.

A. She is there called the Body and Spouse

of Christ, the King's Daughter, the Queen at the right hand of the Messiah, the Lord's Vineyard, the Kingdom of Heaven, of God, of Grace, of Light; the Mountain of the Lord, to which all nations shall flow; the House built on a Rock, the Pillar and Ground of the Truth, the City of God, the Jerusalem which is above, which is the Mother of us all.

<small>CHAP. III.
1 Cor. vi.
15. x. 17.
xii. 12. 27.
Rev. xix. 7.
xxi. 2.
xxii. 17.
Micah iv. 1, 2.
Eph. i. 23.
iv. 12.</small>

[1] Bp. TAYLOR, Sermon xvii. The Marriage Ring, v. p. 254. *This is a great mystery*, but it is the symbolical and sacramental representation of the greatest mysteries of our religion. Christ descended from His Father's bosom, and contracted His Divinity with flesh and blood, and married our nature, and we became a Church, the Spouse of the Bridegroom, which He cleansed with His blood, and gave her His Holy Spirit for a dowry, and Heaven for a jointure; begetting children unto God by the Gospel. This Spouse He hath joined to Himself by an excellent charity; He feeds her at His own table, and lodges her nigh His own heart; provides for all her necessities, relieves her sorrows, determines her doubts, guides her wanderings; He is become her Head, and she is a signet upon His right Hand. Here is the eternal conjunction, the indissoluble knot, the exceeding love of Christ, the obedience of the Spouse, the communicating of goods, the uniting of interests, the fruit of marriage, a celestial generation, a new creature. *Sacramentum hoc magnum est;* this is the Sacramental mystery, represented by the *holy rite of Marriage*.

<small>v. 23. 30.
Ps. xlv. 9. 10.
Matt. xx. 1.
Isa. v. 1.
Ps. lxxx. 8.
Matt. iv. 17.
xvi. 19.
xx. 1.
Dan. ii. 44.
Col. i. 13.
Isa. ii. 2.
Matt. xvi. 18. vii. 24.
1 Tim. iii. 15.
Heb. xii. 22.
Gal. iv. 26.</small>

Q. But do not these latter titles refer to the *Invisible Church*, purified and glorified in heaven?

A. They do indeed specially belong to the Church, as she will be *hereafter* in a state of bliss; but they appertain also to the Universal Church upon Earth, for they describe that which she *is* in tendency, in endeavour, in desire, and in expectation [1].

<small>Eph. ii. 6.
Col. i. 12.</small>

[1] BARROW, Discourse concerning the Unity of the Church, pp. 296-7, ed. 1683.

PART I.

CHAPTER IV.

ON SALVATION IN THE CHURCH.

Q. We have seen that the Visible Church is a *Society;* and since every Society has some essential *characteristics*, by which it is distinguished from *other* Societies, what is that by which the Church is discerned?

A. The profession of the *true* Religion [1].

[1] HOOKER, V. LXVIII. 6. Of the Visible Church of Christ in this present world, we are thus persuaded; *Church* is a word which art hath devised, thereby to sever and distinguish that society of men, which professeth the *true religion*, from the rest which profess it not.

Q. And what is the essential characteristic of this profession of the *true* Religion?

A. *Faith in our* LORD JESUS CHRIST is that which distinguishes the *true* Religion from the *false;* and separates the *Church* from all *other* societies of men; such as Pagans, Jews, Mahometans, Infidels, and Apostates [1].

Acts xi. 26. Hence it is, that when a *name* was to be given to the members of the Church, to distinguish them from all other persons, they received a name derived from *Christ*, and were called *Christians*.

[1] HOOKER, V. LXVIII. 6. There have been in the world, from the very first foundation thereof, but three religions: Paganism, which lived in the blindness of corrupt and depraved nature; Judaism, embracing the law which reformed heathenish impiety, and taught salvation to be looked for through one whom God in the last days would send and exalt to be Lord of all; (and Mahometanism, see Bp. Andrewes, Catechist. Doctr. p. 35;) finally, Christian belief, which yieldeth obedience to the Gospel of Jesus Christ, and acknowledgeth Him the Saviour whom God did promise .... Seeing, then, that *the Church* is a name which art hath given to *professors of true religion* religion being a matter partly of *contemplation*, partly of *action*, we must define the Church, which is a religious

society, by such differences as do properly explain the essence of such things, that is to say, by the object or matter whereabout the contemplations and actions of the Church are properly conversant. For so all knowledges and all virtues are defined. Whereupon because the *only object* which separateth ours from other religions is *Jesus Christ*, and whom none but the Church doth worship, we find that accordingly the Apostles do every where distinguish hereby the Church from infidels and from Jews, accounting them which call upon the name of our Lord Jesus Christ to be His Church.

CHAP. IV.

If we go lower, we shall but add unto this certain casual and variable accidents, which are not *properly* of the *being*, but make only for the *happier and better being*, of the Church of God, either in deed or in men's opinions and conceits. This is the *error* of all *popish definitions* that hitherto have been brought. They define not the Church by that which the Church *essentially is*, but by that wherein *they imagine their own* more *perfect* than the *rest* are. Touching parts of eminency and perfection, parts likewise of imperfection and defect in the Church of God, they are infinite, their degrees and differences no way possible to be drawn unto any certain account. There is not the least contention and variance, but it blemisheth somewhat the Unity that ought to be in the Church of Christ; which notwithstanding may have not only without offence or breach of concord her manifold varieties in rites and ceremonies of religion, but also her strifes and contentions many times, and that about matters of no small importance, yea, her schisms, factions, and such other evils, whereunto the body of the Church is subject, sound and sick remaining both of the same body, as long as both parts retain, by outward profession, that vital substance of truth which maketh Christian religion to differ from theirs which acknowledge not our Lord Jesus Christ, the blessed Saviour of mankind, give no credit to His glorious Gospel, and have His Sacraments, the seals of eternal life, in derision. See also Bp. SANDERSON, Serm. iii. 26, on 1 Pet. ii. 17, and Serm. xv. 15, all who outwardly profess the faith and name of Christ are within the pale of the visible Church.

Q. If we desire to be saved, is it necessary that we should be members of the Christian Church?

A. It is[1].

S. CYPRIAN Ep. iv. p. 9. Domus Dei una est; et

PART I. nemini salus nisi in Ecclesiâ esse potest. See also S. AUG. III. 1985. 1992. 2027.

Q. How does this necessity appear?

Ps. lxvii. 7.
Isa. xxv. 6.
xxxvii. 32.
Ezek. xiii. 9.
Joel ii. 32.
Eph. iv. 11, 12.

A. From the nature of the case. Christ Himself instituted a *Society* on earth, in which men are to receive the means of[1] grace and salvation, and has revealed no *other* way to this end; they therefore who *will not enter* into, and *continue in*, this Society, exclude themselves from participation in the privileges of the Gospel.

[1] S. IREN. adv. Hæreses, iii. 40. Spiritûs Sancti non sunt participes, qui non concurrunt ad Ecclesiam, sed semet ipsos fraudant a vitâ. Ubi enim Ecclesia Dei, ibi Spiritus Dei.

Q. Is this statement, concerning God's dealings with men, confirmed by examples in Holy Scripture?

A. Yes. Holy Scripture presents us with many instances, where God appointed *certain means* for men's preservation; and where *all* were *destroyed*, who refused to avail themselves of those means.

Q. Mention some of these.

Gen. vii. 23.
1 Pet. iii. 20.

Exod. xii. 7. 22. 26, 27.
Josh. ii. 18, 19.

A. It was *necessary* to *enter* and *remain in* the Ark (which is a type of the Church[1]) for safety from the Flood; it was *necessary* to have the door-post[2] sprinkled with blood, and that no one should go out of the doors[2], in order to be safe from the sword of the destroying Angel; and it was *necessary* for the members of the family of Rahab[3] to *abide* in her house, if they wished to escape death.

[1] TERTULLIAN, de Baptism. 8. Ecclesia est Arca figurata: v. de Idol. ad fin. S. CYPRIAN, Ep. lxix. p. 181, et Ep. lxxiv. p. 198. S. HIERON. ad Esa. xi. Quod Arca in Diluvio hoc Ecclesia præstat in Mundo. S. AUG. iv. p. 1315.—De Civ. D. xv. 27. Procul dubio arca Noe figura est peregrinantis in hoc seculo Ecclesiæ, quæ fit salva per lignum in quo pependit Christus.

HOOKER, V. LXVIII. 6. The privilege of the visible

CHAP. IV.

Church is to be herein like the ark of Noah; that for any thing we know to the contrary, all without it are lost sheep.

² S. CYPRIAN de Unit. Eccles. p. 110. Sacramentum Paschæ in Exodi lege nihil aliud continet quam ut agnus qui in figurâ Christi occiditur in domo unâ edatur. Nec alia ulla credentibus præter unam Ecclesiam domus.—Vid. et p. 182.

³ S. IREN. i. 3. ORIGEN in lib. Jesu Naue, Hom. iv. Extra hanc domum, id est, extra Ecclesiam, nemo salvatur.

S. CYPRIAN, Ep. 69. Rahab typum portabat Ecclesiæ, cui dicitur, Omnis, qui *exierit* domus tuæ foras, reus sibi erit.—Quo sacramento declaratur, in *unam domum solam*, hoc est, in Ecclesiam, victuros colligi oportere.

Bp. PEARSON on the Creed, Art. ix. As none were saved from the deluge but such as were within the Ark of Noah, framed for their reception by the command of God; as none of the first-born of Egypt lived but such as were within those habitations, whose door-posts were sprinkled with blood by the appointment of God for their preservation; as none of the inhabitants of Jericho could escape but such as were within the house of Rahab, for whose protection a covenant was made: so none shall ever escape the eternal wrath of God which belong not to the Church of God. These are the Vessels of the Tabernacle, carried up and down, at last to be translated into and fixed in the Temple.

Q. What do we learn from these examples?

A. We are taught by analogy, that, since God has appointed the Church to be the dispenser of the means of pardon, grace, and salvation to men, we may not hope to escape death or inherit life, if we will not belong to it; that is, if we do not enter into it, and abide in it.

Q. Does it appear directly from *Holy Scripture* that there is no sure way to salvation but in the Church of Christ?

A. Yes. The Church is called in Holy Scripture "the Body of Christ:" and while *it is* said in Scripture, that the Lord added to the *Church* such as were being *saved* (τοὺς σωζομένους), and that "Christ is the *Saviour* of His *Body*¹" (σῶμα), which is the Church², salvation is nowhere promised in Scripture to those who are *not* members of that Body³. Col. i. 18.
24.

Acts ii. 47.

PART I.

[1] Eph. v. 23. Σωτὴρ ΤΟΥ σώματος (where the connexion of the Greek words σῶμα and σώζω is made use of by the Apostle). Col. i. 18. αὐτός ἐστι κεφαλὴ ΤΟΥ σώματος, τῆς Ἐκκλησίας. Hence οἱ σωζόμενοι (Acts ii. 47) are the *incorporated* into Christ's σῶμα or Body, the Church, and thus placed in a state of *salvation*.

[2] S. AUGUSTIN in S. Joann. Evan. Tract. xxvi. 13. Vis vivere de Spiritu Christi? In Corpore esto Christi.

[3] Bp. PEARSON on the Creed, Art. ix. Christ never appointed two ways to heaven, nor did He build a Church to save *some*, and make another institution for *other* men's salvation.

Bp. TAYLOR on Repentance, vol. ix. p. 258. There is, in ordinary, no way to heaven but by serving God in the way which He hath commanded us by His Son; that is, in the way of the Church, which is His Body, of which He is the Prince and Head.

Q. But may there not be *more* than *one* Church in which salvation is offered?

A. No: the Church is *Una, Universa*, and *Unica*[1]; *United, Universal*, and *One Only*. Christ is the Head of every man, says St. Paul. As one Head He has but *one* spiritual Body; and this Body, as the Apostle tells us, is the Church, and no one can "hold the Head" who is not in this Body. Further; the Church is called in Scripture the fulness of Him who filleth *all* in *all*. This *universal* fulness admits of *no other* fulness. Again; the Church is the Spouse of Christ, united for ever to Him, Who loved her and gave Himself for her, and Who has *no other* or *second* Spouse besides that which He has sanctified and cleansed with water and the word, that He might "present *the*[2] Church glorious to Himself, not having spot or wrinkle or any such thing." She is the one Spouse of the one Husband[3]. There is one Fold and one Shepherd; "One Lord, one Faith, one Baptism;" and thus the Church is One for us men and for our salvation[4].

1 Cor. xi. 3.
xii. 12. 27.
Col. i. 18.
24. ii. 19.
Eph. iv.
12—25.

Eph. i. 23.
Isa. lxii. 5.

Eph. v.
25—27. 30.
32.

2 Cor. xi. 2.
John x. 16.
Eph. iv. 5.

[1] S. AMBROSE, Hexaëm. iii. 1. Non *multæ* Congregationes sunt; sed *una* est Congregatio, *una* Ecclesia.

[2] Eph. v. 27. ἵνα παραστήσῃ ἑαυτῷ ἔνδοξον ΤΗΝ ἐκ-

πλησίαν. The force of the article in the original (expressive CHAP. IV. of the *oneness* of the Church) is to be observed.

³ S. FIRMILIAN ap. Cyprian. p. 224. Neque enim *multæ* Sponsæ Christi; *una* est, quæ est Ecclesia Catholica, quæ *sola* generat Dei filios.

2 Cor. xi. 2. ἡρμοσάμην ὑμᾶς ἑνὶ ἀνδρὶ παρθένον ἁγνήν· φυβοῦμαι δὲ μήποτε, ὡς ὁ ὄφις Εὔαν ἐξηπάτησεν ἐν τῇ πανουργίᾳ αὐτοῦ, οὕτως φθαρῇ τὰ νοήματα ὑμῶν ἀπὸ τῆς ἁπλότητος τῆς εἰς τὸν Χριστόν.

⁴ CLEMENS ALEXANDRIN. Strom. vii. 17. Ἐκ τῶν εἰρημένων φανερὸν οἶμαι γεγενῆσθαι μίαν εἶναι τὴν ἀληθῆ Ἐκκλησίαν τὴν τῷ ὄντι ἀρχαίαν, εἰς ἣν οἱ κατὰ πρόθεσιν δίκαιοι ἐγκαταλέγονται· ἑνὸς γὰρ ὄντος τοῦ Θεοῦ, καὶ ἑνὸς τοῦ Κυρίου, διὰ τοῦτο καὶ τὸ ἄκρως τίμιον κατὰ μόνωσιν ἐπαινεῖται, μίμημα ὂν ἀρχῆς τῆς μιᾶς.—Καὶ ἡ ἐξοχὴ τῆς Ἐκκλησίας καθάπερ ἡ ἀρχὴ τῆς συστάσεως κατὰ τὴν μονάδα ἐστίν, πάντα τὰ ἄλλα ὑπερβάλλουσα καὶ μηδὲν ἔχουσα ὅμοιον ἢ ἴσον ἑαυτῇ.

S. CYPRIAN, Ep. lxxiv. p. 216. Fell. Deus unus et Christus unus, et una Spes et Fides una, et una Ecclesia. See ibid. p. 83. Sacerdotium novum fieri præter unum altare et unum Sacerdotium non potest. S. CYPRIAN, Ep. lxix. p. 181, ed. Fell. Quod autem Ecclesia *una* sit, declarat in Cantico Canticorum Spiritus Sanctus, 'ex personâ Christi dicens, UNA *est Columba Mea*. De Unit. Eccl. p. 119.

S. OPTATUS, i. 7. Præter unam Ecclesiam altera non est.

S. HIERON. in Esa. xix. Cuncta altaria quæ contra Ecclesiæ eriguntur altare, sciamus esse non Domini.

S. AUGUSTIN, Serm. cxxv. Quia *unica* est Ecclesia, per totum orbem unitas salvatur. Ab unitate ergo noli recedere, si non vis esse immunis a salute.

Bp. PEARSON on the Creed, Art. ix. Except a man be of the *Catholic Church*, he can be of *none*. For being the Church which is truly Catholic containeth within it *all* which are truly Churches, whosoever is not of the Catholic Church cannot be of the true Church. Whatsoever Church pretendeth to a *new beginning*, pretendeth at the same time to a new Churchdome; and whatsoever is so *new*, is *none*.

Q. What other evidence have we of this truth from Holy Scripture?

A. The Church was prefigured by Eve, "the Mother of *all living*:" and, as there is no way to us of being born *naturally*, as *men*, but by descent from Adam and Eve, so is there no way to us of being born *spiritually* as *Christian men*, but from Christ and the Church¹. As Adam was united

Gen. iii. 20.
Gal. iv. 26.

PART I.

1 Cor. xv.47.
Rev. xxi. 2.
Matt. xix. 6.

to Eve, so Christ, "the second Adam," is to his Church, and no one belongs to Christ who does not belong to Christ's Church. "Christianus nor est qui in Christi Ecclesiâ non est²." What God hath joined together, let not man put asunder.

[1] ORIGEN ap. Routh, Rel. Sacr. iii. 265. S. METHODIUS, Conviv. Virg. iii. 8. Galland. Bibl. P. P. iii. p. 688.

S. HIERON. ad Ephes. c. v. Quomodo de Adam et uxore ejus omne hominum nascitur genus, sic de Christo et Ecclesiâ omnis credentium multitudo generata est. S. CHRYSOST. in Ephes. c. v. p. 864, Savil. S. AMBROS. in S. Luc. iii. 22. Adam novissimus Christus est: Costa Christi vita Ecclesiæ. Hæc est Eva mater omnium viventium. S. AUG. Serm. xxii. Parentes qui nos genuerunt ad mortem, Adam et Eva; parentes qui nos genuerunt ad vitam, Christus et Ecclesia. Vide et t. iv. p. 498, et Tractat. in S. Joh. xi. et c. Faustum, xiii. 8. S. AUG. in S. Joann. Tract. ix. Dormit Adam ut fiat Eva; moritur Christus ut fiat Ecclesia. Dormienti Adæ fit Eva de latere; mortuo Christo lanceâ percutitur latus ut profluant sacramenta quibus formetur Ecclesia.

HOOKER, V. LVI. 7. The Church is in Christ, as Eve was in Adam. Yea by grace we are in Christ and in His Church, as by nature we are in our first parents. God made Eve out of Adam. And His Church He framed out of the very flesh, the very wounded and bleeding side, of the Son of Man. His body crucified and His blood shed for the life of the world, are the true elements of that heavenly being which maketh us such as Himself is of Whom we come.

Bp. BEVERIDGE on Article xxv. ii. p. 210.

[2] S. CYPRIAN ad Anton. p. 112.

Q. What was the judgment of the primitive Church upon this point?

A. It declared in its Creeds [1], that the means of grace and salvation can only be obtained in the Church; that remission of sins can only be had there; that the Sacrament of the Eucharist [2], the graces of the Spirit [3], and the Word of God [4], pure and incorrupt, can be received only in the Church; that prayer can only be offered up acceptably to God, and that Benediction can only be received, in Communion with the Church

Below, chap. vi. vii. viii. xiii. xiv. xv.

of Christ[5]. In the words of S. Jerome[6], "Qui matrem Ecclesiam contempserit, morte morietur." And in those of S. Augustin, "Sanctus mons Dei sancta Ecclesia ejus; qui non ei communicant, non exaudiuntur ad vitam æternam." And of S. Ambrose[7], "Ecclesia est Corpus Christi: et ille negat Christum, qui non omnia, quæ Christi sunt, confitetur." And of S. Augustin[6] again, "Ecclesia Catholica sola corpus est Christi, cujus Ille Caput est et Salvator corporis sui. *Extra* hoc corpus *neminem* vivificat Spiritus Sanctus." "*Nulla salus, nisi in Ecclesiâ*," was the concurrent language of all Christian antiquity; and in the words of S. Cyprian[8], and of S. Augustin[6], "*Nemo potest habere* Deum Patrem, *qui non habet* Ecclesiam Matrem."

[1] S. CYPRIAN ad Magn. Credis remissionem peccatorum et vitam æternam per sanctam Ecclesiam.

S. AUG. Enchir. vi. p. 379. Extra Ecclesiam non remittuntur peccata: ipsa nam proprie Spiritûs Sancti pignus accepit sine quo non remittuntur peccata.

See KETTLEWELL on the Creed, pt. ii. chaps. vi. and vii. pp. 323—335, ed. 1718.

[2] S. IGNAT. ad Ephes. v. ἐὰν μή τις ᾖ ἐντὸς τοῦ θυσιαστηρίου, ὑστερεῖται τοῦ ἄρτου τοῦ Θεοῦ. Cf. ad Trall. c. vii.

[3] S. IREN. iii. 40. Spiritûs non sunt participes qui non concurrunt ad Ecclesiam; qui non participant eum neque a mammillis Matris nutriuntur in Vitam, neque percipiunt de Corpore Christi procedentem nitidissimum fontem, sed effodiunt sibi lacus detritos de fossis terrenis, et de cœno putridam bibunt aquam, effugientes fidem Ecclesiæ—nunquam scientiam stabilem habentes, non fundati super unam Petram, sed super arenam.

[4] S. IREN. iii. 4. Non oportet apud alios quærere Veritatem, quam facile est ab Ecclesiâ sumere, cum Apostoli quasi in depositorium dives plenissimè in eam contulerint omnia quæ sint Veritatis, uti omnis quicunque velit sumat ab eâ potum vitæ. Hæc est vitæ introitus. Omnes autem reliqui fures sunt et latrones.

[5] S. PROSPER AQUIT. in Psalm cxlvii. 13. *Benedixit filios in te.* Extra Jerusalem nulla benedictio est: quia non sanctificatur nisi qui Ecclesiæ, quæ est Christi corpus, unitur.

[6] S. HIERON. in Mich. vii. i. S. AUGUSTIN, iv. p. 520. vi. p. 976, in S. Joan. 118, c. Lit. Petil. c. 38.

PART I.

⁷ S. AMBROSE in S. Luc. iv. c. 9. S. CYPRIAN, p. 96, ed. Fell. Cum Apostolus (Eph. v. 31) Christi pariter atque Ecclesiæ unitatem individuis nexibus cohærentem sanctâ suâ voce testatur, quomodo potest esse cum Christo qui cum sponsâ Christi et in Ejus Ecclesiâ non est?

⁸ S. CYPRIAN, p. 109. p. 119, ed. Fell.

Bp. ANDREWES, Sermon on Matt. vi. 17. This is sure: ' *No man hath God to his Father, that hath not the Church for his mother;*' and that once or twice in the Proverbs order is taken, as to "*keep the precepts of our Father, so not to set light by the laws of our Mother.*" *Ira Patris* and *dolor matris* are together in one verse; "he that grieves her, angers Him."

Q. You say that there is no salvation but in the Church, and that the Church is distinguished from all other Societies by Faith in our Lord Jesus Christ; do you hereby intend to say that all who were born *before* the coming of Christ, and all who since His Incarnation have remained in ignorance of Him, are excluded from hope of salvation?

John viii. 56.
1 Cor. x. 1—4.
2 Cor. iv. 13.
Heb. xi. 7—35.

A. No: certainly not. The Church consists of the *covenanted People* of God in *all countries and ages*, whether *before* or *after* the coming of Christ: and the object of its Faith has ever been one and the same, JESUS CHRIST. The members of the Church *before* His coming believed in Him *to come;* we believe in Him *having come*. The *seasons* of the Church are changed, but her *faith* is unchanged and unchangeable ¹, and we doubt not that by that faith men have been saved in every age and country of the world.

¹ S. AUG. Tract. in Joann. xlv. iii. p. 2131. *Ante* adventum Domini Nostri Jesu Christi, quo humilis venit in carne, præcesserunt justi, sic in eum credentes *venturum*, quomodo nos credimus in eum qui *venit*. *Tempora* variata sunt, non *fides*. Diversis quidem temporibus sed per unum fidei ostium videmus ingressos. See also S. AUG. ii. pp. 415. 420, and above, pp. 5, 6, and p. 14. S. IREN. iv. 13—24. Bp. BARLOW's Remains, 582—592. XXXIX ARTICLES. Art. vii. Both in the *Old* and *New* Testament everlasting life is offered to mankind by CHRIST.

Q. But what then should we say of those who remain in entire ignorance of Christ? CHAP. IV.

A. We may not venture to say any thing, except that man's responsibilities vary with his privileges, and that Christ's merits and mercy are infinite[1]; and that those persons are in God's hands, and that "God is Love." Our duty here, is to adore in silence the depth of the riches of the wisdom and knowledge of God, and to discharge those *duties* which the consideration of their case forces upon us.

Luke xii. 48.

1 John iv. 8.

---

[1] BARROW, Sermons on Universal Redemption, iii. p. 464. Bp. BUTLER, Analogy, Pt. ii. chap. vi. "Every man will be dealt equitably with." Cp. Macknight and Whitby on Rom. ii. 14, and Eph. ii. 3.

Q. What are these?

A. First, the duty of thankfulness to God, that "He hath called *us* with a holy calling to His kingdom and glory," by admitting us into Covenant with Himself in Jesus Christ; next, since it is revealed unto us in Scripture, that [1] "no one cometh unto Him but by Christ, Who is the Way, the Truth, and the Life, and that there is none other Name given under heaven whereby men may be saved," we are bound to commiserate the condition of those who have not been admitted into this covenant; and, thirdly, to *pray*[2] God for them; and to do all in our power to promote the cause of Christian *Missions*, in order that all Nations of the world may be brought within the pale of the Church, and become "one fold, under one Shepherd, JESUS CHRIST our Lord."

2 Tim. i. 9.
1 Thess. ii. 12.

John xiv. 6.

Acts iv. 12.

---

[1] CASAUBON, Exerc. Baron. p. 3. Credendum sane, etiam *ante* natum è B. Virgine Dominum, alios quoque salutis factos esse participes, *paucos, qui vel apparent in Scripturis, vel in genere humano latent,* ut ait B. Augustinus in Epistolâ 99, ad Euodium Episcopum; sed illud quoque simul credendum, neminem ullâ unquam ætate ad spiritalem Jerusalem pertinuisse, *nisi cui divinitus revelatus fuerit unus Mediator Dei et hominum, homo Christus Jesus; qui ven-*

PART I. *turus in carne, sic antiquis sanctis prænuntiabatur, quemadmodum nobis venisse nuntiatus est,* ait idem Augustinus, de Civit. Dei, lib. XVIII. cap. xlvii., et in Epistolâ 28, ad Hieronymum, verba illius sunt: *Certus sum, non esse animam ullam in genere humano cui non sit necessarius ad liberationem Mediator Dei et hominum, homo Christus Jesus.*

XXXIX ARTICLES, Art. xviii. *Of obtaining eternal salvation only by the name of Christ.* They also are to be had accursed, that presume to say, that every man shall be saved by the law or sect which he professeth, so that he be diligent to frame his life according to that law, and the light of nature. For holy Scripture doth set out unto us only the name of Jesus Christ, whereby men must be saved.

[2] LEO MAGNUS, ed. Lugduni, 1700, tom. i. pp. 8, 9. De Vocat. omn. Gent. lib. I. cap. xii. *Supplicat* ubique Ecclesia Deo non solum pro sanctis et in Christo jam regeneratis, sed etiam pro omnibus *infidelibus* et inimicis crucis Christi, pro omnibus idolorum cultoribus, pro omnibus qui Christum in membris ipsius persequuntur, pro Judæis quorum cæcitati lumen Evangelii non refulget, pro hæreticis et schismaticis qui ab unitate fidei et charitatis alieni sunt. Quid autem pro istis petit, nisi ut relictis erroribus suis convertantur ad Deum, accipiant fidem, accipiant charitatem, et de ignorantiæ tenebris liberati in agnitionem veniant veritatis? See the Third Collect for Good Friday in the BOOK OF COMMON PRAYER.

CHAPTER V.

ON ERRORS IN THE CHURCH.

Q. CAN the Church *fail?*

A. No. *Particular* Churches *may* fail[1], but the *Catholic* Church *cannot;* for it is Christ's Body; and He has promised that "the gates of hell shall not prevail against it," and that He will be with it "alway, even unto the end of the world." The Church is subject to vicissitudes, but cannot be destroyed; its Light[2] may wane, but will never be extinct. There will always be light in the seven-branched Candlestick of the Universal Church, which will always stand in the World, though *any one* of its branches may be removed.

Rev. ii. 5.
Matt. xvi. 18. xxviii. 20.
Luke xviii. 8.
2 Thess. ii. 3.
1 Tim. iv. 1.
2 Pet. ii. 2.
Rev. xii. 4. xiii. 8.

[1] Abp. BRAMHALL, i. 43. There is a vast difference between the Catholic Church, and a patriarchal one. The Catholic Church can never fail; any patriarchal Church may.

[2] S. AMBROS. Hexaëm. iv. 2, and iv. 8. Ecclesia, sicut Luna, defectus habet et ortus frequentes, sed defectibus suis crevit. S. AUG. Ep. 48, ad Vincent. Ecclesia aliquando obscuratur et tanquam obnubilatur scandalorum multitudine.

Q. Can the Church *err ?*

A. The Invisible Church, or company of God's elect People, is safe from error; and the *whole visible* Church of Christ cannot err; but it may be so much affected by the depraved lives, corrupt tenets, or violent passions of many of its members, that Christ's voice in it may at times be hardly heard [1]; and though there will be always Truth in it by reason of Christ's perpetual presence in the Church, and as it is "the pillar and ground of the Truth," yet *that truth* will be more or less generally and publicly *manifest* at different times.

John x. 29.
1 Pet. i. 5.
Matt. xxiv. 11. 24.
2 Tim. iii. 1

Ps. xlvi. 5.
1 Tim. iii. 15.
Joel ii. 32.
Obad. 17.

[1] S. AUG. lib. ii. c. 3, de Bapt. c. Donat. Provincialia Concilia emendari posse per Plenaria, et Plenaria priora per posteriora. FIELD, on the Church, iv. c. 5. CRAKANTHORPE, Vind. Eccles. Anglican. p. 19. Bp. PEARSON on the Creed, Art. ix. p. 343. (ed. 1715.)

Q. Can you show this from Scripture?

A. Yes. Christ Himself has spoken of a time when *Iniquity will abound* and *Charity* will *wax cold*, and *the Faith* will be hard *to find* [1]. He has said, that as it was in the days of Noah and of Lot, so will it be at his Second Coming, the circumstances of which are also compared to the calamities suffered at the taking of Jerusalem. St. Paul has spoken in like manner of "perilous times" for the Church. Though there will be always good *grain* on the Threshing-floor of the Church, yet the *chaff* may sometimes *nearly* hide it; though pure *wheat* will be ever in the Field, yet it may sometimes be almost choked with *tares.* Therefore, though the *Whole* Church of Christ cannot fall away, yet any *particular* Church, and

Luke xviii. 8. xvii. 26.
Matt. xxiv. 3, &c.
Gen. vii. xix.
1 Tim. iv. 1.
2 Thess. ii. 3—5.
Acts ii. 19—21.

PART I. any particular persons, who may come together in a Council pretending to represent the Church, may err[2].

[1] S. HIERON. in cap. 2. Sophon. Veruntamen veniens Filius hominis, putas, inveniet Fidem supra terram? Non mirabitur de externâ Ecclesiæ vastitate, quod regnante Antichristo redigenda sit in solitudinem? S. AMBROSE in S. Luc. xxi. 25.

S. AUG. de Civ. Dei, xx. 8. Antichristi tempore Diabolus solvendus; et proinde gravior erit illa persecutio, quanto crudelius potest sævire solutus quam ligatus. IDEM, Tract. in S. Joann. xxv. p. 1966.

[2] XXXIX ARTICLES, Art. xix. As the Church of Jerusalem, Alexandria, and Antioch have erred, so also the Church of Rome has erred, not only in their living and manner of ceremonies, but also in matters of faith. Abp. LAUD against Fisher, p. 114, sect. 22; p. 134, sect. 25; and p. 185, sect. 31—33, ed. Oxf. 1839. Bp. BEVERIDGE on XIXth and XXIst Articles. Art. xxi. General *Councils* may err.

Q. But if persons collected together in Councils, and professing to represent the Church, may err, what is the use of Œcumenical or General Councils?

A. Very great: first, though a Council of the Church *may* err[1], yet, if it takes Scripture as its guide, it is not to be *presumed* that it *will* err; and such Councils are of Apostolic institution, and *have* been very serviceable for the maintenance of truth, and suppression of error[2]; and though, *à priori*, it be admitted that any given body of men collected together *may err*, yet, *à posteriori*, it is to be believed, that whatever has been *decreed* and *promulgated* by Church Councils rightly convened, and building their decrees on Holy Scripture, and whatever having been so decreed has been subsequently *received* by the Church Universal,—is *not* erroneous, but true; as, for example, the doctrinal canons of the first four General Councils. And though it should be *thought* that they are in error, yet, until the error be *plainly shown* to be against Scripture[3], *private opinions*

Below, Pt. ii. ch. ix. at end.

ought to give way to *Public Authority*, founding its decisions on the Divine Word, for the end or avoidance of strife[4], and for the sake of Peace and Unity in the Church. In *controverted* points, we ought to stand by the determination of the Church, unless, as has been said, it can be clearly shown to be against Scripture.

CHAP. V.

[1] XXXIX ARTICLES, Art. xxi.
[2] See HOOKER, V. LIV. 10, on the eminent services of the First Four General Councils.
[3] S. ATHANAS. de Synod. c. 6. ἡ γραφὴ πασῶν συνόδων κρείττων.

S. HIERON. in Epist. Galat. Spiritûs Sancti doctrina est, quæ canonicis literis est prodita, contra quam si quid statuant *Concilia*, nefas duco.

[4] HOOKER, II. VII. 5. For it to have been deceived is not impossible. See his Preface, ch. vi. 3, where speaking of controverted questions of Church Discipline he thus writes: "Ye will perhaps make answer, that being persuaded already as touching the truth of your cause, ye are not to hearken unto any sentence. Again, that men, yea, *Councils may err;* and that, unless the judgment given do satisfy your minds, unless it be such as ye can by no further argument oppugn; in a word, unless you perceive and acknowledge it yourselves consonant with *God's Word;* to stand unto it, not allowing it, were to sin against your own consciences.

Gal. i. 8.

. . . . . .

"We wish not that men should do any thing which in their hearts they are persuaded they ought not to do; but *this persuasion* ought (we say) to be *fully settled* in their hearts *that* in litigious and controverted causes of such quality, the will of God is to have them do whatsoever the *sentence of judicial and final decision* shall determine; yea, though it seem in their private opinion to swerve utterly from that which is right: as, no doubt, many times the sentence amongst the Jews did seem unto one part or other contending, and yet in this case God did then allow them to do that which in their private judgment it seemed, yea, and perhaps truly seemed, that the law did disallow. For if God be not the Author of confusion, but of peace, then can He not be the Author of our *refusal*, but of our *contentment* to stand upon some definitive sentence; without which almost impossible it is that either we should avoid confusion, or ever hope to attain peace. To small purpose had the *Council of Jerusalem* been assembled, if once their determination being set down, men might afterwards have

Acts xv.

PART 1. defended their former opinions. When, therefore, they had given their definitive sentence, *all controversy was at an end.* Things were disputed *before* they came to be determined; men *afterwards* were not to *dispute* any longer, but to *obey.* The sentence of judgment *finished their strife,* which their disputes before judgment could not do."

Archbishop LAUD against Fisher, sects. 32 and 33, p. 216. The Church is never more cunningly abused than when men out of this truth that she may err [when represented in a Council called General] infer this falsehood, that she is not to be obeyed. It will never follow, *she may err,* therefore she *may not govern.*

Q. In what respects may individuals in a Church err, as well as national Churches?

A. Principally by Heresies or by Schisms.

Q. What is the meaning of the word Heresy?

A. It comes from the Greek, αἵρεσις, *a choice*[1],

Rom. xvi. 17.
2 Thess. iii. 6. 14.
2 John 10.

and it means an arbitrary adoption, in matters of faith, of opinions at variance with the doctrines delivered by Christ and His Apostles, and received from them by the Catholic Church.

[1] TERTULLIAN, Præscript. Hæret. 6. Sed et in omni pæne epistolâ Paulus Apostolus de adulterinis doctrinis fugiendis inculcans, *hæreses* taxat, quarum opera sunt adulteræ doctrinæ; *Hæreses* dictæ *Græcâ* voce ex interpretatione *electionis,* quâ quis sive ad instituendas sive ad

Titus iii. 11. suscipiendas eas utitur. Ideo et *sibi damnatum* dixit *hæreticum,* quia et in quo damnatur, sibi elegit. Nobis vero nihil ex nostro arbitrio inducere licet, sed nec *eligere* quod aliquis de arbitrio suo induxerit. Apostolos Domini habemus auctores, qui nec ipsi quicquam ex suo arbitrio, quod inducerent, *elegerunt;* sed *acceptam a Christo disciplinam fideliter* nationibus adsignaverunt. Itaque etiamsi *Angelus*

Gal. i. 8, 9. *de cœlis aliter evangelizaret, anathema diceretur* a nobis.

S. HIERON. in Epist. ad Titum, c. 3. *Hæresis* Græce ab *electione* venit, quod scilicet unusquisque id sibi eligat quod ei melius videatur.

Q. Is every one who holds an error in religion to be called a Heretic?

Luke xii. 47.
James iv. 17.
Jude 22.

A. No. Error, which is neither voluntarily adopted, nor pertinaciously defended, *does not,*—but error[1], willingly adopted, publicly avowed, and obstinately maintained, *does,*—make a man a Heretic.

[1] S. Aug. Ep. 43, tom. ii. p. 131. Qui sententiam suam quamvis falsam atque perversam nullâ pertinaci animositate defendunt, præsertim quam non audaciâ præsumptionis suæ pepererunt, sed a seductis atque in errorem lapsis parentibus acceperunt, quærunt autem cautâ solicitudine veritatem, corrigi parati cum invenerint, *nequaquam sunt inter hæreticos deputandi.*

S. Aug. de Civ. D. xviii. 51. Qui in Ecclesiâ morbidum aliquid pravumque sapiunt, resistunt contumaciter, suaque pestifera et mortifera dogmata emendare nolunt, sed defensare persistunt, hæretici fiunt.

Archbishop BRAMHALL, i. p. 110, ed. Oxf. REFORMAT LEGUM, p. 8. HOOKER, V. LXII. 6. S. Cyprian, in the matter of heretical baptism, was "in error, but not in heresy." Bp. TAYLOR. Liberty of Prophesying, caps. i. ii.

Q. In what consists the sin of *Heresy?*

A. In that they who are guilty of it, presume to be wise concerning the things of God "above what is written," and to obtain salvation from Him on terms invented by themselves [1].

1 Cor. iv. 6.

[1] TERTULLIAN, Præscript. Hæret. c. 6. Nobis nihil ex nostro arbitrio inducere licet.—c. 11. Regula a Christo instituta nullas habet apud nos quæstiones nisi quæ Hæreses inferunt.—c. 8. Nobis curiositate non opus est post Christum Jesum, nec inquisitione post Evangelium.

Q. What is the language of Scripture concerning Heresy?

A. Heresy is a corruption of that purity which is the characteristic of Christ's Church, who is described in Scripture as a chaste Virgin [1]. St. Peter speaks of "false teachers bringing in privily damnable heresies." St. Paul compares them to the magicians of Egypt who resisted Moses, and says, "Though we, or an Angel from heaven, preach any other Gospel unto you than that which we have preached unto you, let him be accursed." "A man that is an Heretic after the first and second admonition reject, knowing that he that is such is subverted and sinneth, being condemned *of himself,*" i. e. by his own *choice,* viz. by what he himself has *chosen (elegit)* [2], instead

2 Cor. xi. 2.
2 Pet. ii. 1.
2 Tim. iii. 8
Gal. i. 8.
Titus iii. 10, 11.
2 John 10.

PART I. of framing his will to maintain that which Reason and Religion teach.

[1] S. AMBROSE ad Ev. S. Luc. xv. 18. Vir Christus est, Uxor Ecclesia; caritate Uxor, integritate Virgo. S. PROSPER AQUITAN. Epigr. lxxvi. Virginitas animæ est intemerata fides. S. AUG. Serm. i. de Verb. Dom. Ecclesiæ concessit Christus in Spiritu quod Mater Ejus habuit in corpore, ut et Mater et Virgo sit.—Serm. 16, de Temp. Ecclesia mater est visceribus charitatis, Virgo integritate fidei.
[2] HOOKER, III. VIII. 8.

Q. What is *Schism?*

A. It is an act by which any society of men, or any individual member thereof, voluntarily divides [1], or separates itself or himself from the unity of the Visible Church, or makes divisions in it.

[1] Archbp. BRAMHALL, vol. i. p. 112. Schismatics are,— whosoever doth uncharitably make rupture, or "sets up altar against altar" in Christ's Church, or withdraws his obedience from the Catholic Church . . . . whosoever doth wilfully break the line of Apostolical succession, which is the very nerve and sinew of ecclesiastical unity and communion, both with the present Church, and with the Catholic symbolical Church of all successive ages; he is a schismatic (*quâ talis*), whether he be guilty of heretical pravity or not.

Q. What is the difference between *Heresy* and *Schism?*

A. In the words of S. Jerome [1], "*Heresy* maintains perverse *doctrine*. *Schism* is a separation from the Church," in the nature of what he calls an "*Episcopalis dissensio,*" or dissent from Ecclesiastical governors; when a man wholly or occasionally withdraws himself from communion with his lawful Bishop and Pastor, and takes any part in setting up or maintaining Bishop against Bishop, Pastor against Pastor, or altar against altar. "But," adds S. Jerome, "there is no schism which does not tend to generate some *heresy,*" whence S. Augustin [2] calls heresy a *schisma inveteratum.* Heresy is *contra dogmata,*

1 Kings xii. 27—32.

contra fidem, et contra veritatem; Schism, *contra personas*³, *contra disciplinam, et contra caritatem.*

¹ S. HIERON. in Tit. c. 3. He calls it *dissensio episcopalis;* there being in that age no Christian congregation apart from, or independent of, a Bishop. See below, Pt. i. ch. x.

² S. AUG. c. Crescon. ii. 7.

³ S. CYPRIAN, Ep. lxvi. p. 167. Inde schismata et hæreses, dum Episcopus, qui unus est et Ecclesiæ præest, superbâ præsumptione contemnitur.

S. AUG. de Fide et Symb. c. 10. Hæretici de Deo falsa sentiendo ipsam fidem violant; schismatici autem dissensionibus iniquis a fraternâ caritate dissiliunt, quamvis ea credant quæ credimus.

Q. What do we learn from Holy Scripture concerning Schism?

A. As the punishment and fearful judgment of God on *Nadab* and *Abihu*¹ is a solemn warning against *Heresy*, so is that on *Korah* a warning against *Schism*. *Jeroboam*, who is characterized in Scripture more than twenty times as he that "made Israel to sin," is an example of *both Heresy and Schism.* St. Paul says to the Corinthians, "I beseech you, brethren, by the name of Jesus Christ, that ye all speak the same thing, and that there be no divisions (σχίσματα) among you." And he declares that *nothing*, not even martyrdom², *profiteth* without *charity;* and no one can be said to have charity who is wilfully guilty of schism. Schism is a carnal work, and as such excludes from heaven; it tends to the subversion of a Church, for a kingdom or house divided against itself cannot stand; it is a rending of Christ's blessed Body; a violation of the marriage-compact between Him and the Church (μοιχεία πνευματική); a disregard of His Divine Example, by which He taught His Disciples to love one another; an open contempt of His Prayer, "As Thou, Father, art in Me, and I in Thee; so may they also be one in Us, that they may be one, as We are one;" a breaking of the bond of love, by which Christ's

Levit. x. 1.
Num. iii. 4.
Num. xvi.
Jude 11. 19.
1 Kings xii. 27—32.
1 Cor. i. 10.
1 Cor. xiii. 3.
1 Cor. iii. 3.
Gal. v. 20, 21.
Matt. xii. 25.
John xiii. 34.
John xviii. 21, 22.

John xiii. 35.
Acts ii. 46. iv. 32.
Col. iii. 14.
Gal. v. 22.

disciples are to be known; a falling away from the practice of the members of the Apostolic Church, who were all of one accord, of one heart and one soul[3].

[1] S. IREN. iii. 43. *Hæretici* quidem alienum ignem offerentes ad altare Dei, id est alienas doctrinas, a cœlesti igne comburuntur, quemadmodum *Nadab* et *Abiud*. Qui vero exsurgunt contra veritatem, et alteros adhortantur contra Ecclesiam Dei, remanent apud inferos voragine terræ absorpti, quemadmodum qui circa *Chore, Dathan, et Abiron*.
S. CYPRIAN de Unit. Eccl. p. 116.

[2] S. IGNATIUS concerning Schism, Frag. p. 454, ed. Jacobson. οὐδὲ μαρτυρίου αἷμα ταύτην δύνασθαι ἐξαλείφειν τὴν ἁμαρτίαν.—So S. CYPRIAN, de Unit. Eccles. p. 113. Inexpiabilis culpæ discordiæ nec *passione* purgatur: esse Martyr non potest qui in Ecclesiâ non est; *occidi* talis potest, *coronari* non potest.

[3] Bp. HORNE's Discourse on Schism (in the Scholar Armed, ii. 320—326).

Q. But if the Legislature of a country tolerates or encourages schismatics, does it not make Schism to be innocent?

A. No; this is beyond its power. Although a State may remove all the civil penalties of Schism[1], it cannot diminish its religious guilt; "*Pœna potest demi; culpa perennis erit.*"

[1] NORRIS, John, in Christian Institutes, iii. 302, note.

Q. To consider the case of *wilful* and *obstinate* Heretics and Schismatics; are they in the Church?

Above, pp. 13, 14.
A. We may not say they are in the *Invisible* Church. For *wilful* Heretics[1], *as far as their heresy*, and wilful *Schismatics, as far as their schism*, is concerned, have forsaken the *true* Church of God, which is *sound* in *doctrine*, and joined together in *unity*. But by virtue of the Sacraments[2] which they may have received, and of such articles of the Christian Faith as they may

still continue to hold, they are *so far* in the *Visible* Church. They are in the *field*, but they are *tares* in the field. Being *Heretics* or *Schismatics*, but *not* being *Jews, Saracens, Infidels, Atheists,* or *Apostates*, they are still members of the *Visible* Church, though *peccant* and *unsound* members; they are a part, though a *maimed* and *corrupt* part, of the *Visible* Church. " Sunt in Ecclesiâ, quamvis non[3] *salubriter* in Ecclesiâ[4]." They are *in* the Visible Church, but as long as they are *wilful* Heretics or Schismatics they do not receive benefit *from* it[2]. They are subjects of Christ, but rebellious[5] ones. By breaking the Unity of the Faith and of Worship they forsake *Charity*, without which other things do not profit[3], but rather, it is to be feared, may increase their condemnation. (See further below, Pt. iii. ch. iii.)

CHAP. V.

1 Cor. xiii. 3.

[1] HOOKER, III. I. 7—11, and V. LXIII. 7. V. LXVIII. 6. Many things exclude from the kingdom of God, although from the *visible* Church they separate not.

MASON de Ministerio Anglican. p. 195.

[2] S. AUG. de Bapt. iii. c. 19. *Hæretici aliquo modo sunt in Ecclesiâ*, etiam postquam ex illâ exierunt, propter sacramentorum administrationem.

S. AUG. in Breviculo Collationis 3. Ecclesia est corpus vivum, in quo est *Anima* et *Corpus;* et quidem *Anima* sunt interna Spiritus Sancti dona, Fides, Spes, Caritas. *Corpus* sunt externa professio fidei et sacramentorum communicatio. Ex quo fit, ut quidam sint de *animâ* et de *corpore* Ecclesiæ, et proinde uniti Christo Capiti interius et exterius, et tales sunt *perfectissimè* de Ecclesiâ, sunt enim quasi membra viva in corpore: rursum aliqui sunt de *animâ* et non de *corpore*, ut catechumeni et excommunicati, si fidem et caritatem habeant. Denique aliqui sunt de *corpore* et non de *animâ*, ut qui nullam habeant internam virtutem, et tamen spe aut timore aliquo profiteantur fidem, et in sacramentis communicent, et tales sunt sicut capilli aut ungues aut *mali humores in corpore humano*.

HOOKER, III. I. 7. If by external profession they be *Christians*, they are of the *visible* Church of Christ; yea, although they be impious idolaters, wicked *heretics*, persons excommunicable, yea, and *cast out* for notorious improbity.—Ibid. 8. Of the *Visible* body of the Church those may be, and oftentimes are, in respect of the *main parts* of their outward profession, who, in regard of *some parts* of their very profession are, in the eyes of the sounder part of the Visible Church, most execrable.—Ibid. 11. We must acknowledge even *Heretics* themselves to be, though a *maimed* part, yet a *part* of the Visible Church.—Ibid. 10. *Excommunication* shutteth not out clean from the *Visible* Church, but only from *fellowship* with it in *holy duties.*—Ibid. 12. Where *professed unbelief* is, there can be no Visible Church of Christ: there *may be*, where *sound belief wanteth.*

[3] S. AUG. in Ps. liv. *In multis erat mecum:* Baptismum habebamus utrique, Evangelium utrique legebamus: erant in eo mecum: in schismate non mecum, in hæresi non mecum. Sed in his paucis, in quibus non mecum, *non prosunt multa* in quibus mecum. Etenim videte, fratres, quam multa enarravit apostolus Paulus; (1 Cor. xiii.) *unum* dixit *(caritatem)* si defuerit, frustra sunt illa.

[4] CRAKANTHORPE, Def. Eccl. Angl. p. 83.

[5] S. HIERON. Ephes. i. Dominus noster, cum sit Caput Ecclesiæ, habet membra eos omnes qui in Ecclesiâ congregantur, tam sanctos quam peccatores, sed sanctos voluntate peccatores necessitate sibi conjunctos.

Q. What are the consequent duties of the sounder members of the Church toward Heretics and Schismatics?

A. To feel deep sorrow for them; to act towards them in a spirit of charity; but not to communicate with them in any act of Heresy or Schism, or to encourage or flatter them in it; or to treat it lightly; but to "speak the truth in love" concerning its sin and danger; to pray for them; to offer them counsel and exhortation; and to employ all practicable means for bringing them to the enjoyment of those spiritual [1] blessings which are promised to those who love the peace of the Church, and who dwell together in Unity.

[1] S. AUG. in S. Joann. Tract. xxxiii. 8. Accipimus ergo et nos Spiritum Sanctum, si *amamus Ecclesiam,* si *charitate compaginamur,* si catholico nomine et fide gaudemus. Credamus, fratres, quantum quisque amat Ecclesiam Christi, tantum habet Spiritum Sanctum. See also CLEM. ALEX. Strom. vii. § xv.

CHAPTER VI.

ON PRIVILEGES IN THE CHURCH.

Word of God.—The Church its Witness and Keeper.

Q. WHAT privileges do the members of the Church derive through her means from God?

A. First, the WORD OF GOD pure and entire; which is received from JESUS CHRIST, who is the Head of the Church, and who speaks to us by the HOLY SPIRIT, whom He has sent to abide in His Church.   1 Pet. i. 23. James i. 18. iii. 17. John xiv. 16. 26. xvi. 7. 13.

Q. How is the Word of God received from CHRIST through the Church?

A. As the two Tables of the Law were by God's command consigned to the Ark, so the two Testaments are committed by CHRIST to the Church [1].   Deut. x. 2.

[1] Lord BACON, Confession of Faith, Works, iii. p. 124, ed. 1778. The Church is as the Ark, wherein the Tables of the first Testament were kept and preserved. See also v. 530. De Ecclesiâ et Scripturis. *Contradictiones linguarum* ubique occurrunt *extra tabernaculum Dei.* Quare quocunque te verteris, exitum controversiarum non reperies nisi huc te receperis.

Q. How is the Church a Witness and Keeper of Holy Writ?

A. The *Old Testament* is received by us through the Church of the *Jews,* to whom " were committed the oracles of God," and who received those " lively oracles to give unto us [1]," and by whom " of old time they were read in the Synagogues every Sabbath day;" and they were by them delivered, *pure* and *entire,* into the hands of the *Christian* Church. This we know, from the facts, that the Jews, being dispersed in all parts of the world, could never have conspired [2] to make any change   Isa. viii. 20. Rom. iii. 2. Acts vii. 38. xiii. 14. 15. 27. xv. 21.

PART I. in their sacred books, had they desired to do so, which they were so far from doing, that "they would rather die a thousand deaths³," than allow any change to be made in them; and that every verse and every letter of the sacred text was scrupulously registered in their *Masora*⁴; and also, that CHRIST, when reproving the Scribes and Lawyers, never charges⁵ them with the sin of corrupting the Books of the Law, which He would not have omitted to do, had they been guilty of it. JESUS CHRIST, the Son of God, received the Scriptures of the Old Testament as they existed then amongst the Jews, and He has delivered them to us as the unerring Word of God.

¹ S. AUGUST. tom. ii. 610. iv. 501. 760. v. 47. viii. 391. Judæi Librarii, Capsarii, et Scriniarii Christianorum, iis sparsi per orbem terrarum, quomodo servi, Sacros Codices portant. S. CHRYSOSTOM, i. p. 631, ed. Savil.
² S. AUG. de Civ. Dei, xv. 13.
³ PHILO ap. Euseb. Præp. Evang. viii. 6. JOSEPHUS apud Euseb. iii. 9.
⁴ HOTTINGER, Thesaurus, p. 138.
⁵ S. HIERON. in Esai. vi. Nunquam Dominus et Apostoli, qui cætera crimina arguunt in Scribis et Pharisæis, de hoc crimine, quod erat maximum, reticuissent.
Bp. COSIN on the Canon, pp. 11. 98, ed. 1672. WORDSWORTH on the CANON of SCRIPTURE and on the Apocrypha, 2nd ed. 1851, and "On the INSPIRATION of the Bible," 5th ed., 1864.

Q. Next, what has been the office of the *Christian* Church with respect to the *New Testament?*

A. To deliver it, as well as the Old Testament, down to us also, from age to age, as it was first written.

That these Writings, as we now possess them, are the same as when they were first given to the world, we know from the facts of their having been publicly *received* by Synods of the Church¹; from their having been *openly read*, immediately after their publication, in Congregations of the

Col. iv. 16.
1 Thess. v. 27.

Church in numerous places very distant from each other; from their having been *translated* at an early period into different languages² for the use of various Churches, which Versions thus made are found to coincide with the present text. Lastly, and above all, JESUS CHRIST, who sent the HOLY GHOST to enable the Apostles and Evangelists to *write* Holy Scripture, avouches what they have written, by the *reception* of it by the Universal Church, which is His Body, and to which He promised His Presence and the Holy Spirit. The *reception* of Scripture by the Universal Church is the testimony of JESUS CHRIST Himself speaking thereby³.

CHAP. VI.

Matt. xxviii. 20. John xiv. 16. 26. xvi. 7. 13.

---

¹ Canon lx. Concil. Laodicenum, (about A.D. 352,) p. 79, ed. Bruns., compared with the Sixth Article of the Church of England: the two catalogues coincide, with the exception of the Apocalypse, (on which see Concil. Tolet. iv. can. 16, and Bp. COSIN, pp. 56. 58, and HOOKER, V. xx. 4, with Mr. Keble's note,) not contained in the former; and the book of Baruch, (which however is not in the old Latin Version, Labbe, Concil. i. p. 1521, and see Bp. COSIN, pp. 53. 58,) not received as canonical in the latter. See also the very ancient Fragmentum de Canone SS. Scripturarum, of the New Test. in Routh's Reliquiæ Sacræ, iv. pp. 3–5, with the notes of the Editor; and on the history of the New Test. Canon, see KIRCHHOFER, Quellensammlung, Zürich, 1842, and WORDSWORTH on the CANON, 1851, and WESTCOTT on the Canon, 1855.

S. CYRIL, Cateches. iv. n. xxii. p. 66.

S. CYRIL, Cateches. iv. xxxv. πρὸς τὰ ἀπόκρυφα μηδὲν ἔχε κοινόν· ταύτας μόνας μελέτα (βίβλους) σπουδαίως ἃς ἐν Ἐκκλησίᾳ ἀναγιγνώσκομεν· πολὺ σοῦ φρονιμώτεροι ἦσαν οἱ Ἀπόστολοι, καὶ οἱ ἀρχαῖοι Ἐπίσκοποι οἱ τῆς Ἐκκλησίας προστάται οἱ ταύτας παραδόντες, σὺ οὖν τέκνον τῆς Ἐκκλησίας ὢν μὴ παραχάραττε τοὺς θεσμούς.

S. AUG. Epist. xciii. p. 369. Canonica Scriptura tot linguarum litteris et ordine et successione celebrationis Ecclesiasticæ custoditur.

² S. AUG. c. Faust. xxxii. c. 16. Corrumpi Scripturæ non possunt, quia sunt *in manibus omnium Christianorum: et quisquis hoc primitus ausus esset, multorum codicum* vetustiorum collatione confutaretur; maxime quia *non una lingua* sed *multis* continetur Scriptura.

PART I.   S. CHRYSOST. in S. Joann. i. thus speaks of Translations existing in his time:—Σύροι καὶ Αἰγύπτιοι καὶ Ἰνδοι καὶ Πέρσαι τε καὶ Αἰθίοπες καὶ μυρία ἔθνη ἔτερα, εἰς τὴν ἑαυτῶν γλῶτταν μεταβαλόντες τὰ παρὰ τούτου (εὐαγγελιστοῦ) εἰσαχθέντα δόγματα ἔμαθον.

³ S. AUG. de Civ. Dei, xi. 2. CHRISTUS JESUS priùs per Prophetas, deinde per Se Ipsum, posteà per Apostolos, locutus, Scripturam condidit. C. Faust. ii. 5, and xiii. Nostrorum Librorum Auctoritas tot Gentium consensione, per successiones Apostolorum, Episcoporum, Conciliorumque roboratur.

Q. How do we know that the Books of the New Testament are *genuine*, i. e. were written by those persons whose names they bear?

A. From the testimony of the Church, which *received* them and publicly read them as such¹.

¹ ORIGENES et S. AMBROSIUS in S. Luc. init. TERTULLIAN c. Marcion. iv. 5. Auctoritas Ecclesiarum Apostolicarum patrocinatur Evangeliis, quæ proinde *per* illas et *secundum* illas habemus.

Q. Next, have we any witness of the Church that these writings are *inspired*, i. e. are the Word of God?

1 John iv. 1.
1 Cor. xii. 10.
2 John 7.
2 Pet. iii. 15, 16.
Rev. ii. 2.

A. Yes; JESUS CHRIST endued the Primitive Church with the power of trying and discerning the spirits; and she had the best natural opportunities for ascertaining the truth, and *saw* the *miracles*, by which their Authors established their claim to Inspiration¹; and she *received* and publicly *read* them as inspired; while she *rejected* other writings falsely pretending to be so; and *excommunicated* those who published them².

¹ S. AUG. de Doct. Christ. ii. 13.
RUFFIN. in Symbol. p. 26. (ad calc. Cyprian. ed. Fell.) Novi et Veteris Instrumenti Volumina, quæ secundum majorum traditionem per Ipsum Spiritum Sanctum *inspirata* creduntur et Ecclesiis Christi tradita, competens videtur in hoc loco evidenti numero, sicut ex patrum monumentis accepimus, designare.—He then gives the catalogue.

HOOKER, V. XXII. 2. If with reason we may presume upon things which a few men's dispositions do testify, suppose we that the minds of men are not both at their first access to the school of Christ exceedingly *moved*, yea, and for ever afterwards also *confirmed* much, when they consider the *main consent of all the Churches in the world* witnessing the Sacred Authority of Scripture ever since the first publication thereof even till this present day and hour? See also HOOKER, II. IV. 2.

² BINGHAM, Eccl. Antiq. XVII. v. 18.

Q. Have we *any other foundation* for our belief that the Bible is the Word of God?

A. Yes; we have *internal* evidence, as well as *external*.

1 Cor. x. 15.
xi. 13.
Luke xii. 56, 57.

God gives us *reason* and *grace*; Christ, speaking in and by the Church, *moves* us to this belief by her authority, and by showing us that it is supported by the testimony of all successive ages, even from the time of the Apostles and Evangelists, who were incompetent of themselves to write and do what they wrote and did; and whose lives, actions, and sufferings, with the effects produced by them, prove that they could neither be deceived nor deceive in this matter.

This is *external* evidence.

And then, through the grace of the Spirit of God, the Scripture itself, by its native power, its moral purity, its divine beauty, the wonderful *harmony* and *unity* of all its parts (extending over many thousand years), and by the fulfilment of its prophecies, *confirms*, *establishes*, and *settles* us in the belief of what CHRIST had before *testified* to us by the Church.

And *this* is *internal* evidence that the BIBLE is the WORD of GOD¹.

¹ HOOKER, III. VIII. 14. By experience we all know that the *first outward motive* leading men so to esteem of Scripture is the *authority of Christ's Church: afterwards*, the more we bestow our time in reading and hearing the mysteries thereof, the more we find that the thing itself

PART I. doth answer our received opinions concerning it: so that the former inducement, prevailing somewhat with us before, doth now much more prevail, when the very thing hath ministered further reason. See also HOOKER, I. XIV. 1. Abp. LAUD against Fisher, p. 69.

Q. How does CHRIST employ the instrumentality of the Church in teaching us the true faith by means of Scripture?

A. Both by her language and by her practice, in her own person, and in that of our Parents and Teachers, who act by her guidance and with her authority, she *invites* and *leads us* by the hand to Christ, to Whom she is subject, and
Eph. v. 24. Whom she hears, worships, and obeys, as her Husband, her Head, her Teacher, and her Saviour; she instructs us in His will, she calls us to hear His doctrine, as revealed by Him in Holy Scripture, of which she is the Witness and
Luke i. 70. Guardian; and *then the doctrine itself finally*
John xvi. 13. *persuades, convinces, settles, and stablishes* us in
2 Pet. i. 21. the Faith, through the influence of the Holy Spirit, Whose word the Scripture is, by its own inherent truth and power. The Church, like the Virgin Mary at Cana, tells us "whatso-
John ii. 5. ever He saith unto you, do it." Like the sister
x. 27. of Lazarus, she sits at Christ's feet, and listens
Luke x. 39. to His words. She performs to us the part of
John iv. 29. the Samaritan woman, who brought her friends to Christ; concerning whom we read, that they *first* believed on Him for *her* saying; but when He had remained with them two days, and they had heard HIM, they believed because of His own word, and said unto the woman, as we now
John iv. 42. say to the Church, "*Now* we believe: but no longer (οὐκέτι) because of *thy* saying; for we have *heard Him ourselves*, and know that this is indeed the Christ, the Saviour of the world[1]."

[1] S. AUGUSTIN in S. Joann. iv. Homines, illa muliere, hoc est Ecclesiâ, annuntiante, ad Christum veniunt, cre-

dunt per istam famam: manet Christus apud eos biduo, et multo plures et firmius in Eum credunt quoniam vere ipse est Salvator Mundi. See also FIELD, Of the Church, p. 355. Jo. GERHARD de Ecclesiâ, t. v. pp. 299. 318.

Q. What inferences do we then derive from Scripture with respect to the Church?

A. From Christ speaking to us in Holy Scripture we learn *which is* His true Church. "*In Sacro Codice Ipsum* CAPUT *ostendit nobis corpus suum.*" Christ shows us Scripture by her ministry: the Scripture shows us the Church by Christ speaking therein [1].

[1] S. AUG. de Unit. Ecclesiæ, c. 4, et c. 16. Ecclesiam corpus Christi, sicut ipsum Caput, in ipsis Scripturis debemus agnoscere. See above, chap. iv. S. AUG. de Symb. ad Catechum. iv. c. 13. Scripturæ sunt tabulæ matrimoniales Christi et Sponsæ Ejus, quæ est Ecclesia.

Abp. LAUD, p. 103. After we are moved, prepared, and induced by tradition (of the Church, to believe Scripture to be the Word of God), we resolve our faith into the written Word; in which we find materially, though not in terms, the very tradition that led us thither. And so we are sure, by Divine authority, that we are in the way, because at the end we find the way proved. Bp. CARLETON contra Trident. p. 162.

Q. By what name do we call those writings which are received by the Church as inspired?

A. Canonical [1].

[1] RUFFIN. in Symbol. ad calc. Cypriani. Hæc sunt quæ Patres intra Canonem concluserunt, ex quibus fidei nostræ assertiones constare voluerunt.

S. AUG. de Doct. Christ. lib. iv. tom. iii. p. 113. Canonem in auctoritatis arce salubriter collocatum. In S. Joann. cxii. Libri, quos in auctoritatem Canonicam *recipit Ecclesia.* And ii. pp. 285—287.

XXXIX ARTICLES, Art. vi. *Canonical* Books,— of whose authority was never any doubt in the *Church.*— All the Books of the New Testament, as they are *commonly received,* we do receive.

Q. What is the derivation and meaning of this word *Canonical?*

A. It comes from the Greek, κανών, *a rule;* and *Canonical* Scriptures are those which are the *Rule* of Christian Faith and Practice.

Q. What were the rejected Books called by the *early Church?*

A. *Apocryphal*[1].

[1] BINGHAM, Antiquities, X. I. 7; XIV. III. 15.

Q. Whence is this word derived, and what does it mean?

A. It is derived from the Greek ἀπὸ, *from,* and κρύπτω, *to hide;* and it generally designated those Books which were *kept apart,* and *not read* in the Church[1].

[1] RUFFIN. in Symbol. Apostol. 38. apud Cyprian. p. 26, ed. Fell, ad fin. *Cæteras* Scripturas (beside the Canonical and Ecclesiastical) *Apocryphas* nominarunt, quas in Ecclesiis legi noluerunt.

Q. How then does it happen, that the majority of the Books (seven of the twelve), which are called *Apocrypha* in our English Bible, *are* read in the Church of England?

A. *These* Books, which are so read, were not commonly called *Apocryphal* by the ancient Church, but *Ecclesiastical*[1], and *were* read in the Christian Church (*Ecclesia*), (though not in the Synagogues of the Jews,) "for example of life and instruction of manners, but *not to establish any doctrine*[2];" and are by some authors, in a *restricted sense,* sometimes even called Canonical[3], as being found in the Canon or Sacred Catalogue of certain Churches; and they are not to be confounded with those which were *called Apocryphal* in *early* times, and which were *not* received or read by the Church.

[1] RUFFIN. in Symbol. c. 38. Alii libri sunt qui non *Canonici* sed *Ecclesiastici* a majoribus appellati sunt, ut est Sapientia Solomonis, et alia Sapientia quæ dicitur Filii Sirach, (hence now called κατ' ἐξοχὴν *Ecclesiasticus*,) qui

liber apud Latinos hoc ipso generali vocabulo Ecclesiasticus vocatur, quo non auctor libelli sed scripturæ qualitas cognominata est. Ejusdem ordinis est libellus Tobiæ et Judith et Machabæorum libri—quæ omnia *legi* quidem in *Ecclesiis voluerunt*, non tamen proferri ad auctoritatem ex his fidei confirmandam. Cf. Bp. Cosin, p. 57, et S. Athanas. ibid. p. 58, where he distinguishes between *Apocryphal* and *Ecclesiastical* books, τὰ ἀπόκρυφα οὔτε ἐν τοῖς κανονικοῖς οὔτε ἐν τοῖς ἐκκλησιαστικοῖς ἀριθμεῖται.

Hooker, V. xx. 7—10. We read in our Churches certain books *besides* the Scripture, yet *as* the Scripture we read them not. Bp. Pearson, Vind. Ignat. i. p. 41. Bp. Bull, Def. Fid. Nic. I. ii. 3. Routh, Rel. Sacr. i. p. 251.

[2] S. Hieron. Præf. ad lib. Salomonis. Ad ædificationem plebis, non ad auctoritatem dogmatum.

XXXIX Articles, Art. vi. and Bp. Beveridge on it, i. p. 274.

[3] Bp. Cosin, p. 104. Bp. Jewel, 197, 198.

Q. In what language were the Canonical Books written?

A. Those of the Old Testament, in Hebrew; those of the New Testament, in Greek.

Q. Ought any *Version* or *Translation* of the Scriptures to be received as of *equal* authority with the Original?

A. Certainly not: every Version of the Scriptures, both as a *Version*, and as the work of *man*, must yield to the *original Word of God*[1]. The human stream cannot rise to a level with the Divine source[2].

[1] S. Aug. de Doctr. Christ. ii. 16. Latinæ linguæ homines duabus aliis ad Scripturarum divinarum cognitionem opus habent, *Hebræâ* scilicet et *Græcâ*, ut ad exemplaria præcedentia *recurratur*, si quam dubitationem attulerit Latinorum interpretum infinita varietas: et (ii. 22) Latinis quibuslibet emendandis Græci adhibeantur, in quibus lxxii *Interpretum*, quod ad Vetus Testamentum attinet, excellit auctoritas. Consistently with this statement a distinction may be made to a certain extent in favour of the *Septuagint*, as a *Version* rising in some degree towards the authority of a *Text*, from its use by the Holy Spirit in the New Testament. See Pocock's Life, pp. 307. 321, and Bp. Pearson, Minor Works, ii. 246.

PART I. 259. 264-5. Bp. WALTON's Prolegom. ix. GRINFIELD's Apology for the LXX, p. 140.

² S. HIERON. ad Damas. Ad Hebraicam linguam tanquam ad *fontem* revertendum in Vetere Testamento. S. HIERON. Præf. ad IV. Evangelia. In Novo Testamento ad Græcam originem revertendum. See also his Epist. ad Lucin. Bæt., and particularly his Epistle ad Suniam ii. p. 627, on the two editions of the LXX.

REFORMATIO Legum Eccles. De Fide Cathol. c. 12. Cæterum in lectione D. Scripturarum, si quæ occurrerint ambigua vel obscura in Vetere Testamento, earum interpretatio ex fonte *Hebraicæ* veritatis petatur: in Novo autem *Græci* codices consulantur.

Pietro SOAVE, Storia di Concilio Tridentino, lib. ii. p. 159, ed. 1629. CASAUBON. Exerc. Baron. xiii. p. 243. Dr. R. BENTLEY, Serm. v. Nov. 1715, iii. p. 247, ed. Dyce, and other authorities quoted in the Appendix of the present Author's Volume "On the CANON OF SCRIPTURE," 1851, and his *Introduction* to 2 Peter, pp. 73—78.

CHAPTER VII.

ON PRIVILEGES IN THE CHURCH.

Right Interpretation of the Word of God.

Q. You said that the Church is the *Interpreter* of God's Word; how is this the case?

A. *First*, and that *negatively*, as not being a *Legislator;* that is, not *legislatively*, but *judicially*,—not by *making* laws, but by *explaining* and *declaring* those which God has promulgated. She has no power *against* the truth, but *for* the truth, and may not "so expound one place of Scripture that it be repugnant to another." Scripture is our only Rule of Faith. The Church aids us in the *right application* of the Rule. The doctrinal interpretations of God's Word, which *have* been *generally* declared and received by the *Universal Church* from *the beginning*, and are ascertained from her Creeds, Confessions of

2 Cor. xiii. 8.
Art. xx.

Faith, Liturgies, and the *practice* of the Church; CHAP. VII.
and from Commentaries on Scripture, and from
consentient expositions of the most eminent
Divines and Preachers, are justly concluded to
be true [1]: and those which are *novel* may be
presumed to be false: "Id verius quod prius, id
prius quod ab initio [2]."

[1] ARTICLE XX. Bp. ANDREWES on Decalogue, pp. 54
—56.
[2] TERTULLIAN c. Marcion. iv. 5.
Bp. BULL, ii. p. 238, ed. Oxf. 1827. The primitive Catholic Church ought to be the standard by which we are
to judge of the orthodoxy and purity of all other succeeding Churches, according to that excellent rule of
TERTULLIAN, Præscript. Hæret. c. 21. Constat omnem
doctrinam, quæ cum Ecclesiis Apostolicis matricibus et
originalibus fide conspiret, veritati esse deputandam, sine
dubio tenentem quod Ecclesiæ ab Apostolis, Apostoli a
Christo, Christus a Deo accepit; omnem vero doctrinam
de mendacio præjudicandam, quæ sapiat contra veritatem
Ecclesiarum et Christi et Dei.
King CHARLES I. Fifth Paper to Mr. Henderson. My
conclusion is, that, albeit I never esteemed any authority
equal to the Scriptures, yet *I do think the unanimous
Consent of the Fathers and the universal Practice of the
primitive Church to be the best and most authentical
Interpreters of God's Word.*
Bp. SANDERSON, Prælect. p. 79. Admonendi estis,
judicio et praxi universalis Ecclesiæ in Sacrarum Litera-
rum Interpretatione plurimum deferri oportere. See the
citations from Abp. WAKE, Bp. STILLINGFLEET, and Dr.
WATERLAND, on the Value of Ecclesiastical Antiquity.

Q. But if what you have said be so, might it
not be objected that our faith rests on the authority, not of the Bible, but of the Church?

A. No. The Church and the Bible are *both*
from God: the one is God's Kingdom, the other
is His Word. As soon as we are conscious of
any thing, we *find* the Church with Holy Scripture in her hands, and appointed by God to deliver it to us, and to instruct us in its meaning.
The Church speaks to us ministerially, the Bible
authoritatively [1].

PART I.   ¹ GERHARD de Ecclesiâ, p. 318. Utrumque est res Dei, Ecclesia et Scriptura. Ecclesia est regnum dei, Scriptura est verbum Dei. Regnum Dei administratur per verbum Dei. Verbum Dei auctoritatem habet in Ecclesiam, et in filios Dei, non autem illi auctoritatem habent in Scripturam sive Dei sapientiam: mutuas sibi operas præstant Ecclesia et Scriptura, sed auctoritas est Scripturæ, ministerium verò Ecclesiæ.

Q. She does not, therefore, on her own authority, impose on us any article of faith as necessary to salvation?

Eph. iii. 10.
Jer. xxiii. 28.
Gal. i. 8.
Eph. ii. 20.

2 Cor. i. 24.

A. No. "The manifold wisdom of God is made known to us by the Church;" but she dares not teach any thing, as necessary to salvation, except what she has received from Christ and His Apostles, and is contained in the Written Word; she does not exercise "dominion over our faith," but is a "helper of our joy ¹."

¹ XXXIX ARTICLES, Art. xx. The Church hath power to decree rites or ceremonies, and authority in controversies of faith: and yet it is not lawful for the Church to ordain any thing that is contrary to God's Word written, neither may it so expound one place of Scripture that it be repugnant to another. Wherefore, although the Church be a witness and a keeper of Holy Writ, yet, as it ought not to decree any thing *against* the same, so *besides* the same *ought it not* to enforce any thing to be delivered *for necessity of salvation*. HOOKER, V. XXI. 2. We have no Word of God but Scripture.

See also Art. vi. and below, Pt. ii. ch. v. from middle to end.

Q. Since the Word of God is not, in all places, easy to be understood by all, both from its own nature and from the nature of man, and since man is prone to *forget* and to neglect what he understands, what ordinances are there in the Church for its exposition and perpetual inculcation?

Heb. vi. 1, 2.
Luke i. 4.
2 Tim. iv. 2.

A. Those of Catechizing, or Oral instruction (κατήχησις ¹) by question and answer; and of Public Preaching.

¹ Bp. ANDREWES, Pattern of Catechistical Doctrine, CHAP. VII. p. 4.

Q. What is the subject-matter of Catechizing in the Christian Church?

A. First, the Apostles' Creed; secondly, the Ten Commandments; thirdly, the Lord's Prayer; fourthly, the Two Sacraments.

Q. What do we learn from these?

A. From the Creed¹ we learn *credenda*, i. e. what we are to *believe;* from the Decalogue, *agenda*, what we are to *do;* from the Lord's Prayer, *petenda*, or *postulanda*, what we are to *pray* for: in the Sacraments, we have *adhibenda*, *means* to be *used* for growth in grace.

¹ HOOKER, V. XVIII. 3.

Q. In what does Preaching consist?

A. In the Public Reading¹ and Expounding² of Holy Writ¹.

¹ HOOKER, V. XIX. 1. V. XXI. 4, 5. Bp. TAYLOR, Holy Living, c. iv. § 4. ² HOOKER, V. XXII.

Q. To whom is the ministry of these ordinances committed by Christ?

A. Our Lord commanded His Apostles to "go and teach all nations:" saying, "As my Father hath sent Me, so send I you:" and, "Lo! I am with you alway, even unto the end of the world." His Apostles sent others, as He sent them, and with the same commission, ordering them to commit their doctrine "to faithful men, who should teach others also." Thus Christ made a *permanent, hereditary*, and *successive*, provision of Pastors and Teachers for His Church; and they, who hold the form of sound words of the Apostles, and who derive their commission through them and their successors consecutively from Christ Himself, are the authorized Teachers and Expounders of the Word of God¹. [Matt. xxviii. 19. John xx. 21. Matt. xxviii. 20. 2 Tim. ii. 2. See below, Chap. viii.]

PART I.

[1] S. IREN. iv. 45, p. 345, Grabe. Ibi discere oportet veritatem apud quos est ab Apostolis Ecclesiæ successio, et id quod est sanum et irreprobabile conversationis et inadulteratum et incorruptibile sermonis constat.

S. IREN. iv. 63. Agnitio vera (γνῶσις ἀληθής) est Apostolorum doctrina, et antiquus Ecclesiæ status, in universo mundo, et character corporis Christi *secundum successiones Episcoporum*, quibus illi (Apostoli) eam quæ in unoquoque loco est Ecclesiam tradiderunt. Cf. v. 20.

TERTULLIAN, Præscr. Hær. 21. *Alii non sunt* recipiendi Prædicatores quàm quos Christus instituit.—c. 19. Ubi veritas et *disciplinæ* et fidei, illic veritas Scripturarum et Expositionum. See further below, Part ii. chap. vi.

Q. Is this method of teaching by *human* means consistent with the usual course of God's dispensations?

A. Yes. To the Jews God not only gave a Law, but He appointed a succession of Expounders of it, and of Ministers under it. At St. Paul's conversion Christ sent Ananias to him. The Angel sent Philip the Evangelist to instruct the Ethiopian. And Cornelius was ordered in a dream to send for St. Peter[1]. "Faith cometh by hearing; and hearing by the word of God." "And how shall men hear without a Preacher?" God ordinarily *instructs* the *minds* of men, as He heals their *bodies*, by means of *other men*[2].

Deut. iv. 8, 9. Exod. xxviii. 1. Levit. x. 11. Acts ix. 10 —18. viii. 26. x. 5. Rom. x. 17. 14.

See below, Pt. i. ch. xiv.

[1] S. AUGUST. de Doctrinâ Christianâ, lib. i. (Paris, 1836, vol. iii. pp. 15, 16.) Imò verò et quod per *hominem* discendum est, sine superbiâ discat: et per quem docetur alius, sine superbiâ et sine invidiâ tradat quod accepit: neque tentemus Eum Cui credidimus, ne talibus Inimici versutiis et perversitate decepti, ad ipsum quoque audiendum Evangelium atque discendum nolimus ire in Ecclesias, aut Codicem legere, aut legentem prædicantemque hominem audire; et exspectemus rapi usque in tertium cœlum, sive in corpore, sive extra corpus, sicut dicit Apostolus, et ibi audire ineffabilia verba, quæ non licet homini loqui, aut ibi videre Dominum Jesum Christum, et ab Illo potius quam ab hominibus audire evangelium.

2 Cor. xii. 2.

Caveamus tales tentationes superbissimas et periculosissimas, magisque cogitemus, et ipsum Apostolum Paulum, licet *divinâ et cælesti* voce prostratum et instructum, ad *hominem* tamen missum esse, ut sacramenta perciperet,

Acts ix. 6.

atque copularetur Ecclesiæ: et centurionem Cornelium, CHAP. VII.
quamvis exauditas orationes ejus eleemosynasque respectas
ci *angelus* nuntiaverit, *Petro* tamen traditum imbuendum; Acts x. 5.
per quem non solum sacramenta perciperet, sed etiam quid
credendum, quid sperandum, quid diligendum esset, audiret. Et poterant utique omnia per *angelum* fieri, sed abjecta esset *humana* conditio, si per *homines hominibus* Deus *verbum suum* ministrare nolle videretur. Cf. S. AUG. Prolog. lib. i. de Civ. Dei, p. 131.

² S. AUGUST. de Doct. Christ. p. 131. Sicut enim corporis medicamenta, quæ hominibus ab hominibus adhibentur, non nisi eis prosunt quibus Deus operatur salutem, qui et sine illis mederi potest, cum sine Ipso illa non possint, et tamen adhibentur; et si hoc officiosè fiat, inter opera misericordiæ vel beneficentiæ deputatur, ita et adjumenta doctrinæ tunc prosunt animæ adhibita per hominem, cum Deus operatur ut prosint, qui potuit Evangelium dare *homini,* etiam non ab *hominibus,* neque *per hominem.*

Q. What are the beneficial ends of this arrangement?

A. It is "useful for the humiliation of man's pride, who *would not* be debtor to any one but himself¹." It tends to promote charity between man and man, by a mutual interchange of blessings². It is a condescension to his weakness, and 1 Cor. i. 21.
a trial of his obedience. It is a proof of the truth iii. 6.
and divine origin of the Gospel; which is committed to earthen vessels, in order that all may 2 Cor. iv. 7.
see that the "excellency of its power is not of man but of God."

¹ HOOKER, V. LXXVI. 9.
² S. AUG. de Doct. Christ. i. 6. Ipsa Charitas quæ sibi invicem homines nodo charitatis astringit, non haberet aditum refundendorum et quasi miscendorum sibimet animorum, si homines per homines nihil discerent.

Q. But since authorized Expositors are human, and therefore fallible, why ought we to listen to their expositions?

A. Because they have the professional aids of learning, study, and experience; and because they are publicly known to have given their assent to certain Authorized Confessions of Faith, and are Rom. xii. 6—8.

accountable to their Ecclesiastical Superiors for their public teaching; because also it is their greatest duty and interest to avoid error, and to teach the truth, since "they watch for the souls" of their hearers, "as they that must give account[1];" and because they are Ministers appointed and ordained by God "for this very thing;" and because they have received and do receive Divine grace and help from Him for the execution of their office, which was instituted by Him.

Part I.
1 Cor. ix. 16.
Ezek. xxxiii. 7—9. xxxiv. 2—10.
Heb. xiii. 17.
1 Pet. iv. 5.
Acts xx. 28.
2 Tim. i. 6.
1 Tim. iv. 13 —16.

[1] BARROW on Obedience to our Spiritual Guides and Governors. Sermons lvi. lvii. lviii. lix.

Q. Have we any direct *precept from Scripture, commanding* us to seek for and to receive instruction from them?

A. Yes. Christ charges *them* to *preach;* and by charging them to *preach*, He charges *us* to *hear* them. "The priest's lips should keep knowledge, and we should seek the law at his mouth; for he is the messenger of the Lord of Hosts." On the other hand, the greatest wickedness is described by the words, "Thy people are as they that strive with the priest;" and our Lord said to His Apostles, "He that heareth you heareth Me; and he that despiseth you despiseth Me; and he that despiseth Me despiseth Him that sent Me;" and, "He that receiveth a prophet in the name of a prophet, shall receive a prophet's reward[1]."

Mark xvi. 15.
1 Cor. i. 18. ix. 16.
2 Tim. iv. 1, 2.
Mal ii. 7.
Hos. iv. 4.
Luke x. 16.

Matt. x. 41.

[1] Abp. POTTER on Church Government, ch. v. pp. 221 —240, ed. 1724.

Q. But authorized expositors may err; may we then follow them in their error?

A. No; not when we *know it* to be so. Our Lord has left us the rule, what to follow, and what to avoid. He says, "The Scribes and Pharisees sit (ἐκάθισαν) in Moses' seat (i. e. teach the Law[1], in his place); all therefore whatsoever

OF THE WORD OF GOD. 59

they (so sitting and teaching) bid you to observe, *that* observe and do." But He says also, "Beware of the *leaven* (that is, of the *false doctrine*) of the Pharisees:" that is, we are to follow authorized teachers [2], in as far as they teach by, and according to, Divine authority; but we may not follow them in any errors of doctrine. There may be teachers who do not faithfully keep to their engagements and duties.

CHAP. VII.
Matt. xxiii. 2, 3. xvi. 6. 12.
Luke xii. 1.

[1] S. AUGUST. in S. Joann. Evang. Tract. xlvi. 6. Multi quippe in Ecclesiâ commoda terrena sectantes, *Christum tamen prædicant*, et per eos vox Christi auditur: et sequuntur oves, non *mercenarium*, sed vocem PASTORIS *per mercenarium.* Audite mercenarios ab Ipso Domino demonstratos: *Scribæ,* inquit, *et Pharisæi cathedram Moysi sedent: quæ igitur dicunt, facite; quæ autem faciunt, facere nolite.* Quid aliud dixit, nisi, per *mercenarios* vocem *Pastoris* audite? *Sedendo enim cathedram Moysi,* legem Dei docent: ergo per illos Deus docet. *Sua vero illi si velint docere,* nolite audire, nolite facere. Quod enim facit male, non prædicat de cathedrâ Christi: inde lædit unde *mala facit,* non unde *bona dicit.*
RAINOLD, Conference with Hart, 1598, pp. 255—269.
[2] Below, Pt. iii. ch. iii. toward the end.

Q. May we then make *ourselves* the judges whether they are in error; and if not, to what test and standard of doctrine are we to appeal?

A. We are to "prove all things, and to hold fast what is good," but not to rely on our own reason alone. Holy Scripture, as received, guarded, and interpreted by the Catholic Church from the beginning "according to the proportion of faith," is the Rule and Standard, to which all teaching is to be referred, and *against* which no one is to be heard, no, not even "an angel from heaven." And subordinately and by way of explanation of Scripture, the consent of the Church, speaking in her public Expositions, Creeds [1], Councils, Liturgies, Confessions, and writings of her ancient Bishops and Doctors, is to be regarded [2].

1 Thess. v. 21.

1 Cor. ii 13. Rom. xii. 6.

Gal. i. 8.

PART I.

¹ S. AUG. in Joan. Tract. xviii. 'Neque natæ hæreses, nisi dum Scripturæ bonæ intelliguntur non benè;' and he then enlarges on the necessity of interpreting Scripture 'ad sanam regulam cátholicam;' 'secundum sanam fidei regulam.' See Reformatio Legum, i. 13. Ne quid contra Symbola (the Creeds) aliquando interpretemur.

BARROW, iv. p. 29, on the thesis "*Relaxatio* fidei TRIUM SYMBOLORUM admitti non potest, sine scandalo dato Apostasiæ ab Ecclesiâ Universali."

² RAINOLD'S Conference, p. 46. Bp. ANDREWES on the Decalogue, p. 57.

WATERLAND, Works, v. p. 265. On the Use and Value of Ecclesiastical Antiquity. A very particular regard is due to the *Public Acts* of the Ancient Church appearing in *Creeds* made use of in baptism, and in the *censures* passed upon heretics. It is not at all likely that *any* whole Church of those times should vary from Apostolical doctrine in things of moment; but it is, morally speaking, absurd to imagine, that ALL *the Churches* should combine *in the same error* and *conspire together to corrupt the doctrine of Christ*. Bp. BULL, Def. Fid. Nic. I. 1. 9. Religio mihi est eritque *contra torrentem* omnium Patrum S. Scripturas interpretari, nisi quando me argumenta cogunt evidentissima—quod *nunquam* eventurum credo.

Q. You speak of her ancient Bishops and Doctors; but were not they also fallible?

A. Yes.

Q. What ground then is there for any special deference to their opinions? and what is the nature of that deference?

A. The *first* act of *duty* to them is *not* to attempt to raise them to that place where they themselves are not willing to stand¹; namely, to *a level* with the writers of HOLY SCRIPTURE. Scripture *alone*² can neither deceive nor be deceived. But the expositions of Scripture by the Fathers of the Church are entitled, on many grounds, to special reverence.

¹ TERTULLIANUS adv. Hermogenem. Non recipio quod *extra Scripturam* de tuo infers. See below, Pt. ii. c. v. IDEM, de Carne Christi, 2. Si Apostolicus es, cum Apostolis senti.

S. BASIL de Fide, c. 1. φανερα ἔκπτωσις πιστεως, ἢ

ἀθετεῖν τι τῶν γεγραμμένων, ἢ ἐπεισάγειν τῶν μὴ γεγραμμένων.

S. HIERON. ad Theophilum. Aliter habeo Apostolos, aliter reliquos tractatores. Illos semper vera dicere; istos in quibusdam ut homines errare.

S. AUGUST. Epist. 82. Hieronymo. Ego *solis* eis Scripturarum libris qui jam Canonici appellantur, didici hunc timorem honoremque deferre, ut nullum eorum auctorem scribendo aliquid errasse firmissimè credam. Alios autem ita lego, ut quantâlibet sanctitate doctrinâque præpolleant, non ideo verum putem, quia ipsi ita senserunt, sed quia mihi vel per illos auctores Canonicos, vel ratione probabili, persuadere potuerunt.

² TERTULL. Præscrip. adv. Hæres. c. 3. Non ex personis probamus fidem, sed ex fide personas.

S. AUGUST. lib. iii. de Trinit. Noli meis literis quasi Scripturis Canonicis inservire. Noli meas literas ex tuâ opinione vel contentione, sed ex divinâ lectione vel inconcussâ ratione corrigere.

S. AUGUST. contra Cresconium, lib. ii. cap. 31. Nos nullam facimus Cypriano injuriam, quum ejus quaslibet literas a Canonicâ divinarum Scripturarum auctoritate distinguimus. Neque enim sine causâ tam salubri vigilantiâ *Canon Ecclesiasticus* constitutus est, ad quem certi Prophetarum et Apostolorum libri pertinent, quos omnino judicare non audemus, et secundum quos de cæteris literis vel fidelium vel infidelium judicamus. See also c. Donatistas, ii. c. 3.

Q. On what grounds?

A. First, because they lived in times immediately succeeding those of Christ Himself and His Apostles; next, because the vernacular *language* of many of them was that in which the Evangelists and Apostles themselves wrote; next, because of their undivided *devotion* to the ministry of the *Word;* because, also, they possessed and had the use of religious and other *treatises* which are now *lost;* also, because they habitually used *mutual conference*, publicly and privately, with one another; next, on account of their piety and sufferings urging and requiring them to *examine* the *truth*, as they valued their highest interests, temporal and eternal; and from their special need of and prayers for *Divine Grace*, which we know to have been shed in *abundant supplies* upon the early Church [1]; and, lastly, because their writings have been *approved* and are held in great respect by the *Church*.

[1] Abp. WAKE's Apostolical Fathers, c. x. p. 110. 1. They were contemporary with the Apostles, and instructed by them. 2. They were men of an eminent character in the Church, and therefore such as could not be ignorant of what was taught in it. 3. They were careful to preserve the doctrine of Christ in its purity, and to oppose such as went about to corrupt it. 4. They were men not only of a perfect piety, but of great courage and constancy, and therefore such as cannot be suspected to have had any design to prevaricate in this matter. 5. They were endued with a large portion of the Holy Spirit, and, as such, could hardly err in what they delivered as the Gospel of Christ. 6. Their writings were approved by the Church in those days, which could not be mistaken in its approbation of them.

WATERLAND on the Trinity, vii. On the Use and Value of Ecclesiastical Antiquity, Works, v. pp. 253—333; p. 260. 1. The ancients who lived nearest to the Apostolical times are of some use to us, considered merely as contemporary writers, for their diction and *phraseology*... 2. A further use of the ancient Fathers is seen in the letting us into the knowledge of antiquated *rites* and *customs*, upon the knowledge of which the true interpretation of some Scripture phrases and idioms may depend. 3. They are further useful as giving us an insight into the *history of the age* in which the sacred books (of the New Testament, I mean) were written. 4. The ancientest Fathers may be exceedingly useful for fixing the sense of Scripture in *controverted texts*. Those that lived in or near the Apostolical times might retain in memory what the Apostles themselves or their *immediate* successors said upon such and such points. Their nearness to the time, their known fidelity, and their admirable endowments, ordinary and *extraordinary*, add great weight to their testimony or doctrine, and make it a probable rule of interpretation in the prime things. It deserves our notice, that the Fathers of the third and fourth centuries had the advantage of many written accounts of the doctrine of the former ages, which have since been lost; and therefore their testimonies also are of considerable weight, and are a mark of direction to us, not to be slighted in the main things. .... 5. There is one consideration more, tending still to strengthen the former, and which must by no means be omitted; namely, that the *charismata*, the *extraordinary gifts*, were then frequent, visibly rested in and upon the *Church, and there only*.

Q. What inferences do you thence draw?

A. These considerations show that their works possess great value, especially in a *negative* sense; i. e. *if* any doctrine (such, for example, as the doctrines of the *Trent Creed*, and the dogma of the *Immaculate Conception*, promulgated in 1854) was *unknown* to them, or *contrary* to their teaching, we are sure that such doctrine is *novel*, and ought to be rejected as *false*[1].

[1] WATERLAND, ibid. p. 275. This *negative* way of arguing is generally allowed, and can hardly bear any controversy. Bishop STILLINGFLEET (Rational Account, ii. p. 58) observes, that it is *sufficient prescription* against any thing which can be *alleged* out of Scripture, that *if it appear contrary to the sense of the Catholic Church from the beginning*, it ought not to be looked upon as the *true* meaning of Scripture.

Q. But have not *modern* Expositors special advantages, not possessed by the ancient; and may they not, in certain respects, be preferred to them?

A. Modern Expositors have, no doubt, certain advantages. They have the experience of the past, whence they may see how error has been confuted by truth, which has gained in strength and clearness from the contest, for "Ex hæreticis," says S. Augustine, "asserta est Catholica[1];" and thus we may learn to avoid error and to maintain truth. They have also the benefit of the discoveries in science, and of the critical, geographical, and antiquarian researches of later days.

Both ancient and modern Interpreters have their respective uses: and in the case of two good things, *both* of which are given us for our use by Almighty God, it is unwise to say, "*this* is *worse* than *that*:" our duty is to be thankful to Him for *both*, and according to our means and opportunities to use them accordingly.

Ecclus. xxxix. 34.

[1] S. AUG. i. 1213—1215. iii. 2066. iv. 730. 732. 978. 1729. v. 412. vii. 858. viii. 392, ed. Paris. S. CHRYSOSTOM, ii. 836, ed. Savil. ORIGEN, Hom. 9, in Num. ii. p. 296.

PART I.

Q. I infer, from what you have now said, that you do not allow that there is any *one living, visible, infallible* Judge,—such as the Bishop of Rome,—in controverted causes of Faith?

A. There *is one visible* and *infallible* Judge in such causes, and *one only*, namely, HOLY SCRIPTURE; as S. Augustin [1] says, "Scriptura sancta *sola* nescit fallere, nec falli;" and to this standard,

Isa. viii. 20. "To the Law and to the Testimony," all appeals in such cases must be made, as S. Optatus [2] and S. Augustine said, in their controversies with the Donatists, "On *earth* we can find *no* Judge; we must seek one from *heaven;* but why from heaven, when we have it in the *Gospel?* quid ad *cœlum*, quum habemus in *Evangelio?* Why do we strive together? Quare de hæreditate litigamus? fratres sumus, quare contendimus? Non sine *Testamento* dimisit nos Pater; sedet Christus in cœlo; et contradicitur *Testamento* Ejus—*Aperi, legamus*."

---

[1] S. AUG. de Meritis, i. 22, compared with Epist. lxxxii. *Tantummodo* scripturis hanc debeo servitutem, quâ eas *solas* ita sequar ut conscriptores earum nihil in eis omninò errasse non dubitem. See also his words above, p. 61.

[2] S. OPTATUS adv. Parmen. v. 2. S. AUG. in Psalm. xxi. 30. HOOKER II. VII. 7. Abp. LAUD against Fisher, sect. xxvi. A. C. would know what is to be done for re-uniting of a Church divided in doctrine of the faith, when this remedy by a general council cannot be had. "Sure Christ our Lord," saith he, "hath provided some rule, some judge, in such and such like cases, to procure unity and certainty of belief." I believe so too: for He hath left an infallible rule, the *Scripture*, and that by the *manifest places* in it (which need no dispute, no external judge), is able to settle unity and certainty of belief, in necessaries to salvation: and in *non necessariis*, in and about things not necessary, there ought not to be a contention to a separation.

Q. But Scripture, though a visible and infallible, is not a *living* Judge, and is not a single living Judge necessary?

A. Christ knows best what is necessary for His Church; and He never appointed one.

Q. How do you prove this?

A. *If* there ever had been *one* living Judge (such as the *Pope*), it *must* have existed in the time of the *Apostles;* and they never would have summoned a COUNCIL¹ at Jerusalem, if any *one* living man, and specially any one actually present among them *when* they summoned it, had possessed authority to decide the controversy which occasioned its convocation. And it is absurd to imagine that Bishops would have been put to the pains of coming together from the most distant parts of Christendom to meet in Church Synods, in many *different places*, at many different times, in the early ages of the Church, if the Church had known any thing of any such person as *one* living infallible Judge (such as the *Pope*), existing in *one place*², viz. at *Rome*.

CHAP. VII.

Acts xv. 6, 7.

¹ Abp. LAUD against Fisher, sect. xxvi. To draw all together, to settle controversies in the Church, here is a visible judge and infallible, but not living, and that is the *Scripture* pronouncing by the Church; and there is a visible and a living judge, but not infallible, and that is a general Council, lawfully called and so proceeding.

² See further below, Part ii. chap. ix.

Q. But in cases where *General Councils cannot* be summoned, how are litigated questions to be settled, and necessary Reforms to be made in the Church, since it cannot be by one living Judge?

A. Let each National Church keep itself as near as it can to God's Law ¹: and, whereinsoever it may have gone astray, (whatever *other* Churches may do,) let *it amend itself*². And if, after all, controversies should arise and defects exist in it, —which *will* doubtless always be the case more or less in every part of the Visible Church, even until the Great Day, when "the Son of Man shall send forth His angels, and they shall gather out of His kingdom *all things that do offend*, and them which do iniquity,"—such things must be regarded by us as conducive to our growth in grace. "There must needs be heresies among you,"

See above, pp. 8—16.
Matt. xiii. 41.

1 Cor. xi. 19.

F

says St. Paul, "that they which are approved may be made manifest." They are trials[2] of our faith, incitements to watchfulness, fasting, and prayer, and exercises of our Christian hope, and desire, calling on us to "possess our souls in patience," and to raise our eyes from the present strifes, confusions, failings, and calamities in the Church militant on earth, to the future peace, order, beauty, and felicity of the Church glorified in heaven.

Luke xxi. 19.

---

[1] See HOOKER above, p. 19.

[2] HOOKER, III. I. 10. The indisposition, therefore, of the *Church* of *Rome* to reform herself must be no stay unto *us* from performing our duty to God; even as desire of retaining conformity with them could be no excuse if we did not perform that duty.

Abp. LAUD against Fisher, sect. xxvi. Was it not lawful for Judah to reform herself, when Israel would not join? Sure it was, or else the prophet deceives me, that says expressly, *Though Israel transgress, yet let not Judah sin.* And S. Jerome expounds it of this very particular sin of heresy and error in religion.

Hos. iv. 15.

[3] Abp. LAUD against Fisher, sect. xxiv. When a general Council cannot be had, the Church must pray that it may, and expect till it may; or else reform itself *per partes*, by national or provincial Synods (as hath been said before). And in the mean time it little beseems A. C., or any Christian, to check at the wisdom of Christ, if He have not taken the way they think fitting to settle Church differences; or if, for the Church's sin or trial, the way of composing them be left more uncertain than they would have it, *that they which are approved may be known.* See WATERLAND, v. 21.

1 Cor. xi. 19.

CHAPTER VIII.

ON PRIVILEGES IN THE CHURCH—DUE ADMINISTRATION OF THE SACRAMENTS BY A LAWFUL MINISTRY.

Q. WHAT other privileges are received from God through the medium of the Church?

A. The Sacraments of Baptism and of the Lord's Supper, which are the visible *symbola* and

Matt. xxviii. 19. Mark xvi. 16.

characteres Ecclesiæ,—the signs, badges, and bonds of the Christian Church[1].

[1] S. AUG. contra Faustum, xix. 11. In *nullum nomen religionis,* sive veræ sive falsæ, coagulari homines possunt nisi aliquo *signaculorum* vel *sacramentorum visibilium* consortio colligantur. S. AUG. contra Parmen. ii. c. 13, De Cathechiz. Rudibus. Sacramenta signacula rerum divinarum visibilia, in quibus res ipsæ invisibiles honorantur. S. BASIL, Homil. xiii.

Chap. VIII. Luke xxii. 19. Acts ii. 42. 1 Cor. xi. 24. Tit. iii. 5.

Q. Why is the Administration and Reception of the Sacraments *necessary?*

A. Because it has pleased God, in His infinite wisdom and mercy to us, to ordain them as *federal rites* wherein the new Covenant is ratified to us; and to make them the *instruments* of our incorporation, union, life, and growth, in the Body of Christ; and because He has constituted them the proper and efficacious *means* for the conveyance of His grace, pardon, and goodness to us, and for the quieting of our consciences, the illumination of our minds, and the preservation of our souls and bodies; and because He has made them also to be *memorials* of His *past*, *pledges* of His *present*, and *earnests* of His *future love*, to all who receive them worthily; and because He has appointed them to be visible *symbols* and *tokens* by which the members of Christ are *distinguished* from all who do *not* adore Him as their Lord; and by which they show their love for each other in Him; and thus edify each other, and strengthen the unity of His mystical body by mutual indwelling in Christ; and, finally, because our Saviour Christ Himself *has declared them* to be *necessary* to *salvation*[1].

1 Cor. xii. 12—14. x. 16, 17.

John iii. 3—5. vi. 53. 56. Mark xvi. 16.

[1] HUGO de Sacramentis, lib. cap. 5. Institutio sacramentorum, quantum ad Deum auctorem, *dispensationis* est; quantum vero ad *hominem* obedientem, *necessitatis:* quoniam in potestate Dei est *præter ista* hominem salvare; sed in potestate hominis non est, *sine istis* ad salutem pervenire.

HOOKER, V. LVII. 4. It is not ordinarily God's will to

Part I.

Wisd. xvi. 7.

bestow the grace of Sacraments on any but *by the Sacraments;* which grace also they that receive by Sacraments, or with Sacraments, receive it *from Him,* and not from them. For of Sacraments the very same is true, which Solomon's Wisdom observeth in the brazen serpent, "He that turned towards it was not healed by the thing he saw, but by Thee, O Saviour of all." The use of them is in our hands, the effect in His. HOOKER, V. LX. 4. If Christ Himself, which giveth salvation, do require Baptism, it is not for us, that look for salvation, to examine Him whether unbaptized men may be saved; but seriously to do that which is required; and religiously to fear the danger which may grow from the want thereof. See also the important statements in HOOKER, VI. VI. 10.

John xx. 21, 22.
Matt. xxviii. 19.

℞. By whom are the Sacraments administered?
℟. By persons lawfully called and sent for that purpose¹.

¹ XXXIX ARTICLES, Art. xxiii.

℞. By what name are the Ministers of the Sacraments distinguished from those to whom they minister?

℟. They are called κληρικοὶ, *clerici, clerks,* or *clergy;* and they are thus distinguished from the other members of the Church, who are called λαὸς, or *laity* ¹.

¹ S. CLEMENT, Ep. ad Cor. i. 40. Abp. De MARCA, Dissertatio de discrimine laicorum et clericorum (in the Appendix to his Concordia), p. 84.

℞. What is the origin of these words?

℟. The Clergy are so called from κλῆρος ¹, *a lot* or *portion,* because they are allotted and consecrated to God; or because He and His Church is their lot and inheritance; and the Laity ² of the Christian Church are so termed, as being the chosen nation and peculiar people of God.

¹ SUIDAS, κλῆρος, τὸ σύστημα τῶν διακόνων καὶ πρεσβυτέρων. S. HIERON. ad Nepotian. de vitâ Clericorum. Propterea vocantur *Clerici* vel quia de sorte sunt Domini vel quia Dominus sors, id est pars, Clericorum est.

S. CHRYSOST. in Act. Apost. i. 17, 18, Ἔλαχε τὸν κλῆρον τῆς διακονίας ταύτης· κλῆρον δὲ αὐτὸν καλεῖ δεικνὺς τῆς τοῦ Θεοῦ χάριτος τὸ πᾶν ὄν, καὶ ἀναμιμνήσκων αὐτοὺς τῶν παλαιῶν, ὅτι ὁ Θεὸς αὐτοὺς ἐκληρώσατο καθάπερ τοὺς Λευίτας. See also in Act. i. 26, ἔδωκαν κλήρους αὐτῶν, καὶ ἔπεσεν ὁ κλῆρος ἐπὶ Ματθίαν. CHAP. VIII.

Num. xviii. 24, Vers. LXXII. ἐγὼ ἡ μερίς σου καὶ ἡ κληρονομία σου. The word κληρικοὶ was sometimes, indeed, applied in ancient times to the *inferior* Ministers, the superior being called ἱερεῖς.

[2] Bp. BILSON, Perpet. Government of Christ's Church, chap. x. p. 202, ed. Oxf. 1842. And so the learned know the word λαὸς, whence *lay* is derived, importeth even "the Lord's peculiar people;" which distinction of people from priest is neither profane nor strange in the Scriptures. "There shall be," saith Esay, "like people, like priest." And so saith Osee; as also Jeremy divideth the Church into the "prophet," "priest," and "people." As for the name of Clergymen, Jerome saith, "Therefore are they called Clergymen, or Clerks, either because they are the Lord's portion (to serve the Church of Christ), or for that the Lord is their portion and part (to live on such things as are dedicated to the Lord)."

Isa. xxiv. 2.
Hosea iv. 4.
Jer. xxiii. 11. xxvi. 7.

Q. But how is this assertion, of the necessity of a call and ordination of *special* persons, consistent with the expressions of St. Peter to *whole* congregations, "Ye are a chosen generation, a royal priesthood;" and of St. John, "He hath made us unto our God kings and priests?" Do not these words seem to intimate that *all* Christians are priests to God?

1 Pet. ii. 9.
Rev. i. 6.

A. In a certain sense, they do. *All* men, especially all who are in authority and in eminent stations, as Kings, Nobles, Magistrates, Statesmen, Legislators, Poets, Parents, may be called Priests to God [1] as being consecrated to His service. In the words of S. Augustine [2], "Christians, *whether lay or clergy*, are priests, for they are all members of the one High Priest Jesus Christ. They are a holy Temple of God, and their souls are His altars, on which they do sacrifice to Him." But yet, the *special* ministration of God's Word and Sacraments is committed to certain persons, who have accordingly, in Scripture, particular designations, as being *separated* for the work whereunto they are called [3]; whence

Acts xiii. 2.
1 Cor. ix. 11. 13.

PART I.

Marginal references:
Gal. vi. 6.
1 Thess. v. 12, 13.
Phil. ii. 29.
1 Tim. v. 17.
Heb. xiii. 7. 17.
Acts xx. 28.
Eph. iv. 11, 12.
1 Cor. xii. 29. xiv. 16.
James v. 14.

arise those relative duties of Clergy and Laity, which are enjoined in numerous places of Holy Writ; especially in St. Paul's Epistles to Timothy and Titus. And "*Ecclesia* non *est*," says S. Jerome, "quæ non habet *Sacerdotes*¹." Christ gave, not *all*, but "*some* Apostles, and *some* Prophets, for the work of the *ministry*," says St. Paul, and he asks, "Are *all* Apostles? are *all* Prophets? are *all* Teachers?" No: every one in his own order. And St. James would not have directed Priests to be sent for, if *every one* was a Priest.

And by such a general interpretation of St. Peter's and St. John's words, all degrees, civil as well as ecclesiastical, would be confounded; for then *every one* would be not only a *Priest*, but *every one* would also be a *King*. On the contrary, the expression is itself an evidence and proof that *special Priests* as well as *special Kings* are designed of God; and its true meaning is, that *Christians* are to be distinguished, in spiritual things, from the *rest* of the world, as Kings and Priests, each in their respective functions, are distinguished from others who have not their peculiar duties.

John xii. 26.   ¹ S. AUGUST. in Joan. Evang. Tractatus li. Cum ergo auditis, fratres, Dominum dicentem, *Ubi ego sum, illic et minister meus erit;* nolite *tantummodo* bonos *Episcopos* et *Clericos* cogitare. Etiam *vos,* pro modo vestro, ministrate Christo, bene vivendo, eleemosynas faciendo, nomen doctrinamque ejus quibus potueritis prædicando; ut unusquisque etiam *pater-familias* hoc nomine agnoscat paternum affectum suæ familiæ se debere. Pro Christo et pro vitâ æternâ suos omnes admoneat, doceat, hortetur, corripiat; impendat benevolentiam, exerceat disciplinam; ita in domo suâ ecclesiasticum et *quodammodo Episcopale* implebit officium, ministrans Christo, ut in æternum sit cum Ipso. See also S. AUG. Sermon. xciv.

² S. AUG. de Civ. Dei, xx. 10, and on Psalm xciv. p. 1465.

³ TERTULLIAN de Baptism. 17. Dandi baptismum jus habet summus sacerdos, qui est Episcopus, dehinc Pres-

byteri et Diaconi *non tamen* sine Episcopi auctoritate. CHAP. VIII.
TERTULLIAN de Coron. 3. Eucharistiæ sacramentum non
de aliorum manu quam *præsidentium* sumimus. See S.
HIERON. below, chap. x.

TERTULLIAN de Præscript. Hæret. 39, on the practice
of *heretical* as opposed to that of *Catholic* congregations:
—Ordinationes eorum temerariæ, leves, inconstantes. Itaque alius hodie Episcopus, cras alius; hodie Diaconus qui
cras Lector: *hodie Presbyter* qui *cras Laicus.*

OPTATUS ad Parmen. ii. 25. *Quatuor* genera sunt in
Ecclesiâ, *Episcoporum, Presbyterorum, Diaconorum,* et
Fidelium.

⁴ S. HIERON. adv. Lucif. c. 8. S. CHRYSOSTOM ad 1 Cor.
xiv. 16. ORDINAL of the Church of England. There shall
be a Sermon declaring ... how *necessary* the Order of
Priests is in the Church of Christ. HOOKER, III. XI. 18.
We hold that God's clergy are a state which *hath been and
will be* (as long as there is a Church upon earth) *necessary*,
by the plain *Word of God Himself*, a state, whereunto the
rest of God's people must be subject as touching things
that appertain to their souls' health.

Q. You spoke of special persons, lawfully called
and sent; who are they?

A. Those "who are tried, examined, and known
to have such qualities as are requisite for their
office, and are also, by public prayer and imposition of hands, approved and appointed thereto by
lawful authority [1]."

[1] Pref. to ORDINAL of the Church of England. XXXIX
ARTICLES, Art. xxiii. CANONS of 1603, xxxiii. xxxiv. xxxv.

Q. You mean, therefore, that no man may
undertake *of himself* the duties of the Christian
Ministry?

A. I do. "No one taketh this honour unto
himself [1], but he that is called of God, as was
Aaron." Aaron and his sons were appointed by
God to wait on the Priest's office; and "the
stranger that came nigh" was to be put to death.
"A man can receive nothing unless it be given
him from above." "He that entereth not by the
door into the sheepfold, but climbeth up some
other way, the same is a thief and a robber." The
sons of Sceva, who assumed Apostolic functions,

Isa. xlix. 1.
Jer. xxiii. 21.
Gal. i. 15.
Heb. v. 4.
Exod. xxviii. 1.
Num. iii. 10.
xviii. 3—6.
John x. 1.
Acts xix. 14.

were overcome by the Evil Spirit. And an awful lesson against any such assumption is contained in the history of Korah, and his company, who were destroyed by God for invading the priestly office, a sin against which we are warned by a *Christian Apostle,* St. Jude; and of King Uzziah, who was smitten with leprosy for so doing. Nay, more, Uzzah (who was not a Levite) was smitten by God for touching the ark, though he put forth his hand with a good intention to stay it.

<small>Num. xvi. 32—34.
xvlii. 3.
Jude 11.
2 Chron. xxvi. 16. 19.
2 Sam. vi. 6.
1 Chron. xiii. 10.</small>

<small>¹ S. CYPRIAN de Unit. Eccl. p. 111. Hi sunt, qui se præpositos sine ullâ ordinationis lege constituunt, qui, nemine Episcoporum dante, Episcopi sibi nomen assumunt.
S. CYPRIAN, Ep. 69, p. 182. Quomodo Pastor ille vocari potest, qui, manente vero Pastore et in Ecclesiâ Dei ordinatione succedaneâ præsidente, nemini succedens, et a se ipso incipiens, alienus sit et Dominicæ pacis ac divinæ unitatis inimicus?
Bp. BARLOW on the Necessity of a Lawful Call to the Ministry. Remains, p. 613. On the true meaning of the words "inwardly called and moved," see Bp. SANDERSON, Serm., 1 Cor. vii. 24.</small>

Q. But if Aaron was called by God, why may not a person who *believes* that he has a Divine call take upon him this function?

A. Because a man may be *mistaken*, in supposing himself called by God. Aaron was not only *called by God*, but, at God's express command to Moses, was *visibly ordained by him*. And St. Paul asks, "How shall they preach except they be *sent*¹?"

<small>Exod. xxviii.
Lev. viii. 1—36.
Ecclus. xlv. 16.
Rom. x. 15.</small>

<small>¹ XXXIX ARTICLES, Art. xxiii.
HOOKER, III. XI. 18. A solemn *admittance* to charge in the Church is of such *necessity*, that without it there can be no Church Polity.
LESLIE, Discourse on the Necessity of an outward Commission.</small>

Q. Does the necessity of a due visible *mission* or *sending* appear from the *New* Testament?

A. Yes. Even Christ glorified not Himself to be made an High Priest. He did not enter on

<small>Isa. xlviii. 16. lxi. 1.</small>

His office till He was *visibly* and *audibly* commissioned at His Baptism to do so. And in the same way the Twelve and the Seventy were *chosen, called,* and *sent* by Him [1].

[1] S. AMBROSE, Epist. xliv.

Q. Does not this further appear from the *titles* assigned in Scripture to Christ's Ministers?

A. Yes. An *Apostle* ('Απόστολος) does not signify one who *comes*, but one who is *sent* by another; so Ministers are called in Scripture Κήρυκες, namely, *Heralds*, and Πρέσβεις, *Ambassadors;* that is, they are persons who do *not present themselves* on *their own authority*, but who come with a *commission publicly given them* by *others* [1]; and their office is named in the New Testament a διακονία, λειτουργία, and οἰκονομία, that is, a *ministry, service,* and *stewardship, not* an independent function.

[1] S. AUG. iv. 1375. Dixit Christus (Joh. x. 8), 'Omnes qui *venerunt fures sunt et latrones;'* id est, qui venerunt *suâ sponte, a Me non missi,* qui venerunt sine Me, in quibus Ego non fui.
S. AUG. in S. Joann. xlv. Non *præter* Christum, sed cum Illo, *Prophetæ* venerunt. Venturus Christus illos præcones *misit.*—c. Faust. xvi. 12.
THEOPHYLACT in l. c. S. Joann. x. 8. κλεπταὶ καὶ λησταί—ὅσοι ἦλθον, οὐχ ὅσοι ἀπεστάλησαν· οἱ μὲν γὰρ προφῆται ἀποσταλέντες παρεγένοντο, οἱ δὲ ψευδοπροφῆται οἷοι καὶ οἱ ῥηθέντες στασιασταὶ μηδενὸς ἀποστείλαντος ἦλθον, ἐπὶ διαστροφῇ τῶν ἀπατωμένων.
S. HIERON. Proœm. in S. Matth. In *venientibus* est præsumptio temeritatis, in *missis* est obsequium servitutis.

Q. Since, then, a man cannot take this office upon himself, but must receive it visibly from some lawful authority, *what* is that lawful authority?

A. First, in the beginning, that of Christ Himself; and then after Him, that of those whom Christ sent, saying unto them, "*As My* Father hath sent Me. *even so* send I you:" " and

ADMINISTRATION OF SACRAMENTS.

Part I.
1 Pet. i. 1.
Acts xiii. 3.
xiv. 23.
1 Tim. iv.
14. v. 22.
2 Tim. ii. 2.

lo, I am with you *alway*, even *to the end of the world;*" and who therefore, being thus sent, were commissioned to send others, in a *never-ending succession*, as Christ, Who sent them, was sent of God. Christ was ὁ τοῦ Θεοῦ Ἀπόστολος; the Twelve were Christ's Apostles; and every Minister, lawfully ordained, is an Ἀπόστολος of the Apostles[1].

[1] S. CLEMENS, Ep. ad Cor. cap. xlii. ἐξεπέμφθη ὁ Χριστὸς ἀπὸ τοῦ Θεοῦ, καὶ οἱ ἀπόστολοι ἀπὸ τοῦ Χριστοῦ, οἳ κατὰ χώρας καὶ πόλεις κηρύσσοντες καθέστανον τὰς ἀπαρχὰς αὐτῶν εἰς Ἐπισκόπους καὶ Διακόνους.

HOOKER, V. LXXVII. 1. In that they are Christ's Ambassadors,—who should give them authority, but He Whose most inward affairs they manage? What angel of heaven could have said to man, as our Lord did unto Peter, 'Feed My sheep,—preach,—baptize; do this in remembrance of Me;—whose sins ye retain, they are retained; and their offences in heaven pardoned, whose faults ye shall on earth forgive?'

Q. Together with a lawful call and visible mission, what else is necessary to constitute a person duly and fully a Minister of Christ?

A. He must also receive the *ordaining grace* of the Holy Spirit of God, investing him with the power of dispensing God's word and sacraments; of remitting and retaining sins; of praying for God's people, and of blessing them in His Name; and this the Holy Spirit[1] confers by the hands of the successors of the Apostles, and by their prayers and blessings in the office of Ordination[2].

Matt. xxviii. 19.
John xx. 21. 23. xiv. 27.
Matt. x. 13.

[1] Bp. BILSON, Perpetual Government of Christ's Church, p. 160. To create Ministers by imposing hands, is to give them not only power and leave to preach the Word and dispense the Sacraments, but also *the grace of the Holy Ghost*, to make them able to execute both parts of their function. This *can none give but they that first received the same*.

HOOKER, V. LXXVII. 8. When we take ordination, we receive the presence of the Holy Ghost—Whether we preach, pray, communicate, condemn, give absolution, or whatsoever we do, as disposers of God's mysteries, our words, judgments, acts, and deeds, are not ours, but the Holy Ghost's.

Bp. PEARSON on the Creed, Art. viii. It is the office of the Holy Spirit, to sanctify and set apart persons for the duty of the Ministry, *ordaining* them to *intercede between God and His people*, to *send up prayers to God for them*, to *bless them* in the Name of God, to teach *the doctrine of the Gospel*, to *administer the Sacraments* instituted by Christ, to perform all things necessary "for the perfecting of the saints, for the work of the ministry, for the edifying of the body of Christ." Eph. iv. 12.

[2] ORDINAL of the CHURCH of ENGLAND, the Bishop says: "Receive thou the HOLY GHOST, for the office and work of a Priest in the Church of God, now committed unto thee by the imposition of our hands. Whose sins thou dost forgive, they are forgiven; and whose sins thou dost retain, they are retained." On the Subject of this Chapter, see further below, Part ii. Chapter vi.

CHAPTER IX.

ON THE THREE ORDERS OF MINISTERS IN THE CHURCH.

Q. ARE all ordained Ministers of *equal* rank and dignity?

A. No.

Q. How many degrees are there of them?

A. There are *Three Orders* in the Christian Church, as there were three in the Church of the Jews.

Q. What are they called?

A. The orders of BISHOPS, PRIESTS, and DEACONS[1].

[1] S. IGNAT. ad Trall. iii. χωρὶς τούτων (Ἐπισκόπου, Πρεσβυτέρων καὶ Διακόνων) Ἐκκλησία οὐ καλεῖται.

S. CLEM. cap. xl. p. 142, ed. Jacobson. Τῷ ἀρχιερεῖ (Episcopo) ἴδιαι λειτουργίαι δεδομέναι εἰσὶν, καὶ τοῖς ἱερεῦσι (Presbyteris) ἴδιος ὁ τόπος προστέτακται, καὶ λευΐταις (Diaconis) ἴδιαι διακονίαι ἐπίκεινται. ὁ λαϊκὸς ἄνθρωπος τοῖς λαϊκοῖς προστάγμασιν δέδεται. See THEOPHYL. in S.

PART I. Luc. xix., on the differences and various functions of the *Three Orders*.

OPTATUS de Schismate Donatist. ii. 14. Certa membra sua habet Ecclesia, *Episcopos, Presbyteros, Diaconos, Ministros*, et turbam *fidelium*. OPTATUS, ii. 24. Cum sint (sicut supra dixi) quatuor genera capitum in Ecclesiâ, *Episcoporum, Presbyterorum, Diaconorum*, et *Fidelium*, nec uni parcere voluistis; evertistis animas hominum. Agnoscite vos animas evertisse. Invenistis *Diaconos, Presbyteros, Episcopos;* fecistis *Laicos*. Agnoscite vos animas evertisse. See above, chap. viii. BINGHAM, II. XIX. 15.

Q. To what do they correspond?

A. To those of High Priests, Priests, and Levites[1].

[1] S. HIERON. Ep. lxxxv. ad Evag. Ut sciamus traditiones Apostolicas sumptas de vetere Testamento, quod Aaron et Filii ejus atque Levitæ in Templo fuerunt, hoc sibi Episcopi—(he does not say,—hoc sibi *Papa Romanus*)—et Presbyteri, et Diaconi, vindicent in Ecclesiâ.

Q. What is the derivation and meaning of the word *Bishop?*

A. It is derived from the Greek Ἐπίσκοπος, *Episcopus*, which signifies one who *inspects* or *overlooks* others, for the sake of guiding, governing, and correcting them[1].

[1] S. AUG. ad Ps. cxxvi. Ideo altior locus est Episcopis, ut ipsi *superintendant* et quasi custodiant populum. Nam et Græcè quod dicitur *Episcopus*, hoc Latinè *Superintentor* dicitur. Quo modo Vinitori altior locus ad custodiendam Vineam, sic et Episcopis altior locus factus est.

Q. What is the derivation and meaning of the name of the second order?

A. *Priest*, or *Presbyter*, is derived from the Greek Πρεσβύτερος, and signifies a superior, properly in *age*, and thence also in *worth and gravity*[1].

[1] Bp. BILSON, Perpetual Gov. p. 202. The name of *Presbyter* I use for those whom the Apostles call Πρεσβυτέρους, presbyters, (whence our tongue, following the French, long since derived *Priests*,) who for their age

should be elders, and by their office are Ministers of the Word and Sacraments, and Overseers of the Flock of Christ.

VALCKEN. in Theocr. Adoniaz. pp. 111. 150. Ὁ Προφὺς, vetere linguâ Πρέσβυς, *ætate venerandus*. BLOMF. Gloss. ad Æsch. S. c. Theb. 386, on its *derivative* meanings.

Q. Whence is the word *Deacon* derived?

A. From the Greek Διάκονος, *Diaconus*, a minister, from διήκω, *to go through* or *despatch*[1]; and the term διακονεῖν, *to serve*, is used in the Acts of the Apostles (vi. 12) to designate their office, which was a *holy*[2] function, though partly concerned about secular matters.

[1] BUTTMANN, Lexilogus, p. 232, ed. 1836.
The writers of the Western Church use also the participial form *Diacon*, with a genitive *Diaconis*.

[2] Bp. PEARSON in Acta Apostolorum, p. 345, in cap. vi. 1. Hos (Diaconos) constituerunt ante conspectum Apostolorum, et (Apostoli scilicet) imposuerunt eis manus. Ita Ordo quidam in Ecclesiâ singularis jam tum impositione manuum institutus est. Actus quidem ad quem tum instituti sunt nihil est quam διακονεῖν τραπέζαις.... Officium tamen non fuit merè *civile* aut *œconomicum*, sed *sacrum* etiam sive *Ecclesiasticum*. Mensæ enim tum temporis communes et *sacræ* etiam fuere; hoc est, in communi convictu *Sacramentum Eucharistiæ* celebrabant. Clarum autem est, hos viros septem ad *sacrum* officium electos fuisse atque ordinatos. Eligebantur enim non alii quam qui erant *pleni Spiritu Sancto* et sapientiâ; *ordinabantur* autem *per manuum Apostolicarum impositionem*. Quin et Stephanus paulo post *prædicavit* Evangelium, et Philippus *catechizavit et baptizavit Eunuchum*. Qui quidem ἀπὸ τοῦ διακονεῖν dicti sunt διάκονοι, de quibus sæpe in Epistolis Apostolicis legimus; quorum officium nullibi quàm in hoc loco (Act. vi. 1) legitur institutum. Ut autem hi septem viri Apostolis adjuncti sunt in procurando ministerio quotidiano, ita in primitivâ Ecclesiâ *Diaconi semper Episcopis Apostolorum successoribus juncti sunt*.

Q. How long have these *Three Orders* of Ministers existed in the Christian Church?

A. In and from the times of the Holy Apostles.

Q. How does this appear?

PART I.
2 Tim. i. 6—14. ii. 2.
1 Tim. iii. 2—5.
Titus i. 1—9.
Acts vi. 1—5.
1 Tim. iii. 2. 8—13.
James v. 14.
2 Tim. iv. 1—8.

𝔄. That there are these Three Orders in the Church, and that a religious community is not *duly* and *fully* a *Church* without them, is evident "from Scripture and ancient authors[1];" especially from the writings of S. Ignatius[2], the disciple of St. John, and bishop of Antioch, and martyr; of S. Polycarp[3], the disciple and companion of St. John, and bishop of Smyrna, and martyr; of S. Irenæus, disciple of Polycarp, bishop of Lyons, and martyr; and of S. Cyprian, bishop of Carthage, and marytr; and of other Fathers and Doctors of the Christian Church in succession; from General[4] and Provincial Synods, and from the universal primitive and successive *practice* of the Christian Church.

[1] Preface to the ORDINAL of the United Church of England and Ireland; and Canons of 1603, Canon xxxii. See also Act of Uniformity, 1662, § 13.

[2] S. IGNAT. ad Trall. iii. χωρὶς τούτων (ἐπισκόπου, πρεσ-βυτέρων, καὶ διακόνων) Ἐκκλησία οὐ καλεῖται.—Ibid. 7. ad Magnes. 7. μὴ ὑμεῖς ἄνευ τοῦ ἐπισκόπου καὶ τῶν πρεσβυτέρων μηδὲν πράσσετε.—Ad Phil. 7. ad Smyrn. 8.

[3] Ὃς Ἰωάννῃ καὶ τοῖς ἄλλοις Ἀποστόλοις συνδιέτριψε. (Concil. Lugdun. sub Irenæo. Routh, R. S. i. p. 393.)
S. IREN. iii. 3. TERTULLIAN de Præscr. Hæret. 32.

[4] CONCIL. NICÆN. can. 18. ἐμμενέτωσαν οἱ διάκονοι τοῖς ἰδίοις μέτροις, εἰδότες ὅτι τοῦ μὲν ἐπισκόπου ὑπηρέται εἰσί, τῶν δὲ πρεσβυτέρων ἐλάττους.

HOOKER, V. LXXVII. 9. Whereby (i. e. by Holy Scripture) it clearly appeareth that Churches Apostolic did know but three degrees in the power of ecclesiastical order at the first, Apostles, Presbyters, and Deacons; afterwards, instead of Apostles, Bishops.

LESLIE, C. Supplement to Discourse on the Qualifications requisite to administer the Sacraments (in the Scholar Armed, i. 105).

CHAPTER X.

BISHOPS;

Divine Institution of Episcopacy.

Q. Whom do Bishops succeed and represent?
A. The Holy Apostles[1].

[1] S. IREN. iii. 3. Habemus enumerare eos, qui ab Apostolis instituti sunt Episcopi, et *successores eorum* usque ad nos.
TERTULLIAN, Præscr. Hæret. 32. Edant (sc. hæretici) origines Ecclesiarum suarum; evolvant ordinem Episcoporum suorum ita *per successiones* ab initio decurrentem, ut primus ille Episcopus aliquem ex Apostolis vel Apostolicis viris habuerit auctorem et antecessorem.
S. CYPRIAN, Ep. 66. Episcopi sunt præpositi qui Apostolis vicariâ *ordinatione succedunt.*
S. HIERON. Ep. ad Evag. Omnes Episcopi Apostolorum *successores sunt.* Ad Marcellam, Ep. 5. Apud nos Apostolorum Episcopi locum tenent. S. AUG. in Ps. xliv. *Patres* missi sunt Apostoli, pro Apostolis *Filii* nati sunt Ecclesiæ, constituti sunt *Episcopi.* EPIPHAN. Hæres. 79. ἐξ Ἰακώβου καὶ τῶν προειρημένων Ἀποστόλων κατεστάθησαν διαδοχαὶ ἐπισκόπων καὶ πρεσβυτέρων.

Q. Why then are they not *called* Apostles?
A. Because in the first Christian age the name *Apostle* described one who had been *personally sent* (ἀποσταλεὶς) by CHRIST HIMSELF; it was therefore *reserved*[1] to the Twelve originally appointed by Him when He was upon earth, and to St. Matthias, St. Paul, and St. Barnabas, whose calls were of a peculiar kind, St. Matthias being designated by lot, St. Paul being called by Christ Himself, and he and St. Barnabas being separated for their work by special command of the Holy Ghost; and they are therefore called *Apostles* in Holy Writ.

Matt. x. 5. xxviii. 19. Mark xvi. 15. Acts i. 26. ix. 15. xiii. 2. xiv. 14

[1] See THEODORET, quoted below, p. 80.

Q. The successors of the Apostles could not

PART I. then, it seems, take the name of *Apostle;* but why did they assume that of *Episcopus* or *Bishop?*

A. Because none was more appropriate than *Episcopus* on account of its signification before mentioned (p. 79), and because the term *episcopé*[1] had been already used in the Septuagint version of the Psalms to describe the apostleship of Judas, to which St. Matthias succeeded; and because, in the Apostolic age, *Episcopus* was the name of the order immediately *next* in rank to that of the Apostles. Henceforth, then, *Episcopus* was applied to an *overlooker of (many) pastors*, having previously signified in the Church an *overlooker of a (single) flock*[2].

Ps. cix. 3.

---

[1] Act. Apost. i. 21. Ps. cix. 8. τὴν Ἐπισκοπὴν αὐτοῦ λάβοι ἕτερος.—Cp. Isa. lx. 17. δώσω τοὺς ἄρχοντάς σου ἐν εἰρήνῃ καὶ τοὺς Ἐπισκόπους σου ἐν δικαιοσύνῃ. Compare especially S. Clem. Ep. ad Cor. xlii. xliii. xliv.

[2] Hence St. Peter writes, 1 Pet. v. 1, 2, πρεσβυτέρους παρακαλῶ ὁ συμπρεσβύτερος, ποιμάνατε τὸ ποιμνίον, ἐπισκοποῦντες μὴ ἀναγκάστως.

Q. Had then, before this period, the terms *Bishop* and *Presbyter* signified the *same thing?*

A. No. They never meant the same *thing*, though they sometimes designated the same *person*[1]; who was called *Episcopus* from his *office*, as inspector of a Christian flock, and *Presbyter* from his *age and dignity*.

1 Tim. iii. 1, 2.
Titus i. 5—7.

---

[1] S. CHRYSOSTOM, Theodoret, et Œcumen. in Epist. ad Philipp. c. i. τοὺς πρεσβυτέρους ἐπισκόπους ἐκάλεσε.

THEODORET, in 1 Tim. c. iii. τοὺς αὐτοὺς ἐκάλουν ποτὲ πρεσβυτέρους καὶ ἐπισκόπους, τοὺς δὲ νῦν καλουμένους ἐπισκόπους Ἀποστόλους ὠνόμαζον· τοῦ δὲ χρόνου προϊόντος τὸ μὲν τῆς Ἀποστολῆς ὄνομα τοῖς ἀληθῶς Ἀποστόλοις κατέλιπον, τὸ δὲ τῆς ἐπισκοπῆς τοῖς πάλαι καλουμένοις Ἀποστόλοις ἐπέθεσαν· οὕτω Φιλιππησίων Ἀπόστολος ὁ Ἐπαφρόδιτος ἦν.—Cp. ad Phil. i. 1. This fact of Epaphroditus being *the Bishop* of Philippi, will explain why the Epistle is addressed ἐπισκό—οις καὶ διακόνοις, (ch. i. 1,) for Epaphroditus, their Ἀπόστολος (as he is called by St. Paul) or *Bishop*, was then with St.

Paul (ch. ii. 25); and ἐπισκόποις καὶ διακονο.s therefore (in ch. i. 1) may be rendered, *Priests and Deacons.*

Q. It appears, then, that the same word *Episcopus* was employed to designate two different offices in two successive ages?

A. Not exactly; for even from the beginning the word *Episcopus* was applied to the highest office in the Church, although it did not *exclude* the second order.

1 Pet. ii. 25.
Acts xx. 17, 28.
Tit. i. 5. 7.
1 Tim. iii. 1, 2.

Q. But is it not somewhat surprising that a term (Ἐπίσκοπος), which you say did *not exclude* the *second* order in the *first age* of Christianity, should have *afterwards* been applied *exclusively* to the *first?*

A. No; there is no more cause for surprise that an overlooker of *pastors* should afterwards be specially called *Episcopus,* when an overlooker of a *flock* had been previously called so, than that Augustus and all his successors in the Roman empire should be called *Imperatores,* when in the age preceding him, and indeed in his own age, *all* victorious *Generals,* as Lucullus, Pompey, and Mark Antony, had been called *Imperatores;* or that a large combination of provinces should be called *Diœcesis* by and after the Emperor Constantine, when, before his time, a single province had been termed so [1].

[1] BENTLEY, Remarks upon a late Discourse of Freethinking, Cam. 1743, pp. 136, 137. They (those Bishops), with all Christian Antiquity, never thought themselves and their order to succeed the Scripture Ἐπίσκοποι, but the Scripture Ἀπόστολοι: they were διάδοχοι τῶν Ἀποστόλων, *the successors of the Apostles.* The sum of the matter is this:—Though new institutions are formed, new words are not coined for them, but old ones borrowed and applied. Ἐπίσκοπος, whose general idea is *overseer,* was a word in use long before Christianity; a word of universal relation to œconomical, civil, military, naval, judicial, and religious matters. This word was assumed to denote the governing and presiding persons of the Church, as Διάκονος (another word of vulgar and diffused use) to denote the ministerial.

PART I.

The Presbyters, therefore, while the Apostles lived, were 'Επίσκοποι, *overseers*. But the Apostles, in foresight of their approaching martyrdom, having selected and appointed their successors in the several cities and communities, as *St. Paul* did *Timothy* at *Ephesus*, and *Titus* at *Crete*, A.D. 64, four years before his death; what name were these successors to be called by? not 'Απόστολοι, *Apostles;* their modesty, as it seems, made them refuse it: they would keep that name proper and sacred to the first *extraordinary* messengers of Christ, though they really succeeded them in their office, in due part and measure, as the *ordinary* governors of the Churches.

It was agreed, therefore, over all Christendom at once, in the very next generation after the Apostles, to assign and appropriate to them the word 'Επίσκοπος, or Bishop. From that time to this, that appellation, which before included a *Presbyter,* has been restrained to a superior order. And here's nothing in all this but what has happened in all languages and communities in the world. See the *Notitia* of the *Roman* and *Greek* Empires, and you'll scarce find one name of any state employment, that in course of time did not vary from its primitive signification. The time has been when a commander even of a single regiment was called *Imperator:* and must every such, now-a-days, set up to be *Emperors?*

Q. But does not S. Jerome[1] say that, even in the *Apostolic* times, the Churches were *governed* by *several* Presbyters, who were also called Episcopi, *antequam instinctu diaboli studia in religione fierent, et diceretur in populis,* " *Ego sum*

1 Cor. i. 12. *Apollo, ego sum Cephæ;" postquam autem unusquisque eos quos baptizaverat suos esse putabat non Christi, tum in toto orbe decretum est ut* UNUS *de Presbyteris electus superponeretur cæteris, ad quem omnis cura Ecclesiæ pertineret, et schismatum semina tollerentur?*

A. Yes, he does; but S. Jerome[2] also says that Bishops are the ordained successors of the Apostles; that St. James was Bishop of Jerusalem, immediately after the Ascension of Christ; that Episcopacy is an Apostolic ordinance; that Presbyters cannot ordain; that the safety of the Church consists in the dignity of its Bishop; and his assertion, just quoted, does, when examined, tend rather to confirm the doctrine of the Apostolic and Divine institution of Episcopacy.

¹ S. HIERON. in Tit. i. Ep. lxxxv. ad Evagrium.
² S. HIERON. (See above, note to first question in this chapter.) De Scriptoribus Ecclesiasticis. Jacobus qui appellatur frater Domini,—post passionem Domini statim ab Apostolis Hierosolymorum *Episcopus* ordinatus.
S. HIERON. in Lucif. c. 4. Ecclesiæ salus in summi sacerdotis dignitate consistit, cui si non exsors quædam et eminens detur potestas, tot in Ecclesiâ efficientur schismata quot sacerdotes. Inde venit, ut sine chrismate et *Episcopi jussione neque Presbyter neque Diaconus habeat jus baptizandi.*
S. HIERON. in Evagr. lxxxv. Quid enim facit, *exceptâ ordinatione*, Episcopus, quod Presbyter non faciat? See below, chap. xi.

Q. How do you show this?

A. We do not deny that in the Apostolic age the names *Episcopi* and *Presbyteri* were applied to the same persons; but *then* there were at that time *Bishops* also, in the true sense of the word, namely, the HOLY APOSTLES themselves: and (whatever may be alleged as the *reason* for the institution of Episcopacy) the *fact* and *time* of its institution are the only questions with which we are concerned. Now in this same passage S. Jerome testifies, that it was "*toto orbe* decretum *ut unus* cæteris superponeretur, ad quem omnis Ecclesiæ cura pertineret." And that which was decreed in *the whole world* (and which Jerome himself, in the case of St. James, represents as immediately consequent on our Lord's Ascension), could not be of *human* institution, as is clear from the principle laid down by S. Augustin¹, "Id quod *universa tenet Ecclesia,* (as S. Jerome says is the case with *Episcopacy,*) *nec Conciliis* institutum, (and Councils all *presuppose Bishops,* for they *consist* of them,) sed semper retentum, non nisi *auctoritate Apostolicâ* traditum esse rectissimè creditur." It was instituted by the Holy Ghost,

PART I. who inspired the Holy Apostles, and acted by them.

[1] S. AUG. c. Donat. de Bapt. iv. 24, and v. c. 23. Quæ universa tenet Ecclesia, ob hoc ab Apostolis præcepta bene creduntur.

HOOKER, VII. v. 2, & VII. v. 8. BARROW, de Regimine Episcopali, iv. p. 24, sq. folio ed. 1687. Abp. POTTER, ch. iv. Bp. PEARSON, Vind. Ignat. p. 177.

H. GROTIUS, iv. p. 272. Episcopatum ab *universali Ecclesiâ receptum* fuisse apparet *ex Conciliis Universalibus:* apparet etiam ex collectione Synodorum aut nationalium aut provincialium. *Patres omnes, nemine excepto,* Episcopalem eminentiam testantur, quorum is qui minimum Episcopatui defert est *Hieronymus;* hujus sufficit testimonium, "*In toto orbe* decretum," &c. Episcopatum initium Apostolicis temporibus habuisse testantur *catalogi* Episcoporum apud Irenæum, Eusebium, Socratem.—Episcopatum *divino jure approbatum* fuisse, irrefragabile argumentum præbet divina *Apocalypsis.* See also GROTII Epist. p. 914. Cum quæritur, an Episcopatus juris divini sit—*satis* est Christum in Apostolorum Collegio id dedisse exemplum: Apostolos id secutos et Ecclesiæ Universæ consensum manifestissimum, si pauci et quidem nostri tantùm sæculi novatores excipiantur: cf. p. 923. So writes Grotius, although he was by birth and education a *Presbyterian.* See below, at end of chap. xi.

HOOKER, VII. v. 8. In all this there is no let, why *S. Jerome* might not think the Authors of Episcopal regiment to have been the very blessed *Apostles* themselves, directed therein by the special motion of the Holy Ghost, which the *ancients all before and beside him,* and *himself* also elsewhere, are known to hold. See also Bp. STILLINGFLEET, Eccl. Cases, i. p. 5.

GIBBON, Rom. Hist. ch. xv. "Nulla Ecclesia sine Episcopo" has been a *fact* as well as a maxim since the time of Tertullian and Irenæus; after we have passed over the difficulties of the first century, we find the *Episcopal government universally* established, till it was interrupted by the republican genius of the Swiss and German reformers.

⒜. Inasmuch then as it was very reasonable and right, that such an individual superintendent of pastors as you have described should be called an *Episcopus*, can you prove from Scripture that at the close of the *Apostolic age* there *were in fact* individual superintendents of the Clergy and Laity, besides the Apostles?

A. Yes; such were St. Timothy and St. Titus. They were *not Apostles*[1],—not being of *directly Divine* appointment, as all the Apostles, including St. Matthias, St. Paul, and St. Barnabas, were—they were never so called; and they were not mere *Presbyters;* for they are commanded by St. Paul to *ordain,* to *charge,* to *rebuke* Presbyters[2], and to *superintend* the doctrine and conduct of both *Presbyters* and *Deacons,* and this with *all authority,* but, *Par in parem non habet imperium.*

Chap. X.
Titus i. 5.

1 Tim. v. 17—22.

Titus ii. 15.

[1] Euseb. H. E. iii. 4. iii. 11—15, pp. 148—176, ed. Burton.

[2] Bp. Bilson on the Perpetual Government of Christ's Church, chap. v. p. 89. Oxford, 1842. These were charged by Paul to "require and command" the pastors and preachers to refrain from false doctrine; and to "stop their mouths" or "reject" them that did otherwise; "to ordain elders" according to the necessity of the places, and "receive accusations against them;" and "sharply" and "openly to rebuke" them if they sinned, and that "with all authority." These things the Apostle earnestly requireth, and, before Christ and His elect angels, chargeth Timothie and Tite to do. It is, then, evident they might so do; for how vain and frivolous were all those protestations made by St. Paul, if Timothie and Tite had only voices amongst the rest, and nothing to do but as the rest!

1 Tim. i. 3.
Titus i. 11.
iii. 10.
i. 5. 13.
1 Tim. v. 19, 20.
Titus ii. 15.

Q. You say that they were not Apostles; was then their power Apostolic?

A. Yes: their office was similar to, and in the place of, that of the Holy Apostles.

Q. How do you show this?

A. St. Paul tells Titus, that he had left him in Crete, that he might *perfect* the things which he (St. Paul himself) had left *incomplete*[1].

Titus i. 5.

[1] S. Hieron. ad Tit. c. i. Reliquit Titum Cretæ, ut rudimenta nascentis Ecclesiæ confirmaret, "*ut ea quæ deerant corrigeres.*" Omne autem quod corrigitur imperfectum est. Et in Græco præpositionis adjectio quâ scribitur ἐπὶ διορθώσῃς non id ipsum sonat quod διορθώσῃς *corrigeres,* sed *super corrigeres;* ut quæ a *me* correcta

Part I. sunt nedum ad plenam veri lineam retracta, a *te* corrigantur, et normam æqualitatis accipiant.

Q. Does this superintending and governing power, resident in one individual, appear in any other part of Scripture?

A. Yes; in the Revelation of St. John, where each of the seven Asiatic Churches is represented as having a chief pastor, who is called by the Holy Spirit the *Angel* of that Church [1].

[1] S. Aug. Ep. xliii. Divinâ voce laudatur sub *Angeli* nomine Præpositus Ecclesiæ. (S. Aug. ?) in Apocalyps. Hom. ii. Ecclesiæ et angeli Ecclesiarum intelligi debent Episcopi aut Præpositi Ecclesiarum.

Saravia, de Minist. Eccl. p. 29, observes, that the Spirit blames some of the Angels of the Churches, but that He never blames them *for being Angels.* On the contrary, He recognizes them as the Rulers of the Churches, which He addresses *through them.* See Wordsworth on the Apocalypse, pp. 83—103, and p. 490, 2nd edit. Grotius, quoted above, p. 84.

Q. But to ascend higher; does the succession of the chief pastors to the Apostles appear to have been directly *authorized* by Christ?

A. It does. The Episcopal Government of the Church was originally *founded* in the *person* and *office* of our Blessed Lord Himself.

Q. How does this appear?

A. As follows: Christ, being sent by His Heb. iii. 1, 2. Father [1], to be the great Apostle, Bishop, and 1 Pet. ii. 25. Pastor of the Church, as He is called in Scripture, and being visibly consecrated to that office by the Holy Ghost, sent His Apostles, as His Father had sent Him. He gave to them the John xx. 21, Holy Ghost, as His Father had given to Him; 22. xvii. 18. and commissioned them to execute the same apostolic, episcopal, and pastoral office, in their own 2 Tim. ii. 2. persons, and in that of their successors, for the governing of His Church until His coming again, Matt. xxviii. promising to be with them "alway, even unto 18—20. the end of the world."

Q. Do we read in Scripture of any *act* of the Apostles done with a view to *continue* this succession from themselves?

A. Yes: their very *first* act after the Ascension of Christ was done with a view to the appointment of one to take part in the ministry of the Apostleship (ἐπισκοπή), from which Judas by transgression fell, and whose *office* (ἐπισκοπή) was to be *taken* by *another*.

Acts i. 20.— 25. Ps. cix. 8.

Q. It is justly said, that the best *Commentary* upon a law is *practice*, especially contemporary, universal, and uninterrupted *practice*[1]. And how does the *practice* of the Church bear on the present question concerning the institution, authority, and obligation of Episcopacy?

A. The *universal practice* of the Church of Christ, *from its foundation* for more than [2] *fifteen hundred years without interruption*, shows Episcopacy to be of Divine institution, and to have been regarded by the Church as of inviolable authority. "*Exitus variâsse debuerat error; cæterùm quod apud* multos unum *invenitur,* non *est* erratum *sed traditum; et id* Dominicum *est et* verum *quod* priùs *traditum, id* extraneum *et* falsum *quod* posteriùs *immissum*[3]."

---

[1] Ch. Justice COKE. *Consuetudo* optimus legum interpres. Contemporanea expositio optima.

[2] Bp. BILSON, Perpetual Government of Christ's Church, xiii. p. 348, ed. Oxf. 1842. *No example* before our age can be showed, that ever the Church of Christ, *in any place or time*, since the Apostles died, had any other form of government than by *Bishops*, succeeding and ruling as well the Presbyters as the people that were under them.

HOOKER, Pref. IV. 1. We require you to find out *one* Church *upon the face of the whole earth*, that hath not been ordered by Episcopal Regiment, since the time that the blessed Apostles were here conversant. See also Bp. ANDREWES on Worshipping of Imaginations, p. 32.

Abp. LAUD, Sermon iii. A *Paritie* they would have;

[Bp. SANDERSON, Postscript to "Episcopacy not prejudicial to Regal Power," pp. 137. 140, 1673. — CHAP. X.]

PART I. no Bishop, no Governor; but a Parochial Consistory. This paritie was never left to the Church of Christ. He left Apostles, and Disciples under them. It was never in use with the Church. *No* Church *ever any where*, till this last age, *without a Bishop.* GROTIUS, tom. iv. p. 273. Episcopatus est ab Ecclesiâ Universali receptus; initium habuit ab Apostolicis temporibus, et divino judicio est approbatus. Compare above, p. 86; below, p. 93.

³ TERTULLIAN, Præscr. Hæret. c. 28, c. 31, adv. Marcion. iv. 5.

℞. Does any *other* form of Church Government appear to have existed in any of the Apostolic Churches?

1 Cor. xi. 16.

℞. No. "We have *no* such *custom*, nor the Churches of God." In *every case*, where Catalogues¹ of Church Governors are extant, the series of pastors is traced back through individual and successive (and not through many, equal, co-existent, and contemporaneous) Governors, the first of them being some Apostle or some disciple of the Apostles; and as has been before said, there is *no* example of a Church *without a Bishop* for *fifteen centuries after Christ.*

¹ S. IREN. iii. 3. EUSEB. H. E. iii. 4. 10. v. 5. 22. 24. vii. 32. HOOKER, VII. v. 9. Bp. BILSON, Perpet. Gov. ch. xiii. pp. 334—340. BINGHAM, Antiq. ii. 1. 3, 4.

℞. What additional proof is there of the Divine institution of Episcopacy from ancient practice?

℞. There is a strong confirmation of it in the fact, that not only *catholics*, but also *heretics* and *schismatics*¹, differing from the Church and from each other in many other respects, *all agreed* in recognizing the *necessity* of *Episcopal Government*, with one single exception, that of Aerius² (of Sebastia, in Pontus), in the fourth century, who on that account, as well as for other reasons, is placed among *heretics* by the Fathers of the

OF EPISCOPACY.   89

Church, and whose doctrine on that point was condemned by the Church as *sacrilegious*[3]. CHAP. X.

---

[1] Bp. PEARSON, Vind. Ignat. c. 13.

[2] S. AUG. de Hæres. § 53. Aerius dicebat Presbyterum ab Episcopo nullâ differentiâ debere discerni.

BARROW, vol. iii. Serm. xxiv. p. 273 (vol. iii. Serm. lvi. p. 112, ed. Oxf.). All Arians, Macedonians, Novatians, Donatists, maintained the distinction of Ecclesiastical Orders, and the duty of the inferior Clergy to their Bishops; and of this distinction was never made any question, except by Aerius, who found very few followers in his heterodoxy.

EPIPHAN. de Hæreticis, § 66 or § 76.

[3] The General Council of Chalcedon declared, can. 39, Ἐπίσκοπον εἰς Πρεσβυτέρου βαθμὸν φέρειν ἱεροσυλία ἐστίν. Cp. Bp. ANDREWES, in Christian Institutes, iii. 234, and HOOKER, VII. IX.

Q. What are the words in which Hooker concludes his argument upon this subject?

A. "Let us not fear," he says, "to be herein bold and peremptory, that if *any thing* in the Church's government, surely the first institution of Bishops was from heaven, even of God; the HOLY GHOST was the Author of it[1]."

---

[1] HOOKER, VII. VI. 1. Compare VII. I. 4. Add to this the summary of the argument by Dr. ISAAC BARROW. "The *primitive general use* of Christians most effectually doth back the Scripture, and interpret it in favour of this distinction (of Episcopal Government); for how otherwise is it imaginable, that all the *Churches*, founded by the *Apostles* in several most distant and disjoined places (at *Jerusalem*, at *Antioch*, at *Alexandria*, at *Ephesus*, at *Corinth*, at *Rome*) should presently conspire in acknowledgment and use of it? how could it without apparent confederacy be formed? how could it creep in without notable clatter, how could it be admitted without considerable opposition, if it were not in the foundation of those Churches laid by the *Apostles*? How is it likely that in those times of grievous persecution falling chiefly upon the *Bishops* (when to be eminent among Christians yielded slender reward, and exposed to extreme hazard; when to seek pre-eminence was in effect to court danger and trouble, torture and ruin), an ambition of irregularly advancing themselves above their brethren should so gene-

PART I. rally prevail among the ablest and best Christians? How could those famous Martyrs for the Christian truth be some of them so unconscionable as to affect, others so irresolute as to yield to, such injurious encroachments? and how could all the holy Fathers (persons of so renowned, so approved wisdom and integrity) be so blind as not to discern such a corruption, or so bad as to abet it? How, indeed, could all God's Church be so weak as to consent in judgment, so base as to comply in practice with it? In fine, how can we conceive, that all the best monuments of antiquity down from the beginning (the *Acts*, the *Epistles*, the *Histories*, the *Commentaries*, the *writings* of all sorts coming from the blessed *Martyrs* and most holy *Confessors* of our faith), should conspire to abuse us? the which do speak nothing but *Bishops*."

See Dr. ISAAC BARROW's Works, London, 1686, Folio, Serm. xxiv. vol. iii. p. 273. *See also* BARROW's Latin Treatise (iv. 18). "Rejectio regiminis Episcopalis, ubi habentur orthodoxi et legitimi Episcopi, facit propriè schisma mortale." The learned BISHOP PATRICK, when a young man, was a Presbyterian, and received Presbyterian orders; but he was convinced by the study of Holy Scripture and of Church History that they were defective, and he sought for and received Holy Orders in 1654 at the hands of Bishop Hall. See THORNDIKE's Works, vol. vi. p. 184. See also Bp. PEARSON, Minor Works, i. pp. 271—286. CHILLINGWORTH, Apostolical Institution of Episcopacy demonstrated (in Christian Institutes, iii. pp. 210. 214), and WORDSWORTH's notes on the Greek Testament on 1 Tim. iii. p. 445, and Revelation, p. 167.

CHAPTER XI.

FUNCTIONS OF BISHOPS.

Q. WHEN you say that Bishops are the successors of the Apostles, do you mean that they succeed them in *all* their Apostolic functions?

A. No. *Some* of the functions of the Apostles were *ordinary* and *permanent* in their nature, such as those of ¹preaching, administering the Sacraments, feeding the flock of Christ, giving attendance to reading, to exhortation, to doctrine, exercising discipline, judging controversies, conferring with each other in Councils and Synods, confirming the baptized, ordaining[2] and superintending ministers.

But *other* functions of the Apostles were *extraordinary* and *temporary*, such as healing the sick, casting out devils, and speaking with tongues.

Bishops succeed the Apostles in their *ordinary* functions, but *not* in their *extraordinary* offices[3].

---

[1] BINGHAM, Antiquities, ii. 3.

[2] S. CHRYSOST. in Tit. i. 5. Ἵνα καταστήσῃς κατὰ πόλιν πρεσβυτέρους—τῶν ἐπισκόπων λέγω τὰς χειροτονίας. In Philip. i. 1. οὐκ ἂν πρεσβύτεροι ἐπίσκοπον ἐχειροτόνησαν.
AMMONIUS ad Act. Apost. xiv. 23. οἱ περὶ Παῦλον ἐπισκόπων εἶχον ἀξίαν, ἐξ ὧν ἐχειροτόνουν οὐ μόνον διακόνους ἀλλὰ καὶ πρεσβυτέρους. Timothy is said to have received the χάρισμα of Holy Orders μετὰ ἐπιθέσεως τῶν χειρῶν τοῦ πρεσβυτερίου (1 Tim. iv. 14), but διὰ τῆς ἐπιθέσεως τῶν χειρῶν of St. Paul, 2 Tim. i. 6.

[3] K. CHARLES I. in Christian Institutes, iii. p. 220. The *mission* both for teaching and governing (at least for the substance of it) was *ordinary*, and to continue to the end of the world; and, therefore, necessarily to descend, and be by them transmitted to others, as their substitutes and successors. But the *unction*, whereby they were enabled to both offices or functions, by the effusion of the Holy Ghost in such a plenteous measure of knowledge, tongues, miracles, prophesyings, healing, infallibility of doctrine, discerning of spirits, and such like, was, indeed, *extraordinary* in them, and in some few others, though in an inferior measure, as God saw it needful for the planting of the Churches and propagation of the Gospel in those primitive times; and in this (which was indeed *extraordinary* in them) they were not necessarily to have successors. (Matt. xxvii. 18—20.)

His Majesty conceives that the succession of Bishops to the Apostles into so much of their office as was *ordinary and perpetual*, and such a distinction of Bishops and Presbyters as His Majesty has formerly expressed, needs no further confirmation from Scripture to such as are willing to make use of their *reason* also; which, in interpreting Scripture, upon all other occasions they are enforced to do.

Bp. CARLETON de Ecclesiâ, cap. xi. p. 278. *Extraordinaria* Apostolorum potestas cum ipsis finem habuit; *ordinaria* vero Episcopis commendata fuit, atque in illis permansit.

Q. You speak of *Ordinations*—do you intend

PART 1. to say that no one can confer Holy Orders except Bishops?

A. Yes; "cases of inevitable necessity excepted, none may ordain but only Bishops [1];" and all other ordinations, whether by Presbyters or any one else, have ever been regarded by the Christian Church as invalid [2].

[1] HOOKER, VII. XIV. 11.
[2] LEO M. Ep. 88. *Nunquam* auditum est, quòd Presbyteri Presbyteros aut Diaconos nedum Episcopos *ordinaverint*.

Bp. CARLETON de Consensu Ecclesiæ contra Tridentinos, ii. p. 277. Si omnia Ecclesiæ sæcula lustremus ab Apostolis usque ad Patrum nostrorum memoriam, *non alia* ordinandi ratio invenitur nisi per *Episcopos*. SARAVIA de Div. Minist. Grad. p. 33. Bp. BILSON, Perpet. Gov. of Christ's Church, p. 321.

Bp. PEARSON, Minor Works, ed. Churton, ii. 75. Per traditionem Apostolicam *tota* ordinandi potestas in Episcopis resedit; *nulli alii* unquam in Novo Testamento indulta est; nulli in vetere Ecclesiâ permissa. See also ibid. on Promiscuous Ordinations, pp. 232 – 237.

Abp. POTTER, on Church Government, p. 285. The opinion of the primitive Church in this matter will be put beyond dispute, if we compare the judgment concerning Ischyras, who was ordained by one Coluthus, a mere *presbyter*, with that about the presbyters ordained by Meletius, a schismatical *bishop*. The latter, having been ordained by one who had the episcopal character, were received as presbyters without being re-ordained; whereas Ischyras, having received his orders from one who had not power to give them, was reckoned as a mere layman. This appears from the synodical epistles of the bishops of Egypt, Thebais, Libya, and Pentapolis.

On this subject, see CABASSUTIUS, Concilia, cap. xi. p. 44. Osius Alexandriæ Concilium indixit, cujus meminit Athanasius, Apol. 2, vocatque generale Concilium, meminit ejus Socrates, iii. 5.—Addit Athanasius in eâ synodo Coluthum *presbyterum* Alexandrinum, eò quod episcopus non esset, munus tamen episcopale obire et ordinare clericos attentasset, fuisse redactum in ordinem.—Ibid. cap. ii. p. 18. Synodus Alexandrina synodicam (epistolam) scripsit ad Julium Romæ episcopum, cæterosque omnes orbis Christiani præsules, quam integram epistolam refert Athanasius; ea fidem facit Ischyram ne *presbyterum* quidem esse sed *laicum*, quippe qui a Colutho manuum suscepisset ordinationem, qui non erat *episcopus* sed *presbyter*.

FUNCTIONS OF BISHOPS. 93

Hence the Church of England has decreed in her Ordinal, CHAP. XI.
"that no man shall be accounted or taken to be a lawful
bishop, priest, or deacon in her communion, or suffered to
execute any of the said functions, except he hath had
episcopal consecration or ordination."

STREITWOLF, Libri Symbolici in Catechism. Conc. Trid.
c. vii. p. 442. Etiam schismaticis atque hæreticis persuasum
fuisse *solas* ordinationes ab *episcopis* factas ratas esse de-
ducitur ex iis, quæ Cornel. P. de Novatiano tradit in Ep.
ap. Euseb. H. E. vi. 43; and the Greek Church expressly
condemned the opinion that non-episcopal ordinations are
valid, in the Synodus Hierosolymitana, 1672, pp. 436-7, ed.
Kimmel, 1843.

Q. In maintaining the necessity of Episcopal
Government, are we not guilty of want of charity
by condemning those who are *without it?*

A. VERITAS est maxima CARITAS; TRUTH is
the greatest CHARITY. It is no *charity*, to con-
nive at error, and to suppress truth; but it *is*
charity, to endeavour to remove error, and to
maintain and communicate truth. Therefore our
duty is, if we enjoy Episcopal Government, to
thank God for it; and to pray to Him that they
who have it not, whether from necessity [1], real or
supposed, from inadvertence, indifference, or deliberate purpose, may at length become able and
willing to receive it; and we are bound to be
ready and desirous [2], as far as we are able, to
encourage and promote such reception [3].

[1] HOOKER, III. XI. 14. BRAMHALL, ii. 70.
Cp. Note to Christian Institutes, vol. iii. p. 258.
GERHARD de Ecclesiâ, p. 372. vi. 183. 231. Art. Smal-
cald. Art. x.; and the words of Calvin, Inst. iv. 4. 1.
The following is the very important testimony of the
writers of the AUGSBURGH CONFESSION on this subject,
subscribed by CALVIN himself, showing the desires of its
framers for the preservation of Episcopacy in the foreign
Reformed Churches. See De la Motte, Correspondence
fraternelle, p. 424, and Calvin, Opera, ix. p. 113.
LIBRI SYMBOLICI Ecclesiæ Evangelicæ, &c. Lipsiæ,
1837, p. 204. Apologia Confessionis, (a P. MELANCHTHON,)
Art. vii. § 24. "Hâc de re in hoc conventu sæpe testati
sumus, nos summâ voluntate *cupere conservare politiam
Ecclesiasticam*, et gradus in Ecclesiâ factos etiam humanâ

PART I. auctoritate. Scimus enim bono et utili consilio a Patribus Ecclesiasticam disciplinam hoc modo, ut veteres canones describunt, constitutam esse. Sed Episcopi sacerdotes nostros aut cogunt hoc doctrinæ genus, quod confessi sumus, abjicere et damnare, aut novâ et inauditâ crudelitate miseros et innocentes occidunt. Hæ causæ impediunt, quo minus agnoscant hos Episcopos nostri sacerdotes. Ita sævitia Episcoporum in causâ est, quare alicubi dissolvitur illa canonica politia, quam nos *magnoperè cupiebamus conservare*. Ipsi viderint, quomodo rationem Deo reddituri sint, quod *dissipant Ecclesiam*.

"Porro hic iterum volumus testatum, nos libenter conservaturos esse Ecclesiasticam et Canonicam politiam, si modo Episcopi desinant in nostras Ecclesias sævire. Hæc nostra voluntas et coram Deo, et *apud omnes gentes*, ad omnem *posteritatem excusabit* nos, ne *nobis imputari possit quod Episcoporum auctoritas labefactatur*, ubi legerint atque audierint homines, nos injustam sævitiam Episcoporum deprecantes, nihil æqui impetrare potuisse."

The above is the LUTHERAN statement; for the ARMINIAN, the language of GROTIUS (above, pp. 84. 88, and below, pt. ii. ch. v.) may be referred to; and the following are the words of CALVIN and BEZA:—

CALVINUS, Epist. ad Cardinal. Sadolet. Disciplinam, qualem habuit *vetus Ecclesia, nobis deesse* non diffitemur —sed cujus erit æquitatis nos eversæ disciplinæ ab iis accusari qui eam penitus sustulerunt? *Episcopatus* a *Deo* profectus est; *Episcopi* munus *Dei* authoritate constitutum est et legibus definitum. CALVINUS, de Necessit. Reform. Eccles. Talem nobis hierarchiam si exhibeant in quâ sic emineant *Episcopi* ut Christo subesse non recusent, ut ab Illo tanquam ab unico Capite pendeant et ad Ipsum referantur; tum vero *nullo non anathemate dignos fatear*, si qui erunt, qui non eam revereantur, summâque obedientiâ observent. See also STRYPE's Parker, A.D. 1560, i. pp. 139, 140.

BEZA ad Sarav. Tract. de Ministrorum Gradibus. Si qui sunt qui omnem *Episcoporum* ordinem rejiciant, absit ut quisquam sanæ mentis *furoribus illorum* assentiatur!

On this subject, see the avowals of the Reformers quoted by Bishop WORDSWORTH, of St. Andrew's, in his Discourse on the Scottish Reformation, p. viii. p. 29.

[2] See the *desires* to this effect expressed by Abp. LAUD, Bps. ANDREWES and SANDERSON, Christian Institutes, iii. pp. 261. 216—219.

[3] The exhortation of GROTIUS to the *Reformed* Churches of his own times may be reiterated now.—Epist. p. 975. Suaderem eis ut constituerent inter se quosdam in eminentiore gradu ut Episcopos, et ut ius χειροθεσίαν sume-

rent ab Archiepiscopo Hiberno, qui ibi est, et ita ordinati ordinarent, deinde pastores cæteros, atque sic initium facerent *redeundi* ad mores et antiquos et salutares; quibus contemptis licentia invaluit pro *novis opinionibus* faciendi *novas Ecclesias,* quæ *quid* post *aliquot annos creditura sint,* nescimus. How fully have the melancholy forebodings of these last words been realized in Germany, Switzerland, Holland, and elsewhere!

CHAPTER XII.

OF BISHOPS AS DIOCESANS, METROPOLITANS, AND PATRIARCHS.

Q. You have spoken of Bishops in general, and of their institution and offices; is not the performance of their duty, individually, and the *exercise* and *application* of their powers, restrained habitually in Christian States by laws ecclesiastical and civil, within certain limits?

A. Yes.

Q. And do not Bishops bear certain titles according to the limits within which their functions are exercised?

A. They do.

Q. Can you give any instances of such restrictions from Holy Scripture?

A. Yes. Our Lord Himself says, He was not "sent but to the lost sheep of the House of Israel." St. Peter was specially the Apostle of the circumcision, and St. Paul of the Gentiles. St. James had special jurisdiction at Jerusalem; St. Timothy at Ephesus; St. Titus in Crete; and the seven Asiatic Churches had each their own Bishop respectively [1].

Matt. xv. 24.
Gal. ii. 7—9.
Rom. xi. 13.
Acts xii. 17.
xv. 13. xxi.
18. Gal. i.
19. ii. 12.
1 Tim. i. 3.
Tit. i. 5.
Rev. i. 20.

[1] Archbp. USHER, Original of Bishops and Metropolitans, Oxford, 1641. Archbp. De MARCA de Concordiâ, vi. 1. WORDSWORTH on the Apocalypse, pp. 83—103.

Q. Does this principle of distribution and restriction appear to have been generally received in the Church in ancient times?

A. Yes: and there were certain circumstances of a providential nature which rendered the uniform reception of it very easy and natural.

Q. What were these?

A. The *civil* divisions of the Roman *Empire*[1], that is to say, of the greater part of the civilized world, in the early ages of Christianity, were admirably adapted to, and prepared for, the application of this distributive system and economy of *Church* government, throughout the whole extent of the Roman sway.

[1] HOOKER, VII. VIII. 7. BARROW on the Pope's Supremacy, p. 163. BINGHAM, Antiquities, II. xvi. xvii. ix. i. 7.

Hence the expression of S. OPTATUS, iii. 3. Non Respublica in Ecclesiâ, sed Ecclesia in Republicâ, i. e. in Imperio Romano. PANCIROLI, Notitia Dignitatum utriusque Imperii, in Græv1i Thesaur. Antiq. vii. p. 1308. Bp. BEVERIDGE, Codex Canonum, v. 13, de Metropolitanis, in Patres Apostolici, ed. Cotelerii, n. 2, p. 87. JOHNSON'S Code of the Universal Church (in vol. n. of Clergyman's Vade Mecum, 1709).—CANONES Apostol. et Concil. Sæculorum IV. V. VI. VII. Bruns. Berolin. 1839.

Q. You mean, that the system of *civil* government invited the application of a similar system of *ecclesiastical* polity?

A. Yes: and this aptitude was recognized by General Councils of the Church, and made by them the groundwork[1] of their own legislation; so that, when the Empire became Christian, (i. e. early in the fourth century,) the lines of the ecclesiastical map coincided very nearly with those of the civil chart of the whole empire.

[1] Concil. Antioch. A.D. 341, can. 9, p. 80, ed. Bruns. τοὺς καθ' ἑκάστην ἐπαρχίαν ἐπισκόπους εἰδέναι χρὴ τὸν ἐν τῇ μητροπόλει προεστῶτα ἐπίσκοπον, καὶ τὴν φροντίδα ἀναδέχεσθαι πάσης τῆς ἐπαρχίας διὰ τὸ ἐν τῇ μητροπόλει πανταχόθεν συντρέχειν πάντας τοὺς τὰ πράγματα ἔχοντας —ἕκαστον ἐπίσκοπον ἐξουσίαν ἔχειν τῆς ἑαυτοῦ παροικίας —περαιτέρω δὲ μηδὲν πράττειν ἐπιχειρεῖν δίχα τοῦ τῆς

μητροπόλεως ἐπισκόπου. See also Archbp. De MARCA Chap. XII. de Concordiâ, vi. cap. 1. BARROW on the Pope's Supremacy, p. 165. DUPIN de Ant. Eccles. Discipl. 1, § 8.

Q. As, then, at that time, the Eastern Empire consisted, *politically*, of seven districts called *Dioceses* (διοικήσεις), and seven also composed the Western, there were, I suppose, seven *ecclesiastical* districts coinciding with them in the East, and seven in the West also?

A. Yes; and these *ecclesiastical* districts were *also* termed *Dioceses*.

Q. And as in these fourteen dioceses there were altogether about one hundred and eighteen minor territorial divisions called *Provinces* (ἐπαρχίαι), so there were as many sub-divisions in the Church?

A. Yes; and these *ecclesiastical* sub-divisions were also termed *Provinces*.

Q. And as in each province there were several cities, with their respective *precincts* (παροικίαι) attached to them, so there were several chief *Churches*, each having its own territorial range allotted to it?

A. There were; and these too were called παροικίαι[1], *Parœciæ*, which word in English has now *descended* to describe a *Parish*, from signifying what we *now* term a Diocese; as διοίκησις has also *descended* to designate a *Diocese*, from signifying, as it once did, a *combination* of several Dioceses.

---

[1] Bp. BILSON, Appendix to Perpetual Government of Christ's Church, p. 540. Παροικία *Parœcia* non civitatem solùm in quâ Episcopus sedem habuerit, sed totam regionem finitimam civitati assignatam sive subjectam significat. CABASSUTIUS, Concil. cap. xxviii. and cap. xxvii. p. 114. Iste Canon (Antioch. 9) tres commemorat Ecclesiasticæ Præfecturæ gradus, scilicet

1. ἐπαρχίαν, *Provinciam*, sub Metropolitano Præsule;
2. παροικίαν, *Parœciam*, sub comprovinciali sive suffraganeo Episcopo;

PART I.

3. χώραν, *locum,* seu minorem locum, unde χωρεπίσκοποι dicti, locorum particularium intra Parœciam præfecti;

Sed omnes gradus illos antecellebat *Diœcesis,* habens plures Provincias, qualis erat singulorum *Patriarcharum* ditio.

Nunc vero *Diœcesis* usurpari pro Parœciâ solet, ipsa verò *Parœcia* pro intimâ Præfecturâ pagorum, quorum præfectus vulgo *Parochus* audit, meliùs tamen juxta Græcorum Canonum expressionem *Parœcus* diceretur. On the word παροικία see also Vales. ad Euseb. i. 1.

Q. And now, to *ascend* in an inverted order, what, first, were the rulers of these *chief Churches* called?

A. *Bishops.*

Q. Could there be more than *one* Bishop in a city?

A. No[1]; there could not; this was specially prohibited by the laws of the Church, and censured by them as schismatical; and a *second* Bishop in a city is regarded by them as *no* Bishop[2].

[1] Concil. Nicæn. c. 8. Ἵνα μὴ ἐν τῇ πόλει δύο ἐπίσκοποι ὦσι. S. HIERON. ad Ep. Philipp. i. Non in *unâ* urbe *plures Episcopi* esse potuissent. S. CORNEL. ap. Euseb. vi. 43. εἷς ἐπίσκοπος ἐν καθολικῇ ἐκκλησίᾳ. There were, however, Bishops of various *nations*, speaking different languages, in the same city. See Le Moyne, Varia Sacra, vol. ii. * 28. 2.

[2] S. CYPRIAN ad Antonian. ep. 52. Quisquis post *unum* (Episcopum) factus est, non jam *secundus* ille, sed *nullus* est.

S. CYPRIAN ad Step. ep. 67. *Foris* esse cœpit, qui, Episcopo Cornelio ordinato, *profanum altare* erigere, adulteram cathedram collocare, et sacrilega sacrificia offerre tentaverit. See also S. CHRYSOST. Theodoret. et Œcumen. in Epist. ad Phil. i., and BINGHAM, II. xiii. 1. XVII. v. 3.

Q. What were the Episcopal Rulers of the *Provinces* styled?

A. *Metropolitans,* (Ecclesiastical Governors of the mother city, μητρόπολις,) and sometimes Archbishops, though this latter title was more generally applied to a still more dignified ecclesiastical office; and all were called *Apostolici.*

Q. And what were those of the *Dioceses* called?

A. *Patriarchs* [1], *Exarchs*, or *Archbishops* [2].

[1] Conc. Chalcedon., Act. ii. vol. iv. p. 338, ed. Labbé. ὁσιώτατοι πατριάρχαι διοικήσεως ἑκάστης.—Act. iii. p. 395. ἀρχιεπισκόπῳ καὶ πατριάρχῃ τῆς μεγάλης Ῥώμης Λέοντι.

[2] Concil. Chalcedon. can. 30. Justin. Novell. ii. Concerning their limits, see Conc. Const. c. 2. Conc. Ephes. i. Act. 7.

Q. So that there were, on the whole, fourteen *Patriarchs* in the Roman Empire?

A. Yes [1].

[1] BINGHAM, II. xvii. 20.
CABASSUTIUS, Notit. Concil. xxvii. xxviii.
The importance of this subject will justify the insertion of the following luminous statement from Dr. R. CRAKANTHORPE's Defensio Ecclesiæ Anglicanæ, Lond. 1625, p. 144. Ecclesiam, in suâ Diœcesium et Provinciarum divisione ac regimine, civilem formam et Regimen sequutam esse, neminem qui antiquitatis paulò studiosior est, latere arbitror. Docet hoc præter alia Concilium Chalcedonense. Hinc factum, ut sicut Imperium Romanum in duas generales partes, seu duos *orbes* (sic vocari solebant) divideretur, ita Ecclesiam generaliter primo, in *Orientalem* et *Occidentalem* partirentur.

Ut in Oriente septem erant Imperii *Diœceses*, in *Occidente*, præter Romanæ urbis *Præfecturam*, sex: itidem et *quatuordecim diœceses* antiquitus habuit Ecclesia. Septem Orientis tam Imperii quam Ecclesiæ Diœceses hæ erant, 1. *Ægyptus*, cujus ut et Libyæ, Thebaidis, ac Pentapolis Provinciæ, Alexandrino suberant Patriarchæ. 2. *Oriens*, cujus provinciæ *Antiocheno* Patriarchæ subjectæ. 3. *Asiana*, cujus olim Provinciæ *Ephesino* Primati, post *Constantinopolitano* Patriarchæ subditæ. 4. *Pontica*, cujus metropolis *Cæsarea*. 5. *Thracia*, cujus Provinciæ Græcia, Achaia, aliæque *Thessalonicensi* olim Episcopo, ut primati, Diœcescos, post *Constantinopolitano* Patriarchæ subjectæ fuerunt. 6. *Macedonia*, et 7. *Dacia*.

Septem quoque in Occidente. Prima omnium erat Romana, cujus propria, et, ut Hincmarus vocat, *specialis Diœcesis*, erant illæ Provinciæ quæ *suburbicariæ* dictæ sunt, quia *Vicario Imperatoris* in civilibus, in Ecclesiasticis *Romano Patriarchæ* suberant; quæque ab *Italiæ* Provinciis omnino secernuntur.

Quis vel certius cognoscere potuit, vel rectius explicare

PART I.
Canon 6.

Romani pontificis antiquos limites, quam Ruffinus, Presbyter ipse *Romanæ Ecclesiæ*, in eâ *enutritus*, in his pervestigandis *diligenter versatus?* Is de industriâ quasi *explicans Nicænum Canonem*, Romano Episcopo non alias quam *suburbicarias attribuit Provincias*, aut Ecclesias. Hæ in universum decem erant Provinciæ. Insulæ tres, Sicilia, Corsica, et Sardinia, et septem aliæ in eo Italiæ tractu, qui ad Orientem vergit et Austrum, ad Occidentem vero non ultra Magram fluvium, qui Hetruriæ limes, et *Asium* fluvium (*Esis* Plinio et Blondo vocatur) non longe ab Anconâ protendebantur. Cujus illud certum omnino iudicium, quod Piceni (in quo Ancona sita) pars una *Picenum suburbicarium* dictum sit, altera, *Annonarium*, quia in Picenâ regione *suburbicarum provinciarum* terminus. Si igitur Italia juxta Antonini Itinerarium in sedecim, aut rectius juxta *Notitiam* in *septemdecim*, *Provincias* dividatur, præter tres illas Insulas, 4. Campania, 5. Tuscia, 6. Picenum suburbicarium, 7. Apulia cum Calabriâ, 8. Bruttium, 9. Samnium, et 10. Valeria, quia *suburbicariæ regiones, et Provinciæ* erant, *Romano* subjectæ Patriarchæ, illiusque *Diœcesis* propria ac peculiaris fuerunt.

Secunda, *Italica Diœcesis* dicta est, quæ septem alias Italiæ complectebatur Provincias. 1. Venetias nempe, cum Istriâ, 2. Æmiliam, 3. Liguriam, 4. Flaminiam cum Piceno Annonario, 5. Alpes Cottias, 6. Rhætiam primam, 7. et Rhætiam secundam ; quæ omnes Provinciæ, ut in civilibus suo ab Imperatore illis dato vicario, ita in Ecclesiasticis, *Mediolanensi Primati*, ut suo Metropolitano, parebant. Quare ab Athanasio *Mediolanum Italiæ Metropolis, sicut Romanæ ditionis Metropolis Roma*, nominatur. Ita in *duas Diœceses* Italia olim divisa, una *Italicæ* appellationem retinuit, altera ab *urbe* et *Suburbicariis Provinciis* nomen accepit : illa *Romano*, hæc *Mediolanensi* Episcopo subjecta. Tertia, Africana diœcesis erat, in quâ Episcopi olim plusquam ducenti, Metropolitani etiam complures; qui omnes et ipsorum Provinciæ, Carthaginiensi Episcopo ut *Primati totius diœcesis* suberant. Quarta *Illyrium*, quæ ut suas Provincias, ita suum, qui eis præerat, *Primatem* olim habuit, sed post, tota ipsa Diœcesis Constantinopolitano subjecta erat Patriarchæ. Quinta est *Gallia*, cujus olim *Metropolis* fuit Augusta Treverorum, et totius Diœcesis Primas Treverensis Episcopus; sed ea dignitas ad *Arclatensem* postea translata. Sexta, *Hispaniarum*, cujus ut Regia, ita Metropolis quoque *Hispalis* fuisse videtur : posteâ unâ cum Regiâ, primatus quoque dignitas *Toletano* concessit Episcopo. Septima et *Brittanniarum*, cujus ut olim Regia, ita et Metropolis *Eboracum* fuisse conjicitur : sed istæ à multis retrò sæculis, *Cantuariensi* Episcopo ut Primati, aut (ut eum Malmsburiensis, et Glossa Juris vocant) *Patriarchæ*, Diœcesis tota subjecta.

Et quidem antiquitùs hæc Diœcesium in Ecclesiâ, juxta Imperii formam facta divisio; sed ea et mutata sæpiùs à Conciliis, et ab Imperatoribus.

Nec in divisione solùm *Diœcesium* Imperium sequuta est Ecclesia, sed et in ipsius regimine, mirum omninò est, quàm illius formam imitata sit. Nam sicut in *quatuordecim* illis *Diœcesibus* erant in universum *Provinciæ centum* et *octodecim;* ita et totidem Provincias numerabat Ecclesia. Ut in singulis Provinciis erant complures Urbes, quibus singulis inferioris ordinis Judices civiles, quos *Defensores civitatum* ferè vocabant, præponebantur; ita in singulis civitatibus *Episcopos* suos, qui eas cum parœciâ totâ circumjacente gubernabant, præficiebat Ecclesia. Ut Provinciæ singulæ suos habebant *Proconsules Consulares,* aut *Provinciarum præsides*, qui in Metropoli Provinciæ residentes, aliis in eâ Provinciâ authoritate præibant: itidem habuit et Ecclesia *Episcopos suos Metropolitanos,* seu *Archiepiscopos*, quibus ut Præsidi Provinciæ, cæteri illius Provinciæ Episcopi subjecti erant. Ut singulæ illæ *quatuordecim Diœcesis Vicarios Imperatoris Augustales, Præfectos, Prætorio,* aut alio nomine vocatos, in primariâ urbe, seu *Metropoli totius Diœcesis,* velut generales illius Rectores habuerint, quorum tanta autoritas, ut nulla post Imperatorem major: itidem et Ecclesia in singulis suis *quatuordecim Diœcesibus*, Primarios quosdam et præ omnibus eminentes suos habuit Episcopos, qui κατ' ἐξοχήν *Patriarchæ*, vel *Primates Patriarchales* dicebantur, qui in primariâ sede et totius *Diœcesis Metropoli* constituti, non Episcopis solùm qui *Parœcias*, sed et Metropolitanis qui *Provincias* regebant, præponebantur, quorum singulorum tanta est in Ecclesiâ autoritas, ut non sit in Episcopo ullo post Imperatorem Jesum Christum ulla major.

Ut in toto Imperio antiquitùs tres inter omnes eminebant civitates, "Prima urbes inter, divûm domus, aurea *Roma;*" secunda, *Alexandria,* quæ a Dione Chrysostomo per excellentiam *Civitas*, et *secunda omnium quæ sub sole sunt*, vocatur. Tertia, *Antiochia*, quæ teste Hegesippo *tertium omnium in orbe civitatum locum obtinet:* itidem in Ecclesiâ, tres illarum urbium Episcopi præ aliis omnibus insignes erant et spectabiles: ideòque per excellentiam *Patriarchæ* dicti: cùm reliqui *undecim Diœcesium* Episcopi, licèt *Patriarchali omni potestate* illis pares, non *Patriarchæ*, sed *Primates* dicerentur: *Primates*, inquam, *Patriarchales*, non solùm *Metropolitani:* et *Primates Diœcesium* suarum Patriarchalium, non *unius Provinciæ Primates*.

Hæc antiquitùs et divisio et regimen in Ecclesiis in-

PART I. stituta. Nec certè vel ad *pacem* in Ecclesiâ conservandam, vel ad jurisdictionem cuique Episcopo suam sartam tectam tuendam, aut facilior aut commodior ulla *Parœciarum, Provinciarum,* et *Diœcesium* distributio fieri potuit aut inveniri.

Q. We have before seen what are the functions of a Bishop; what next is the office of a *Metropolitan?*

A. To consecrate or confirm his suffragan Bishops [1], and no one could be ordained a Bishop in his province without his consent and approbation, and any such ordination was null and void; to receive appeals, and decide controversies among the Bishops of his province, either by himself, or by commission, or by reference to a Provincial Synod [2]; to convoke and to preside in Provincial Synods [3], (generally summoned twice a year,) which all his Suffragans were bound to attend; to give to his suffragans *literæ formatæ* when going into foreign parts [4], to publish imperial decrees on ecclesiastical matters; and, together with the Suffragans of his Province, to pronounce judicial sentence on any Clerk or Bishop of his Province, charged with heresy; and from this judicial sentence of the Provincial Synod there was *no appeal* [5] to any other Tribunal.

[1] Concil. Nic. can. 4. τὸ κῦρος (confirmation of Bishop) διδόσθω καθ' ἑκάστην ἐπαρχίαν τῷ μητροπολίτῃ.—Can. 6. χωρὶς γνώμης τοῦ μητροπολίτου μὴ δεῖν εἶναι ἐπίσκοπον.— Conc. Sardic. c. 6.—Conc. Ephes. Decret. et Episc. Cypr. —Conc. Chalc. Act. 16. Antioch. 9. Laodic. 12. Chalced. 19. 25. Carth. 11, 12. Arelat. 5, 6.

[2] Cod. Justin. I. v. 29. Conc. Const. 6. 35. Conc. Nic. 5. Chalced. 19. Antioch. 9. 20. 38. Arelat. 19.

[3] Conc. Nic. c. 5. Chalced. 19.

[4] Conc. Carth. iii. 28.

[5] See below, Part iii. chap. vii.

Q. What is the office of a *Patriarch?*

A. To ordain or confirm the Metropolitans of his Diœcesis or Patriarchate [1]; to convoke them to Synods, which they were obliged to attend [2]; to receive appeals from the Metropolitans [3] and from the Synods [4] in his jurisdiction; to communicate imperial decrees [5] to his Metropolitans.

CHAP. XII.

[1] Justin. Novell. 7. 131, c. 3.   [2] Theodoret, Epist. 81.
[3] Conc. Chalc. c. 9, c. 17.   Justin. Novell. 123. 137.
[4] Concil. Chalced. can. 9.
[5] Justinian, Epilog. Novell. 6.

Q. Were any of the Cities, in which the fourteen Patriarchs resided, superior in civil dignity to the rest?

A. Yes, three: *Rome*, *Alexandria*, and *Antioch*. See above, p. 101.

Q. And were the Patriarchs of these superior in ecclesiastical rank to the other eleven?

A. They were *not higher* in *order*, (for all Patriarchs possess co-ordinate and independent authority,) but they had *precedence* of the others in *place*.

Q. And was this precedence *liable to change?*

A. Yes: it was [1]. If a city rose or declined in civil power and importance, then, after mature consideration of the circumstances of the case, its ecclesiastical precedence was modified. Thus, for instance, the Bishop of *Constantinople*, from not being a Patriarch at all, was raised, A.D. 381, under Theodosius the Great, to the dignity of the *second* among the fourteen Patriarchs [2].

[1] By Concil. Constantinop. A.D. 381, can. 3, [and Concilium Chalcedon. A.D. 451, can. 28,] the second place is assigned to Constantinople, διὰ τὸ εἶναι νέαν 'Ρώμην: and in Concil. Chalcedon. A.D. 451, can. 28, Constantinople is declared to be on a *parity* with Rome (τῶν ἴσων ἀπολαύουσαν πρεσβείων τῇ πρεσβυτέρᾳ βασιλίδι 'Ρώμῃ). See Concil. Trull. or Quini-Sext. can. 36. On the same principle as the first place had been given to Rome, διὰ τὸ βασιλεύειν τὴν πόλιν ἐκείνην. Cp. Act. 16. Conc. Chalced. Constantinople is called the Head of all the Churches (Constantinopolitana Ecclesia omnium aliarum est caput) by Justinian, Cod. i. Tit. 3, c. 24.

Compare Concil. Trullan. A.D. 692, can. 38. Concil.

PART 1. Chalcedon. can. 17. εἴ τις ἐκ βασιλικῆς ἐξουσίας ἐκαινίσθη πόλις ἢ αὖθις καινισθείη, τοῖς πολιτικοῖς καὶ δημοσίοις τύποις καὶ τῶν ἐκκλησιαστικῶν παροικιῶν ἡ τάξις ἀκολουθείτω.

BINGHAM, Antiq. IX. I. 7.
[2] Abp. BRAMHALL, i. 130. 177.

Q. By what process were these variations effected?

A. It was unlawful[1] for a Bishop to take any steps to obtain the elevation of his own see; but it was competent to a General Council, convoked by the Emperor, to deliberate, and decide, with the imperial sanction, on questions of this nature.

[1] Concil. Chalced. 12. BINGHAM, XVII. v. 37.

Q. It appears, then, that while the *Episcopal Office* is of *Divine institution*, and cannot, in its *spiritual* nature and ministrations, be affected by *any human* laws, the actual *exercise* of *authority* of Bishops, as Diocesans, Metropolitans, and Patriarchs, may depend, for its distribution and apportionment, upon various circumstances, and be subject to modifications, from time to time, according to the varying condition of Kingdoms and Churches.

A. Certainly. The history of the Church affords many proofs and examples[1] of this. By the order of God's Providence in the world, king-
Dan. ii. 21. doms are augmented and diminished, they are
v. 30, 31. transferred from one sceptre to another, as He wills in His supreme wisdom and power; and the bounds of ecclesiastical jurisdiction have been usually modelled accordingly[2].

[1] Concil. Constant. A.D. 381, can. 2. Concil. Ephes. A.D. 431, tom. iii. p. 801, Labbè. Chalcedon. A.D. 451, can. 12. Justin. Novell. 11, case of Justiniana Prima.
[2] BARROW, Treatise on the Pope's Supremacy, pp. 171, 172, London, 1683, thus states the law and practice of the Church on this subject. *Patriarchs are an human institution.* As they were erected by the power and prudence of men, so they may be dissolved by the same. They were

erected by the leave and confirmation of Princes; and by the same they may be dejected, if great reason do appear. *No ecclesiastical power can interpose in the management of any affairs within the territory of any Prince without his concession.* By the laws of God, and according to ancient practice, Princes may *model the bounds of ecclesiastical jurisdiction.* Wherefore, each Prince (having supreme power in his own dominion, and equal to what the Emperor had in his) may exclude any foreign Prelate from jurisdiction in his territories. It is expedient for peace and public good that he should do thus. Such Prelate, according to the rules of Christianity, ought to be content with his doing so. Any Prelate exercising power in the dominion of any Prince, is *eatenus* his subject; as the Popes and all Bishops were to the Roman emperors.

Abp. BRAMHALL, i. pp 177, 178. ii. pp. 185, 186, ed. Oxf.

In A.D. 1721 the Church of Russia, and in A.D. 1833 the Church of Greece, was detached from the Patriarchate of Constantinople.

Q. How does the practice or adoption of such ecclesiastical modification appear to be consequent on God's government of the world?

A. Kings and Emperors would not be what God has made them, namely [1], His deputies and vicegerents upon earth, and He would not be "the *only* Ruler of Princes," *if any* of their subjects, and,—in the case supposed,—if the Ecclesiastical Persons of their Realm,—were under *foreign* allegiance, so that they acknowledged an *external* authority (such, for example, as that which is now claimed by the Bishop of *Rome*) as the source of their jurisdiction, and could be summoned by it out of their own country, and be deprived of their office by a power over which their lawful sovereign had no control.

Rom. xiii. 1—5.
Tit. iii. 1.
1 Pet. ii. 13—17.

[1] TERTULLIAN ad Scap. 2. Colimus Imperatorem, ut hominem a Deo secundum et solo Deo minorem.

OPTATUS, iii. 3. Super Imperatorem non est nisi solus Deus, qui fecit Imperatorem.

S. CHRYSOSTOM ad Rom. xiii. 1. Every one is bound to obey the higher powers; κἂν τις ἀπόστολος ᾖ, κἂν εὐαγγελιστὴς, κἂν προφήτης—ταῦτα διατάττεται ἱερεῦσι, οὐχὶ τοῖς βιωτικοῖς (*laicis*) μόνον.

PART I.

Rom. xiii. 1.

S. BERNARD de Officio Episcoporum, ed. Paris, 1839, tom. ii. cap. viii. p. 1123. Intelligitis quæ dico: cui honorem, honorem. *Omnis anima,* inquit, *potestatibus sublimioribus subdita sit. Si omnis,* et vestra. Quis vos excipit ab universitate? Si quis tentat excipere, conatur decipere. Nolite illorum acquiescere consiliis, qui cum sint Christiani, Christi tamen vel sequi facta, vel obsequi dictis opprobrio ducunt. Ipsi sunt qui vobis dicere solent; "Servate vestræ sedis honorem. Decebat quidem ex vobis, vobis commissam Ecclesiam crescere: nunc vero saltem in illâ, quâ suscepistis, maneat dignitate. Et vos enim vestro prædecessore impotentiores? Si non crescit per vos, non decrescat per vos." Hæc isti: Christus aliter et jussit, et gessit. *Reddite,* ait, *quæ sunt Cæsaris, Cæsari; et quæ sunt Dei, Deo.* Quod ore locutus est, mox opere implere curavit. Conditor Cæsaris Cæsari non cunctatus est reddere censum: exemplum enim dedit vobis, ut et vos ita faciatis.

Matt. xxii. 21.

See further, below, Pt. iii. chap. v.

CHAPTER XIII.

PRIVILEGES IN THE CHURCH.

Discipline.—Power of the Keys.

Q. WE have spoken of the Word of God, and of the ministration of the Word and Sacraments; what other privilege must we next notice as possessed by the Church?

A. That of *Discipline*[1].

---

[1] HOMILIES, Homily for Whitsunday, Part II. ed. Oxon. 1822, p. 428. The true Church hath always three notes or marks whereby it is known: pure and sound doctrine, the Sacraments ministered according to Christ's holy institution, and *the right use of Ecclesiastical discipline.* This description of the Church is agreeable both to the Scriptures of God, and also to the doctrine of the ancient Fathers, so that none may justly find fault therewith.

On this subject the student may consult MARSHALL'S Penitential Discipline, Lond. 1714.

Q. What is this power of exercising Church Discipline usually called?

A. It is usually termed by Divines *the power of the Keys*[1], of which it is one main and primary part.

[1] Abp. CRANMER's Catechism, pp. 193—204, ed. Oxf. 1829.

Q. Whence did it receive this name?

A. From the words of Christ to St. Peter, and in him to all Presbyters: "I will give to thee the *Keys* of the kingdom of heaven." Matt. xvi. 19.

Q. You say, "in St. Peter to *all* Presbyters[1];" how does this appear?

A. From the fact, that the power which our Lord here gave to St. Peter, He gave to *all the Apostles*[2], and to the *Church*[3] generally; and this is further apparent from the universal language and practice of the Church, according to which *all Presbyters* have ever *used* this power. Matt. xviii. 17, 18. John xx. 23.

[1] ORDERING OF PRIESTS, in the Book of Common Prayer of the United Church of England and Ireland. Receive the Holy Ghost for the Office and Work of a Priest in the Church of God, now committed unto thee by the Imposition of our Hands. Whose sins thou dost forgive, they are forgiven; and whose sins thou dost retain, they are retained. And be thou a faithful Dispenser of the Word of God, and of His Holy Sacraments; in the Name of the Father, and of the Son, and of the Holy Ghost. Amen.

[2] See below, S. CHRYSOST., S. AUG., S. AMBROSE, at the close of this chapter, and the beginning of the next, and Pt. ii. last chapter.

S. AUG. in Joannis Evang. Tract. cxviii. Sicut in Apostolis cum esset etiam ipse numerus duodenarius, id est, quadripartitus in ternos, et omnes essent interrogati, solus Petrus respondit, *Tu es Christus Filius Dei vivi:* et ei dicitur, *Tibi dabo claves regni cœlorum*, tanquam ligandi et solvendi solus acceperit potestatem: cùm et illud unus pro omnibus dixerit, et hoc *cum omnibus* tanquam personam gerens ipsius unitatis acceperit: ideo unus pro omnibus, quia unitas est in omnibus. Matt. xvi. 17—19.

S. CYPRIAN de Unitate Ecclesiæ, p. 106. Loquitur Dominus ad Petrum, *Ego tibi dico*, inquit, *quia tu es* Matt. xvi. 18.

PART I.

John xxi. 15. 17.

John xx. 23

Petrus, &c. Et iterum eidem post resurrectionem suam dicit: *Pasce oves meas.* Super unum ædificat Ecclesiam suam. Et quamvis Apostolis omnibus *parem* potestatem tribuat et dicat: *Sicut misit me Pater, et Ego mitto vos, accipite Spiritum Sanctum. Si cui remiseritis peccata, remittantur illi; si cui tenueritis, tenebuntur:* tamen ut unitatem manifestaret, unitatis ejusdem originem ab uno incipientem suâ auctoritate disposuit. Hoc erant utique et ceteri Apostoli, quod fuit Petrus, *pari consortio* præditi et honoris et potestatis, sed exordium ab unitate proficiscitur, ut Ecclesia una monstretur.

S. Firmilian, Epist. apud Cyprian. p. 225. Potestas peccatorum remittendorum *Apostolis* data est, et *Episcopis* qui eis vicariâ ordinatione succedunt. Casaubon, Exc. Baron. p. 377. Ecclesia semper credidit ex verbis Domini ad Petrum cuivis presbytero legitime ordinato hoc jus competere.

[3] S. Aug. in Joannis Evang. Tract. cxxiv. 5. Quando ei dictum est *Tibi dabo claves regni cœlorum, universam* significabat *Ecclesiam*, quæ in hoc sæculo diversis tentationibus velut imbribus, flaminibus, tempestatibus quatitur, et non cadit, quoniam fundata est super petram, unde Petrus nomen accepit. Non enim a Petro petra, sed Petrus a petra; sicut non Christus a christiano, sed christianus a Christo vocatur. Ideo quippe ait Dominus, *Super hanc petram ædificabo Ecclesiam meam*, quia dixerat Petrus, *Tu es Christus Filius Dei vivi.* Super hanc ergo, inquit, Petram quam confessus es, ædificabo Ecclesiam meam. *Petra enim erat Christus:* super quod fundamentum etiam

1 Cor. iii. 11. ipse ædificatus est Petrus. "Fundamentum quippe aliud nemo potest ponere præter id quod positum est, quod est Christus Jesus." *Ecclesia* ergo quæ fundatur in Christo, claves ab eo regni cœlorum accepit in Petro, id est, potestatem ligandi solvendique peccata.

Q. In what respects are Keys an emblem of ecclesiastical authority?

A. Keys are wont to be given to stewards, treasurers, warders, and other officers, domestic

Isa. xxii. 22. Rev. i. 18. iii. 7. xx. 1. Job xii. 24.

and civil, as badges of trust and power[1]. The proper use of Keys is to open, to admit, to shut in or shut out, and to re-admit: and so Christ has given to His Ministers the power, in subordination to Himself, of admitting to the Kingdom of Heaven, of excluding from it, and of re-admitting to it; and this is what is meant, when it is said that they have from Christ *the power of the Keys*[2].

CHAP. XIII.

[1] Thence Christ's Ministers are called ταμίαι, οἰκονόμοι. See 1 Cor. iv. 1. 2 Cor. vi. 4. Col. i. 25. Titus i. 7. 1 Pet. iv. 10.

[2] HOOKER, VI. IV. 1. They that have the *keys* of the kingdom of heaven are hereby signified to be stewards of the house of God, under whom they guide, command, and judge His family. The souls of men are God's treasure, committed to the trust and fidelity of such as must render a strict account for the very least which is under their custody.

See also BARROW *de Potestate Clavium*, iv. p. 50, ed. 1687. This *Latin* Treatise is fuller and more complete than the *English* one of the same Author, entitled, *On the Power of the Keys*.

Q. You speak of admitting to the *Kingdom of Heaven*; when so speaking, what do you mean by the Kingdom of Heaven?

A. I mean, first, the *Visible Church*, or the *Kingdom of Grace*; and, secondly, that to which it leads the faithful Christian [1],—namely, the *Invisible Church*, or the *Kingdom of Glory*.

[1] See above, chaps. ii. and iii.

Q. How do Christ's Ministers *admit* persons into the kingdom of heaven in the former sense?

A. By the Ministry of the Word of God, that is, by Preaching; and by Holy Baptism.

Q. How do they *exclude* from the kingdom of heaven?

A. By Church censures after solemn investigation, trial, and admonition, and specially by the judicial sentence of excommunication.

1 Cor. v. 3—5.
2 Tim. ii. 17.
1 Tim. i. 20.

Q. What are the intents and ends of Church censures?

A. With respect to Christ, the ends and aims of Church censures are, to maintain His honour; with respect to the Church, to preserve her holiness, purity, and unity; with respect to offenders, to warn them by a *pre-announcement* of the final

Lev. x. 9.
Ezek. xxii.
26. xliv. 23.
Deut. xxvii. 13.
Joel ii. 12.

PART I.
2 Chron. xxiv. 20.
1 Cor. v. 4—7.
2 Cor. vii. 9—12.
1 Tim. i. 20.

Judgment[1], to inspire them with godly sorrow, to the intent that "they may learn not to blaspheme," and "that their spirits may be saved in the day of the Lord;" and with respect to all others, to deter them from similar offences. For, *Impunitas semper ad deteriora invitat*[2], and, *Minatur innocentibus, qui parcit nocentibus*[3].

[1] TERTULLIAN, Apol. 38. Summum futuri *judicii præjudicium est*, si quis ita deliquerit, ut a communicatione orationis et conventûs et omnis sancti commercii relegetur.

S. CYPRIAN de Habitu Virginum, p. 92. This treatise commences with a recital of the benefits of Church Discipline.

COMMINATION Office of the Church of England.
[2] 5 COKE, 109.   [3] 4 COKE, 45.

Q. What, further, is the true character of Church censures?

2 Cor. ii. 4.
vii. 9.

A. They are acts of *charity* to the offender and to others; and the omission of them, when they ought to be exercised, is an act of *injury* and *cruelty*[1]. Knowing God's wrath against sin, the Church must censure it. *Terreo, quia timeo*[2], is her motto, and *Si perdo, pereo*.

2 Cor. v. 11.
Heb. x. 31.

[1] WISDOM vi. 17. The very true beginning of Wisdom is the desire of Discipline, and the care of Discipline is Love, and Love is the keeping of her laws.

ECCLUS. xxiii. 1—3. O Lord, . . . who will set scourges over my thoughts, and the Discipline of wisdom over mine heart? that they spare me not for mine ignorances, and it pass not by my sins; lest mine ignorance increase, and my sins abound to my destruction, and I fall before mine adversaries, and mine enemy rejoice over me, whose hope is far from Thy mercy.

EPISTOLA Cleri Rom. ap. S. Cyprian. ep. 31. Ubi poterit medicina indulgentiæ proficere si etiam ipse medicus, interceptâ pœnitentiâ, indulget periculis? si tantummodo *operit* vulnus! Hoc est non *curare*, sed *occidere*.

S. CHRYSOSTOM, ii. 112, ed. Savil. ὁ μηδεμίαν αὐτοῖς τιμωρίαν τιθεὶς, μονονουχὶ ὁπλίζει τῇ ἀδείᾳ.

S. AUG. Serm. xiii. *Disciplinam* qui *abjicit, infelix* est; qui *negat, crudelis* est.

[2] S. AUG. in Ps. lxiii. iv. 895, et ad Litt. Petilian. iii. 4.

Ecclesiastica Disciplina, medicinalis vindicta, terribilis lenitas, charitatis severitas.

CHAP. XIII.

Q. Is it, then, to be considered a matter of *choice* with the Ministers of Christ whether they will exercise such discipline or no?

A. No. Christ never said or did any thing in vain. When He said[1], "If he will not *hear* the Church," He ordered the Church to *speak;* and when He gave the Apostles power for the government of His Church, He *commanded* them to *exercise* it; and, accordingly, St. Titus and St. Timothy are commanded by St. Paul to rebuke with all authority; and the Bishops[2] of Pergamus and Thyatira are severely reproved by St. John for suffering false doctrines and corrupt practices in their Churches. *Non regit,* says S. Augustin, *qui non corrigit*[3].

Matt. xviii. 17.
Mark vi. 7—13.
Luke ix. 1—6.
xxiv. 47.
1 Tim. v. 20.
2 Tim. iv. 2.
Titus ii. 15.
Rev. ii. 14, 15. 20.

---

[1] S. CHRYSOSTOM, ii. p. 160, ed. Savil. καὶ ὁ Χριστὸς ἐπέστησε (τοὺς ἀποστόλους) ἐπιτιμῶντας, καὶ οὐ μόνον ἐπιτιμῶντας ἀλλὰ καὶ κολάζοντας, τὸν γὰρ οὐδενὸς τούτων ἀκούσαντα ἐκέλευσεν ὡς ἐθνικὸν εἶναι καὶ τελώνην· πῶς δὲ αὐτοῖς τὰς κλεῖς ἔδωκεν; εἰ γὰρ μὴ μέλλουσι κρίνειν, ἁπάντων ἔσονται ἄκυροι, καὶ μάτην τὴν ἐξουσίαν τοῦ δεσμεῖν καὶ τοῦ λύειν εἰλήφασι, καὶ ἄλλως δέ, εἰ τοῦτο κρατήσειεν, ἅπαντα οἰχήσεται καὶ τὰ ἐν ταῖς ἐκκλησίαις, καὶ τὰ ἐν ταῖς πόλεσι, καὶ τὰ ἐν ταῖς οἰκίαις—καὶ ἄνω καὶ κάτω πάντα γενήσεται.

[2] S. HIERON. in Mich. c. v. Legamus Apocalypsin Joannis Apostoli, in quâ laudantur accusanturque *Angeli Ecclesiarum* pro virtutibus vitiisque eorum quibus præesse dicuntur.

It is observable, that in the original Greek of the Revelation of St. John (ii. 9, 10. iii. 2. 15—18), the epithets assigned to the several *Churches agree in gender* with the word *Angel,* and *not* with the word *Church,* so that the Holy Spirit seems emphatically to identify each Church with its respective Bishop, and to lay on *him* the responsibility of its failings and corruptions.

[3] S. AUG. in Ps. xliv. iv. p. 552. Tractat. in Joann. xlvi. Qui sua quærit, non quæ Jesu Christi, peccantem non liberè audet arguere. Ecce nescio quis peccavit; graviter peccavit; increpandus est, excommunicandus est. Sed excommunicatus, inimicus erit. Jam ille qui sua quærit, non

Part I. quæ Jesu Christi, ne inimicitiarum humanarum incurrat molestiam, tacet, non corripit. Ecce lupus ovi guttur apprehendit; tu taces, non increpas! O mercenarie, lupum venientem vidisti, et fugisti! Fugisti, quia tacuisti; tacuisti, quia timuisti. Fuga animi timor est.

On the measure and rule of Church Discipline, see S. AUG. de Fide, vi. p. 291, &c.

Archbp. CRANMER'S Catechism, ed. Oxon. 1829, p. 201. And this also is to be reproved, that some men, whiche continue in manyfest and open synne, and go not about to amend their lyfes, yet they wil be counted Christen men, and interpoyse to receaue the same sacramentes that other do, to come to the Churche, to worship God, and to pray with other. Suche muste be warned of their fautes, and yf they refuse to heare and amende, then they ought to be excommunicate and put out of the Christen congregation, vntil they repente and amende their lyfes; lest by suche manifest sinne and euil examples, other men might be provoked to do the lyke, and so at length many might be infected, and the Christen relygyon despised and euil spoken of, as though it were the worst relygyon, forasmuche as Christian men shoulde then leade a shameful and ungodly lyfe.

CHAPTER XIV.

PRIVILEGES IN THE CHURCH.

Absolution.

Q. YOU spoke of re-admission to the *Visible Church,* or *Kingdom of Grace;* and, secondly, by its means, to the *Invisible Church,* or *Kingdom of Glory;* how do the Ministers of Christ *re-admit* offenders into the Church or Kingdom of Heaven, both Visible and Invisible?

A. By *disposing* them to repentance through application of the salutary medicine of the promises to penitence, and threats against sin, revealed in the Word of God, and thus producing compunction and contrition in them; then by *declaring,* as God's heralds, His readiness to pardon all who truly *repent* and *believe* in Him;

then, by *pronouncing* their pardon and restoring them, on their repentance and faith, and confession of sins, through the ministry of reconciliation, which has been appointed and entrusted to them as Ministers in the Church of God [1].

CHAP. XIV.

2 Cor. v. 19.
Gal. vi. 1.

[1] S. AUG. Serm. ccxiv. *Ecclesia* Dei vivi claves accepit regni cœlorum, ut in illâ per sanguinem Christi, operante Spiritu Sancto, fiat remissio peccatorum. In hâc Ecclesiâ reviviscit anima quæ mortua fuerat peccatis, ut convivificetur Christo, cujus gratiâ sumus salvi facti.

F. MASON de Ministerio, v. 10. Minister Evangelicus dupliciter peccata remittit, *dispositivè* et *declarativè : dispositivè*, quia homines ad remissionem peccatorum consequendam *disponit* perducendo ad fidem et pœnitentiam; *declarativè*, quia *jam pœnitentibus* et *credentibus* peccatorum remissionem tanquam divinus præco declarat. Ita teneras conscientias cum peccatorum mole et desperatione luctantes per promissiones evangelicas spe veniæ erigimus, jamque pœnitentibus et credentibus remissa peccata pronunciamus. See also BARROW de Potestate Clavium, p. 58.

Q. By what other figure beside that of *opening* and *shutting* by the Keys does Christ describe the exercise of Church authority?

A. By that of *binding* and *loosing.* "Whosoever sins ye remit," says He to His Apostles, "they are remitted; and whose soever sins ye retain, they are retained."

Matt. xviii. 18.
John xx. 23.

Q. Have *men* then the power of absolving their fellow-men from sin committed against God?

A. No, they have not: for "who can forgive sins but God alone [1]?" They do not *give* pardon to the sinner, any more than the Physician *gives* health to the sick, or the Judge *gives* release to the accused: but they *apply* the *means* appointed and given by *God* for its attainment; and God blesses the means, and He works by them.

Mark ii. 7.
Luke v. 21.
viii. 47.
Rev. iii. 7.

[1] S. CYPRIAN de Lapsis, p. 129. Nemo se fallat, nemo se decipiat. Solus Dominus misereri potest. Veniam peccatis, quæ in ipsum commissa sunt, solus potest Ille largiri,

PART I. qui peccata nostra portavit, qui pro nobis doluit, quem Deus tradidit pro peccatis nostris.

S. AMBROSE in S. Luc. v. 19. Quis potest peccata dimittere nisi solus Deus, Qui per eos quoque dimittit, quibus dimittendi tribuit potestatem?

S. AUG. Serm. xcix. 7. Homo non potest dimittere peccata.

Q. Would it not then be more reverential to God to reserve the office of remitting sins to Him alone?

A. Obedience to God is true reverence. It would be grievous disrespect to Him, and great wrong to His heritage, to rescind and refuse His gifts. The Church shows her reverence to God, by obeying Him, and by using them; i. e. by remitting and retaining sins[1].

[1] S. AMBROSE de Pœnitentiâ, lib. i. cap. 2. 6. Sed aiunt se Domino deferre reverentiam, Cui soli remittendorum criminum potestatem reservent. Immò nulli majorem injuriam faciunt, quam qui ejus volunt mandata rescindere, commissum munus refundere. Nam cum Ipse in Evangelio suo dixerit Dominus Jesus: *Accipite Spiritum sanctum; quorum remiseritis peccata, remittuntur eis; et quorum detinueritis, detenta erunt;* quis est ergo qui magis honorat, utrum qui mandatis obtemperat, an qui resistit? Ecclesia in utroque servat obedientiam, ut peccatum et alliget et relaxet.

See also HOOKER, VI. IV. 7. "The Novatianists presume to plead against the Church, that every man ought to be his own Penitentiary. The truth is otherwise."

On the office of Penitentiary, see HOOKER, VI. IV. 8. VI. IV. 14. "We every where find the use of confession, especially public, allowed of, and commended by, the Fathers; but that extreme and rigorous necessity of *auricular* confession, which is upheld by the Church of Rome, we find not."

Q. But if no one can forgive sins but God, how can *men* be said to bind or loose?

A. The Priest is like a civil[1] Judge, who does not sit on the judicial tribunal to *make* laws, but to *administer* them. He does not pronounce sentence of forgiveness, in his own name, or on his own authority, but in the Name of God[2], the

Father, Son, and Holy Spirit; and upon the conditions of repentance and faith prescribed by Christ, and required and ascertained after careful investigation by the Priest in the exercise of his ministry. The penitent must resort to the Priest, and the Priest must examine, exhort, and make trial of his sincerity. Christ's power is here αὐτοκρατορικὴ, or *imperial;* the Priest's is διακονικὴ, or *ministerial.* It is CHRIST who raises the sinner from the death of sin [3]; but when He has raised him by His Spirit, His Word, and His Ministry, Christ then says to His Ministers, "Loose him, and let him go."

Acts x. 43. xiii. 38. xx. 21. Mark xvi. 16. Acts iii. 19. 2 Cor. v. 20. John xi. 43. 44.

[1] F. MASON de Ministerio, v. 10. Absolutio non est declaratoria tantum, est etiam judicatoria: Sacerdotem judicem esse fatetur Apologia Ecclesiæ Anglicanæ (non longè a principio); requiritur autem judicium non discretionis modo sed authoritatis etiam et potestatis; siquidem personæ absolvendæ fidem suam et pœnitentiam palam profitentur, hìc est causæ cognitio; dein Minister iisdem peccatorum indulgentiam declarat et obsignat; hìc est sententiæ dictio. See also Bp. SANDERSON, Cases, ii. 13, on Confession and Absolution, and CANONS of 1603, Canon 113.

[2] S. CHRYS. in S. Joann. p. 923, Savil. Πατὴρ καὶ ὁ Υἱὸς καὶ τὸ ἅγιον Πνεῦμα πάντα οἰκονομεῖ, ὁ δὲ ἱερεὺς τὴν ἑαυτοῦ δανείζει γλῶσσαν, καὶ τὴν ἑαυτοῦ παρέχει χεῖρα.

S. AMBROSE de Pœnitentiâ, cap. 2. *Munus* Spiritûs Sancti est Officium Sacerdotis; *jus* autem Spiritûs Sancti in solvendis ligandisque criminibus est. Cap. 8. Omnia dedit Christus discipulis suis; sed *nulla* in his *hominis* potestas est, ubi *divini muneris* gratia viget.

[3] S. AUG. Serm. ccxcv. Quatriduano mortuo dicitur, "Lazare, prodi foras." Excitat Dominus, si cor tangit. Per se excitat, per discipulos solvit.

Q. Are then *all* who are absolved by Christ's ministers pardoned by Christ? or are *all* they who are condemned by Christ's ministers condemned by Christ?

A. No; a *right* sentence is the only one which Christ has authorized, and the only one which He will ratify, by giving it validity, spiritually and internally [1]. "Clavis *potestatis* nihil operatur

PART I.

Rev. iii. 7.

sine clave *scientiæ*." The key of *knowledge* or *discretion* is necessary to give effect to that of *power*. No one can be admitted through the door of Pardon, who has not passed through that of Penitence. Christ alone "openeth, and no man shutteth; and shutteth, and no man openeth;" and He turns the key in the hand of His ministers *only* when it is moved *aright* in the wards of repentance and of faith.

> [1] HOOKER, VI. IV. 2. Whether they remit or retain sins, whatsoever is done by way of *orderly* and *lawful proceeding*, the Lord Himself hath promised to ratify.

Q. If this be so, is not the sentence of the Priest superfluous?

Wisd. xvi. 7.
John ix. 7.

A. No; for God, in this as in other cases, is pleased to work by *means*, and to use the agency of His creatures, especially of men, as *instruments* in conferring His benefits upon other men. And though *His power* is not tied to means, yet, when *He* has vouchsafed to *appoint* certain means for dispensing His grace, *we are tied* to the due and reverent *use* of them. He remits the punishment of *original* sin [1] by means of the Sacrament of Baptism; and, in the case of *actual* sin, He confers the grace of His own pardon by the *instrumentality* [2] of priestly Absolution [3], ordinarily and where it may be had, and whenever justly pronounced and duly received; and thus He makes *repentance available* to the true penitent, through the declaration and pronunciation of pardon by the Minister of Christ, acting by His authority, at His command, and by His power. Absolution does not *give* repentance, but *makes* it *effectual;* as the *loosing* of Lazarus did not give him *life*, but the full and free *use* of it.

Acts ii. 38.
xxii. 16.
Rom. vi.
2—7.

John xi. 43,
44.

> [1] S. AMBROSE de Pœnit. lib. i. cap. 8. Cur præsumitis aliquos a colluvione diaboli per vos mundari posse? Cur baptizatis, si per hominem peccata dimitti non licet? In Baptismo utique remissio peccatorum omnium est: quid

interest, utrum per pœnitentiam, an per lavacrum hoc jus sibi datum sacerdotes vindicent ? Unum in utroque mysterium est.

S. AUG. Tractat. in S. Joann. xii. iii. p. 1815. Regeneratio spiritualis una est, sicut generatio carnalis una est: sicut ad nativitatem carnalem valent muliebria viscera ad semel pariendum, sic ad nativitatem spiritualem valent viscera Ecclesiæ, ut semel quisque baptizetur. With regard to *Infant* Baptism, see ibid. p. 1830. Quomodo non caruit populus Israel pressurâ Ægyptiorum, nisi cum venisset ad mare Rubrum, sic pressurâ peccatorum nemo caret nisi cum ad fontem Baptismi venerit. P. 2070. Propter hoc etiam *sugens parvulus* a matre piis manibus ad Ecclesiam fertur, ne sine Baptismo exeat et in peccato quo natus est moriatur. Serm. 174. 9. Regula antiqua fidei *baptizare parvulos ;* and Serm. 176. Hoc Ecclesia *semper* habuit, *semper* tenuit. See also Serm. 294. Baptizandos esse parvulos nemo dubitat.

OFFICE for Public BAPTISM of Infants in the Church of England and Ireland. We call upon Thee for *this infant*, that *he* coming to Thy Holy Baptism, may receive remission of *his* sins by spiritual regeneration.... It is certain that children which are baptized, dying before they commit actual sin, are undoubtedly saved.—OFFICE of Private BAPTISM. Seeing now that this Child is by Baptism regenerate and grafted into the Body of Christ's Church.—ORDER of CONFIRMATION. Almighty and everliving God, Who hast vouchsafed to regenerate these Thy servants by Water and the Holy Ghost, and hast given unto them forgiveness of all their sins.—See also HOMILIES, 2 B. III., and 2 B. IV. 1. HOOKER, V. LXII. 5. We are by baptism born anew. Bp. PEARSON on the Creed, Art. x. p. 368.

WATERLAND, Regeneration stated and explained, Works, vi. p. 356. Bp. BETHELL, General View of Regeneration in Baptism, Lond. 1850.

² F. MASON de Ministerio, v. 12. Minister est *efficax* Dei *instrumentum* ad remissionem efficiendam, et præco ad promulgandam.... Ministri tanquam viva Dei *instrumenta* Deo cooperantia primo animas ad credendum et pœnitendum perducunt, deinde iisdem peccatorum remissionem ex officio idque secundum Christi institutum annunciant. Quod munus quoties quâ decet reverentiâ præstatur, singularis benedictio a Deo expectari potest.

³ S. AMBROSE de Cain et Abel, ii. 4. Remittuntur peccata per officium sacerdotis sacrumque ministerium.

S. HIERON. ad Esai. iii. Secunda post naufragium tabula Pœnitentia est. See also the FORM of ABSOLUTION in the Visitation of the Sick.

PART I. HOMILY on Common Prayer, p. 330 (ed. 1822). Absolution hath the promise of forgiveness of sins.

Bp. JEWELL, Apol. ii. Sententiam quamcumque ministri ad hunc modum tulerunt, Deus ipse comprobat.

Abp. CRANMER on the Power of the Keyes, Catech. p. 202. God hath given the keys of the kingdom of heaven, and authority to forgyve sin, to the ministers of the Church. And when the minister does so, then I ought stedfastly to believe that my sins are truly forgyven me.—Compare CRANMER'S Works, iv. p. 283, ed. Jenkyns.

Bp. SPARROW, Rationale, p. 14, ed. 1704. If our confession be serious and hearty, this absolution is effectual, as if God did pronounce it from heaven: so says the Confession of Saxony and Bohemia, and the Augsburgh Confession, (xi. xii. xiii.,) and so says S. Chrysostom in his Fifth Homily on Esay, "Heaven waits and expects the Priest's sentence here on earth; and what the servant rightly binds or looses on earth, that the Lord confirms in heaven." S. Augustin and S. Cyprian, and general Antiquity, say the same. See also HOOKER, VI. IV. 14, and VI. VI. 8.

Bp. MONTAGUE, Appello Cæsarem, 25. Protestants hold that Priests have power, not only to pronounce, but to give, remission of sins.

CHILLINGWORTH, p. 409. (Serm. vii.) Come to your spiritual physician, not only as to a learned man, experienced in the Scriptures, as one that can speak quieting words to you, but as to one who hath Authority delegated to him from God Himself, to absolve and acquit your sins.

Q. What are the effects produced by Absolution, as respects the relation of the person absolved to the *Visible* Church?

A. First, a *declarative* one; for, even though the penitent sinner may indeed be pardoned by God without Absolution, yet he is not regarded so to be in *the eye of the Church* without the sacerdotal *declaration* of it; just as the lepers among the Jews, when healed, were not regarded as clean, and restored as such to society, till they had been *pronounced* to be clean by the Priest.

Levit. xiii. 17—23. xiv. 2. Matt. viii. 4. Luke xvii. 14.

Q. Is not some other *visible effect* produced by absolution?

A. Yes. When a person under Church censures is, on his repentance, reconciled to the Church by absolution, he is restored to a participation in the Holy Communion, and in the other *means of grace* in the Church, which is the *depository of grace*[1] as well as the *house of discipline*[2].

[1] See above, ch. iv.
[2] S. AUGUSTIN de Disciplinâ Christ. vi. p. 977. Dicente Scripturâ, Accipite disciplinam in *domo disciplinæ*, (where Ecclus. li. 31. 36, is called 'Scriptura,' though an Ecclesiastical book; see above, chap. vi.)—*Disciplinæ domus* est *Ecclesia* Christi.—S. AUG. de Moribus Eccl. i. 1146.

See the citation from Peter Lombard in HOOKER, VI. VI. 8. Albeit a man be already cleared before God, yet he is not in the *face of the Church* so taken, but by virtue of the priest's sentence, who likewise may be said to *bind* by imposing satisfaction, (and by censures constraining to amend their lives he doth *more* than *declare* and signify what God hath wrought. VI. VI. 5,) and to *loose* by admitting to the Holy Communion.

Q. These are *visible* effects; but what influence has absolution on a man's relation to the *Invisible* Church?

A. The *visible* effects lead to *invisible* results, which follow, as we have seen, from the *right use* of the *means of grace* in the Church; but, in addition to the grace conveyed by these means, the sincere penitent, for whose benefit Absolution was intended, will derive spiritual comfort and assurance from it.

Q. In what respects?

A. First, in *obeying* God, by using the ordinance which God has appointed for his good. Next, he will receive aid and encouragement in his own supplications for pardon and grace, from the further co-operation of the prayers of God's Minister, and of His Church[1], that his sins may be forgiven, and stedfastness confirmed; and he will feel his scruples removed[2], and his faith, hope, and love to God increased, by an *assurance* of pardon from God, delivered to him by His ambassador[3], authorized and commanded to act in His Name. And thus he is openly and effectually

Luke vii. 47
—50.
Luke xxiv. 47.
2 Cor. v. 18
—20.

PART I. re-admitted by Absolution into the Kingdom of Heaven.

[1] S. AMBROSE de Pœnitentiâ, ii. c. 10. Fleat pro te Mater Ecclesia, et culpam tuam lachrymis lavet.—Amat Christus ut pro uno multi rogent.
TERTULLIAN de Pœn. c. 9.

[2] HOOKER, VI. VI. 14. The last and sometimes hardest to be satisfied by repentance are our own minds; are we not bound, then, with all thankfulness to acknowledge His infinite goodness whom it hath pleased (VI. VI. 17) to ordain for men's spiritual comfort consecrated persons, who by sentence of power and authority given from above, may as it were out of His mouth ascertain timorous and doubtful minds, ease them of their scrupulosities, leave them settled in peace, and satisfied of God's mercy to them?

[3] HOOKER, VI. VI. 5. Having first the promises of God for pardon generally unto all offenders penitent; and for our own unfeigned meaning, the infallible testimony of a good conscience, then the sentence of God's appointed officer and vicegerent to approve the quality of what we have done, and as from his tribunal to assoil us of any crime, I see no cause but we may rest ourselves very well assured touching God's most merciful pardon and grace.

CHAPTER XV.

PRIVILEGES IN THE CHURCH.

Sacerdotal Intercession and Benediction.

Q. WHAT other benefits, besides those already considered, of doctrine, the sacraments, and the exercise of the keys, do we derive from God through the ministry of the Church?

A. Those of *sacerdotal Intercession* (ἔντευξις) and *Benediction* (εὐλογία).

Q. You speak of *sacerdotal Intercession;* what do you understand by that term?

A. I mean the act of the Minister praying for the people, and presenting their prayers to God[1].

¹ Abp. POTTER on Church Government, ch. v. To present the people's prayers to God, and to intercede with Him to bless them, has always been reckoned an essential part of the Sacerdotal Office.

Q. What authority have we for believing that the prayers of special persons, as of Christian Ministers, have any peculiar efficacy with God?

A. The authority of God's own Word, and the records therein contained of the *Patriarchal*, *Mosaic*, and *Christian* Dispensations¹.

¹ HOOKER, V. xxv. 3. As the *place* of public prayer is a circumstance in the outward form thereof which hath moment to help devotion, so the *Person much more* with whom the people of God do join themselves in action, as with him that standeth and speaketh in the presence of God for them. The authority of his *calling* is a furtherance, because if God have so far received him into favour as to impose upon him by the hands of men that office of *blessing* the people in His name, and making *intercession* to Him in theirs, which office he hath sanctified with His own most gracious promise (Numbers vi. 23), and ratified that promise by manifest actual performance thereof, when (2 Chron. xxx. 27) others before in like place have done the same; is not his very Ordination a seal, as it were, to us that the self-same Divine Love that hath chosen the Instrument to work with, will by that instrument effect the thing whereto He ordained it, in blessing His people, and accepting the prayers which His servant offereth up unto God for them?

Q. To speak, first, of the efficacy of *sacerdotal Intercession* in *Patriarchal* times, can you give examples of it from Holy Writ?

A. Yes. God says to Abimelech, that He would heal him, *when* Abraham had prayed for him, "for he is a *prophet*." He says to Job's friends, "My servant Job shall pray for you, for him will I accept ¹." Abraham and Job in the Patriarchal dispensation were not only Fathers but *Priests*, the *priesthood* in that dispensation being in the *first-born* of each family in hereditary succession².

Gen. xx. 7. 17
Job xlii. 8.
i. 4, 5.
Gen. xxii.
Job i. 5.

¹ Bp. ANDREWES, v. 355. It is an opinion very erroneous, that we have no other use of the Apostles of Christ

PART I.

and their successors, but only for *preaching;* whereas, as it is a thing no less hard to *pray* well, than to *preach* well, so the people reap as great benefit by the *Intercession* of their Pastors which they continually make to God, both privately and publicly, as they do by their preaching. For this cause the Priests are *called the Lord's Remembrancers*, because they put God in mind of His people, desiring Him continually to help and bless them with things needful; for God hath a greater respect to the prayers of those who have a spiritual charge, than to those that are of the common sort. Thus the Lord would have Abimelech deal well with Abraham and deliver him his wife, 'because he is a Prophet, and should pray for him that he may live.' So to the friends of Job the Lord said, 'My servant Job shall pray for you, and I will accept him.' (Sermon on Luke xi. 1.)

Isa. lxii. 6. [See Margin, and Lowth's note.]

² Bp. BILSON on the Perpetual Government of Christ's Church, p. 37, ed. 1842. God did consecrate the first-born of their family as holy to Himself to be Priests in His Church.

SCULTETUS in Job i. 4. *Sacrificabat* Job tanquam Primogenitus, et Pater-familias, ut ante Legem fieri solebat. And see Bp. Patrick and Mercer on Job xlii. 8. Jobus *sacerdos* a Deo eligitur. See also Gen. xiv. 18. xviii. 19. xx. 7. xxi. 33. xxvi. 25. xxxiii. 20. Psalm cv. 22. Heb. vii. 7. 2 Pet. ii. 5. 7. Jude 14.

Q. Have we further evidence of the efficacy of sacerdotal Intercession in the *Mosaic Dispensation* also?

Num. xvi. 48.
Joel ii. 17, 18.
1 Kings xiii. 6.

A. Yes; Aaron the Priest¹ stood between the dead and the living, (as Moses commanded him by God's order,) and the plague was stayed. The Lord says by the Prophet Joel, "Let the Priests, the Ministers of the Lord, weep between the porch and the altar, and let them say, Spare thy people, O Lord, ... and then will the Lord pity His people."

¹ Bp. ANDREWES, Sermons, v. 231. Prayer is good, and that Phinehas' Prayer. Phinehas was a Priest, the son of Eleazar, the nephew of Aaron. So as there is virtue, as in the prayer, so in the person that did pray, in Phinehas himself. ... Every Priest being taken from among men, and ordained for men in things pertaining to God, that he may offer prayers; the prayers he offereth he offereth out of his *office*, and so, even in that respect there is, *cæteris paribus*, a more force and energy in them, as coming from

him whose *calling* it is to offer them, than in those that come from another whose calling it is not so to do.

CHAP. XV.

Q. And have we any evidence of the special virtue of priestly Intercession under the *Christian Dispensation?*

A. Yes; St. James says, "Is any sick among you? let him call for the *Elders of the Church*, and let them pray over him: and the prayer of faith shall save the sick: and if he have committed sins, they shall be forgiven him." So Christian Priests pray *with* and *for* the people, and "it is the office of the Holy Spirit to set apart persons for the duty of the Ministry, ordaining them to *intercede* between God and His people, and send up prayers to God for them[1]."

James v. 14, 15.
Acts vi. 4.
viii. 15. 24.
Col. iv. 12.
1 Cor. xiv. 16.

[1] Bp. PEARSON on the Creed, Art. viii. Abp. POTTER on the Church, chap. v. BINGHAM, Antiq. II. XIX. 15. It was one act of the Priest's office to offer up the sacrifice of the people's prayers, praises, and thanksgivings, to God, as their mouth and orator, and to make intercession to God for them. Another part of the office was, in God's name, to bless the people, particularly by admitting them to the benefit and privilege of remission of sins by spiritual regeneration or baptism. See also HOOKER, quoted below, p. 129.

Q. But is not all Priestly Intercession superseded and taken away by the *Intercession of Christ?*

A. There is indeed to us but One Mediator between God and man, Christ Jesus; and no intercessions are available except only by and through Him[1]; and the intercession of His Ministers, acting in His name, and by His authority and appointment, is to be considered, in a certain sense, His act and His Intercession[2].

John x. 9.
xiv. 6.
1 Tim. ii. 5.
Heb. vii. 25.
Acts viii. 24. ix. 34.

[1] S. AUG. c. Ep. Parmen. ii. 16.
[2] COTELERIUS in Const. Apost. II. xxv. p. 240. WATERLAND, Works, vii. p. 349. Authorized Ministers perform the office of proper Evangelical Priests in the Communion Service, in three ways:—1. as commemorating; 2. as handing up, if I may so speak, those prayers and services

PART I. of Christians to Christ our Lord, Who, as High Priest in heaven, recommends the same in heaven to God the Father; 3. as offering up to God all the faithful who are under their care and ministry, and who are sanctified by the Spirit. In these three ways the Christian Officers are priests or Liturgs to very excellent purposes far above the *legal* ones, in a sense worth the pursuing with the utmost zeal and assiduity.

RICHARD BAXTER, Christian Directory, p. 714, fol. ed. 1673. Christ's Ministers are to be the Guides of the Congregation in Public Worship, and to stand between them and Christ in things pertaining to God as subservient to Christ in his Priestly office; and so both *for* the People, and *in their names*, to put up the public Prayers and Praises of the Church to God. It is their duty to administer to them, as in the *name* and *stead* of Christ, His Body and Blood; and to subserve Christ, especially in His Priestly Office, and to be *their agent in offering themselves* to God.

Q. You spoke of *Sacerdotal Benediction;* what do you intend by this expression?

A. I mean the act of the Bishop or Priest presenting persons to God by *Prayer*[1], (and thus being an act of *Intercession*, of which we have already spoken,) and imploring and pronouncing His blessing upon them.

[1] S. AUG. Epist. cxlix. 17. Interpellationes (ἐντεύξεις, intercessions, 1 Tim. ii. 1, on which passage he is commenting) fiunt, cùm populus *benedicitur;* tunc enim Antistites velut *advocati* susceptos suos per manûs impositionem misericordissimæ offerunt Potestati. S. AUG. de Baptism. iii. 16. Quid aliud est impositio manûs, nisi *oratio* super hominem?

HOOKER, V. LXX. 1. To pray for others is to bless them for whom we pray, because Prayer procureth the blessing of God upon them, especially the Prayer of such as God either most respecteth for their piety or zeal that way, or else regardeth for that their place and calling bindeth them above others unto this duty, as it doth both natural and spiritual Fathers. See HOOKER, below, p. 127.

Q. Have then any particular persons a special power of conveying blessings from God to men?

A. Yes. It has pleased God that certain individuals, *as His Ministers*[1], by virtue of their office and appointment from Him, and of the

ordaining grace of the Holy Spirit, should com- CHAP. XV.
municate His blessings which are given *by Him*
through the ministry of *man* to all who by faith
and love have the capacity of receiving them.

¹ S. CHRYSOST. ii. p. 222, ed. Savil. ἐν τῇ ἐκκλησίᾳ ὁ προ
εστὼς δίδωσιν εἰρήνην, καὶ τοῦτο Χριστοῦ τύπος ἐστί· καὶ
δεῖ μετὰ πάσης αὐτὴν δέχεσθαι τῆς προθυμίας.

Bp. TAYLOR, Preface to Apology for Authorized and
Set Forms of Liturgy, Works, vii. p. 307. The blessings
of religion do descend most properly from our spiritual
fathers and with most plentiful emanation. And this hath
been the religion of all the world, to derive very much
of their blessings by the Priest's particular and signal
benediction.

℺. Can you give Examples of this being the
case from the *Old Testament?*

℟. Yes; Melchizedek, the type of Christ, Gen. xiv.
blessed Abraham. "The Lord spake unto Moses, 18, 19.
saying, Speak unto Aaron and unto his sons, 1—10.
saying, On this wise ye shall bless the children Num. vi. 22,
of Israel, saying unto them, The Lord bless thee &c.
and keep thee: the Lord make His face shine 20, 21.
upon thee, and be gracious unto thee: the Lord
lift up His countenance upon thee, and give thee
peace. And they shall put My Name upon the
children of Israel; and *I will bless them.*" And Deut. xxi.
again, "The priests, the sons of Levi, shall come 5. xxvii. 11.
near; for them the Lord thy God hath chosen to xxiii. 13.
bless in the Name of the Lord."

℺. Can you give similar Examples from the
New Testament?

℟. Yes. Our Lord thus charged both His
Apostles and His Seventy Disciples, "Into Matt. x. 13.
whatsoever house ye enter, first say, Peace be Luke x. 5.
to this house. And if the son of peace be there, 27.
your peace shall rest upon it; if not, it shall Rom. xv.
turn to you again." And Christ says, "Peace 1 Cor. i. 3.
I leave with you, My peace I give unto you." 2 Cor. i. 2.
And in conformity with these words the Apos- xiii. 11.
tles of Christ imparted their benedictions to Eph. i. 2.

PART I.
1 Thess. v. 23.
2 Thess. iii. 16.
1 Tim. i. 2.
2 Tim. i. 2.
Titus i. 4.
Philem. 3.

individual Christians and Christian Churches, not only by word of mouth, but in their letters also [1].

[1] S. CHRYSOSTOM ap. Damascen. Par. Sac. ii. p. 514.
GEORGE HERBERT, Country Parson, chap. xxxvi. The Country Parson wonders that the *Blessing* the people is in so little use with his brethren, whereas he thinks it not only a grave and reverend thing, but a beneficial also. That which the Apostles used in their writings, nay, which our Saviour Himself used, Mark x. 16, cannot be vain and superfluous. But this was not proper to Christ, or the Apostles only, no more than to be a spiritual Father was appropriated to them. . . . But the Parson first values the gift, and then teacheth his Parish to value it. The same is to be observed in writing *letters* also.

Q. By what significant action has the communication of spiritual grace and blessing to single individuals been always accompanied in the Church?

A. By the laying on of hands upon the head of the recipient of the benediction [1].

[1] See references on the next question.

Q. In what rites and offices of the Church is it imparted in this manner?

A. In the Confirmation [1] of those who have been baptized,—wherein spiritual *weapons* are given to those who *enlisted* themselves as *soldiers* of Christ at *baptism;*—in the re-admission of penitent sinners [2]; and in the making, ordaining, and consecrating of Bishops, Priests, and Deacons [3].

[1] In *blessing*, Gen. xlviii. 14. Matt. xix. 15. Mark x. 16. *Ordaining*, Numb. viii. 10. 20. xxvii. 18. Acts xi. 6. xiii. 3. 1 Tim. iv. 14. v. 22. 2 Tim. i. 6. *Confirming*, see the Author's notes on Acts viii. 17. xix. 6, and on Heb. vi. 2.
S. HIERON. adv. Lucif. 4. Ad eos qui longe in minoribus urbibus per presbyteros et diaconos baptizati sunt, Episcopus ad invocationem Sancti Spiritûs manum impositurus excurrit. See HOOKER, V. LXVI. HAMMOND de Confirmatione, iv. p. 851. Bp. TAYLOR, χρίσις τελειω-

τικὴ, xi. p. 215. COMBER, iii. p. 451. BINGHAM, Bk. xii. c. ii. CHAP. XV

Among Manuals preparatory to Confirmation, may be specially noticed, "CATECHESIS; or Christian Instruction, &c. By CHARLES WORDSWORTH, D.D., Bishop of St. Andrew's, Lond. 1849;" and that of Dr. GOULBURN.

[2] S. HIERON. adv. Lucif. 11. 173. Recipio pœnitentem per manûs impositionem et invocationem Spiritûs Sancti.

Concil. Nicæn. 8, 9. Antioch. 17. 22.—S. AUG. ix. p. 267.

HOOKER, VII. VI. 5.

[3] Concil. Nic. c. 19. Chalced. c. 15.

S. HIERON. in Esai. c. 58. Χειροτονία, id est, ordinatio clericorum non solum ad imprecationem vocis, sed ad impositionem impletur manûs; ne scilicet vocis imprecatio clandestina *clericos ordinet nescientes*.

HOOKER, V. LXVI. 1. With prayers of spiritual and personal benediction the manner hath been in all ages to use *imposition of hands*, as a ceremony betokening our *restrained* desires to the party whom we present unto God by prayer.

FULLER, Moderation of the Church of England, chap. 8, § 9. Our Church doth rightly suppose its Ministers to have a special commission given them to pray for God's people and bless them: as the Priests under the Law had commission to bless the people in the name of God, Num. vi. 22. Deut. x. 8. 1 Chron. xxiii. 13. Which practice had nothing ceremonial in it and peculiar to the Law. Wherefore Christ put His hands upon the little children and blessed them, Matt. xix. 13, and commanded His Apostles and Ministers to bless His people, Matt. x. 13. Luke x. 5. And without all contradiction the less is blessed of the greater, Heb. vii. 7. Wherefore for the dignity of the Episcopal Office, the Church doth especially delegate that power to her Bishops, for Confirmation, with imposition of hands, and in Ordination. Neither do our religious Kings refuse the benedictions of the Church's ministers at their Coronations.

Q. You have spoken of the sacerdotal benediction of *persons;* have we any Scriptural authority for the blessing of particular *things* also?

A. Yes. St. Paul says, "The cup of blessing which we bless, is it not the Communion of the blood of Christ?" Hence at the Holy Communion the Priest lays his hand on the Sacramental Elements [1], when he offers up the prayer of Consecration.

1 Cor. x. 16.

PART I.   [1] S. AUG. iii. p. 2290. Accedit verbum ad elementum et fit sacramentum. The words of Institution "*Hoc est corpus Meum*," pronounced in the *Prayer of Consecration* at the Holy Table, have the force of consecration. CHRYSOSTOM, Hom. 1, de prodit. Judæ, ii. p. 384. τοῦτο τὸ ῥῆμα μεταρρυθμίζει τὰ προκείμενα κ.τ.λ. S. AMBROS. de Sacr. iv. c. 4. Sermo Christi hoc confecit Sacramentum.

Q. You have given Scriptural examples of the efficacy of Sacerdotal Intercession and Benediction; does this efficacy appear, further, from the constitution of the Church of Christ?

A. Yes. The Christian Church is One spiritual Body (p. 3), and, since its members are joined together in this one Body, all their solemn public acts must partake of this character of Unity; and one of the chief of those acts is the making of their wants known to God, which is Prayer; another is the reception of His grace, by Blessing. Accordingly, Christ Himself has declared that there is special efficacy[1] in *united* Prayer; and for the maintenance and public exhibition of this unity in the sacred assemblies of the Church, God has appointed certain Persons to be His Orators for the People, who are, as it were, *Angeli ascendentes et descendentes*[2], messengers ascending to Him with Prayer *from* the people, and descending from Him with Blessing *to* them. And since Unity is the divinely appointed character of the Church, God will assuredly bless those means which conduce to maintain that Unity, and which He has appointed for its attainment and preservation.

Matt. v. 24.
xviii. 19, 20.
Acts ii. 1.

Mal. iii. 7.

[1] S. AUGUST. de Bapt. lib. ii. cap. 13. Multùm valet ad propitiandum Deum fraterna concordia. "Si duobus ex vobis," ait Dominus, "convenerit in terrâ, quicquid petieritis, fiet vobis." Si duobus hominibus, quantò magis duobus populis! Simul nos Domino prosternamus, participamini nobiscum unitatem, participemur vobiscum dolorem, et charitas cooperiat multitudinem peccatorum.

[2] Bp. ANDREWES, v. 355. (Sermon on Luke xi. 2.) Thus much are we to learn from hence, that the Priests

are *Angeli Domini exercituum*. If Angels, then they must not only *descend* to the people to teach them the will of God, but *ascend* to the presence of God to make intercession for the people. HAMMOND on Rev. i. 23. They are like *Angels ascending* and *descending* between God and His people, in ruling them, in delivering God's messages to them, and also returning their messages or prayers to God. HOOKER, V. xxv. 2. God hath imposed on the Priest the office of *blessing* the People in His Name, and *making intercession* to Him in theirs.

Q. You say that these Ministrations of Sacerdotal Intercession and Benediction conduce to maintain Church Unity; how is this the case?

A. It has been shown from Scripture, that Public Prayer derives its efficacy from being offered in a spirit of Unity, that is, not only in a special Place, but also in communion with special Persons, and that God has appointed that Public Prayer should be offered, and His Benedictions be received, in this manner[1]. It follows, therefore, that we shall be careful not to separate ourselves from such appointed Places and Persons[2], lest we forfeit the benefits promised and conferred, in and through them, by Prayer and Blessing, on those "who are gathered together in *Christ's Name*," i. e. in a spirit of love to Him and to His Church. Thus we ourselves shall "maintain the Unity of the Spirit in the bond of Peace;" "not forsaking the assembling of ourselves together," but being assembled all "with one accord in one place," and being all "of one heart, and of one soul," united in one holy bond of Truth and Peace, of Faith and Charity, we shall with one mind and *one mouth* glorify God.

Matt. v. 24.
xviii. 19, 20.
1 Tim. ii. 8.
1 Cor. xiii. 1.
Exod. xx. 25.
xxv. 1. 8.
2 Chron. vii. 1. 12—16.
Deut. xii. 5. 13.
xxxi. 11—13.
Ps. cvii. 32.
Isa. ii. 3.
Luke xxiv. 53.
Acts ii. 1.
46. iii. 1.
Heb. x. 25.
Prayer for Unity.
Ps. xxvii. 4.
lxxxiv. 1, 2.

---

[1] HAMMOND's Practical Catechism, lib. iii. sect. 2, p. 200. The union of so many hearts being most likely to prevail, and the presence of some godly to bring down mercies on others, especially if the service of prayer be performed by a consecrated person, whose office it is to draw nigh unto God, namely, to offer up Prayer, &c. to

PART I. Him, and to be the ambassador and messenger between God and man, God's ambassador to the people, *in God's stead beseeching them to be reconciled;* and the people's ambassador to God, to offer up our requests for grace, for pardon, for mercies to Him. See also HOOKER, V. XXIV.

² BINGHAM's Antiquities, XVI. 1. p. 5. The fifth Canon (of the Council of Gangra) is to the same effect: "If any one teach that the House of God, and the assemblies held therein, are to be despised, let him be anathema." The sixth forbids all private and irregular assemblies: "If any hold other assemblies privately out of the Church, and contemning the Church will have ecclesiastical offices performed without a Presbyter licensed by the Bishop, let him be anathema."

Q. How was this principle for the maintenance of Unity by these Ministrations practically carried out in the Primitive Church?

A. In the early ages of the Church, Christendom consisted of co-ordinate Provinces, as has been shown, (chapter xii.) and these were subdivided into what are now termed Dioceses, each of which had a Bishop as its *Centre of Unity*¹, the Presbyters of the Diocese being subject to and united with their Bishop, and the People being in communion with their respective Pastors². And as the Bishop was the Centre of Unity¹, for the purposes of diffusing Grace to all, and of joining all together², and of presenting them unitedly to God, so the Cathedral³ was the common Mother Church of the whole Diocese; and thus, by personal and local communion, the Faithful of each Diocese were united together as one man in the offices of Public Worship, and were partakers of those Graces⁴ which are specially promised by God to all who "dwell together in Unity."

Ps cxxxiii. 1.

¹ BINGHAM, XVI. 1. p. 6. The *standing rule* of the Catholic Church was to have but one Bishop in a Church as the *Centre of Unity.*

² S. CYPRIAN, Ep. lxix. al. lxvi. ad Florent. p. 168. Ecclesia est plebs sacerdoti adunata, et pastori suo grex

adhærens. Unde scire debes Episcopum in Ecclesiâ esse, CHAP. XV. et Ecclesiam in Episcopo.

S. CYPRIAN, Ep. xxvii. al. xxxiii. ad Lapsos, p. 66. Inde per temporum et successionum vices Episcoporum ordinatio et Ecclesiæ ratio decurrit, ut Ecclesia super Episcopos constituatur, et omnis actus Ecclesiæ per eosdem præpositos gubernetur.

³ Bp. GIBSON, Codex, p. 171. The *Cathedral* Church is the *Parish Church* of the *whole Diocese*.

⁴ S. IGNATIUS ad Ephes. v. εἰ ἑνὸς καὶ δευτέρου προσευχὴ ταύτην ἰσχὺν ἔχει, πόσῳ μᾶλλον ἥ τε τοῦ Ἐπισκόπου καὶ πάσης τῆς Ἐκκλησίας; Ad Magnes. μὴ ὑμεῖς μηδὲν ἄνευ Ἐπισκόπου πράσσετε, ἀλλ' ἐπὶ τὸ αὐτὸ μία προσευχή, μία δέησις, on which passage see

HAMMOND, iv. p. 750. Palam est de unitarum Ecclesiæ Precum beneficio sermonem institui. Hanc inquit *Unitatem* in eo consistere ut omnes Episcopo morem gerant. Hic ἐντὸς τοῦ θυσιαστηρίου εἶναι significat Unitatis illius potissimam partem, sic Episcopo ut Capiti concorporari, ut *precum Ecclesiasticarum* participes fiat.

S. CHRYSOSTOM, vi. p. 408, Savil. εὔχεσθαι μὲν ἐπὶ τῆς ἰδίας οἰκίας δυνατὸν, οὕτω δὲ εὔχεσθαι ὡς ἐπὶ τῆς ἐκκλησίας ἀδύνατον, ὅπου πατέρων πλῆθος τοσοῦτον, ὅπου βοὴ πρὸς τὸν Θεὸν ὁμοθυμαδὸν ἀναπέμπεται—ἐνταῦθα γάρ ἐστι τὶ πλεῖον, οἷον ἡ ὁμόνοια, ἡ συμφωνία, καὶ τῆς ἀγάπης ὁ σύνδεσμος καὶ αἱ τῶν ἱερέων εὐχαί. See also vi. p. 663.

Prayer for UNITY, in Form of Prayer for Queen's Accession.

HOOKER, V. xxxix. p. 1. If the Prophet David did think that the very meeting of men together, and their accompanying one another to the House of God, should make the bond of their love insoluble, and tie them in a league of inviolable amity, (Ps. lv. 14,) how much more may we judge it reasonable to hope, that the like effects may grow in each of the people towards other, in them all towards their pastor, and in their pastor towards every of them, between whom there daily and interchangeably pass in the hearing of God Himself, and in the presence of His holy Angels, so many heavenly acclamations, exultations, provocations, petitions, songs of comfort, psalms of praise and thanksgiving, as when the pastor maketh their suits, and they with one voice testify a general assent thereunto.

On this and the two preceding chapters the reader may consult W. LAW's Three Letters to Bp. Hoadly, i. p. 364 (in the Scholar Armed). See also i. p. 362, on Benediction; i. pp. 368—370, on Intercession; i. pp. 382—391. 495, on Absolution; i. p. 500, on Excommunication.

K 2

CHAPTER XVI.

PRIVILEGES IN THE CHURCH.

Set Forms of Public Prayer.

Q. What other benefit do we receive through the Church, besides the pure Word of God, the Administration of the Sacraments, Discipline, Intercession, and Benediction? (Chaps. vi.—xv.)

A. That of *sound set Forms of Common Prayer.*

Q. How do we receive them by the Church?

A. Because, even if the Church could exist without them, they could not exist without the Church: that is, they could not exist without stated Times, Places, and Persons, set apart for the exercise of Christian worship.

Q. What authority have we for expecting to receive special benefits from *Common,* or *Public Prayer?*

A. When our Lord described the Temple, He called it a *"House of Prayer;"* and to *Public Prayers,* as distinguished from *Private,* a special blessing is promised by Christ Himself: "Where two or three are *gathered together* in My Name there am I in the midst of them[1]."

Matt. xxi. 13.
Isa. lvi. 7.
Matt. xviii. 20.

---

[1] Hooker, V. xxiv. V. xxv. The House of Prayer is a place beautified with the presence of celestial powers; there we stand, we pray, we sound forth hymns to God, having His Angels intermingled as our associates.

Q. In what way are *set Forms* of Public Prayer advantageous?

A. Set forms of sound words, as distinguished from extemporaneous Prayers, are free[1] from the danger of offending the majesty of God by irrelevant and irreverent expressions, and "endless and senseless effusions of indigested prayers, and of thus disgracing the worthiest[2] part of Christian duty towards God[3];" they are formed according to the precept[4] of Almighty God in the Old Testament, and of our Blessed Lord in the New; they impart fervour to the lukewarm, and are a restraint on fanaticism; they are public, solemn professions of true Religion, to which they give life and vigour; they maintain unimpaired "*the proportion of faith*," τὴν ἀναλογίαν τῆς πίστεως: Rom. xii. 6. they deliver the Minister from the peril of pride, and of unduly exalting and dwelling upon one doctrine, and depressing and neglecting another; they are a standard of preaching, and a rule for hearing; they unite the hearts and voices of Christian men and of Christian congregations with each other, with the Saints departed, and with Angels in heaven; they give public significations of Christian charity for those who cannot or will not communicate in them; they serve to maintain Unity by Unison and Uniformity; they are like a sacred anchor, by which the Church is safely moored in the peaceful harbour of Evangelical Truth, Apostolical Order, and Catholic Love.

[1] Bp. TAYLOR, vol. vii. pp. 285—307.

[2] HOOKER, V. VI. p. 2. This present world affordeth not any thing comparable unto the Public Duties of Religion.

[3] HOOKER, V. xxv. p. 5. ibid. p. 4. No doubt from God it hath proceeded, and by us it must be acknowledged a work of His singular Care and Providence, that the Church hath *evermore* held a *prescript form* of *Common Prayer*, although not in all things every where the same, yet for the most part retaining still the same analogy.... If the liturgies of all ancient Churches be compared, it may easily be perceived that the public prayers in churches thoroughly settled, did never use to be voluntary dictates proceeding from any man's extemporal wits. King CHARLES I. Works, *Icón Basiliké*, chap. xvi. Bp. BULL, Serm. xiii. vol. i. p. 336.

[4] HOOKER, V. XXVI. p. 2. God Himself did frame to His Priests the very speech wherewith they were charged to bless the people (Num. vi. 23)..... Our Saviour Christ hath left us of His own framing a Prayer which might both remain as a *part* of the Church Liturgy, and serve as a *pattern* whereby to frame all other prayers with efficacy.

PART II.

On the Anglican Branch of the Catholic Church.

CHAPTER I.

CHURCH OF ENGLAND. ITS ORIGIN.

Part II.

Q. The Catholic Church is compared by the Christian Fathers to the Sea[1], as being diffused throughout all the world; as being, like the Sea, one; as having one name, that of the Catholic Church; and as containing within it many Catholic Churches with various names, as the Sea has many various bays and harbours in it. Is the Church of England one of these Churches?

A. Yes.

---

[1] S. Theophil. Antioch. Autolyc. ii. p. 14.
See the beautiful comparison of S. Ambrose, Hexaëm. iii. p. 5. Bene Mari plerumque comparatur Ecclesia, &c.

S. Ambrose de Benedict. Patriarch. lib. i. cap. 5. Ecclesia, spectans Hæreticorum procellas et naufragia Judæorum, tanquam Portus salutis, quæ expansis brachiis in gremium tranquillitatis suæ vocet periclitantes, locum fidæ stationis ostendens. Ecclesiæ igitur in hoc sæculo tamquam Portus maritimi per littora diffusi occurrunt laborantibus, dicentes esse credentibus refugium præparatum, quo ventis quassata navigia possint subducere.

Hooker, III. i. p. 14. As the main body of the Sea being one, yet within divers precincts hath divers names, so the Catholic Church is in like sort divided into a number of distinct societies, every one of which is termed a Church within itself.

Q. How do you prove that she is a part of the Catholic Church?

A. Because she is united with it in Origin, in Doctrine, and in Government.

Q. How in *Origin?*

A. By means of the unbroken succession of her Bishops and Pastors, through whom she traces her origin [1] from the Apostles; some of whom are recorded to have preached the Gospel in the British Isles.

[1] TERTULLIAN, Præscr. Hæret. c. 20. Omne genus ad Originem suam censeatur necesse est. Itaque tot et tantæ Ecclesiæ Una est Illa ab Apostolis Prima, ex quâ Omnes. Sic omnes Prima et Apostolica, dum una omnes probant unitatem.

Ibid. Apostoli Ecclesias condiderunt a quibus traducem fidei et semina doctrinæ cæteræ Ecclesiæ mutuatæ sunt et quotidie mutuantur ut *Ecclesiæ fiant,* ac per hoc Apostolicæ deputantur, ut soboles Ecclesiarum Apostolicarum.

See below, Pt. ii. chap. vi. On the Apostolical Succession in the Church of England.

Q. You say that the Church of England was founded in the Apostolic age; how is this consistent with the opinion sometimes expressed, that its inhabitants were first converted to Christianity by S. Augustin, sent from Rome for that purpose by Pope Gregory the First, at the close of the sixth century (A.D. 596)?

A. S. Augustin converted the *Saxon* inhabitants of a *part* of England [1] (Kent), who had invaded that region and dispossessed the ancient *British* inhabitants; but they *relapsed* into *heathenism* in a little more than twenty years after the arrival of Augustin [2]; and there were Christian Bishops in Britain several hundred years *before* Augustin landed there [3].

[1] Abp. BRAMHALL, i. pp. 266—8.

[2] Archd. CHURTON, Early English Church, chaps. i. ii. See also the Brief Account, in the form of a chronicle, of the Scottish and Italian Missions to the Anglo-Saxons, by the Rev. D. I. HEATH, Lond. 1845, p. 4.

[3] GILDAS, Britannus Sapiens, (sæculi vi^{ti},) de Excid. Brit. § 8, ed. Stevenson. See below, p. 138.

CRAKANTHORPE, Defens. Eccl. Anglic. p. 25. Amplificavit Augustinus inter Anglos Ecclesiam, *non fundavit*.

Q. What proof have you of this?

A. Eusebius[1] asserts that some of the Apostles passed over to Britain. Tertullian, who lived in the *second* century after Christ, speaks of "*Britannorum inaccessa Romanis loca, Christo vero subdita.*" Origen, who lived in the next age, speaks of Britain consenting in the worship of the true God. And S. Alban was martyred under Diocletian (A.D. 305), nearly three hundred years before the landing of S. Augustin.

[1] EUSEB. Præp. Evang. iii. p. 7. TERTULL. c. Judæos, c. vii. ORIGEN, Hom. in Ezek. iv. in S. Luc. i. hom. 6. See also S. CHRYSOSTOM, tom. ii. p. 499. v. p. 919. vi. p. 638. viii. p. 3, ed. Savil. BEDE, Hist. Eccl. i. p. 6.

Q. Since, then, there were *Christians* in England even from the Apostolic times, can you further show that there were Christian *Bishops?*

A. Yes; it follows, first from the very nature of the case. *Ecclesia in Episcopo* was the motto of primitive Christianity; and also, *Ubi Ecclesia, ibi Episcopus*[1]. There was in those ages no idea of such a thing as a Church without a Bishop[2].

[1] S. IGNAT. ad Trall. vii. ad Phil. iv. ad Smyrn. vii.

S. CYPRIAN, Ep. 66, p. 168, ed. Fell. Scire debes Episcopum in Ecclesiâ esse, et Ecclesiam in Episcopo; et si qui cum Episcopo non sunt, in Ecclesiâ non esse.

[2] GRABE ad S. Irenæum, p. 199. CASAUBON, Exerc. Baron. pp. 307-8, ed. 1654. See above, Pt. i. ch. x.

Q. Does the existence of British Bishops antecedently to Augustin appear from any other evidence?

A. Yes. British Bishops were present at the earliest Councils of the Church; viz. at the

Council of Arles [1], A.D. 314; at which time there were three Metropolitans in Britain, as there were three Provinces, one Maxima Cæsariensis, the other Britannia Prima, the third Britannia Secunda; the seat of the Metropolitan of the first being York; of the second, London; of the third, Caerleon on Usk in Monmouthshire. Again, at the Council of Sardica [2], A.D. 347; and again, probably, at that of Ariminum [3], A.D. 359; and there were, we know, *seven* British Bishops and a British Archbishop when Augustin landed in England [4].

[1] CONCIL. ARELAT. Labbe, i. p. 1430. (Contra Donatistas, Concilium convocante Constantino M.) to which are attached the following subscriptions:—
Eborius, Episcopus de civitate Eboracensi, provinciâ Britanniâ.—Restitutus, Episcopus de civitate Londinensi, provinciâ suprascriptâ.—Adelphinus, *Episcopus* de civitate coloniâ Londinensium, (Coloniâ Lindi, *Lincoln*. Bingham, ix. pp. 6. 20. Cave, Hist. Lit. i. p. 350,) exinde sacerdos *Presbyter*, Arminius *Diaconus*.

From the above signatures it is clear that in A.D. 314 there were in England the three Orders of *Bishops, Priests*, and *Deacons*.

Abp. USSHER, Brit. Eccles. Antiq. p. 73. BREDEWOOD, in Abp. Ussher's Original of Bishops and Metropolitans, Oxford, 1641. CRAKANTHORPE, Defens. Eccles. Anglic. p. 23. Bp. STILLINGFLEET, Orig. Brit. p. 78, ed. 1837.

[2] S. ATHANAS. Apol. ii. init. BINGHAM, IX. I. p. 5.
[3] SULP. SEVER. H. S. ii. ad fin.
[4] GILFRID de Gest. Brit. viii. Eo tempore, quo Augustinus Monachus in Britanniam missus est a Gregorio, Christianismus viguit, cum fuerint in eâ *septem Episcopatus* et *unus Archiepiscopatus*. Vide Bed. ii. p. 2. The Archbishop was the *Menevensis Episcopus* (Bp. of St. David's). Concerning the transfer of the archiepiscopal see, first from Caerleon to Llandaff, and thence to St. David's, Sir H. SPELMAN thus speaks: Discesserat hæc dignitas archiepiscopalis a Caerlegione ad Landaviam sub Dubritio, primo Landavensis ecclesiæ archiepiscopo, A.D. 512; mox a Landaviâ ad Meneviam cum S. Davide proximo ejus successore, annos plus minus 80 ante istam Augustini synodum, translationi aspirante Arthuro rege invictissimo; sed *retento pariter Caerlegionis titulo* (WILKINS, Concil. i. p. 24, not.). See below, chap. iii.

Bishop BEVERIDGE, ad Canon. Concil. Nicæn. i. p. 58.

PART II. Ecclesia Britannica erat αὐτοκέφαλος, nulli extraneo Episcopo sed suo soli Metropolitano subjacens.

It may here be added, that not only the Britons, but also the Scots and Picts, had received the Gospel before the time of Augustin. See MASON de Ministerio Anglicano, ii. p. 4.

CHAPTER II.

CHURCH OF ENGLAND INDEPENDENT OF ROME.

Period before the Arrival of S. Augustin.

Q. THERE were, then, Christians and Christian Bishops in Britain from the Apostolic times[1]; but can you show, further, that the British Church did not derive its origin from that of *Rome*, and was not dependent on it?

A. There is no evidence whatever of any such dependence. *No trace whatever* can be found of the Bishop of Rome having exercised any ecclesiastical authority in England for the first *six hundred years after Christ*[2]*;* and it is certain that England did not receive her Christianity at first through Rome; indeed, there is very good ground for believing that the Church of *England* is *older* than that of *Rome*[3].

[1] BINGHAM, Antiquities, IX. VI. p. 20. Indeed it would appear that there were *more* Bishops in England and Wales at the time of the *Saxon Invasion* [i. e. 150 years *before* the arrival of Augustin], than there *are at this day*.

[2] Abp. BRAMHALL, p. 158.

[3] CRAKANTHORPE, Defensio Eccl. Angl. p. 23. De Britannicâ Ecclesiâ nostrâ liquidum est fuisse eam aliquot *ante* Romanam *annis* fundatam..... *Glaciali* (inquit Gildas) frigore rigenti insulæ (de Britanniâ agit) Christus suos radios, id est sua præcepta, indulget, tempore ut scimus summo Tiberii Cæsaris. Supremum Tiberii tempus incidit in xvii. kal. April. A.D. xxxix. natalitia vero *Romanæ* Ecclesiæ in xv. kal. Feb. A.D. xlv. (teste Baronio.) Disce jam hinc sapere. Disce Romanam Ecclesiam Britannicæ nostræ non *matrem* sed *sororem* atque *sororem* integro

quinquennio *minorem.* See also F. MASON de Ministerio, n. 72. Apparet Evangelium in Britanniâ citiùs quàm Romæ emicuisse.

Q. Give evidence of this non-reception of Christianity, in the first instance, from *Rome.*

A. To omit other proofs, we may appeal to the English word *Church*[1], which is derived, as has been before said (Part i. chap. i.), from the *Greek* Κυριακὴ, a term which no *Roman* ever applied to the Church (which he called *Ecclesia*, and by no other name) : and it is not credible that, *if* the Church of England had been derived from *Rome*, it should have been designated by a title *foreign* to Rome.

[1] Bp. BEVERIDGE in Canon xv. Concil. Ancyran., and on Art. xix.—Routh, Rel. Sacr. iii. p. 489. It is probable that this word is due to the Irish, Scottish, and Saxon missionaries under AIDAN, who followed the Eastern Church in the time of observing Easter.

Q. Yes. The word *Church* is, no doubt, of *Greek* origin, and is unknown to the *Roman* tongue; is there any other proof that the English Church was derived from some country where the *Greek*, and not *Roman*, language was spoken?

A. Yes. The facts that the British Church, and indeed a great portion of the Saxon Church, from A.D. 635 till A.D. 664, followed the Asiatic custom in keeping Easter, and in its manner of administering Baptism—(points in which they *differed* from the *Roman Church*, as Augustin himself said in his speech to the British Bishops, adding, that there were also other things "*quæ agitis moribus nostris contraria* [1]")—seem to show that the Church of England was derived, through a Greek or Asiatic channel[2], from *that* whence the *Roman* itself came, namely, from the *Mother of all Churches*, the Church of *Jerusalem*[3].

Isa. ii. 3.
Micah iv. 2
Luke xxiv. 47.

[1] BEDA, Ecclesiast. Histor. Gentis Anglorum, ii. c. 2. LAPPENBERG, Hist. of England under the Saxons, i. p. 134, ed. Lond. 1845.

PART II.

² Sir ROGER TWISDEN, Historical Vindication of the Church of England in point of Schism, p. 7.
CRAKANTHORPE, Def. Eccl. Angl. p. 24.
³ CONCIL. CONST. (i. e. the second General Council) in Synodic. Epist. Theodoret, v. 9. μήτηρ ἁπασῶν τῶν ἐκκλησιῶν ἡ ἐν ῾Ιεροσολύμοις. S. HIERON. in Esai. ii. In *Hierusalem* primùm fundata Ecclesia *totius Orbis Ecclesias* seminavit. Bp. BULL, ii. pp. 192. 199, ed. 1827. GIESELER, Eccl. Hist. § 94, note 40.

Q. The Church of England, then, was not planted by Rome: was it in any way dependent on it?

A. As has been before said[1], for the first six centuries after Christ, no ecclesiastical authority was exercised in Britain by the Bishop of Rome. So true is this, that Gregory himself, about A.D. 590, being told that certain children whom he saw at Rome were "*de Britanniâ insulâ*," did not even know[2], but inquired for information whether England was *Pagan* or *Christian?* and the British Bishops declared to S. Augustin that they were under a Metropolitan of their own, the Bishop of Caerleon, and that they knew nothing of the Bishop of Rome as an ecclesiastical *superior*[3].

[1] P. 138; cp. INETT, Church History. Origines Anglicanæ, ii. p. 488.
[2] JOH. DIAC. Vit. Gregor. i. c. 21. GREG. M. Opera, tom. iv. p. 8.
[3] See speech of Dinoth, Abbot of Bangor, to Augustin (Wilkins, Concilia, i. p. 26, compared with Bingham, IX. I. p. 11). Bp. Nicolson's Hist. Library, i. p. 91. And even as late as A.D. 787, the legate of Pope Adrian the First writes to him from England thus: *Ut scitis*, a tempore Sancti Augustini Pontificis sacerdos *nullus* illuc (i. e. to England) missus est nisi nos. (Wilkins, Concil. i. p. 146.) And Girald. Cambr. Itinerar. ii. c. 1, states that all the Bishops of Wales received their consecration from their own Metropolitan (Menevensi Antistite) the Bishop of St. David's, till the time of Henry I. "nullâ penitus alii Ecclesiæ factâ professione vel subjectione." BEDA, Eccl. Hist. ii. c. 2, and Professor Hussey's note there. See also above, p. 136; and below, chap. iii.

Q. But did not the first General Council, that

of Nicæa in Bithynia (A.D. 325), acknowledge the Bishop of Rome to be *Patriarch* of the *West* (Canon 6)?

A. No; the Nicene Council[1] recognized the Bishop of Alexandria as having authority over the Churches of Egypt, Libya, and Pentapolis, as the Bishops of Rome, Antioch, and other patriarchal Churches had over their own Ecclesiastical Districts respectively; and *no further*. And the Bishop of Rome's jurisdiction extended only, as has been shown (see above, Pt. i. ch. xii.), to what were called the *Suburbicariæ Ecclesiæ*[2], that is, to the Churches near the *Urbs* or *City* of Rome, viz. those of *middle and southern Italy, Sicily, Sardinia, and Corsica*. Certainly the Bishops of Milan, Ravenna, and Aquileia, in Italy, were not ordained by, nor dependent on, the Bishop of Rome, for more than six hundred years after Christ. So far, then, from his being *Patriarch of the West*, in the fourth century, the Bishop of Rome's Patriarchate did *not* even include all *Italy;* for the ordination or confirmation of Metropolitans in a Patriarchate is an essential part of patriarchal power. (See Pt. i. ch. xii.)

[1] Canones et Concil. Bruns, p. 16.
[2] RUFFIN. Hist. Eccles. ii. 6. Apud Alexandriam et in urbe Româ vetusta consuetudo servetur, ut ille (Alexandrinus Episcopus) Ægypti, hic Suburbicariarum Ecclesiarum sollicitudinem gerat. Ruffinus was a Roman Presbyter, and flourished in the next century to the Nicene Council, and therefore his evidence concerning the limits of the Roman Patriarchate, and on the meaning of this Nicene canon, is unexceptionable.

The language of the Church-historian, DUPIN, himself a member of the Church of Rome, is explicit as to this point (viz. the limits of the *Roman Patriarchate*), as follows:

DUPIN de Antiq. Eccles. Disc. p. 32. Patriarchatûs Romani limites non videntur excessisse provincias eas, quæ Vicario *Urbis* parebant, dicunturque a Ruffino *suburbicariæ*. Nam extra istas provincias etiam in Italiâ Metropolitani Episcopos omnes ordinabant, et ipsi ab Episcopis provinciæ ordinabantur... At in aliis provinciis minime suburbicariis jus ordinationum pontificem Romanum habuisse probari

PART II. non potest. Imo constat, non tantum Episcopos omnes a Metropolitanis sed et Metropolitanos ipsos ab Episcopis cujusque provinciæ fuisse ordinatos : ergo extra controversiam esse debet, Rom. pontificem in solis provinciis suburbicariis primum ac præcipuum patriarcharum jus habuisse. . . . Nihilominus tamen successu temporis Romanus Pontifex patriarchatûs sui limites, quantum potuit, extendit: ac primo Illyricum ditioni suæ per vicarios adjicere conatus est : deinde vero non modo totam Italiam, sed et Gallias atque Hispaniam patriarchatûs sui limitibus comprehendi voluit.

DUPIN de Antiq. Eccles. Disc. p. 70. Provinciæ autem suburbicariæ aliæ dici non possunt, quam illæ, quæ circa Romam adjacebant: quæ *Urbs* dicitur ἀντονομαστικῶς. Docet id vel ipsum nomen, quod regiones ab *urbe* non longe positas significat, tum etiam imperatoriarum legum auctoritas, in quibus provinciæ suburbicariæ adpellantur eæ, quæ circa Romam adjacebant. Et procul dissitis ab urbe regionibus, ut Africæ, Galliæ, et Hispaniæ, opponuntur.

S. LEONIS Opera, ii. p. 452, ed. 1700. The *note* in this edition, published by P. Quesnel, another member of the Church of Rome, proves this. See also on this point the Abbé FLEURY, Histoire Ecclésiastique, Bruxelles, 1721, tom. viii. p. 41. Saint Grégoire n'entroit dans ce détail que pour les Eglises qui dépendoient particulièrement du Saint Siége, et que par cette raison on nommoit *Suburbicaires;* sçavoir celles de la *partie méridionale d'Italie*, où il étoit seul Archevêque, celles de Sicile et des autres îles, quoiqu'elles eussent de Métropolitains. Mais on ne *trouvera pas qu'il exerçât le même pouvoir immédiat dans les provinces dépendantes de Milan, d'Aquilée,* ni dans *l'Espagne* et les *Gaules;* cp. WORDSWORTH'S Italy, ii. p. 332—343.

Archbp. LAUD against Fisher, sect. 25. In ancient times Britain was never subject to the see of Rome; for it was one of the dioceses of the Western Empire (Notitia Prov. Occident. Panciroli, ii. c. 48), and had a Primate of its own; whence Pope Urban the Second, at the Council of Bari, accounted S. Anselm (of Canterbury) as his own compeer, and said he was the Apostolic and *Patriarch* of the other world. (Guil. Malmesbur. de Gestis Pontif. Angl. p. 223.) Now the Britons, having a Primate of their own, (which is greater than a Metropolitan,) yea, *a Patriarch*, if you will, (ibi Cantuariæ prima sedes archiepiscopi habetur, qui est totius Angliæ *Primas* et *Patriarcha*, says William of Malmesbury, in Prol. lib. i. de Gestis Pont. Ang. p. 195,) he could not be appealed from to Rome, by S. Gregory's own doctrine, Epist. xi. 54, *Patriarcha* secundum canones et leges præbeat finem. See also CRAKANTHORPE, Def. Eccl. Angl. p. 96. BINGHAM, Antiq. IX. I. 9—11. PALMER on the Church, ii. 538—543.

Q. But did not the Council of Arles in Gaul, A.D. 314, at which three British Bishops were present, in their synodical letter to Pope Sylvester[1], acknowledge him as holding the *majores Diœceses* ?

A. Yes, certainly it did; but the term *Diocese*[2] did not *then* mean a Patriarchal *Province*, but one of several *subdivisions of* a Province; and it is certain that the Fathers of that Council never understood these *majores Diœceses* to extend beyond the *Suburbicarian Churches* above mentioned: and they never conceived the Bishop of Rome, who was not present there, to have any jurisdiction over themselves, as is clear from their enacting Canons without him, and from the following words in the same synodical letter, "Te *pariter nobiscum* judicante, cœtus noster majore lætitiâ exultasset;" and from the appellation "*frater* carissime," by which they address him.

[1] Ep. Synod. Concil. Arelat. i. p. 1426, ed. Labbe, 1671. Placuit ergo, præsente Spiritu Sancto et angelis Ejus, ut et his qui singulos quos movebat judicare proferremus de quiete præsenti. Placuit etiam antequam a te qui *majores diœceses* tenes, per te potissimum omnibus insinuari. The text of both these sentences is corrupt; for conjectural emendations of the latter, see Bingham, IX. I. 11. ROUTH, Rel. Sac. iv. 87.

[2] Suiceri Thesaur. p. 919. Diviso a Constantino imperio latior fuit διοικήσεως appellatio. *Tunc* enim *Diœcesis* non fuit una provincia, sed administratio multarum simul provinciarum. See above, Pt. i. ch. xii.

Q. But what do you say to the appellate jurisdiction *given* to the see of Rome by the Council of Sardica, in Illyria, A.D. 347 (Canons 3, 4. 7) ?

A. If *given then*, we may infer that it was not *possessed before*, and, whatever it may be, it is therefore not only of *human*, but *not* of *primitive*

PART II. nor very *early* institution. But further, the Council of Sardica, wishing to have means of meeting a *particular* case, that of S. Athanasius, *permits*[1], but does not *require*, that a reference may be made, not to the Bishop of Rome generally[2], but personally to Julius, the *then* Bishop of that see, if a Bishop thinks himself aggrieved in a judicial matter : and this reference is to be made by the judges who tried the cause; in which case the Bishop of Rome *may desire* the cause to be re-heard by the *neighbouring Bishops, in the country* where it arose, and may *send* assessors to them. So far was the Council of Sardica from giving a right of appeal *to Rome* in the common sense of the term. And further still, it is to be observed that this Council of Sardica was *not* a *General* one[3]; that its decrees were not received in the Eastern Church; and that this decree was subsequently *reversed* by a General Council, that of Chalcedon (Can. ix. xvii. xxv.).

[1] Canones Concil. Sard. Bruns. p. 90. Ὅσιος ἐπίσκοπος εἶπε—εἴ τις ἐπισκόπων ἔν τινι πράγματι δόξει κατακρίνεσθαι, καὶ ὑπολαμβάνει ἑαυτὸν μὴ σαθρὸν ἀλλὰ καλὸν ἔχειν τὸ πρᾶγμα, ἵνα αὖθις ἡ κρίσις ἀνανεωθῇ, εἰ δοκεῖ ὑμῶν τῇ ἀγάπῃ, Πέτρου τοῦ ἀποστόλου τὴν μνήμην τιμήσωμεν καὶ γραφῆναι παρὰ τούτων τῶν κοινάντων Ἰουλίῳ τῷ ἐπισκόπῳ Ῥώμης ὥστε διὰ τῶν γειτνιώντων τῇ ἐπαρχίᾳ ἐπισκόπων, εἰ δέοι, ἀνανεωθῆναι τὸ δικαστήριον καὶ ἐπιγνώμονας αὐτὸς παράσχοι.

[2] CRAKANTH. Def. Eccl. Ang. Ad Julium, non ad Papam Romanum ; privilegium Sardicense personale fuit, ideoque cum personâ Julii extinctum.

[3] This is clearly stated by Casaubon de Lib. Eccles. p. 223, ad finem; Abp. Bramhall, ii. p. 533, ed. Oxf. ; Bp. Stillingfleet, Orig. Brit. ch. iii. p. 146; Bingham, IX. I. 11. XVII. v. 14; Routh, Præf. ad Script. Eccl. p. iii. : and also by *Romanist* writers, as Archbp. De Marca de Conciliis, vii. c. ii.—iv. Dupin, Dissert. Eccl. 11, § 3, pp. 84. 89. 110. and P. Quesnel, in his edition of Pope Leo's Works, ii p. 256, who says, Illi (Sardicensi) Concilio debetur earum appellationum origo, et inde appellationum usui ratio quæsita est a Romanis Pontificibus, licet revera *nihil de appellationibus* decernant Sardicenses Patres, sed tantum retractationis seu revisionis causæ decernendæ potestatem

faciant Romano Episcopo. Quæ potestas retractationis in ipsâ Provinciâ decernendæ, etsi jure appellationum longè inferior sit, trepidè tamen et dubitanter admodum ab Osio proposita est, qui rem *novam* canonibus Nicænis minimè consonam, constantique adversam consuetudini quasi supplex et honorandam S. Petri memoriam prætendens exoravit; *si vobis placet*, inquit, Petri Apostoli memoriam honoremus. Vide ibid. pp. 307, 308.

Archbp. De MARCA de Concordiâ, vi. 30, also refutes the notion that this Council gave any right of appeal to Rome.—vii. 3. 2. Satis modestè hæc lex Synodi Sardicensis observata *est usque* ad seculum x.—till the time of Gregory VII. who elevated the Legatine authority above that of all Provincial Bishops.—Vide ibid. v. 47. vi. 30. 9.

DUPIN thus expresses himself on the same subject, Eccles. Dissertat. ii. p. 89. Sciunt omnes quantum sit discrimen inter jus istud revisionis decernendæ, et jus adpellationis admittendæ; nam adpellatio, ut definit Petrus de Marca, *causam inferiori tribunali judicatam ad superiorem transfert, ut litem excutiat, et definiat in suo tribunali, ita ut quamdiu durat adpellatio, sententia inferioris judicis non possit exsequutioni demandari.* At nihil simile est in eo privilegio, quod Romano pontifici concedit Synodus Sardicensis.—P. 91. Porro canones isti Sardicenses nunquam in oriente et serò in occidente recepti sunt. De oriente jam constat illo ipso tempore, quo condebantur, orientes episcopos contrarium prorsus statuisse. Deinceps autem tum in concilio Constantinopolitano, tum in Chalcedonensi, tum in Trullano, nullam hujus revisionis mentionem fecerunt, jusseruntque causas omnes synodi provincialis, aut ad summum patriarchalis judicio finiri. In occidente porro post hanc synodum adversus disciplinam in ea sancitam reclamarunt Africani, reclamarunt et Galli, ut dicemus infra, imo ne ipsi quidem Itali illos in authoritatem admiserunt.—P. 110. At non ita se gessit *Concilium Tridentinum*, nam illud omnem prorsus judicandorum Episcoporum potestatem Episcopis aliis ademit, et *soli Pontifici Romano* reservavit, sessione vigesima quarta de reform. cap. v.

The correspondence of S. Augustin (of Hippo) and the African Bishops with Pope Zosimus, A.D. 418, shows that the Sardican Canons were unknown in Africa in the fifth century, and that Rome was not then acknowledged to have any such appellate jurisdiction as, on the ground of those Sardican Canons, it has since claimed. See Cabassutii Concilia, p. 236, and see below, Pt. iii. ch. vii.

After all, it is not certain that these Sardican Canons are genuine. See BARROW's arguments, lately published for the first time, at the close of his work on the Papal

PART II. Supremacy, edited for the 'Society for Promoting Christian Knowledge.'

CHAPTER III.

CHURCH OF ENGLAND INDEPENDENT OF ROME.

Mission of S. Augustin.

Q. You have said that the Bishop of Rome exercised no jurisdiction in England during the first six centuries; but may it not be justly alleged, that he might *acquire* Patriarchal authority over England by the *conversion* of the Saxons to Christianity by Augustin, sent from Rome by Pope Gregory the First, A.D. 596?

1 Cor. i. 12, 13. iii. 5. 7.

A. No. By *conversion* they became not Gregory's nor Augustin's, but CHRIST's.

Augustin, it is true, converted Ethelbert, king of the *Cantii*, and the inhabitants of *part* of *his* kingdom; but Bertha, his queen, was a Christian already; and there was a Christian Bishop, Liudhard, and a Christian Church in his capital city, Canterbury, before Augustin's arrival[1]: and even *if* Augustin had converted the *whole Heptarchy*, no such right could by that act have been acquired[2]. *If* such right were to accrue by *conversion*, all Christian Churches, and Rome among them, would be subject to "the Mother of all Churches, the Church of Jerusalem," p. 139.

[1] BEDA, Hist. Eccles. i. p. 25. Cp. LAPPENBERG, i. p. 138.
[2] Archbp. BRAMHALL, i. pp. 266—268.

Q. But might not the Bishop of Rome *obtain* Patriarchal authority by the *ordination* of S. Augustin, and of those who were ordained by him?

Ⓐ. No. This plea is, under another form, the same as that of *conversion;* for *that* supposes the planting of a Church, and a Church supposes an *ordained ministry* of Bishops, Priests, and Deacons [1].

Besides, as Britain had never been under the Bishop of Rome's jurisdiction, but had been always governed by her own Bishops, the assertion of such authority on the part of the Popes of Rome is an infraction of the Canon of the General Council of Ephesus (A.D. 431); which Pope Gregory himself declared that he regarded, as he did the three other General Councils, with the highest veneration [2].

[1] S. IGNAT. ad Trall. 3. χωρὶς τούτων 'Εκκλησία οὐ καλεῖται. See above, Pt. i. ch. ix.
[2] GREG. Mag. ii. pp. 515. 632. Sicut quatuor Evangelii libros, sic *quatuor Concilia* suscipere et *venerari* me fateor, *totâ devotione complector, integerrimâ approbatione custodio.*

Ⓠ. What is the tenour of that Ephesine non?

Ⓐ. It is expressed as follows: " Rheginus and his fellow-Bishops of the province of CYPRUS, Zeno and Evagrius, having brought under our notice an innovation against the laws of the Church and the Canons of the Holy Fathers, and affecting the liberty of all; this holy Synod, seeing that public disorders require greater remedies, inasmuch as they bring greater damage, decrees that, if no ancient custom has prevailed for the Bishop of Antioch to ordain in CYPRUS—as the depositions made to us attest there has *not*—the Prelates of the Cyprian Churches shall, according to the decrees of the Holy Fathers and to ancient practice, exercise the right of ordaining in the said Church unmolested and inviolable. And the same rule shall be observed *in all other dioceses and provinces* whatsoever, so that no

PART II. Bishop shall occupy another province which has not been subject to him *from the beginning;* and if *he shall have made any such occupation or seizure, let him make restitution,* lest the Canons of the Holy Fathers [1] be transgressed; and lest under pretext of sacerdocy, the pride of power should creep in, and thus we should, by little and little, lose the liberty which the Liberator of all men, JESUS CHRIST, has purchased for us with His own blood [2]." On the principle embodied in this law, which is called the "JUS CYPRIUM [3]," the Church of England is independent of all foreign jurisdiction; and on the same ground the Bishop of Rome, in claiming any such authority, is guilty of unwarrantable usurpation.

[1] EPISTOLA Episcoporum Ægypti ad Melet. circa A.D. 306. Routh, Reliq. Sacr. iii. p. 382. Lex et Patrum et Propatrum, constituta secundum Divinum et Ecclesiasticum ordinem, in alienis Parœciis non licere alicui Episcoporum ordinationes celebrare. Cp. ibid. p. 391, and vol. iv. p. iv.

[2] CONCILIA Generalia, iii. p. 802, ed. Labbe, 1671. And this was again affirmed by the Council of Trullo (Conc. Quini-Sextum), the Vth and VIth General Council, canon 39.

[3] BINGHAM, Antiquities, bk. ii. chap. xviii. § 3. And this (jus Cyprium) was also the ancient liberty of the Britannic Church before the coming of Austin the Monk, when the seven British bishops paid obedience to the Archbishop of Caer-Leon, and acknowledged no superior in spirituals over him: as Dionothus, the learned Abbot of Bangor, told Austin in the name of all the Britannic Churches; 'that they owed no other obedience to the Pope of Rome than they did to every godly Christian, to love every one in his degree in perfect charity; other obedience than this they knew none due to him whom *he* named pope. But they were under the government of the Bishop of Caer-Leon upon Uske, who was their overseer under God.' On the genuineness of this document see LAPPENBERG, i. p. 135, and cp. BINGHAM, IX. ch. i. pp. 11, 12; and above, chap. i. at the end.

HAMMOND's Works, Reply on Schism, ii. pp. 31. 93. Abp. BRAMHALL, ii. p. 406.

And this is confessed even by some Roman Catholic writers, as by BARNS, *Cath. Rom. Pacif.* sect. 3, in the Appendix to Brown's Fasciculus Rerum Expetendarum, p. 839. Insula Britannia gavisa est olim *privilegio Cyprio*. Hoc autem privilegium cum tempore Henrici Octavi totius Regni consensu fuerit *restitutum*, videtur pacis ergo retineri debere, absque *schismatis ullius notâ*. See also ibid. pp. 841, 842.

Q. But is not the case of England very different from that of Cyprus, inasmuch as in Cyprus, at the time of the Council of Ephesus, there were Christian Bishops discharging their spiritual functions; whereas, when Augustin landed in England, the greater part of it had fallen into heathenism, and without him, it is alleged, there would have been no Church in this country; and did not Pope Gregory, therefore, it is asked, obtain a patriarchal jurisdiction over England by giving it what is called the *grace of Holy Orders?*

A. The *grace* of Holy Orders, like all other spiritual grace, is not to be dispensed for private advantage; "*gratia* vocatur, quia *gratis* datur [1];" "*gratis* accepistis, *gratis* date." It might also first be inquired, whether Augustin used all proper means to enter into [2] and maintain communion with the existing *British* Bishops. Next it may be asked, whether, on the ground of a mere ceremonial difference concerning the time of observing Easter, and one or two similar matters, such as had *not* interrupted the communion of S. Polycarp [3] and Pope Anicetus, and concerning which S. Irenæus [4], in his letter to Pope Victor, had left both a warning and a rule, he ought to have stood apart from them, and required a change of their customs as a condition of communion with Rome?

Lastly, it may well be doubted whether, because the British Bishops were unwilling to renounce obedience to their own Primate [5], and to

Luke xix. 45.
Acts viii. 18—20.

PART II. swear allegiance to the Bishop of Rome, the rights of these native Bishops and of the British Church ought to have been set at nought by him, and sacrificed.

But even *on the supposition* that Augustin proceeded *regularly* in all this, yet the ordination of Augustin, and of those who were ordained by him, gave to the Bishop of Rome no patriarchal jurisdiction over the country in which Augustin was *received*.

---

[1] S. AUG. Tract. iii. in S. Joan.
S. AMBROSE in S. Luc. xix. p. 40.
[2] Augustin's conference with the British Bishops did not take place till near the *close* of his mission and life: and this, Bede says, was *adjutorio Regis Ethelberti*, lib. ii. p. 1.—Sir H. SPELMAN, in WILKINS' Concilia, i. p. 26, animadverts on the proceedings of Augustin in his intercourse with the British Bishops.

MASON, F. Vindiciæ Eccl. Angl. lib. ii. cap. 5 says, Augustinus ipse, nisi superbo et elato fuisset animo, rogásset ut suam in prædicando Anglis operam Britanni unà collocarent, non etiam ut sibi et domino suo obtemperarent: and again, Quicquid in Augustino resplendet boni, illud amplectimur atque laudamus; quicquid vero in eo reperitur mali, in ipsâ radice flaccescat. Sanctum paganos convertendi desiderium, et pia in Principem desideria, aureis literis inscribi merentur; at, ut cœremoniarum quas intulit redundantiam et nimiam fimbriæ pontificiæ dilationem silentio præteream, negari non potest quin erga Britannos superbè se gesserit atque superciliosè.

[3] EVANS, R. W., Biography of the Early Church, 1837, p. 81. The Churches of Asia differed from the Western Churches with respect to the day of termination of the fast which introduced the festival of Easter. Each side claimed apostolical authority for their usage—the former that of St. John, the latter of their predecessors. This difference, which, within forty years after, very nearly produced a schism in the Church (under Pope Victor), broke no bonds of love between Polycarp and the Roman Bishop Anicetus, the heads of the two parties at this day. So far from it, they partook together of the body and blood of the Lord. In this rite, too, Anicetus showed his deep sense of the character and services of his illustrious guest, by conceding to him, in his own Church, the post of consecrating the elements of the Eucharist. Here was indeed a proof of spiritual unity. See USSHER, Brit. Eccl.

Ant. p. 925, and GIESELER's History, § 126, and KING's Primer of Irish Church, B. ii. c. 6, p. 190, concerning the controversy with regard to Easter and the tonsure, between S. Augustin and the British Bishops.

⁴ EVANS, p. 263. S. Irenæus stepped forward to check Victor's violent proceedings, and the successor of Anicetus was obliged to bear a rebuke from the successor of Polycarp. Nor did Irenæus address Victor only, but also the rest of the Bishops on the same side as Victor himself had done: on this Victor was obliged to retire from his bold position.

⁵ See above, note ³ to the last question.

MASON, Vindiciæ Eccl. Anglic. ii. p. 5. Ne Augustini jugo Britanni colla sua subderent, causa erat justissima; ne scilicet Archiepiscopi Menevensis auctoritatem minuerent, quod per Canonem Nicænum, (Canon vi.) quo cautum est ut suis privilegia serventur Ecclesiis, non licuit.

Q. You say that the ordination of S. Augustin gave the Bishop of Rome no jurisdiction over England; explain the grounds on which this assertion rests.

A. It is one thing to give a *power*, and another thing to give the *privileges*, which may accrue, by the will of a *third independent* party, to the recipient of that power. Gregory *had*, indeed, the power to *ordain* Augustin a Bishop, and so to give him the *power* of ordaining others, (though, be it remembered, Augustin was not consecrated by Gregory at Rome, but by the Archbishop of Arles, in Gaul¹,) but he had no power to *place* Augustin at Canterbury as *Metropolitan* and *Patriarch* of England, and to give him Jurisdiction as such over the Bishops and Clergy of England.

¹ BEDE, Hist. i. p. 27.

Q. To whom, then, did this power of *placing* belong?

A. In *Christian* kingdoms and states, the *placing* of Bishops as Diocesans, Metropolitans, and Patriarchs, depends on the permission of the

See below, Pt. iii. ch. vii.

PART II. governing power of the country[1]; thus even Pope Gregory himself, as he himself declares[2], could not have become Bishop of Rome and Metropolitan of the Suburbicarian Churches, without the consent of the Roman Emperor Maurice; and, again, in the words also of Gregory[3] himself, "Kings have from God supreme power over all their subjects."

It was no more in Pope Gregory's power to *place* Augustin at Canterbury as *Metropolitan* in England, than it was in King Ethelbert's to have *made* Augustin *a Bishop* of the Church. Ethelbert did not lose any of his royalties by becoming a Christian king, (for Christianity gives new rights, but does not take away old ones[4],) and Augustin became an English subject by being *received* and *placed* on English ground.

---

[1] BARROW, Pope's Supremacy, p. 288. It is notorious that most Princes in the West, in Germany, France, and England, did *invest* Bishops till the time of Gregory VII. See also BURKE, quoted in Eccl. Biog. i. p. 34.

[2] S. GREGORIUS, tom. ii. lib. i. Indictione ix. Epist. v. p. 492. Paris, 1705. Sed mihi hæc difficilia sunt, quia et valde onerosa: et quod mens voluntariè non recepit, congruè non disponit. *Ecce serenissimus Dominus Imperator fieri simiam leonem jussit.* Et quidem pro jussione illius *vocari* leo potest, *fieri* autem leo non potest. Unde necesse est, ut omnes culpas ac negligentias meas non mihi, sed suæ pietati deputet, qui virtutis *ministerium* infirmo *commisit*.

VITA S. GREGORII, Opera, Paris, 1705, ed. Benedict. lib. i. cap. vii. p. 216. Nonnullorum quoque mentem haud dubiè pulsabit, quod narrat laudatus scriptor, de petito et *expectato Imperatoris consensu, antequam Gregorius electus ordinaretur*. Neque verò Gregorius, qui sacrum *sibi ministerium ab Imperatore commissum agnoscit*, hunc morem usquam damnare visus est, aut improbasse.—Restituto in Occidente Imperio, Carolus Magnus ejusque posteri hoc jure confirmandi summi Pontificis, nullo repugnante, potiti sunt, ut ex Anastasio Ecclesiæ Romanæ Bibliothecario, et ex aliis passim non iniquis erga sedem Apostolicam scriptoribus constat.—So Gregory IV., A.D. 820, could not become Pope without the Emperor's consent.

Cp. Abp. De MARCA de Concordiâ, viii. p. 14; and JUS
CANONICUM, pp. 204-8, ed. Richter, Lips. 1839.

[3] S. GREGOR. Epist. iii. p. 65. Potestas super *omnes* homines Dominorum meorum (Imperatorum) pietati *cœlitus* data est. *Ego* indignus famulus vester.

[4] HOOKER, VIII. VI. 13.

Q. And does Augustin in fact also appear to have been *placed* in England by King Ethelbert, and *not* by the Bishop of Rome?

A. Yes, certainly. Ethelbert gave him permission[1] to land, and to preach in his realm. Even his place at *Canterbury* is a proof of the exercise of the royal power: for *Ethelbert* placed him at *Canterbury* (as being the civil *Metropolis* of his kingdom), and *not* at *London*[2], which *Gregory* had desired; and Ethelbert endowed the Cathedral Churches of Canterbury, London, and Rochester, which were the only Episcopal Sees founded or restored in England in the life of Augustin.

[1] BEDE, ii. p. 1. Ut Augustinus in urbe Regis sedem Episcopatûs *acceperit.*—i. p. 25. *Rex Edelberthus* in Cantio potentissimus, qui ad confinium usque Humbri fluminis maximi fines imperii tetenderat ... *dedit* eis mansionem in civitate Dorovernensi (i. e. *Canterbury*), quæ imperii sui totius erat metropolis. *Et* locum sedis in Doverniâ metropoli suâ *donavit.*—Similarly, ii. p. 3. Rex Edelberthus fecit in civitate Londiniâ Ecclesiam sancti Pauli Apostoli, in quâ *locum* sedis Episcopalis Mellitus et successores ejus haberent.—Similarly, at Rochester, *Rex Edelbertus* Ecclesiam B. Andreæ Apostoli fecit, qui etiam Episcopis utriusque hujus Ecclesiæ dona multa, sicut et Doroverniensis, *obtulit*, sed et *territoria* ac *possessiones* in usum eorum qui erant cum Episcopis adjecit. No other sees were founded in Augustin's lifetime but these three, viz., Canterbury, London, Rochester; and from a comparison of Bede's account with Gregory's letter (quoted in the next note) it will appear that the *placing* and *endowment* of the English Bishops was the work, not of Gregory, but of Ethelbert, acting in this respect independently of him, and indeed not consistently with his plans for the ordering of the *external* polity of the Church. Cp. Bp. STILLINGFLEET on the True Antiquity

PART II. of London, p. 550, and CODEX Diplomat. Anglo-Saxonum, p. i. sq.

Bp. BILSON on Christian Subjection, p. 57 They that came (with S. Austin from Gregory) would not enter this land, nor preach there without the king's express licence.

Archbp. BRAMHALL, i. p. 132. When Austin first arrived in England, he stayed in the Isle of Thanet until he knew the King's pleasure; and offered not to preach in Kent, until he had the king's licence for him and his followers to preach throughout his dominions. (Bed. Hist. i. pp. 25, 26.) So not only their *jurisdiction* but even the *exercise* of their pastoral function within that realm was by the king's leave and authority. See vol. ii. p. 133.

² S. GREGOR. lib. xi. p. 1163, ep. lxv. (to Augustin.) Per loca *singula duodecim Episcopos* ordines, qui tuæ ditioni subjaceant: quatenus *Londoniensis* civitatis Episcopus semper in posterum à Synodo propriâ debeat consecrari, atque honoris Pallium ab hâc sanctâ et apostolicâ, cui auctore Deo deservio, sedc percipiat, ad Eboracam verò civitatem te volumus Episcopum mittere, quem ipse judicaveris ordinandum; ita ut si eadem civitas cum finitimis locis verbum Dei receperit, ipse quoque *duodecim Episcopos* ordinet, et Metropolitani honore perfruatur: quia ei quoque, si vita comes fuerit, Pallium tribuere Domino favente disponimus, quem tamen tuæ Fraternitatis volumus dispositioni subjacere. Post obitum verò tuum ita Episcopis quos ordinaverit præsit, ut *Londoniensis* Episcopi nullo modo ditioni subjaceat. Sit verò inter *Londoniæ* et *Eboracæ* civitatis Episcopos in posterum honoris ista distinctio, ut ipse prior habeatur qui priùs fuerit ordinatus.

The reader will have observed, that it appears from the

---

* On which Alteserra, the Canonist of Toulouse, thus writes: Anglis recens conversis ad fidem, prædicante Augustino et sociis, Gregorius duas metropolitanas sedes constituit in Britanniâ, unam *Londini*, alteram *Eboraci:* ita ut per singulas metropoles ordinarentur duodecim episcopi: de quo Beda, lib. i. cap. 29. Sed postquam Cantuaria, *quæ erat caput regni Cantii et sedes regia*, ab Ethelberto Rege *concessa est Augustino*, qui sedem sibi et successoribus suis hic locavit, ibique diem obiit et sepultus est—, Metropolitica dignitas, quæ a Gregorio statuta fuerat Londini, Cantuariam translata est, ut patet ex Kenulfi *Regis* Merciorum ad Leon. III. Pontificem, quæ est apud Wilhelmum Malmesbur. de Regum Angliæ Gestis, lib. i. cap. 4.

above passage that, according to the plan there specified, there were to be *twenty-four* sees erected in *England;* and there already existed *eight sees in Wales* at this time; so that the number of Bishops in England and Wales, in A.D. 600, was to be *thirty-two*.

Mason de Ministerio, iv. c. xvi.

Q. Reserving, then, to the *British* Bishops their jurisdiction, within their own limits, we may consider Augustin and his successors as holding the place of the ancient *Metropolitans* and *Patriarchs* of England, and succeeding to the privileges secured to them by the Canons of the Church?

A. Yes[1], so far as was allowed by the governing power; and since it cannot be pleaded that any act of a General or Provincial Council canonically done with the Sovereign's consent, and received in will and deed by the Nation at large, has ever placed Britain in the *patriarchate* of *Rome*, in which it never was *before* the landing of Augustin, the Bishop of Rome's subsequent usurpation of the Metropolitan and Patriarchal rights of the English Primate, is an invasion of the Royal Prerogative, an aggression on the Rights and Liberties of the English People, and an infraction of the *Canons* of the *Universal Church*[2], and a violation of the precept of *Scripture* concerning the removal of a neighbour's landmark. Deut. xxvii. 17.

[1] Vita S. Augustini Archiepiscopi (vid. Lanfranci Opera, Venet. 1745, p. 329). Augustinus, transfretato æquore, (after his consecration at Arles,) accepto Apostolatu à Domino *primarium* Anglicæ genti retulit *Patriarchatum* et *Patriarchale* patrocinium.

[2] Not only of those of the Council of Ephesus, but of those which, like the 'Decreta Nicæna, Clericos et Episcopos suis Metropolitanis apertissimè commiserunt.' Syn. Afr. in Ep. ad P. Cœlestiu. Conc. Constant. can. 2. 4. 6. Chalced. c. 8. 17. Milev. c. 22.

Q. And therefore the Patriarch of Rome can-

PART II. not claim jurisdiction over the Patriarch of England on the alleged ground of the mission and ordination of S. Augustin or any other?

A. No; all Patriarchs are independent of each other (p. 103); and with respect to this plea of ordination, the Bishop of Rome might as well claim jurisdiction over the Patriarch of Alexandria, and over the Bishops and Clergy of his patriarchate, on the ground of St. Mark, the first Bishop of Alexandria, having been sent into Egypt by St. Peter, as over the Patriarch of England[1], (and such the Archbishop of Canterbury was acknowledged by Pope Urban II. to be,) and over his patriarchate, on the ground of the mission of Augustin by Gregory.

[1] Sir R. TWISDEN, p. 18. After the erection of Canterbury into an archbishopric, the Bishop of that see was held *quasi alterius orbis Papa*, as Urban II. styled him (Wil. Malmes. de Gestis Pont. Angl. i. Eadmer, ii. p. 52); and is, therefore, called frequently in our writers Princeps Episcoporum Angliæ, Pontifex summus, Patriarcha Primas, and his seat *Cathedra Patriarchatûs Anglorum*. See above, Abp. LAUD, chap. ii. p. 162.

Q. In speaking thus, you do not mean to disparage the labours of S. Gregory and S. Augustin in propagating Christianity in England?

A. By no means. In that holy and pious work of religion let Almighty God first be blessed and praised, for putting it into the hearts of its

1 Cor. iii. 6. various agents to do what they did; let a grateful remembrance be preserved of Gregory the Great for sending S. Augustin, and of S. Augustin for coming into England; of Queen[1] Bertha for assisting and encouraging, and of King Ethelbert for receiving, protecting, and maintaining him, and for establishing him and his followers, and their successors in this country, by the building and endowment of Cathedral

Churches. But we may not suppose that we can show our gratitude to Augustin, or to Gregory, and above all to Almighty God, by disparaging the prerogatives of Ethelbert and his successors, by surrendering the *liberty wherewith Christ has made us free*, and by doing injury to the rights of the lawful Sovereign Princes whom God has set over us, and of the Church which is our spiritual Mother in Jesus Christ.

CHAP. IV.

Gal. v. 1.

[1] Gregory himself, in his Epistles, compares King Ethelbert to Constantine, and Queen Bertha to Helena, on account of their pious munificence to the English Church. See Vita S. Augustini, l. c. pp. 330, 331.

CHAPTER IV.

CHURCH OF ENGLAND INDEPENDENT OF ROME.

Period between the Mission of S. Augustin and the Reformation.

Q. Even on the supposition that the Bishops of Rome *had* possessed a patriarchal jurisdiction in England before or during the papacy of Gregory, could they have had any such power after it?

A. No. As was before said, *that part* of England, which was converted by Augustin, and his companions, relapsed into Paganism a few years after his decease; and not only that part, but a very large portion of the whole country was Christianized in the seventh century, by *Irish*, and *Scottish*, and *Saxon* Missionaries, under AIDAN and Finan, of Iona and Lindisfarn, and other Bishops and Priests, (e. g. S. Chad and

PART II. his brother Cedd, and Diuma,) who were *independent* of *Rome*[1]. But, further, a year and a half after the death of Gregory, Boniface III. occupied the papal chair, and by his assumption of the anti-scriptural and anti-catholic title (condemned as such by Gregory his predecessor[2]) of *Universal Bishop*, by which he violated the Unity of the Church, he may even be thought to have forfeited[3] the name of *Patriarch;* as one of the greatest of the Popes[4] says, *Propria perdit, qui indebita concupiscit.*

[1] BEDE, iii. pp. 3 and 5, iii. pp. 22, 23. Archbp. USSHER, Religion of Anct. Irish, c. 10. FULLER, Ch. Hist. book ii. cent. vii., and see the authorities in HEATH's Brief Account, p. 18, who observes that "Aidan had little suspicion that a Bishop not in the Patriarchate of Rome *could* be considered a schismatic solely for preserving the independence of his character: he had not so read the decrees of Ephesus."
[2] See below, Part ii. chap. ix.
[3] Abp. BRAMHALL, i. pp. 260—263. F. MASON, Vind. Eccl. Angl. pp. 536—541.
[4] Pope LEO I. Epist. 54.

Q. But *after* this time did not the Bishops of Rome *in fact* exercise a patriarchal jurisdiction over the British Metropolitans, by sending them their *Pallium*, or archiepiscopal *pall*[1], at their consecration?

A. Unhappily after the age of Gregory there was a maxim in Romish state-policy[2], "*Da, ut habeas*," *Give*, in order that you may *have*. The Pall was at first a badge given by the *Emperors* to Patriarchs[3]; when it came to be *given* by Popes, it was for some time nothing but a *symbolum fraternitatis*—a mark of communion with Rome: it was no necessary part of the archiepiscopal dignity, and many archbishops never had it[4]. At length, however, it was *imposed* by Rome as essential to them, about A.D. 1235[5], and was *sold*[6] for vast sums of money.

¹ STANDA, Onomas. Eccles. p. 241, Rom. 1764. *Pallium* est fascia lanea candida, in modum circuli contexta, quæ super humeros imponitur, ex quo circulo alia similis fascia ante pectus, alia deorsum ex opposito pendet, quæ super humeros demittuntur.

² Sir ROGER TWISDEN's Vindication of the Church of England in point of Schism, 1675, p. 45.

³ HAMMOND's Works, ii. p. 97, folio, ed. 1684. The Pall was an honorary ornament, which the *Emperors* first gave to the Patriarchs, and the Patriarchs sent to Archbishops and Metropolitans, and was then far from being a sign of *subjection* to him that sends it. BRAMHALL, i. p. 193.

The following are the testimonies of *Romanists* concerning the Pallium :—Abp. De MARCA de Concordiâ, vi. c. 6. (p. 332.) *Pallium* antiquitùs fuit genus quoddam *imperatorii* indumenti, cujus usum *Imperatores* permisere Patriarchis, a quibus dein communicatum est cum Metropolitanis, sed non absque *Imperatorum consensu.*—P. 331. Optabant olim Pontifices (Romani), ut Metropolitani aliquod confirmationis genus a sede Apostolicâ acciperent. Verùm, quia *ubique receptum* erat *consecrationes fieri posse extra Italiam absque eorum consensu,* vim ei legi palam afferre noluerunt; sed Metropolitanos rei cujusdam *novæ* miraculo veluti obstupefecerunt, quæ in initio magnifica, paulatim tamen earum libertatem per cuniculos infregit, et synodorum provincialium auctoritatem pessumdedit. De *Pallii* usu loquor.

DUPIN de Antiq. Eccles. Discipl. i. § 12, p. 53. Succedente vero tempore, Pontifices Romani ordinandorum per universum occidentem Episcoporum potestatem non sine multâ contradictione sibi vindicavere, et omnium Metropolitanorum jura paulatim pessumdederunt.

Primum quidem Metropolitica ordinationum jura ad se trahere conati sunt per concessionem *pallii;* eò enim dabatur a pontificibus, ut possent plena auctoritate suæ provinciæ Episcopos ordinare: unde sequebatur hanc potestatem a Pontifice Metropolitanis simul cum pallio concedi. Hinc postea novo jure Metropolitanis interdictum est universis functionibus episcopalibus, donec pallium recepissent, *Juramentumque fidei introductum est.* See also the definition of the *Pallium* in Bp. GIBSON's Codex, p. 105, note.

⁴ TWISDEN, pp. 43, 44. After Paulinus, five in the catalogue of York are said expressly to have wanted it (the Pallium), yet are reputed both archbishops and saints.

⁵ TWISDEN, p. 47.   ⁶ TWISDEN, p. 45.

Q. Did not those Metropolitans then take an *Oath* of Canonical Obedience to the see of Rome?

PART II.   **A.** No. The Oath of Bishops at Consecration, to whomsoever it was taken, was anciently only a *Profession of the Christian Faith* [1]; and any other oath was *prohibited* by a Council regarded as General by Rome (A.D. 870) [1]. Nor was any *oath* imposed *with* the Pall before the year A.D. 1115; and the oath of Canonical obedience, when it *came* to be taken to the Pope, even under Gregory VII., Hildebrand (A.D. 1073—1085), obliged a Bishop to observe the *Regulas Sanctorum Patrum* [2], and not, as these words were afterwards *transformed*, to maintain the *Regalia Sancti Petri;* and the Oath *now* taken [3] to the Pope by Roman Catholic Bishops dates only from Pope Clement VIII. (A.D. 1592—1605.)

[1] CONCIL. CONSTANT. iv. tom. viii. p. 1131, Labbe. Visum est sanctæ huic et Universali-Synodo nequaquam id ex hoc a quopiam fieri, excepto eo quod, secundum formam et consuetudinem, pro *sincerâ fide* nostrâ, tempore *consecrationis Episcoporum* exigitur; quod enim *aliter* fit omninò non expedit, sed neque ad ædificationem Ecclesiæ pertinet. Quisquis ergo *ausus* fuerit solvere hanc definitionem nostram, aut expetierit aut paruerit expetentibus, *honore proprio decidat.*

The following are corroborating testimonies from *Romanist* writers:—Archbp. De MARCA de Concordiâ, vi c. 7. Res eo devenit, ut coacti sint Europæ Metropolitani scripto polliceri subjectionem et obedientiam Apostolicæ Sedi. *Novi* hujus juris repertor erat Bonifacius Moguntinus in Synodo ab eo celebratâ anno 742. Gregorius VII. formulam auxit quibusdam clausis, quæ illam obedientiæ sponsionem prorsus convertunt in *juramentum fidelitatis* quod *vassallus domino suo* præstare tenetur. Adeò autem *principum jura* violavit hæc formula, ut Gregorius *prohibuerit* ne quis Episcopus *homagium regibus* præstaret, quod a successoribus ejus Urbano II. et Paschali II. confirmatum est. Attamen Gregorius potuit animadvertere *canonem octavum octavæ synodi* (A.D. 870) prohibere ne Patriarchæ ab Episcopis aliam sponsionem exigerent quam eam quæ fieri consueverat, nimirum illos *veram fidem* servaturos.

Father WALSH, Defence of Church of Rome, sect. 25. In the beginning, there was no such Oath or any other, nor any promise of fidelity or obedience made by the Bishops to the Pope, but only a bare *profession of the common faith,* even such as he also made to them by his encyclical letters: and afterwards, when promises began, they were *only* of *canonical obedience* in general terms.

Dr. O'CONNOR, Columbanus 3. 159. Even those Bishops who were consecrated by the Pope himself, swore no other oath than that they would, to the best of their power, maintain the *Catholic religion* in their dioceses.

See also, DIGEST of the Evidence, &c. &c. concerning Ireland. London, 1826, Part ii. chap. i. p. 2, note *a*.

² These were the terms of the Oath even under Gregory VII. A.D. 1079. Concerning the *changes* in its terms, see BARROW, Pope's Supremacy, xiv. TWISDEN, p. 46. The present Oath may be seen in the Roman Pontifical, p. 62, ed. Rom. 1818.

Archbp. BRAMHALL, i. p. 148, and note. During the wars between the houses of York and Lancaster, the Popes sometimes invaded this undoubted right of our kings, *de facto*, not *de jure;* and tendered to the Bishops, at their investitures, another Oath, at first modest and innocent enough, that they should observe *Regulas Sanctorum Patrum;* but after they altered the oath, changing it into *Regalia Sancti Petri.* Bp. GIBSON, Codex, p. 117.

³ VAN ESPEN, Jus Ecclesiast. I. XV. ii. p. 8.

Q. But was not the Pall received by English Archbishops, and the Oath to maintain the *Regalia Sancti Petri* taken by English Bishops, from the beginning of the twelfth century?

A. Yes; that Oath was framed by Pope Paschalis II. (1099—1118), and was imposed by him, to the surprise[1] of Kings, Nobles, and Ecclesiastics, on Archbishops; and afterwards by Gregory IX. (1227—1241) on Bishops. But neither could the Pall be lawfully received from a foreign prelate under conditions of allegiance to him, nor an Oath of obedience taken to him by any subject *without* the consent of his Prince, and much *less* so *against* it; for it is essential to the goodness of an oath, that it should be *in possibilibus et licitis*[2], or, as the Holy Scripture expresses it, *in veritate, judicio et justitiâ.* And further, as the papal decretals[3] themselves declare, *non* valet *juramentum in præjudicium juris superioris*[4]. Hence, when an English Bishop had received the Pall, and taken the oath, King

Jer. iv. 2.
Num. xxx. 2—10.
1 Sam. xiv. 28. 45. xxv. 34.
Mark vi. 23.
Acts xxiii. 12.

PART II. William II. declared that he would banish him from England, if he violated his allegiance to the Crown under plea of compliance with the oath⁵.

¹ JUS CANON. Decret. Greg. IX. De Elect. c. 4. Significasti, (says Pope Paschalis to the Abp. of Palermo, which was even in the Roman Patriarchate; see above, p. 100,) *reges* et *regni majores admiratione* permotos, quod *pallium* tibi ab apocrisiariis nostris tali conditione oblatum fuerit, si *sacramentum* quod a *nobis* scriptum detulerant exhiberes. See also BARON. Anno 1102. MASON, Vind. Ecc. Angl. iv. 16, p. 539.

² Bp. ANDREWES on the Decalogue, p. 245,
S. HIERON. in Jerem. iv. 2. Animadvertendum quod jusjurandum hos habet comites, *Veritatem, Judicium* atque *Justitiam;* si ista defuerint, nequaquam erit juramentum, sed perjurium.

ART. XXXIX. A man may swear, when the magistrate requireth, in a cause of Faith and Charity, so it be done according to the Prophet's (Jerem. iv. 2) teaching, *in Justice, Judgment, and Truth.*

HOMILIES, p. 77, ed. 1822, Oxon. "Whosoever maketh any promise, binding himself thereunto by an oath, let him *foresee* that the thing he promiseth be good and honest, and not against the commandment of God, and that it be in his *own power* to perform it justly; and such promises must men keep evermore assuredly. But if a man at any time shall, either of ignorance or of malice, promise and swear to do any thing, which is either against the law of Almighty God, or not in his power to perform, let him take it for an unlawful and ungodly oath." Of an unlawful oath the same Homily declares in the case of *Herod,* "that as he took a wicked oath, so he more wickedly performed the same." Upon these determinations of the Church, the *Abjuration of the Solemn League and Covenant,* "as an unlawful oath, and imposed on the subjects of this realm against the known laws and liberties of this kingdom," was required in the Act of Uniformity, A.D. 1661, 13 and 14 Car. II. cap. 4.

³ DECRETAL. ii. xxiv. 4.

⁴ Compare Bp. SANDERSON'S Prælectiones de Juramenti Obligatione, ii. p. 31. Rei illicitæ Nulla Obligatio, p. 66. Juramentum ejus, qui sub alterius potestate est, absque illius consensu, nec *licitum* neque *obligatorium.* See also Prælect. vii. p. 140.

⁵ MATTH. PARIS in Guil. Ruf. The King said, neque Archiepiscopum neque Episcopum sui regni Papæ subesse. Si juramento suscepto promitteret (Anselmus) se neque Apostolorum limina visitaturum, nec Romauæ sedis audien-

tiam appellaturum, rebus suis frueretur. Si secus faciat, exilium perpetuum ei denunciat.

Q. But the Pall being received, and the Oath taken, did not the Popes acquire a Patriarchal right in England by *practice?*

A. No; the Pope both *quitted* and *forfeited* whatever Patriarchal jurisdiction he possessed any where, by his assumption of *Universal Supermacy* over the Church, and by his acts of tyranny, usurpation, exaction, and rebellion against Church-Canons and lawful Sovereigns [1]: and the *exercise* of such Patriarchal jurisdiction on his part was never acknowledged *in England*, but, on the contrary, was resisted *by protests* continually made by the Kings of England, by the Church in her Synods, and by the State in Parliament. Besides, as it rested not on any sound basis of right [2], but, on the contrary, was destructive of the fundamental rights of the Crown and of the Church, (and *nullum tempus occurrit Regi aut Ecclesiæ,*) and as Patriarchal authority depends on the consent of both, (see above, Pt. i. ch. xii., and below, p. 165,) it never could have acquired legal validity, for, as Pope Boniface the VIIIth [3] says, *Non firmatur tractu temporis quod de jure ab initio non subsistit* [4].

[1] Abp. BRAMHALL, i. p. 261.
[2] Abbé FLEURY, iv. Discours sur l'Histoire Ecclésiastique. See below, chap. vii.
[3] REGULÆ JURIS, xviii.
[4] Sir R. TWISDEN thus emphatically concludes his examination of this subject ... "I dare boldly say, that whoever will, without partiality, look back, will find that the reverence yielded by this Church of England to Rome, for more than 1000 years after Christ, was no other than the respect of love, not of duty."—p. 67.

Q. What evidence is there of opposition to the Papal encroachments?

A. Protests, such as have been mentioned, were made by Egfrid [1], King of Northumberland, and his successor King Alfred, on occasion of the

PART II. first great appeal to Rome; by King Edward the Confessor; by Henry the First, and succeeding sovereigns; and the same spirit which dictated these remonstrances, declared itself publicly and legislatively in the [2] *Constitutions of Clarendon*, A.D. 1164; and again, A.D. 1246; in the *Statute of Carlisle*, A.D. 1297; in the *Articles of the Clergy*, in the *Statutes of Provisors*, A.D. 1350, A.D. 1363, and A.D. 1389; of *Mortmain* and of *Præmunire*, A.D. 1391-2; and, finally, in the Statutes of Henry VIII., from A.D. 1531 to A.D. 1543, which, in the opinion of the soundest English lawyers, were only *declaratory* acts; that is, they were *not new* laws, but vindicated and enforced *the old* [3].

[1] TWISDEN, pp. 29—37. Egfrid, styled by Bede *piissimus et Deo dilectissimus*, imprisoned Wilfrid, Archbishop of York, with the advice of his Bishops, for appealing to Rome, about A.D. 680. No papal legate came into England between A.D. 595 and A.D. 787. BRAMHALL, i. pp. 37. 133. 136. 144. Bp. STILLINGFLEET, Eccles. Jurisd. pp. 87—91.

[2] Constitutions of Clarendon on the Controversy between Henry II. and Becket. BRAMHALL, i. pp. 136—143. ARTICULI CLERI, made at Lincoln 9 Edw. II. A.D. 1315.

Bp. GIBSON, Codex, p. 175. Election of dignities of the Church to be free. BRAMHALL, i. p. 146. Concerning the Protest in A.D. 1246, see BRAMHALL, i. p. 194.

STATUTES for the CLERGY, 14 and 18 Edw. III. A.D. 1340, 1344.

The STATUTES of PROVISORS, i. e. 'that the king and other lords shall present unto benefices of their own or their ancestors' foundation, and not the Bishop of Rome,' 25 Edw. III. A.D. 1350. GIBSON's Codex, p. 65, and 38 Edw. III. A.D. 1363. Ibid. p. 69, and 13 Rich. II. c. 2, A.D. 1389. Ibid. p. 71.

PRÆMUNIRE 'for suing in a foreign realm, or impeaching judgment given,' 27 Edw. III. c. 1; 'for purchasing of bulls from Rome; the Crown of England subject to none,' 16 Rich. II. c. 5, A.D. 1392, ibid. p. 73; against appeals to Rome, 25 Henry VIII. c. 19, ibid. p. 86.

For RESTRAINT of APPEALS to Rome, 'in all cases whatsoever, prohibited,' 24 Henry VIII. c. 12, A.D. 1532; ibid. p. 83; and 'to *restore* to the Crown *its ancient* jurisdiction,' ibid. p. 86; against payment of *annates* and first-fruits, 23 Henry VIII. p. 105. An act for taking away the burden of *Peter-pence*, and other papal exactions, 25 Henry VIII. c. 21, A.D. 1533; for taking away *dispensations*, 25 Henry VIII. c. 21, A.D. 1533, p. 87; against the Pope's *supremacy*, 26 Henry VIII. c. 1, A.D. 1534, ibid. p. 23; 35 Henry VIII. c. 3, A.D. 1513, 'for ratification of the *King's Majesty's style*,' ibid. p. 29.

Archbp. COURTENAY, Archbishop of Canterbury, (A.D. 1395,—Parl. Hist. vol. i. p. 219,) and Primate of all England, made protestation in open Parliament, "that the Pope ought not to excommunicate any Bishop, or intermeddle as to presentations to any ecclesiastical dignity recovered in the king's courts. That the said holy father ought not to make translations to any bishopric within the realm without the king's leave; for that this practice tended to the destruction of the Realm and Crown of England, which had always been free and subject to no earthly power, but to God only, as to regalities, and no other." See *ibidem*, p. 257. "The Crown of the kingdom of England, and the rights of the said Crown, and the kingdom itself, have in all time past been so free, that our Lord the Pope, nor any other without the kingdom, ought to concern himself about the same."

[3] As Lord Chief Justice COKE and others. See Abp. BRAMHALL, i. p. 151, and Bp. GIBSON's Codex, p. 42.

Q. Supposing that no such protests had been made, could the Bishop of Rome have *acquired* ecclesiastical jurisdiction in England, so that it should be his indefeasibly?

A. No, he could not. The Christian Sovereigns of England are the LORD's Vicegerents in that country; and it is their " Prerogative to rule all Estates and Degrees committed to their charge by God, whether they be Ecclesiastical or Temporal," and to see that all persons, ecclesiastical[1] and civil, do their duty; and Kings cannot execute this function, unless they have supreme authority in causes ecclesiastical. It is indisputable that *Patriarchal* jurisdiction is purely a matter of *human law*, and liable to be *altered*, according to the circumstances of countries and of times[2]. And as the Christian Emperors, with advice of their Synods, *transferred* Pontus and Asia to the Patriarchate of Constan-

PART II. tinople, which they had created; as in Britain the Primacy had been transferred[2], A.D. 516, from Caerleon to Llandaff, A.D. 512, thence in the reign of King Arthur, A.D. 516, to St. David's, and thence by Henry the First to Canterbury; so, even *if* England had ever been legally and canonically in the Patriarchate of Rome, *which it never was,* our Christian Princes, in a Church Synod, might have *transferred* their kingdom from it to some other Patriarchate[4]; and much more they ought to *maintain* it in its reasonable, undoubted, ancient, and primitive ecclesiastical relation both of right and duty to a Patriarch of their own Realm of England[5].

---

[1] XXXIX ARTICLES, Art. xxxvii. See below, Part iii. chapters ii. iii. iv. v., and above, Part i. ch. xii.

LEGES EDVARDI CONFESSORIS, c. xvii. Rex, quia Vicarius Summi REGIS est, ad hoc est constitutus, ut regnum terrenum et populum Domini et super omnia sanctam veneretur Ecclesiam Ejus et regat et ab injuriosis defendat.

Ibid. Debet Rex Sanctam Ecclesiam regni sui cum omni integritate et libertate juxta constitutiones Patrum et Praedecessorum servare, fovere, manu tenere, regere.

[2] Abp. BRAMHALL, i. p. 162, note; i. pp. 178. 260—264; ii. pp. 303—305; and above, Pt. i. ch. xii.

[3] MASON, Vind. Eccl. Angl. iv. p. 16. Qui *jure humano* niti non vult nobis patriarcha esse non potest; cum patriarchatus sit *juris humani.* See also BARROW, above, p. 104, and HAMMOND in following note, and Abp. BRAMHALL, i. pp. 260—264; ii. pp. 303—305.

[4] HAMMOND on Schism, i. p. 520. "It is and always hath been in the power of Christian Emperors and Princes, within their own dominions, to erect patriarchates, or to translate them from one city to another; and therefore" (even on the supposition that the Pope had acquired any title on the first planting of the Gospel here) "the Kings of England *may freely remove* that power from Rome to Canterbury, and subject all the Christians of this Island to the spiritual power of that Archbishop or Primate."—p. 522. And this power, vested in the Regal Power, *cannot* be taken away by foreign laws, nor be *alienated by prescription.*

[5] HAMMOND, Works, ii. pp. 28. 119. 126. 132. BRAM-

HALL, i. p. 178. The pledges of the SOVEREIGN to this effect may be seen in the English CORONATION OATH.

Q. But did not King Henry the First resign his right of Investiture of Bishops to the Pope? and did not King Stephen, and more fully King Henry the Second, concede the right of Appeal to Rome, and admit the Legatine Power claimed by that See? and did not King John give up to him the Supremacy of the Crown?

A. Whether they did or no, matters little[1]; for Kings have their Kingdoms from God to *rule*, and not to *give away;* and *nihil potest Rex nisi quod* jure *potest*. As Lord Chancellor Clarendon[2] says, "The King hath no power to release a single grain of the allegiance which is due to him as such." Therefore those acts, whatever they were, were of no validity whatsoever[3].

---

[1] Abp. BRAMHALL, i. p. 188. The answer of Sir Thomas More (himself a Romanist) is beyond all exception, that if either King Henry II. or King John had done such a thing, it was not worth a rush, nor signified any thing but the greediness of the Popes.

[2] See the authorities in Wordsworth's Eccl. Biog. i. pp. 23—25, ed. 1839. For the history, see INETT, ibid. p. 33, and pp. 134-7.

GERHARD de Magistratu Politico, vi. p. 513. Princeps non diminuere debet imperium sed augere. § 2, Prooem. Inst. Jur. Nec *potest Regalia in præjudicium successorum alienare.* HAMMOND, vol. ii. p. 133. The King *cannot* alienate his Regality.

[3] The following will show the *national* recorded opinion and judgment of this transaction: PARLIAMENTARY HISTORY, vol. i. p. 130. "His Majesty (King Edward III.) had lately received notice that the Pope, in consideration of the homage which John, king of England, had formerly paid to the see of Rome, intended by process to cite his Majesty to appear at his court at Avignon, to answer for his defaults, in not performing what the said king, his predecessor, had so undertaken for him and his heirs, kings of England. Whereupon the king required the advice of his parliament what course he had best take if any such process should come out against him. The Bishops, Lords,

PART II. and Commons, desired until the following day to give in their answer, when they declared as follows, 'That neither King John, nor any other king, *could* bring himself, his realm and people, under such subjection without their assent; and *if* it was done, it was without consent of parliament, and contrary to his Coronation Oath: that he was notoriously compelled to it by the necessity of his affairs and the iniquity of the times; wherefore the said Estates *enacted,* that in case the Pope should attempt any thing by process or any other way, to constrain the king and his subjects to perform what he says he lays claim to in this respect, they would *resist and withstand him to the utmost of their power.'*"

Q. But was not the English Reformation brought about by Henry VIII. to gratify his own evil passions; and was it not attended with corrupt and sacrilegious practices?

A. *We* might ask in reply, "Is not the Papal Supremacy due to the Emperor Phocas, a murderer[1]?" But, admitting, for argument's sake, all that has been said against King Henry VIII. by the adversaries of the Reformation; admitting also, that he was a leading agent in effecting it; still the workman is not the work. The Temple of Solomon was constructed with cedars of Lebanon hewn by workmen of heathen Tyre. Jehu did not please God; but his Reformation did. Nebuchadnezzar and Ahasuerus were idolatrous; but their Edicts for God's service were religious. The Temple in which our Lord was presented, and in which He preached and worshipped, had been repaired and restored by the impious and cruel Herod, who sought our Lord's life. And so with respect to the charge of sacrilege, we are not careful to defend the character and conduct of all those who had any part in the Reformation; but we bless God for His own work, and for many of the instruments He raised up for it, and for overruling and directing others to His own glory, and to the good of His Church[2].

1 Kings v. 6.
2 Chron. ii. 8.
2 Kings x. 30, 31.
Dan. iii. 1—29.
Esther ix. 29.

¹ Platina de Vitis Pontificum, in Bonifac. III., below, Chap. IV, chap. ix.
² Abp. Bramhall, i. p. 123.

Q. What is the conclusion from the arguments against the Pope's exercise of any Patriarchal jurisdiction in England?

A. In the words of a learned English Bishop¹, "By God's law, the Pope of Rome hath no such jurisdiction; for six hundred years after Christ *he had none;* for the last six hundred years, as looking to greater matters, (i. e. to be Universal Bishop,) he *would have none;* above or against the Prince he *can have none;* to the subversion of thé faith, or oppression of his brethren, he *ought² to have none;* therefore this land oweth him none."

¹ Bp. Bilson, True Difference between Christian Subjection and Unchristian Rebellion, pt. ii. p. 321. Mason, Vind. Eccl. Angl. p. 541.
² Oath of Queen's Sovereignty and Supremacy, to be taken by Bishops, Priests, and Deacons, in the Ordinal of the Church of England,—I do declare that no foreign Prince, Person, Prelate, State, or Potentate, hath, or *ought to have*, any Jurisdiction, Power, Superiority, Pre-eminence, or Authority, Ecclesiastical or Spiritual, within this realm. *So help me God.*
XXXIX Articles, Art. xxxvii. The Queen's Majesty hath the chief power in this realm of England, and other her dominions, unto whom the chief government of all estates in this realm, whether they be ecclesiastical or civil, in all causes doth appertain; and *is not, nor ought to be,* subject to *any foreign jurisdiction.*
The Bishop of *Rome* hath no jurisdiction in this realm of England.
Bp. Gardiner de Verâ Obedientiâ (in Brown, Fasciculus, pp. 812. 817). No foreign Bishop hath authority among us. . . . All sorts of people are agreed with us in this point, that *no manner* of persons bred or brought up in *England hath aught to do with Rome.*
Attorney and Solicitor Generals' (R. Gifford and J. S. Copley) Reply to Letter of Right Hon. George Canning, &c. We beg leave to state, that advisedly and wittingly to attribute by any speech, open deed, or act,

PART II. any manner of jurisdiction, &c. to the *see of Rome*, or to *any Bishop* of the same, within this realm, subjects a party for the first offence to the penalties of *præmunire*, &c.—See PHILLIMORE'S BURN'S Eccl. Law, iii. p. 145, ed. 1842.

CHAPTER V.

THE REFORMATION IN ENGLAND A REMOVAL OF WHAT WAS NEW, AND A RESTORATION OF WHAT WAS OLD.

Q. Is it not sometimes said that the Church of England, as she now exists, arose at the Reformation, and is therefore a *new* Church, not more than 300 years old? How then can she be united *by origin* with the Catholic Church?

A. The language of the Church of England, when she reformed herself, was similar to that of the Fathers at the Nicene Council, in A.D. 325, ΤΑ ΑΡΧΑΙΑ ΕΘΗ ΚΡΑΤΕΙΤΩ, "*Let the primitive customs prevail*[1]."

[1] HAMMOND contr. Blondell. in Prælim. c. xiv. f. 13 Ecclesia Anglicana hoc se universo orbi charactere dignoscendam, hoc æquæ posteritati æstimandam proponit, quod in controversiis fidei aut praxeos decernendis, illud firmum ratumque semper habuerit, et huic basi Reformationem Britannicam niti voluerit, ut SCRIPTURIS primæ, dein primorum sæculorum *episcopis, martyribus, scriptoribus, ecclesiasticis secundæ* deferantur.

The following are the testimonies of three eminently learned *foreigners*, Isaac CASAUBON, Hugo GROTIUS, and Dr. Hadrian SARAVIA, to the *restorative* character of the Reformation in ENGLAND.

CASAUBON ad Salmas. Epist. 837, p. 489, A.D. 1612. Quod si me conjectura non fallit, totius Reformationis pars integerrima est in ANGLIA, ubi cum studio Veritatis viget studium Antiquitatis. CASAUBON, Epist. ad Cardinal. Perron. p. 494. (See below, ch. v.) Parata est ECCLESIA ANGLICANA fidei suæ reddere rationem, et rebus ipsis evincere, auctoribus Reformationis hîc institutæ non fuisse propositum, *novam aliquam* Ecclesiam condere, ut imperiti et malevoli calumniantur; sed quæ erant collapsa, ad formam revocare quàm fieri posset optimam; optimam autem judicarunt nascenti Ecclesiæ ab Apostolis traditam, et proximis seculis usurpatam.

HUGO GROTIUS, Epist. ad Boetselaer. (Ep. 62, p. 21, ed. 1687.) Certum est mihi λειτουργίαν ANGLICANAM, item morem imponendi manus adolescentibus in memoriam Baptismi, auctoritatem *Episcoporum*, et Presbyteria ex solis Pastoribus composita, multaque alia ejusmodi satis congruere institutis *vetustioris Ecclesiæ*, a quibus in Galliâ et Belgio recessum negare non possumus. GROTIUS, Epist. ad Corvinum, Epist. p. 434. Qui illam optimam antiquitatem sequuntur ducem, iis non eveniet ut multùm sibi ipsis sint discolores. In ANGLIA vides quam bene processerit dogmatum noxiorum repurgatio; hâc maxime de causâ, quod qui id sanctissimum negotium procurandum suscepere, *nihil* admiserint *novi, nihil sui*, sed ad *meliora secula* intentam habuere oculorum aciem.

HADRIAN SARAVIA, cited by Dr. Puller, Moderation of the Church of England, chap. xvi. p. 427. Among others that have reformed their Churches, I have often (saith Saravia) admired the wisdom of those who restored the true worship of God to the Church of ENGLAND,—who so tempered themselves, that they cannot be reproved for having departed from the *ancient and primitive customs of the Church of God;* and that moderation they have used, that by their example they have invited others to reform, and deterred none.

See also the references to the next question.

Q. But you say she *reformed* herself; did she not thus become a *new* Church?

A. No. She reformed herself, because she loved what was *old*, and did *not* love what was *new*[1]. As was before shown, (Part ii. chapters i. and ii.) she was founded in the *Apostolic age;* at the Reformation, she *recovered* herself from the errors into which in course of time she had fallen; and she proceeded in all this gradually and moderately, lawfully[2] and wisely, with the joint deliberation and co-operation of her Universities, her Clergy, and the People of England in Parliament assembled; and finally, with

PART II. the ratification of the Crown. The *errors* of the English Church were *not the Church;* and in quitting those errors she did not quit the Church³, any more than a man *changes* his skin when he *cleanses* it, or *loses* his identity when he *recovers* from a disease. The English Church after the Reformation was as much the English Church, as Naaman was Naaman after he had washed in the river Jordan: indeed, *as " his flesh then came again,"* so was she *restored* to her *healthful* self at the Reformation. She might then have applied to herself the language of the Bishop of Carthage⁴, "In quo nutaverit Veritas, ad *Originem Dominicam* et *Evangelicam* et *Apostolicam Traditionem* revertamur, et *inde* surgat *actûs* nostri Ratio, unde et *Ordo* et *Origo* surrexit."

2 Kings v. 14.

¹ CASAUBON, Dedicat. Exerc. Baron. p. 128, ed. 1709. Quâ fronte hæc *novationis* criminatio in Reformationis auctores aut assertores hodie confertur, qui à centum fere jam annis hoc *unum* clamant, "Reddite populis Christianis *Primam Fidem!* Reddite primitivæ Ecclesiæ *ritus;* desinite *nuper* inventa pro credendis necessario, et quidem sub anathemate, gregibus magni Pastoris obtrudere.— Volumus scire, quæ sit vera fides: ea est, auctore Juda Apostolo, (v. 3,) quæ *semel* fuit tradita."

² Archbp. LAUD against Fisher, sect. 24. In the English Reformation, our *Princes* had their parts, and the *Clergy* theirs: and to these two principally the power and direction for Reformation belong. That our Princes had their parts is manifest, by their calling together of the Bishops and other of the Clergy to consider of what might seem worthy of Reformation. And the Clergy did their part: for being then called together by Regal Power, they met in the National Synod of sixty-two, and the Articles then agreed on were afterwards confirmed by acts of State and the Royal assent.—And it is more than clear, that if the Roman Church will neither reform nor suffer Reformation, it is lawful for any other particular Church to reform itself, so long as it doth it peaceably and orderly. See also Bp. PEARSON, Minor Works, ii. p. 233.

Archbp. WAKE, Letter to the learned Gallican, Dupin, in 1718, in Mosheim, Eccl. Hist. App. iii. No. v. Tandem defatigato regno dura necessitas sua jura tuendi oculos omnium aperuit. Proponitur quæstio *Episcopis* ac *Clero* in utriusque Provinciæ *Synodo* congregatis, an Episcopus Romanus in Sacris Scripturis habeat aliquam majorem jurisdictionem in regno Angliæ quam quivis alius externus Episcopus? In partem sanam, justam, veram utriusque concilii suffragia concurrere. Quod Episcopi cum suo Clero statuerant, etiam regni *Academiæ* calculo suo approbarunt, *Rex* cum *Parliamento* sancivit; adeoque tandem, quod unicè fieri poterat, sublata penitus potestas, quam nullæ leges, nulla jura, vel civilia vel ecclesiastica, intra debitos fines unquam poterant continere.

Siquam prærogativam Ecclesiæ concilia Sedis Imperialis Episcopo concesserint (etsi, cadente imperio, etiam ea prærogativa excidisse merito possit censeri); tamen quod ad me attinet, servatis semper Regnorum juribus, Ecclesiarum libertatibus, Episcoporum dignitate, modo in cæteris conveniatur, per me licet, suo fruatur qualicunque primatu. At in alias ecclesias dominari; episcopatum, cujus partem Christus unicuique episcopo *in solidum* reliquit, tantum non in solidum sibi soli vindicare; siquis ejus injustæ tyrannidi sese opposuerit, cœlum ac terram in illius perniciem commovere; hæc nec nos unquam ferre potuimus, nec vos debetis. In hoc pacis fundamento si inter nos semel conveniatur, in cæteris aut idem sentiemus omnes, aut facile alii aliis dissentiendi libertatem absque pacis jacturâ concedemus.

³ Bp. JEWELL, Apology, c. vi. in Christian Institutes, p. 352, and ibid. p. 312, and *note*. HOOKER, III. I. 10. As if we were of opinion that *Luther* did erect a *new* Church of CHRIST! Bp. HARSNETT, Parl. Hist. i. p. 1481. We fetch not our Reformation from Wickliffe, Huss, and Luther, of latter times, but from the first 400 years next after Christ. Bp. SANDERSON, Pref. to Sermons, § xv. Our godly forefathers had no purpose,—nor had they any warrant, to *set* up a *new Religion;* but to *reform* the *old*. Archbp. BRAMHALL, i. p. 119. We do not arrogate to ourselves a new Church, a new Religion, or new Holy Orders. Our Religion is the same as it was, our Church the same, our Holy Orders the same, differing from what they were only as a garden weeded from a garden unweeded. Bp. BULL, ii. p. 205. We maintain that our Church, and the Pastors thereof, did always acknowledge the same Rule of Faith, the same fundamental Articles of the Christian Religion, both *before* and *since* the *Reformation;* but with this difference, that we *then* professed the Rule of Faith, with the additional corruptions of the Church of Rome, but *now*, God be thanked, without them.

See also the valuable remarks of Bp. BULL, Apolog. pro Harmon. § 4, 5.

⁴ S. CYPRIAN, Ep. 74.

PART II.

Q. But since the English Church was, as you affirm, *restored at* the Reformation, can we say that she could have been properly called a *Church*, while she was infected with so many Papal corruptions as she was *before* the Reformation?

A. Yes; under Popery she was a Church, though an *erring* one. The Israelitish Church still remained a Church even under Ahab; the Jewish Church still existed under the Pharisees; the Scribes sat in Moses' seat, and were to be obeyed in all things lawful and indifferent. Jerusalem is called "the Holy City," even after the Death of Christ. The Christian Church existed still, when the "world groaned that it had become *Arian*[1]." The Ark of God was still the Ark of God, even when in the hands of the Philistines; and the vessels of the Temple were holy, even at Babylon. So the Church of England, though she had fallen from her former purity, was still a Church while under the Pope[2]. *If* she was *not a Church then*, we admit that she *is no Church now;* and we would then allow that she was *founded* at the Reformation, that is, that she was the work of *men*, and not of *God;* that she sprang from *earth*, and not from heaven; that she is a *new* Church, and therefore *no* Church. But no; we believe her to have been a *true* Church, and (*corruptions excepted*) the *same* Church *before* Papal times, *in* them, and *after* them.

Matt. xxiii. 2. xxvii. 53.

---

[1] S. HIERON. adv. Lucif. c. 7. Ingemuit totus Orbis, et Arianum se esse factum miratus est.

[2] Archbp. LAUD against Fisher, p. 105, ed. Oxf. 1839. A Church that is exceedingly corrupt is yet *a true* Church in verity of *essence*, but it is not a *right* Church: as a thief is a true *man* in the verity of essence, but is not a *right* man.

Archbp. BRAMHALL, ii. p. 38. "A Church may be said to be a *true* Church in two senses, *metaphysically* and *morally;* and every Church which hath the essentials of a

Church, how tainted soever it be in other things, is *meta-physically* a *true"* (though *not morally a right*) " Church." See also ii. pp. 26. 55.

HOOKER, V. LXVIII. 9. We earnestly advise them to consider their oversight, in suffering indignation at the faults of the Church of Rome to blind and withhold their judgments from seeing that which withal they should acknowledge, concerning so much nevertheless still due to the same Church, as to be held and reputed a part of the House of God, a limb of the Visible Church of Christ. See also HOOKER, Serm. ii. § 27, and his citations from Calvin, Mornay, Zanchius, &c., acknowledging the same truth.

Bp. SANDERSON, Preface to his Sermons, p. xviii. "The great *promoters* of the *Roman* interest among us, and betrayers of the Protestant cause, are they who, among other false principles, maintain that the Church of Rome is no true Church." The truth of the above assertion of Bp. Sanderson will appear on examination of the use which Bossuet makes of the allegation, that "Rome is no true Church," in his Variations, xv. pp. 26, 27. See also Dr. PULLER, Moderation of the Church of England, chap. xvii. p. 454. "CASAUBON had good reason to say, The denying the Church of Rome the *being* of a Church, hath been a great hindrance of Reformation: and I verily believe the opinion most Papists are kept in, that the religion of Protestants is *a new religion,* is not of little force to make them averse from it to this day."

Q. But can you explain further, how she could be a Church in *Papal times?*

A. Because as both the Israelites and Jews had the Law and the Prophets and a Priesthood in the worst times, and were so God's people[1], as we have seen, and were recognized by Him and by Christ as such; as the apostolical and apocalyptic Churches, although tainted with sundry corruptions, (see above, p. 9,) did not therefore cease to be Churches, and are called Churches in Holy Writ; so in Popish times, the Church of England had, by God's mercy, the *essentials of a Church,* though greatly marred and obscured. She had the Christian Sacraments; the Holy Scriptures; an Apostolic succession of Ministers; the Lord's Prayer; the

PART II. three Creeds, and the Ten Commandments[2], and she was therefore a Church.

[1] HOOKER, III. I. 8—10.
[2] The words of the Reformers on this important point, as for instance of MARTIN LUTHER, in S. Joann. c. xvi. and contra Anabaptistas, tom. iv. p. 409, are very observable. Nos fatemur sub Papatu plurimum esse boni Christiani, imo omne bonum Christianum, atque etiam *illinc ad nos advenisse;* quippe fatemur in Papatu veram esse Sacram Scripturam, verum Sacramentum Altaris, veras claves ad remissionem peccatorum, verum prædicandi officium, verum Catechismum, ut sunt Oratio Dominica, Decem Præcepta, Articuli Fidei: dico insuper sub Papatu veram Christianitatem imo verum Christianitatis nucleum esse.

See also CALVIN, Instit. iv. 11, 12. Hinc patet nos *minime negare* quin sub Romani quoque Pontificis tyrannide *Ecclesiæ* maneant. See also, concerning the *English Reformers*, NEAL, History of the Puritans, pt. i. ch. iv. "It was admitted by the Court-Reformers," (by which the writer means Abp. PARKER, Bps. JEWELL, GRINDAL, &c.,) "that the Church of Rome was a *true Church*, though corrupt in some points of doctrine and government; that all her ministrations were valid, and that the Pope was a true Bishop of Rome, though not [Supreme Head] of the Universal Church." And, finally, Rome is called a Church in the XXXIX ARTICLES, Art. xix., on which Dr. Hey,— "The Church of Rome is here allowed the *essence* of a true Church." IV. xix. 8, tom. ii. p. 373, ed. 1841, and in the CANONS (Canon 29) it is said, "So far was it from the purpose of the Church of England to forsake and reject the *Churches of Italy*," &c.

Q. You speak of the Church of England as existing *before* Popery, and as holding the *ancient faith;* but is she not called a *Protestant* Church, and is it then *consistent* to say, that she is *older* than Popery, when Protestantism is a *renunciation* of Popery; and how then can she be united by doctrine with the Catholic Church?

Above, Pt. ii. chap. i.

A. The Church of England, *as a Church*, is as old as Christianity. Her *Protestantism* is indeed comparatively recent, and *this* for a good reason, because the *Romish errors* and *corruptions*, against which she *protests*, are *recent:* but the fact is, that, as the *Universal* Church, for the maintenance of her Catholicity, was *protesting* at the first four General Councils; as she *protested* at Nicæa against the heresy of Arius, and at Constantinople against Macedonius; as she *protested* at Ephesus against Nestorius, and at Chalcedon against Eutyches; so the Church of *England became Protestant*[1] at the Reformation, in order that she might be more truly and purely *Catholic;* and, as far as Papal errors are concerned, if Rome will *become* truly *Catholic*, then, but not *till then*, the Church of England will cease to be *Protestant*.

[1] Archbp. LAUD, Conference with Fisher, sect. 21. The Protestants did not get their name by protesting against the *Church of* Rome, but by protesting (and that when nothing else would serve) against her *errors* and *superstitions.* Do you *remove them* from the Church of Rome, and our *Protestation* is *ended*, and the *separation* too.— Thus far Abp. LAUD; and it may be added, that *if* Rome would become *Catholic, Popery* would cease too; for, as GROTIUS observes, Epist. p. 5, Fermè verum est quod quidam magni nominis theologi prodiderunt, omnia quæ vera sunt, et quæ nos credimus, etiam à Papistis agnosci; sed addi insuper falsa alia, quorum quædam sunt talia ut cum primis illis additis veris nequeant consistere. Unde sequitur, redactâ Religione ad ea in quæ omnes Ecclesiæ omnium temporum consentiunt, *collabi Papismum*, ut qui conflatus sit ex *privatis opinionibus*. See also Bp. ANDREWES ad Card. Bellarmin. cap. i. p. 20.

BURKE, v. p. 180. We are Protestants, not from indifference, but *zeal*.

Q. But do not the *Thirty-nine Articles of Religion* contain an exposition of the doctrines of the Church of England, and were they not first drawn up, as they now stand, in the year 1562? and if so, where was the Faith of the English Church *before* that time? and if she had no Articles of Faith, how could she be a Church? and how therefore could she be united in doctrine with the Catholic Church?

A. Where, we might ask in reply, was the

PART II.

Jude 3.

1 Tim. vi. 3
—5. 20.
Art. vi.

Art. vi.
Art. viii.

Art. xxiv.

Gal. 1. 8, 9.

faith of the *Universal Church* of Christ before the year 325, when the Nicene Creed was promulgated?—And the answer would be—It was in the *Holy Scriptures* as interpreted by the Church from the beginning. So the Church of England holds neither more nor less than '*the Faith once (for all, ἅπαξ) delivered to the saints.*' The Thirty-nine Articles contain no *enactment* of any thing *new* in doctrine, but they are only a *declaration* of what is *old*. In them, the Church of *England* affirms that HOLY SCRIPTURE[1] "containeth *all things* necessary to salvation," and that by Holy Scripture she means "those Canonical books of whose authority was never any doubt in the *Church;*" in them she asserts that the three CREEDS[1], which have been received by the Catholic Church ever since they were framed, "ought thoroughly to be received and believed." She rejects the practice of public prayer in a tongue not understood by the people as "plainly repugnant to the Word of God, and the *custom of the primitive Church.*" Similarly, she appeals to "*Ancient Authors*," "*Ancient Canons*," "*Fathers*," and "*Decrees*" of the Church in her Ordinal[2], Homilies, and Canons. She is ready to be judged by the earliest and best ages of the Church[3]. *But*, on the contrary, the Church of *Rome*, on other occasions, and especially at the *Council of Trent* in the sixteenth century (A.D. 1545-63), in defiance of the prohibition of the Third General Council[4] (that of Ephesus), imposed *Twelve new Articles of faith*[5] (which she does not pretend to rest on Holy Scripture) to be believed, on pain of damnation, on *the authority* of this *Council*, which was uncanonical[6] in its convocation, illegal in its convention, and uncatholic in its constitution; and thus she claims to herself the power of publishing a *new Gospel;* in despite of St. Paul's anathema against those who do so; she *convicts herself* of obtruding on the world a *New Religion*, and of being, so far, a *New Church*.

CHAP. V.

---

[1] XXXIX ARTICLES, Art. vi. Art. viii. Art. xxiv.

[2] Preface to the Ordinal, A.D. 1552. See the passage below cited, chap. vi., also OFFICE for Consecration of Bishops; "Brother, forasmuch as the Holy Scripture and the *ancient Canons* command," &c.

HOMILIES *passim*. As a specimen, see the Homily against Peril of Idolatry, pt. ii. p. 178. "It shall be declared that this truth and doctrine ... was believed and taught of the *old holy Fathers*, and *most ancient learned Doctors*, and received *in the old Primitive Church*, which was *most uncorrupt and pure;* and this declaration shall be made out of the said holy Doctors' own writings, and out of the ancient Histories Ecclesiastical to the same belonging."

CANONS of 1603; in the 31st Canon, Forasmuch as the ancient Fathers of the Church, led by the example of the Apostles, appointed, &c., we following their holy and religious example, do constitute and decree, &c.—Canon 32, According to the judgment of the *ancient Fathers*, and the practice of the primitive Church, We do ordain, &c.—Canon 33, It hath been long since provided by many *decrees of ancient Fathers*, That, &c. According to which example we do ordain.—Canon 60, Forasmuch as it hath been a solemn, ancient, and laudable *custom in the Church* of God, *continued from the Apostles' time*, That, &c. We will and appoint, &c.

[3] Of the Scriptural, Primitive, and Catholic foundation of the doctrine of the Church of England, a very clear and emphatic statement was made by KING JAMES I., aided by Bishop ANDREWES and Isaac CASAUBON, to Cardinal PERRON, (Casauboni Epist. p. 493,) as follows (see above, p. 172, and below, chap. vii.). Beatus Chrysostomus, cum alibi, tum ex professo in Homiliâ, in Acta, xxxiii. tractans illam quæstionem, *Quo pacto vera Ecclesia inter plures societates, quæ hoc sibi nomen vindicant, possit discerni?* duo docet esse instrumenta judicandi, et quæstionis hujus decidendæ; primò quidem *Verbum Dei*, tum autem *antiquitatem doctrinæ*, non ab aliquo recentiore excogitatæ, sed ab ipso Ecclesiæ nascentis *principio semper* cognitæ. Hæc duo κριτήρια REX cum ECCLESIA ANGLICANA totâ voluntate amplectens pronuntiat eam demum sc doctrinam pro verâ simul et necessariâ ad salutem agnoscere, quæ e fonte Scripturæ Sacræ manans per consensum Ecclesiæ veteris, ceu per canalem, ad hæc tempora fuerit

PART II. derivata. Pag. 498. REX igitur et ECCLESIA ANGLICANA, *quatuor prima Concilia œcumenica* quum admittant, eo ipso satis declarant, veræ ac legitimæ Ecclesiæ tempus non includere se uno aut altero demum seculo; verùm multò longius producere, et Marciani Imperatoris, sub quo Chalcedonense concilium est celebratum, tempus complecti. . . . *Primitivæ Ecclesiæ* testimonio et pondere sublato, controversias hodiernas finem nunquam τὸ κατ' ἀνθρώπους accepturas, neque ullâ disputatione fore terminandas, ultro Serenissimus Rex agnoscit. Dogmata fidei, et quicquid ad salutem necessarium meretur credi, è *solâ Scripturâ sacrâ* peti debere, neque a quorumvis mortalium auctoritate pendere, sed è *Verbo Dei* duntaxat, quo suam Ipse nobis voluntatem per Spiritum Sanctum declaravit. *Patribus* enim et *Ecclesiæ veteri* Fidei Articulos *eliciendi* è Sacrâ Scripturâ, et *explicandi*, jus fuisse; *novos articulos comminiscendi* nullum jus fuisse. Isto posito fundamento, et τῇ θεοπνεύστῳ paginæ sua majestas manebit sarta, tecta; et piis Patribus quæ debetur reverentia præstabitur. Hoc voluisse omnes veteris Ecclesiæ Doctores facilè potest ex eorum scriptis demonstrari.

Cui jam nota non sunt verba aurea Basilii Magni, in libello de Fide? c. 2. Φανερὰ ἔκπτωσις πίστεως, ἢ ἀθετεῖν τι τῶν γεγραμμένων, ἢ ἐπεισάγειν τῶν μὴ γεγραμμένων.

[4] CONCIL. GENERAL. Labbe, iii. p. 689, A; see below, chap. vii. ὥρισεν ἡ ἁγία σύνοδος ἑτέραν πίστιν μηδενὶ ἐξεῖναι προσφέρειν ἢ συντιθέναι παρὰ τὴν ὁρισθεῖσαν παρὰ τῶν ἁγίων πατέρων τῶν ἐν τῇ Νικαίᾳ συναχθέντων σὺν ἁγίῳ πνεύματι—and it anathematizes all who dare to do so.

[5] Abp. LAUD, Conference, sect. 38. The Council of Trent having added *twelve new* articles to the *Creed* adds this statement; '*Hæc est vera Catholica Fides, extra quam nemo salvus esse potest.*' (Bulla Pii IV. super Formâ Juramenti Prof. Fid. in fine Conc. Tridentini.)

BARROW on the Pope's Supremacy, p. 290. The New Creed of Pius IV. (i. e. of the Council of Trent) containeth these novelties and heterodoxies, which follow;

1. Seven Sacraments. 2. Trent Doctrine of Justification and Original Sin. 3. Propitiatory Sacrifice of the Mass. 4. Transubstantiation. 5. Communicating under one kind. 6. Purgatory. 7. Invocation of Saints. 8. Veneration of Reliques. 9. Worship of Images. 10. The Roman Church to be the Mother and Mistress of all Churches. 11. Swearing obedience to the Pope. 12. Receiving the decrees of all Synods and of Trent.

The Oath declares, Hanc veram Catholicam Fidem, *extra quam nemo salvus esse potest*—voveo, spondeo et juro— A.D. 1564. This Oath is to be taken by all Romish Priests, lay and secular, and by all members of monastic orders, teachers, and graduates. Libri Symbol. Eccl. Cath. i. p. 98; ii. p. 317.

⁶ XXXIX ARTICLES, Art. xxi. General Councils may not be gathered together without the commandment and will of princes.

Abp. LAUD, Conference, sect. 27, 28, 29. The Council of Trent was *not legal* in the necessary conditions to be observed in a General Council—both through defect of legal *convocation* and of legal *presidency*, and therefore without synodical order; for there is no such thing as a General Council without *imperial* or *royal convocation* and *presidency*.—(It was *partial* in its constitution,) there being more *Italian* Bishops than of all Christendom besides; and in some sessions scarce forty or fifty Bishops present. See also BRAMHALL, i. pp. 258, 259, and note, and CASAUBON, Exerc. Baron. xv. p. 214.

Q. But may not a similar defence be made for these twelve articles of the *Council of Trent*, as was just now alleged in behalf of the *Thirty-nine Articles?* May it not be said that *they also* were only *declaratory*, and that, though first *enounced* at that Council, they had been *believed* by the Catholic Church from the beginning?

A. *Some* Romanists say this. But it is written in Scripture, that "the *Holy Scriptures* are 2 Tim. iii. *the things* that are able (τὰ δυνάμενα) to make 15. men wise unto salvation;" that, "if any man 1 Pet. iv. 11. speak, let him speak as the Oracles of God," and he that interpreteth (προφητεύων), "let him in- Rom. xii. 6. terpret according to the proportion of faith;" that "the faith was *once for all* (ἅπαξ) delivered Jude 3. to the saints;" that we are to hold fast the form of sound words, and that, "if any man, or even an Angel from heaven, preach any thing to us *besides* (παρ' ὃ) what the Apostles have delivered, and the Apostolic Churches have received, let him be anathema;" and it is incredible Gal. i. 9. that the Church should have *believed* from the beginning so many articles which it did not *publicly profess* till the Council of Trent; and no *proof* has ever been adduced of such a belief as is here affirmed; and *other* Romanists take refuge in the plea, that the Pope has power to '*develope*' doctrines as he may think fit.

And further, the Thirty-nine Articles not only do not enforce *any new* doctrine, but they affirm (Article xx.) that none *can be enforced* which is not found in Scripture; whereas the greater number of these articles of the Council of Trent *were first declared then:* and they, be it observed, are articles of *doctrine;* and are required *on oath, and* under solemn anathemas, to be believed as *necessary to salvation.* Now, a Communion which enforces articles *of faith* which it does not find in Scripture, and which it allows to have been first *declared* in the sixteenth century after Christ, and which it cannot show to have been held in the early ages of the Church, does, in that respect, what is very unwarrantable; and, also, it leaves the world in uncertainty as to what it may *hereafter declare* to be necessary to salvation; it convicts itself of having been very remiss in not having *before* declared doctrines which it asserts to be *necessary to salvation;* it removes the Faith from the rock on which Christ has set it, and places it on the shifting sand; it overthrows the authority of SCRIPTURE; it sets at defiance the Divine command, "To the Law and to the Testimony!" and it subjects itself to the anathema, "Adoro Scripturæ plenitudinem; si non est *scriptum*, timeant VÆ illud adjicientibus, aut detrahentibus destinatum[1]!"

Deut. iv. 2.
xii. 32.
xviii. 20.
Prov. xxx. 5, 6.
Isa. viii. 20.
Matt. xv. 9.
Rom. xv. 4.
Gal. i. 9.
iii. 15.
2 Tim. iii. 15.
1 Pet. iv. 11.
Rev. xxii. 18.

[1] On the Supremacy and Sufficiency of the HOLY SCRIPTURES, see TERTULLIAN c. Hermog. c. 22. de Virg. Vel. i. Regula Fidei una omninò est sola *immobilis*, et *irreformabilis.* The words of the ancient SCRIPTOR ANONYMUS ap. Euseb. H. E. v. 16. Routh, Rel. Sacræ, ii. p. 73, are very worthy of remark; δεδιὼς καὶ ἐξευλαβούμενος, μή τῃ δόξω τισὶν ἐπισυγγράφειν ἢ ἐπιδιατάττεσθαι τῷ τῆς τοῦ εὐαγγελίου Καινῆς Διαθήκης λόγῳ, ᾧ μήτε προσθεῖναι μήτ' ἀφελεῖν δυνατὸν τῷ

κατὰ τὸ Εὐαγγέλιον αὐτὸ πολιτεύεσθαι προῃρημένῳ. S. HIERON. in Aggeum, cap. i. Quæ absque auctoritate et testimoniis *Scripturarum*, quasi *Traditione* Apostolicâ sponte reperiunt atque confingunt, percutit gladius Dei.

S. ATHANAS. cont. Gentes, tom. i. p. 1, ed. Bened. αὐταρκεῖς μὲν γάρ εἰσιν αἱ ἅγιαι καὶ θεόπνευστοι γραφαὶ πρὸς τὴν τῆς ἀληθείας ἀπαγγελίαν.

S. ATHANAS. ex festali Epistola xxxix., tom. ii. p. 962. ταῦτα [βιβλία] πηγαὶ τοῦ σωτηρίου, ὥστε τὸν διψῶντα ἐμφορεῖσθαι τῶν ἐν τούτοις λογίων· ἐν τούτοις μόνον τὸ τῆς εὐσεβείας διδασκαλεῖον εὐαγγελίζεται· μηδεὶς τούτοις ἐπιβαλλέτω, μηδὲ τούτων ἀφαιρείσθω.

S. AUG. de doct. Chr. ii. p. 9. In iis, quæ apertè in Scripturâ posita sunt inveniuntur illa omnia quæ continent fidem moresque vivendi.

S. AUG. c. liter. Petil. iii. p. 6. Si angelus de cœlo vobis annuntiaverit *præterquam* (παρ' ὃ Galat. i. 8) quod in *Scripturis* Legalibus et Evangelicis accepistis, Anathema sit!

ORIGEN, Homil. v. in Levit. t. ii. p. 212. In hoc biduo puto duo Testamenta posse intelligi, in quibus liceat omne verbum quod ad Deum pertinet requiri et discuti, atque ex ipsis omnem rerum scientiam capi. Si quid autem superfuerit, quod non Divina Scriptura decernat, nullam aliam tertiam Scripturam debere ad auctoritatem scientiæ suscipi . . . . Sed igui tradamus quod superest, id est, Deo reservemus. Neque enim in præsenti vita Deus scire nos omnia voluit.

ORIGEN, Hom. i. in Jer. Quapropter necesse nobis est Scripturas sanctas in testimonium vocare: sensus quippe et enarrationes, sine his testibus, non habent fidem.

S. HIPPOLYT. adv. Noetum, ch. ix. Quemadmodum enim, si quis vellet sapientiam hujus sæculi exercere, non aliter hoc consequi poterit, nisi dogmata philosophorum legat; sic quicunque volumus pietatem in Deum exercere, non aliunde discemus quam ex Scripturis sacris.

HOOKER, II. v. 4. To urge any thing upon the Church requireuto thereunto that religious assent of Christian belief wherewith the words of the Holy Prophets are received, to urge any thing as part of that supernatural and celestially revealed truth, which God hath taught, and not to show it in *Scripture*, this did the *Ancient Fathers* evermore think *unlawful, impious, execrable*. See also Bp. SANDERSON, Prælect. iv. p. 19, and CASAUBON, Epist. Ded. Exerc. Baron. p. 16.

Q. But, although the Church of England declares that the Scriptures contain all things ne-

PART II. cessary to salvation, yet she is often said to admit the right of *private judgment* also, and may not therefore *novel expositions* of the Scriptures be publicly propounded with her permission by Ministers in her communion?

A. The term *private judgment* is often used very erroneously by those who do not consider its true meaning. Every one is bound to use his reason; but by *private judgment* we mean the act of a member or minister of the Church setting up his *own private opinions* in *opposition* to the *declared public sentence of the Church* [1].

The Church of England no where sanctions any *such* judgment, but, on the contrary, openly and strongly *condemns it*. Thus in her xxth Article, she asserts the power of the *Church* to decree rites and ceremonies, and that it has "authority in controversies of faith." And with respect to *discipline* also, she says in her xxxivth Article, "Whosoever through his *private judgment* willingly and purposely doth break the *traditions* of God's *Church*, which be not repugnant to God's Word, and be *ordained* and *approved by common Authority*, ought to be rebuked openly, that others may fear to do the like." She denies not indeed the liberty to any one to determine whether *he will engage to expound* according to her public formularies; but she admits *no* right in any one who *has made* such an engagement, to alter, weaken, and subvert, what he is by his own act pledged to maintain: on the contrary, she censures [2] all impugners of her doctrine and discipline; and no Minister of her communion may expound [3] at all, unless examined, approved, and licensed by the Bishop; and all Preachers are under the jurisdiction of their Ordinary [4]. She affirms (Art. viii.) that "the Three Creeds ought thoroughly to be received and believed;" and she has emphatically declared her reverence for Scripture, as expounded by Antiquity, in her Canon of 1571, concerning Preachers; In primis *videbunt Concionatores, nequid unquam doceant pro concione quod à populo religiosè teneri et credi velint, nisi quod consentaneum sit* doctrinæ Veteris aut Novi Testamenti, *quodque ex* illâ ipsâ doctrinâ Catholici Patres et veteres Episcopi collegerint⁵.

---

¹ HOOKER, Pref. vi. 6. When public consent of the whole hath established any thing, every man's judgment, being compared thereunto, is private.
² Canons of 1603. Canons 5, 6, 7, 9, 36.
³ Canons 48, 49.   ⁴ Canon 53.
⁵ Called by Bp. COSIN "the Golden Rule of the Church of England." On the Canon of Scripture, Table, ad finem. See also Bp. BEVERIDGE, vol. i. Serm. vi. p. 126, on this Canon. "So wisely hath our Church provided against novelties; insomuch that had this one rule been duly observed as it ought, there would have been no such thing as heresy or schism amongst us; but we should all have continued firm both to the doctrine and discipline of the Universal Church, and so should have 'held fast the form of sound words' according to the Apostle's counsel." And HUGO GROTIUS de Imperio Sum. Pot. circa Sacra, vi. 8. Non possum non laudare *præclarum* Angliæ Canonem, '*Imprimis,*' &c. See also Bp. PEARSON, Posthumous Works, i. 436.

Q. But if the Church of Rome be chargeable with error and corruption in doctrine and discipline, is not the Church of England tainted with error and corruption, since she has derived so much from that of Rome? and if she wishes to be a pure Church, ought she not to renounce and utterly destroy what she has so received?

A. Let it be allowed for argument's sake, that the Church of England *has* received from the Primitive Church many things *through* that of *Rome*, and not rather *through* the *medium* of the ancient *British*, *Irish*, and *Scotch* Churches; and some things *from* that of Rome herself. But the nature of the former, as, for example, the Sacraments, the Word of God, Holy Orders,

PART II. Episcopal Government, Prayers, Creeds, Places for Divine Worship, the observance of the Lord's Day and of Fasts and Festivals, has not been impaired by transmission; and if, because they had been abused [1], she had lost these, she would have lost herself; for the *abuse* of a thing does not take away its lawful *use*, but, on the contrary, "*Is confirmat usum, qui tollit abusum.*" The latter, such as certain Prayers and Ceremonies, were not derived from Romanists, *as such*, but from them as being therein reasonable and Christian men; and the Church of England, by retaining both, has prudently, charitably, and piously vindicated and restored God's things to God's service [2]: whereas, if she had permitted the accidental association of bad with good to deprive her of the good, and had chosen to *destroy*, instead of to *restore*, she would have been guilty of the folly and of the sin of promoting the cause of evil against Almighty God and against herself [3].

[1] CANONS of 1603. Canon xxx. See further below, Pt. iii. ch. ii., last question but one.

[2] HOOKER, IV. III.

[3] IV. VII. 6. When God did by His good Spirit put it into our hearts first to *reform ourselves*, (whence grew our separation,) and then by all good means to seek also their reformation, had we not only cut off their *corruptions*, but also estranged ourselves from them in things *indifferent*, who seeth not how prejudicial this might have been to so good a cause? See Bp. SANDERSON's Preface to his Sermons, § xv., and HOOKER, IV. VIII. IX. 2. IV. x. V. XII. 6. V. XVII. V. XXVIII.

CHAPTER VI.

UNINTERRUPTED SUCCESSION OF HOLY ORDERS IN THE CHURCH OF ENGLAND.

Q. I would now ask, whether the Church of England can stand the test applied by the ancient Fathers to try Christian communities, as to their soundness as branches of the Catholic Church?

A. Of what test do you speak?

Q. That before mentioned (Chapter viii.); viz. whether her Ministers derive their commission by succession from the Apostles[1].

A. Yes; the Church of England traces the Holy Orders of her Bishops and Presbyters in an unbroken line from the Apostles of Christ[2]; and she declares in her Ordinal, (approved in her Articles [Art. xxxvi.] and Canons [Canon xxxvi.], and subscribed by all her Ministers and by all who have taken Academic Degrees in her Universities of Oxford and Cambridge,) that "there have ever been Three Orders in Christ's Church, those of *Bishops*, *Priests*, and *Deacons*, from the Apostles' times;" and she recognizes none as having these orders, who have not received *Episcopal Ordination*[3]. (See above, Pt. i. ch. xi. Pt. ii. ch. i.)

---

[1] S. IREN. iv. 43, p. 343. Grabe. Oportet obedire ns, qui, cùm *successionem* habent *ab Apostolis*, cùm Episcopatûs successione charisma veritatis certum, secundum placitum Patris, acceperunt.

TERTULLIAN, Præscript. Heret. c. 31. Edant (*Hæretici*) origines Ecclesiarum suarum; evolvant ordinem Episcoporum suorum, ita *per successiones* ab initio decurrentem, ut primus ille Episcopus aliquem *ex Apostolis* vel Apostolicis viris habuerit auctorem et antecessorem.

S. CYPRIAN, Ep. 69. Non Episcopus computari potest, qui nemini succedens à se ipso ortus est; such an one S.

PART II. CORNELIUS calls ἐπίσκοπον ὥσπερ ἐκ μαγγάνου τινὸς εἰς μέσον ῥιφθέντα. Routh, Rel. Sacr. ii. p. 10.

S. AUGUST. in Joannis Evang. Tract. xxxvii. 6. Catholica fides veniens de doctrinâ *Apostolorum*, plantata in nobis, per seriem *successionis* accepta, sana ad posteros transmittenda, inter utrosque, id est, inter utrumque errorem, tenuit veritatem.

Abp. BRAMHALL, i. p. 112. Apostolical succession is the nerve and sinew of Apostolic Unity. See Bp. PEARSON, Minor Works, ii. 232.

² Bp. BEVERIDGE, Serm. i. vol. i. p. 23, on Matt. xxviii. 20. They certainly hazard their salvation at a strange rate, who separate themselves from such a Church as ours, wherein the *Apostolical succession, the root of all Christian communion,* hath been so entirely preserved, and the Word and Sacraments are so effectually administered; and all to go into such assemblies and meetings as can have no pretence to the great promise in my text. For it is manifest that this promise was made only to the Apostles, *and their successors,* to the end of the world. Whereas in the private meetings, where their teachers have no Apostolical or Episcopal imposition of hands, they have no ground to pretend to succeed the Apostles, nor, by consequence, any right to the Spirit which her Lord here promiseth.

³ BOOK OF COMMON PRAYER of the United Church of England and Ireland; Preface to Ordination Service. It is evident unto all men diligently reading the Holy Scripture and ancient authors, that from *the Apostles' time* there have been these *orders* of Ministers in Christ's Church, *Bishops, Priests, and Deacons.* Which offices were evermore had in such reverent estimation, that no man might presume to execute any of them, except he were first called, tried, examined, and known to have such qualities as are requisite for the same; and also by publick Prayer, with Imposition of Hands, were approved and admitted thereunto by lawful authority. And therefore, to the intent that these Orders might be continued and reverently used and esteemed in the *United Church of England and Ireland, no man shall be accounted* or taken to be a lawful Bishop, Priest, or Deacon in the United Church of England and Ireland, or suffered to execute any of the said functions, except he be called, tried, examined, and admitted thereunto, according *to the Form hereafter following,* or hath had formerly *Episcopal Consecration or Ordination.*—See also ACT OF UNIFORMITY, xiii. xiv.

Q. And this series was never interrupted ?

𝔄. No; never [1].

[1] Abp. BRAMHALL, ii. 203. We have set up no new Chairs, nor new Altars, nor new Successions, but have *continued* those which were from the beginning. MASON, F. Vindiciæ Eccles. ch. viii. xvii. See CASAUBON, below, Pt. ii. ch. vii.

The story of the Ordination of our first Bishop in Queen Elizabeth's reign at the Nag's Head Tavern in Cheapside thoroughly examined, and proved to be a late invented, inconsistent, self-contradictory, and absurd fable, &c. By THOMAS BROWNE, B.D., formerly Fellow of St. John's College, Cambridge, 1731, 8vo. COURAYER'S (P. F. Le) Dissertation sur la Validité des Ordinations des Anglois, 1733. Bp. BULL, ii. 204. "The story of the Nag's Head Ordination is so putid a fable, that the more learned and ingenuous Papists" (and Puritans, see NEAL, I. iv. p. 99) "are now ashamed to make use of it." PERCEVAL on Apostolical Succession, with an Appendix on the English Orders, 1841. See also the recent very able Preface to Abp. BRAMHALL's Works, vol. iii. Oxford, 1844, p. 4, and of the Validity of the Matter and Form of English Orders, see Bp. PEARSON's Minor Works, i. 296. PRIDEAUX's Tracts, 1716, pp. 72—144. BRAMHALL, i. 271; and on the *novelty* in the form of the *Romish* Orders, see BRAMHALL, ii. 36. 40.

The following are testimonies of *Romanists* to the validity of *English* Orders : - COLBERT, Bishop of Montpellier, in the Catechism published by his authority for the use of the Clergy of his Diocese, 1701, pt. i. sect. ii. ch. iii. § 7, p. 297, ed. 1795. *Demande.* Vous ne pouvez pas nier au moins que la *succession Apostolique* ne convienne à plusieurs Evêques de l'*Eglise* qu'on nomme *Anglicane*, même depuis qu'ils se sont séparés de la communion de l'Eglise Romaine ? *Réponse.* Je *conviens* qu'il peut y avoir quelques-uns de ces Evêques qui aient cette succession. For the testimony of BOSSUET on this subject, see Courayer, Preuves Justif. § 1 ; and PALMER on the Church, ii. 453 ; and the Preface by the late ARCHBISHOP of PARIS to the work of Cardinal de la Luzerne sur les Droits des Evêques :—L'Eglise Anglicane fut la seule des sectes Protestantes qui *conserva* son *Episcopat*. Paris, 1845; and Dr. LINGARD, Hist. of England, vol. vii. note i. says, "The Ceremony (of Archbishop Parker's Consecration) was performed, though with a little variation, according to the Ordinal of Edward VI. Two of the consecrators, Barlow and Hodgskins, had been ordained Bishops, according to the Roman Pontifical; the other two according to the Reformed Ordinal. (Wilk. Conc. iv. 198.) *Of this con-*

PART II. *secration, on the 17th of December (1559), there can be no doubt."*

Q. Did, then, the Romish Church give an Apostolic commission to those teachers who preached against herself?

A. No. It was not *Rome*, but it is CHRIST, and Christ alone, Who *gives the commission* to preach and to send preachers, and Who prescribes what is to be preached, viz. *His own Gospel*. The Church of Rome was only *one*[1] of the *channels through which* that commission *flowed*, and not the *Source from* which it *rose*.

[1] Archbp. BRAMHALL, ii. 94. Before Austin, there were in Britain British Bishops and Scottish Bishops, to which he added English Bishops. These three successions, in tract of time, came to be united into *one;* so as every English Bishop now derives his succession from British, Scottish, and English Bishops.

Q. And this commission was not invalidated by the errors of those through whose hands it passed, so that the continuity of the Apostolic succession could thus have received any interruption?

A. No. The *divine office* must be distinguished from the *human officers*. The Grace of Holy Orders which was transmitted by them was not the Grace of men, but of Christ and of the Holy Spirit, and could not be impaired by any personal defects or demerits of the Ministers who transmitted it. In the communication of God's ordinances *non merita personarum consideranda sunt, sed officia sacerdotum*[1].

Num. xxiv. 2.
1 Sam. x. 11.
Matt. xxiii. 2, 3.
John xi. 49.
Acts i. 25.
1 Cor. iii. 7.

[1] See S. AMBROSE, Epist. i. ad Chromatium. S. OPTATUS, v. 4. *Sacramenta per se sancta sunt, non per homines.*

HOOKER V. LXXVII. 3. Much less is iteration necessary, which some have urged concerning the *re-ordination* of such as others in times more corrupt did consecrate before. Which error, already quelled by S. Jerome (in Dialog.

c. Luciferianos), doth not now require any further refutation.

GERHARD de Sacramentis, tom. iv. p. 233, and vi. 148, 149, where he cites passages from Martin Luther, resting his claim to the ministerial office on his *Episcopal Ordination* under the *Papacy* in 1507.

Bp. ANDREWES, vol. iii. p. 278, Sermon on the Sending of the Holy Ghost. Hath not the Church long since defined it positively, that the Baptism Peter gave was no better than that which Judas, and exemplified it that a seal of iron will give as perfect a stamp as one of gold? (Greg. Naz. Orat. de Baptism.) Semblably is it with these; they that by the word, the sacraments, the keys, are unto other the *conduits* of Grace, to make them fructify in all good works, may well so be, though themselves remain unfruitful, as do the *pipes* of *wood* or *lead*, that by transmitting the water make the garden bear both herbs and flowers, though themselves never bear any. (S. Aug. Tract. v. in S. Joann.) Sever the *office* from the *men*; leave the *men* to God, to whom they stand or fall; *let the ordinance of God stand fast*.

XXXIX ARTICLES, Art. xxvi. and BEVERIDGE and BROWNE on it: "On the unworthiness of the Ministers, which hinders not the effect" of Christ's sacraments ministered by them; and see above, Pt. ii. ch. v., and below, Pt. iii. ch. iii.

Q. But were not the Churches, in which those Teachers preached, built and endowed by *Roman Catholics*, many of whose religious opinions the Church of England has declared to be erroneous, and ought those Churches therefore to belong to *her?*

A. These Churches, by whomsoever they were built, were dedicated "DEO ET ECCLESIÆ;" and by Consecration they ceased to be the possessions of man, and became the property and the dwelling-places of the MOST HIGH [1]. Since then they do not belong to *man*, but *God*, and since God is TRUTH, therefore whatever doctrine and whatever worship is *true*, *may*, nay, *must*, be taught and offered therein. Moreover, to speak of the *intention* with which they were *founded*, they were built for *Christian* preaching and worship, and not for the promotion of *Popery, as*

John xiv. 6
xvii. 17.
1 Tim. ii. 7
1 John v. 6

PART II. *such;* much less for the promotion of Popery such as it *became* in the sixteenth century at the Council of Trent, and as it now *is.* Their founders built and endowed them for the maintenance of *truth;* and their endowments, though given, indeed, in some cases, to an *erring* Church, were *not* given to its *errors.* And further (as the Churches of the Donatists in Africa and their endowments were transferred to the Catholic Church by Christian Emperors in the fifth century, and this was done *legibus religiosis*[2], as S. Augustin calls them; so) when the whole body of the Church and State of England, Sovereign and People, Clergy and Laity, (doubts and questions having arisen concerning divers points of doctrine and discipline,) did, after consulting Reason, Scripture, and Antiquity, in a lawful and deliberate manner[3] consider and decide the question, *what is* Truth and what is Error, and so the plea of *ignorance* on these matters was taken away, it would have been inconsistent with the duty of Rulers and People to Almighty God, and injurious to the Founders of those Churches, and to the Nation at large, to have suffered Error mixed with Truth, and corrupting it in teaching and worship, to be perpetuated in them, instead of Truth alone. The Pantheon at Rome was once a heathen temple, built by Heathens, and dedicated to all the gods, and it is now a Christian Church; and the members of the Church of England might ask the Romanist, why sacrifices are not there offered to Jupiter, if he should inquire of them why saints are not invoked, and why images are not worshipped, in our Churches.

---

[1] Ecclesia (says the English Law, 2 Inst. 64) est domus mansionalis OMNIPOTENTIS DEI. Cp. HOOKER, V. XII. 3. The Dedication of Churches serveth to *surrender* up that right which otherwise their founders might have in them,

and to make GOD Himself their *Owner*. See also SOUTH, in Christian Institutes, iii. p. 429.

² S. AUGUSTIN, Epist. 50, ad Bonifac. Quicquid nomine Ecclesiarum partis *Donati* possidebatur, Christiani Imperatores *legibus religiosis* cum ipsis Ecclesiis ad *Catholicam* transire jusserunt.

SARAVIA de Sacrilegio, p. 88. In Reformatione Ecclesia fit casta conjux, et vero suo Christo reconciliatur: quare bona mariti tanquam uxor sibi vendicat legitima Ecclesia.

³ See above, ch. v. pp. 170—174. Of 9400 beneficed Clergy, only 243 (according to Neal, i. ch. iv.) or 199 (according to Bp. Burnet) did not conform to the Doctrine and Discipline of the Church of England as reformed in 1559.

Q. You have before spoken of the Church of England as *Protestant* (p. 176); is she not then liable to a charge of inconsistency and partiality in recognizing the Holy Orders of the Church of *Rome*, while she does not acknowledge those of such *Protestant Communities* as do not possess *Episcopal* Government; and does she not, in so doing, prefer Romanists to Protestants?

Preface to the Ordinal of the Church of England.

A. No. The Church of England does not prefer any *persons, as such*, to *any other persons*. But, as the baptism given by Judas was the baptism of Christ not less than that given by Peter or by John, and therefore the primitive Church¹ did *not re-baptize* those who had been baptized by Judas, but *did baptize* those who had been baptized by John the Baptist; and in so doing, did *not* prefer *Judas* to *John*, but preferred the baptism of *Christ*, though given by *Judas*, to the baptism of *John the Baptist*, though given by *John himself*; so the Church of England prefers the Holy Orders of *Christ*², by *whomsoever* they may be given, to a commission from *man*, whoever he may be. In this matter, therefore, she is resolved to "follow the perfection of them that like not her, rather than the defect of them whom she loves³."

Ecclus. xlii. 1.
James ii. 1.
Jude 16.

Acts xix. 5.

¹ S. AUGUST. in Joannis Evang. Tract. v. p. 18. Bap-

PART II. tismum Christi das, ideo non *post te* baptizatur. *post Joannem* (Baptistam) ideo baptizatum est, quia non *Christi* baptismum dabat, sed *suum*. Non ergo tu melior quàm Joannes: sed baptismus, qui per te datur, melior quàm Joannis. Ipse enim *Christi* est, iste autem Joannis. Et quod dabatur à Paulo, et quod dabatur à Petro, Christi erat: et si datum est à *Judâ*, Christi erat. Dedit Judas, et non baptizatum est *post Judam;* dedit Joannes, et baptizatum est post Joannem : quia si datus est à Judâ baptismus, Christi erat: qui autem à Joanne datus est, Joannis erat. Non Judam Joanni, sed baptismum *Christi*, etiam per *Judæ* manus datum, baptismo *Joannis* etiam per manus *Joannis* dato rectè præponimus.

² See above, p. 149.
³ HOOKER, V. XXVIII. 1.

Q. But it is asked, since a Church cannot exist without a *priesthood*¹, nor a priesthood without a *sacrifice*, can it be said that there is any sacrifice in the Church of England; and if not, has she a true priesthood, and is she a true Church?

A. We must first understand clearly what is meant by the word *Sacrifice*. A true sacrifice (says S. Augustin²) is every act which is performed in order that we may hold fast to God, and is referred to Him as our sovereign good, in whom we may enjoy true felicity.

Heb. x

The Church of England has *all* the sacrifice which the Catholic Church has, and she dares not have more. In her Office for the Holy Communion she has a sacrificium *primitivum*, i. e. a sacrifice in which she offers "alms and oblations,"

Phil. iv. 18.
Heb. xiii. 16.

primitiæ, or *first-fruits*, of His own gifts³, to God, as the Creator and Giver of all; she has a sacrificium *eucharisticum*, i. e. a "sacrifice of praise and thanksgiving;" she has a sacrificium

Ps. cxvi. 12.
1 Cor. vi. 20.
xi. 23—26.
Heb. xiii. 1.
Rom. xii. 15.
16.
1 Pet. ii. 5.

votivum, in which the communicant presents *himself*, his "soul and body, to be a reasonable sacrifice to God," and in which the Church offers herself, which is "Christ's mystical body," to God³; a sacrificium *commemorativum*, commemorative of the death and sacrifice of Christ⁴;

a sacrificium *repræsentativum*, which represents and pleads His meritorious sufferings to God; a sacrificium *impetrativum*, which implores the benefits of Christ's death from Him; and she has a sacrificium *applicativum*, which applies them to the worthy receiver. But she has *no* sacrificium *defectivum*, in which the cup is denied to the lay communicant; nor, on the other hand, has she a sacrificium *suppletivum*, to make up any supposed defects in the One great sacrifice offered once for all for the sins of the world, upon the cross, by Him Who "remaineth a Priest for ever after the order of Melchizedek[5]."

CHAP. VI.

John vi. 51 —56.

Heb. vii. 27. x. 12. 14.

Heb. vii. 15.

[1] S. HIERON. adv. Lucif. c. 8. Ecclesia non est quæ non habet *Sacerdotes*.

[2] S. AUGUST. de Civ. Dei x. p. 6. *Verum* Sacrificium est *omne* opus quod agitur ut sancta societate inhæreamus Deo, relatum scilicet ad Illum finem boni, quo veraciter beati esse possimus. Ibid. 5. Illud quod ab omnibus appellatur sacrificium *signum* est veri sacrificii.

[3] GRABE ad S. Iren. III. xxxii. Ante consecrationem, veluti *primitias* creaturarum, in recognitionem supremi Ejus super universa domini. pp. 323—328, and p. 396. "Hoc est" (says GROTIUS, Annot. in Cassand, Art. x. p. 620) "quod dicitur in Liturgiis, τὰ Σὰ ἐκ τῶν Σῶν."

[4] S. AUG. de Civ. Dei x. p. 6. In sacramento altaris, Ecclesia, in câ re quam offert, ipsa offertur. GROTIUS, iv. p. 620. Tertium sacrificium est quod facit Ecclesia *offerens corpus Christi, quod est Ipsa*, ut loquitur Augustinus. Offerunt enim fideles suum corpus et sanguinem Deo, parati, si res ita tulerit, pro Ejus gloriâ vitam profundere. Sic Abraham dicitur filium obtulisse defunctione cordis, ut explicat Salvianus.

[5] S. CHRYSOST. in Hebr. Hom. xvii. μᾶλλον ἀνάμνησιν ἐργαζόμεθα θυσίας. S. AUG. c. Faust. xx. c. 18. *Peracti* sacrificii *memoriam* celebrant. Archbp. LAUD against Fisher, p. 35. In the Eucharist we offer up to God three sacrifices; one by the priest only, that is the *commemorative* sacrifice of Christ's death, *represented* in bread broken and wine poured out; another by the priest and people jointly, and that is the sacrifice of *praise* and *thanksgiving* for all the benefits and graces we receive by the precious death of Christ; the third by every particular man for himself, and that is the sacrifice of every man's *body and soul* to serve Him in both all the rest of his life.

PART II. With respect to the true nature of "the Eucharistic Sacrifice," see also Bp. ANDREWES, v. p. 67, on Worshipping of Imaginations, p. 35, fol. 1641. Archbp. BRAMHALL, ii. p. 276. v. p. 221. Bp. VAN MILDERT's Preface to Waterland's Works, i. pp. 267—276, and WATERLAND, Works, vii. p. 349. viii. p. 161 (who regards the "unbloody sacrifice" as a sacrifice of the heart). GROTIUS in Cassand. Art. x. p. 620; and Bp. BULL's Answer to Bp. of Meaux, Queries, Sect. iii. vol. ii. pp. 251, 252; and NELSON's Life of Bp. Bull, pp. 414. 416.

CHAPTER VII.

THE CHURCH OF ROME IS GUILTY OF THE SCHISM BETWEEN HERSELF AND THE CHURCH OF ENGLAND.

Matt. v. 14. **Q.** IT is one of the marks of the true Church to be *always visible:* was then, it is asked, the Protestant Church of England visible before the Reformation? and if not, can it be a true Church?

A. Yes, (as has been before stated, chap. i.—vi.,) the Church of England has been *always* visible since the time of the Apostles. not indeed *as Protestant*, but as a branch of the Catholic Church. A man is a man, and a visible man, even when he is labouring under a sore disease. Job was visibly Job when he was covered with sores. So was the Church of England visible in the worst times. She was visible in her Churches, in her ordained ministry, and in her religious assemblies; she was visible in the Holy Sacraments, in the Holy Scriptures, in the Decalogue, in the Lord's Prayer, and in the Creeds, which she retained[1] even in the worst times; she was visible in the flames of her Martyrs, who suffered for the TRUTH.

[1] HOOKER, III. I. 8—10. See above, chap. v. pp. 175—195.

Q. But if the Church of England was still a Church in Papal times, was she not guilty of the *sin of schism* in separating herself from the Church of Rome?

A. Schism is a *voluntary* separation (Part i. p. 38). The Church of England did never *separate herself* voluntarily from *any* Christian Church[1], or make a division in the universal Church; she purified herself indeed from *Romish errors, usurpations,* and *corruptions;* but she did not sever herself from the Catholic Church, nor even from the *Church* of Rome, as far as that Church still retains any thing which belongs to Christ[2].

---

[1] The following is the language of the Church herself on this subject. CANONS, 1603. Canon xxx. *So far* was it from the purpose of the Church of England to *forsake and reject the Churches of Italy,* France, Spain, Germany, or any such like Churches, that it doth with reverence retain those ceremonies which do neither endamage the Church of God, nor offend the minds of sober men; and only departed from them in those particular points, wherein they were fallen from themselves in their ancient integrity, and from the Apostolical Churches which were their first founders.

HOOKER, III. I. 10. We hope that to *reform ourselves*, if at any time we have done amiss, is not to *sever* ourselves from the Church we were of before.

Archbp. BRAMHALL, ii. p. 39. We have not left the *Roman Church in essentials.*—We retain the same *Creed* to a *word*, and in the same *sense*, by which all the Primitive Fathers were saved, which they held to be so *sufficient*, that in a General Council (Council of Ephesus, A.D. 431, pt. ii. act. vi. cap. 7. Labbe, Concil. iii. p. 689, A.) they did forbid all persons, under pain of deposition to Bishops and Clerks, and anathematization to laymen, to compose or obtrude *any other* upon any persons converted from Paganism or Judaism. We retain the same *Sacraments* and *Discipline* which they retained; we derive our *Holy Orders* by lineal succession from them. It is not we who have forsaken the *essence* of the *modern* Roman Church by *subtraction,* but they who have forsaken the *ancient* Roman Church by *addition.* Can we not forsake their New Creed, unless we forsake their Old Faith? See above, p. 173.

[2] CASAUBONI Epistolæ, Roterodami, 1709, p. 483. Ec-

PART II. clesiam enim Anglicanam adeò non descivisse à fide veteris Ecclesiæ Catholicæ, quam veneratur et suspicit, ut ne à fide quidem *Romanæ* Ecclesiæ desciverit, *quatenus* illa cum vetere Catholicâ consentit. Si quæritur successio personarum, in promptu sunt nomina Episcoporum et series à primo uusquam interrupta. Si successio doctrinæ, agite, periculum facite. See above, chaps. iv. and vi., and below chap. viii., and Bp. BILSON, Perpet. Gov. c. 15.

Q. How can you further show this?

A. Even by the confession and practice of Popes and Romanists themselves. The doctrine and discipline of the Church of England is to be found in her Book of *Common Prayer*. Now the Popes of Rome, Paul the Fourth and Pius the Fourth, offered to confirm this [1] Book, if Queen Elizabeth would acknowledge the Pope's Supremacy; and Roman Catholics in these realms habitually conformed to the worship of the Church of England for the first ten years of Queen Elizabeth's reign [2], after which time they were prevented from doing so by the bull of Pius V. (dated Feb. 23, 1569), which excommunicated that sovereign [3].

[1] TWISDEN, p. 175. BRAMHALL, ii. p. 85, Lord CLARENDON, Religion and Policy, p. 381.

[2] CAMDEN, Annal. 1570. SANDERS de Schism. Angl. p. 292, ed. 1588. Bp. ANDREWES, Tortura Torti, pp. 130—132.

Archbp. BRAMHALL, i. p. 248. For divers years in Queen Elizabeth's reign there was no recusant known in England; but even they who were most addicted to Roman opinions yet frequented our Churches and public assemblies, and did join with us in the use of the same prayers and divine offices, without any scruple, till they were prohibited by a papal bull for the interest of the Roman court. Bp. TAYLOR, vii. pp. 289, 290. Bp. BULL, ii. p. 207. See authorities quoted in Christian Institutes, iv. p. 251; PHELAN's Church in Ireland, App. A. p. 215; and PALMER on the Church, i. p. 457.

[3] BULLARIUM ROMANUM, viii. p. 98.

Q. How was this separation from Romish errors occasioned?

CHAP. VII.

𝔄. *First*, through the unjust claims[1], usurpations, encroachments, and exactions of the Bishop of Rome with respect to *Investiture, Annates, Peter-pence, Papal Bulls, Appeals, &c.;* which claims rested on *forged* Papal Decretals[2] published by Dionysius Exiguus in the sixth century, and by Pseudo-Isidorus in the ninth century, and the Decretum of Gratian in the twelfth; and which were enforced with great rigour and rapacity, in defiance of reason, law, custom, and long and oft-repeated remonstrance[3]; and, *secondly*, through the principles of state-policy propounded by the See of Rome, which rendered resistance to its domination on the part of Princes and Governments necessary for their own preservation; *thirdly*, and mainly, because the *Church* of Rome presumed to impose, and still continues to impose, new and corrupt *doctrines*, as *necessary to salvation*, and as *terms* of Communion with herself[4].

[1] Sir R. TWISDEN, pp. 117. 134. 176. 179. Archbp. BRAMHALL, i. pp. 149—151. Bp. BULL, ii. p. 207. Bp. STILLINGFLEET on Eccles. Jurisdict. p. 52 (in Eccl. Cases, vol. ii.). PALMER on the Church, i. pp. 434—439.

[2] BUDDEI Isagoge, i. pp. 757. 759. 763. LABBE, Concil. i. p. 78. Abbé FLEURY, Discours IV. de l'Histoire Ecclésiastique, pp. 159. 290. GIESELER, Eccl. Hist. Div. ii. § 20. PUETTER, Historical Development of the Constitution of the German Empire—Dornford's Translation, i. p. 79. It had been customary for the learned to employ themselves in collecting the decrees of the ancient synods of the Church, and sometimes the letters of the Bishops of Rome. A certain *Dionysius Exiguus* had published such a collection at Rome about A.D. 526, from Pope Siricius, A.D. 385, to Pope Anastasius, A.D. 498. *Isidorus*, Bp. of Seville in Spain, who died A.D. 636, made a similar collection. An impostor about the middle of the ninth century made use of the name of Isidorus to promote the circulation of a collection he had fabricated, which he pretended contained the letters of Bishops of Rome from as far back as A.D. 93. The subjects of them tended chiefly to prove that the Bishop of Rome was the successor of the Apostle Peter, that the keys of Heaven were in his hands, and that the foundation of the Church rested on him; that all Arch-

PART II. bishops and Bishops were subject to the Pope, from whom they derived all the power they enjoyed; that it was his prerogative to excommunicate both kings and princes, and to declare them incapable of reigning. The decrees of councils were falsified; no less than fifty forged decrees were added to the Council of Nice, and the sense of other passages, in which the patriarchs of Alexandria and Constantinople were placed on an equality with the Bishop of Rome, was reversed by the insertion of a negative. The authors of this scheme contrived to disperse the collection, which was at last so universally received as genuine, that the greatest part of it was received into the *Papal Code, which is still the source of Roman Catholic Ecclesiastical law;* and whole nations and general Councils of the Church were unable to resist the consequences of the Collection of Isidorus, the spurious character of which was first exposed to the world by the divines who compiled a laborious work on Ecclesiastical History, called the Centuries of Magdeburgh, about the middle of the sixteenth century. The establishment of the Isidorian principles was reserved for a man who carried them even far beyond their original design. This was the object of Hildebrand, as counsellor of the Popes, till he ascended the pontific throne as Gregory VII. Concerning the formation of the CANON LAW, see note in WORDSWORTH's Eccl. Biog. i. p. 129, and Pref. to BURN's Eccl. Law.

[3] Bp. BILSON, Christian Subjection, pt. i. p. 105.
[4] See above, pp. 178—181; below, pp. 200—202.
Abp. BRAMHALL, ii. pp. 56. 199, 200.

Q. Mention some of these main principles of Romish State Policy.

A. The Bishop of Rome, in his public enactments [1], never yet revoked, claimed power to dethrone Kings, to dispose of their Kingdoms, to prohibit Ecclesiastics from taking Oaths of Allegiance, and to release all subjects from the obligation of such oaths to their lawful Sovereigns [2].

[1] The following are the statements of the PAPAL SEE concerning *its own powers;* they are all derived from the CANON LAW, approved and published by its authority (*jussu*). See the Bull of Pope GREGORY XIII. prefixed to the Canon Law.

The Bishop of Rome claims power to absolve subjects from their Oaths of Allegiance to Kings.

DECRETI ii. Pars. Causo xv. Qu. vi. Gratian. A fidelitatis juramento Romanus Pontifex nonnullos absolvit cùm aliquos à suâ dignitate deponit.

Oaths of Allegiance, if against the interest of the Church of Rome, are affirmed by her to be Perjuries.

Pope GREG. IX. Decret. lib. ii. Tit. xxiv. de jurejurando. INNOCENT III. ibid. Tit. xxvii. Circa A.D. 1204. Non juramenta sed *perjuria* potius sunt dicenda, quæ contra utilitatem Ecclesiasticam attentantur.

The Church of Rome affirms that oaths of Allegiance cannot be imposed on Roman Ecclesiastics.

Pope INNOCENT III. ibid. Tit. xxiv. Circa A.D. 1216. Nimis de jure divino quidam laici usurpare nituntur, cùm viros *Ecclesiasticos* ad præstandum sibi fidelitatis juramenta compellunt. Sacri concilii (Lateranensis) auctoritate prohibemus, ne tales Clerici personis secularibus præstare cogantur hujusmodi juramenta.

She says, that oaths of Allegiance, which are repugnant to the interests of the See of Rome, are not binding.

Pope HONORIUS III. ibid. Tit. xxiv. Princeps Antiochenus timens conspirationes aliquas fieri contra eum, à vobis juramentum extorsit, quòd contra ipsum non essetis. Interpretatione congruâ declaramus vos *juramento hujusmodi non teneri*, quin pro juribus et honoribus ipsius Ecclesiæ ac etiam *specialibus vestris* legitimè defendendis *contra* ipsum *principem* stare liberè valeatis.

The Bishop of Rome claims power to depose Kings even for private reasons, and to absolve soldiers from their oaths.

Pope GREG. III. A.D. 1080. ibid. Alius Romanus Pontifex, Zacharias scilicet, Regem Francorum non tam pro suis iniquitatibus quàm pro eo quod *tantæ potestati erat inutilis*, regno deposuit, omnesque Francigenas à juramento fidelitatis, quod illi fecerant, absolvit. Quod etiam *ex auctoritate frequenti* agit sancta Ecclesia, cùm milites absolvit à vinculo juramenti. See also Pope GREG. VII. apud Thom. Aquin., Secunda Secundæ, Qu. xii. Art. 2.

The Papal power claims to be paramount to the Royal.

Pope GREG. IX. Decret. lib. i. Tit. xxxiii. Pope INNOCENT III. A.D. 1198. Nosse debueras, quod fecit Deus duo magna luminaria in firmamento cœli. Ad firmamentum igitur cœli, hoc est universalis Ecclesiæ, fecit Deus duo magna luminaria, id est duas instituit dignitates, quæ sunt Pontificialis autoritas et Regalis potestas. Sed illa quæ præest diebus, id est spiritualibus, major est, quæ

PART II. verò carnalibus, minor; ut *quanta inter solem et lunam, tanta inter Pontifices et Reges,* differentia cognoscatur.

The Church of Rome affirms that subjection to the Pope is necessary to salvation.

Pope BONIFACE VIII. Extrav. Com. lib. i. Tit. viii. Circa an. 1302. (Bull *Unam Sanctam.*) *Uterque* gladius est in potestate Ecclesiæ, spiritalis scilicet gladius et materialis. De Ecclesiâ et Ecclesiasticâ potestate verificatur vaticinium Hieremiæ (Hier. i.), *Ecce constitui Te hodie super gentes et regna.* Est autem hæc autoritas non humana sed potius *divina,* ore divino Petro data, sibique suisque successoribus, in ipso quem confessus fuit, Petrâ firmata. *Porro subesse Romano Pontifici, omni humanæ creaturæ declaramus, dicimus, definimus, et pronuntiamus omninò esse de necessitate salutis.*

² The *secular* claims of the popedom are thus stated by Cardinal BELLARMIN de Pontifice Romano, v. c. 6. Pontifex, ut Pontifex, etsi non habet ullam merè temporalem potestatem, tamen habet in ordine ad bonum spirituale, [of which, who is to be judge but himself?] *summam potestatem disponendi* de temporalibus rebus *omnium Christianorum.* Yet, vast as this claim is, it is to be remembered, that Pope SIXTUS V. placed the work of Bellarmin among the prohibited books on account of this reservation, "*in ordine ad spiritualia.*"

HOMILIES, p. 540, ed. 1822. The Bishop of Rome, being by the order of God's word none other than the Bishop of that Church and Diocese, did challenge not only to be Head of all the Church dispersed throughout all the world, but also to be Lord of all the kingdoms of the world, as is expressly set forth in *the book of his own canon laws.*

TOWNSON's Works, ed. Lond. 1810, vol. ii. p. 252. This is declared with great solemnity from the portico of St. Peter's Church, in the presence of a numerous assembly, at the Coronation of a Pope; when a Cardinal Deacon having taken the Mitre from his head, another places on it the Triple Crown, and says, *Accipe Tiaram tribus coronis ornatam, et scias te esse Patrem Principum et Regum, Rectorem orbis, in terrâ Vicarium Salvatoris nostri* Jesu Christi. See also C. LESLIE, Case Stated, p. 75.

Archbp. LAUD, Conference with Fisher, sect. 25. In a synod at Rome, about the year 1076, Pope Gregory the Seventh established certain brief conclusions, twenty-seven in number, upon which stands almost all the greatness of the papacy. These conclusions are called *Dictatus Papæ,* and they are reckoned up by BARONIUS in the year 1076, num. 31, 32, &c. But whether this dictatorship did now first invade the Church, I cannot certainly say.

The chief of those propositions are as follows:

'Quod solus Rom. pontifex jure dicatur *universalis*.'
'Quod solius Papæ pedes omnes Principes deosculentur.'
'Quod liceat illi Imperatores deponere.' 'Quod nulla Synodus absque præcepto ejus debet Generalis vocari.'
'Quod nullum Capitulum, nullusque Liber Canonicus habeatur absque illius authoritate.' 'Quod sententia illius à nullo debet retractari, et ipse omnium solus retractare potest.' 'Quod *Rom. Ecclesia nunquam erravit, nec* in perpetuum, Scripturâ testante, *errabit*.' 'Quod Rom. Pontifex, si canonicè fuerit ordinatus, meritis B. Petri indubitanter efficitur sanctus.' 'Quod à fidelitate iniquorum subditos potest absolvere.' See CASAUBON, Exc. Baron. xv. p. 373.

Q. But were these such grievances as concerned the *Church* of England as well as the *State?*

A. Yes, certainly, they concerned both; and any remonstrance against them was treated by the Bishop of Rome as resistance to his *spiritual* authority, and denounced by him *as heresy*: and, in addition to these, there were other grievances purely spiritual.

Q. What were these?

A. Sundry Articles of Doctrine promulgated by the Bishop of Rome.

Q. Specify them.

A. In the year A.D. 606, Pope Boniface the Third demanded that the Bishop of Rome should be recognized by Christendom as *Episcopus Episcoporum*, or *Universal Bishop;* A.D. 787, Pope Hadrian the First ordered that *images* should be *worshipped;* A.D. 1302, Pope Boniface the Eighth[1] decreed that subjection to the Pope was *necessary to salvation;* A.D. 1516, Leo the Tenth decreed that the Pope was superior *to all general councils*[2] *of the Church.*

[1] Pope BONIFACE VIII. Extravag. Commun. 1, viii. p. 1. Qui in Potestate Petri temporalem esse gladium negat, male verbum attendit Domini proferentis, 'Converte gladium tuum in vaginam.'—*Porro* subesse Romano Pontifici, *omni humanæ creaturæ* declaramus, dicimus, definimus, et pronuntiamus *omnino esse de necessitate salutis.* Dat. Late-

PART II. rani, Pont. Nost. Ao. viii. Decretal. p. 1160, ed. Lips. 1839 On which, says Cardinal BARONIUS, (Annal. anno 1303, § 14,) Hæc Bonifacius, cui *assentiuntur omnes* nisi qui dissidio ab Ecclesiâ excidit; and his constitution was affirmed by Pope LEO X. Concil. Lateran. Sess. ii. tom. xiv. p. 309, Labbe. Christus .. Petrum ejusque successores vicarios suos instituit, quibus ex libri Regum testimonio ita obedire necesse est, ut, qui non *obedierit, morte moriatur;* and the Bull in Cœnâ Domini (declared by JULIUS II. in 1511, to be of universal obligation) *anathematizes* all who appeal from a Pope to a General Council.

[2] CRAKANTHORPE, Defens. Eccl. Angl. pp. 20. 87. Abp. BRAMHALL, i. pp. 247. 249. 257. Bp. BULL, ii. pp. 248. 273.

Q. But although these tenets were novel and false, and were condemned by the Church in her Councils [1], and had been opposed even by Popes [1] of Rome, still, since a Church may err, and yet Pt. i. ch. v. continue a Church, as we have before seen, did Pt. ii ch. v. the maintenance of these errors render all intercourse with the Church of Rome impossible?

A. Not absolutely in themselves, and therefore the Church of England, though it could not communicate with that of Rome *in these errors* [2], and was *bound* to *reform* [3] *herself*, whatever Rome might do, yet she did not separate from Rome, *as far* as Rome retained *the truth;* ' *Nam,*' as Luther said, ' *Christum propter diabolum non deseri debere ;*' and, by allowing the baptism and holy orders of the Church of Rome, she *still* communicates with her, in a certain sense, and *as far* as Rome still communicates with Christ. But the Church of Rome showed no disposition to reform herself, or even to *tolerate communion* with *herself* on *Scriptural* terms; and was not satisfied with *propounding* these errors, but proceeded to *exact a belief* in them from all, as an indispensable *condition* of *communion with her*, and as *necessary to salvation :* and she persecuted, excommunicated, condemned, and anathematized as heretics, those who could not believe them; and this she continues to do to this day.

Therefore the Separation between the Church CHAP. VII of England and the Church of Rome was not caused by the Church of England, but by that of Rome, who, on these accounts, is so far from being, as she professes to be, a Centre of Spiritual Unity, that she is rather the main cause of the unhappy Schism which rends Christendom asunder[4].

[1] Image-worship was condemned in the Council of Frankfort; the Hildebrandine principles in the Councils of Mayence, Worms, and others; the Leonine at Constance and Basle; and they had been previously condemned by some of the Popes themselves: Pope GREGORY the Great, Epist. ii. p. 62, says, *Regia Potestas cœlitus* est Imperatori *super omnes* homines data.—Epist. vii. p. 3. Ab *imaginum* adoratione *prohibeat*, et zelum eorum laudet qui nihil *manufactum* adorare volunt.—In Ezechiel i. Hom. 9. In volumine sacro scripta sunt et continentur *omnia* quæ erudiunt. *His* opinion of the title *Episcopus Episcoporum* is quoted below, chap. ix.

[2] HOOKER, III. i. 10. With Rome we dare not communicate, concerning sundry her gross and grievous abominations; yet touching those main parts of Christian truth wherein they constantly still persist, we gladly acknowledge them to be of the family of Jesus Christ. BRAMHALL, ii. pp. 35. 39. 41.

[3] Archbp. LAUD, Conference, sect. 24. Was it not lawful for Judah to reform itself when Israel would not join? Sure it was, or else the prophet (Hos. iv. 15) deceives me that says, 'Though Israel transgress, yet let not Judah sin.' See also HOOKER, III. i. 10.

[4] Bp. SANDERSON, Serm. xi. p. 9. The *Bishops of Rome* by obtruding their own inventions both in faith and manners, and those inventions to be received under pain of damnation, became the *authors* and still are the *continuers* of the widest *schism* that ever was in the Church of Christ.

Q. When did the Church of Rome enforce these articles as terms of communion with herself?

A. On several occasions, but especially and emphatically at the illegal, uncatholic, and uncanonical Council of Trent[1], when she anathematized all who did not believe these and other new, unscriptural, and anti-scriptural² articles, *as necessary to salvation, on her authority.*

¹ BULLA PII IVti Concil. Trident. pp. 209, 210. Lips. 1837. For the true character of this council, see above, pp. 178—181.
² See above, Pt. ii. chap. v. pp. 178—181.

Q. This was a *general* denunciation; but has she not gone further than this in her conduct towards the Church of *England?*

A. Yes. In the year 1535, Pope Paul the Third excommunicated the supreme governor of the Church of England, Henry the Eighth¹, and forbad his subjects to obey him, commanded his nobles to rebel against him, and ordered all Bishops and Pastors to leave England, having first placed it under an Interdict. In 1558², Paul the Fourth excommunicated and *deprived of their kingdoms* ALL heretical princes, both *present and to come.* He sent in the same year a menacing message to Queen Elizabeth². In 1570³, Pius the Fifth (who was *canonized* as a Saint by the Church of Rome in the year 1712) issued a Bull denouncing and dethroning Queen Elizabeth, and commanding her subjects to rise in insurrection against her. This bull was renewed by Gregory XIII. in 1580, and Sixtus V. in 1587. Paul V. by his brief Oct. 1, 1606, and Urban VIII. by his bull dated May 30, 1626, forbad all English Roman Catholic subjects to take the oath of allegiance to their lawful Sovereign, as injurious to the *Catholic faith;* and in the year 1613 Paul V., and in 1671 Clement the Tenth, excommunicated and anathematized the members of all Protestant Churches in a bull expressly ratified and renewed by more than twenty Popes, and annually read every Maunday Thursday⁴ at Rome till the year 1740, and which is *still in full force*⁵.

And in the Oath to the Pope which all Roman Catholic Bishops now take on their consecration, is the following clause, "I will persecute and assail all heretics and schismatics" (i. e. *protestants*, &c.) "to the utmost of my power." "Hæreticos omnes, Schismaticos, et rebelles eidem Domino nostro (Papæ) vel successoribus, *pro posse, persequar et impugnabo*⁶."

Hence, with respect to the separation from Rome, the Church of England non *schisma fecit* sed *patitur*⁷; and her members may well say, with Bp. Jewell⁸, 'Non *tam discessimus, quàm ejecti sumus*;' and with King James the First, '*Non fugimus, sed fugamur*⁹.'

---

[1] Bullarium Romanum, vi. p. 129.
[2] Bullar. Rom. vi. p. 355.
[3] Bull. Rom. vii. p. 99.
[4] Thence called the BULL *in Cœnâ Domini*, Bull. Rom. v. p. 319. xxi. p. 95. For the history of this Bull, see FLEURY, Histoire Ecclésiastique, xxxiv. p. 532, an. 1568. Quelques-uns ont cru qu'elle commença à paroître en 1420. D'autres la font remonter à Clément V. et même au pontificat de Boniface VII., élu en 1224. Jules II. statua eu 1511 qu'elle obligeait partout.
See also, on this Bull, LESLIE, Case Stated, &c. Lond. 1714, Appendix, where the Bull is printed, as also in H. WARTON's Tracts; and see the full details given in LIBRI SYMBOLICI ECCL. CATH. ed. Steitwolf, Gott. 1838, p. xcix.
[5] Cardinal ERSKINE (Promotore della Fede, and Uditore del Papa) in his letter to Sir J. C. Hippisley, Aug. 1793, says, "This bull, though the formality of its publication is *now* omitted, is nevertheless implicitly in vigour *in all its extension*, and is likewise observed in all cases where there is no impediment to the exercise of the Pope's authority. It must therefore be looked upon as a *public declaration* to preserve his *rights*." See Report of Committee on Rom. Cath. Subjects, p. 340, 1816.
[6] This clause is *dispensed* with in *some countries*, where the *civil* Power will not allow it to be taken, but it stands in the ROMAN PONTIFICAL, p. 63, ed. Rom. 1818. See also MENDHAM's Life of Pius V. p. 281.
[7] Archbp. LAUD against Fisher, p. 109. I never said or thought that the Protestants made this rent. The cause of the schism is yours; for you thrust us from you, because we called for truth and redress of abuses. A schism must

PART II. needs be theirs whose the *cause* of it is. The woe is against him that *gives* the offence. (Matt. xviii. 7.) *The Protestants did not depart, for departure is voluntary.*

Archbp. LAUD, Sermons, 1651, p. 19. The Church of Rome challengeth us for breach of this peace in our separation from them: but we say, and justly, *the breach was theirs by their separation not only from disputable but from evident truth.* Nor are we fallers out of the *Church,* but they fallers off from *verity.* Let them return to primitive truth, and our quarrel is ended. See also HOOKER, III. i. 10. Bp. SANDERSON'S Last Will and Testament (in his Life by Isaac Walton): I am abundantly satisfied that the schism which the Papists lay to our charge is very justly chargeable upon themselves.

⁸ Bp. JEWELL, Apol. iv.

⁹ CASAUBONI Epist. p. 494. Postremò addit Rex (Jacobus Primus) magnum se quidem crimen judicare, defectionem ab Ecclesiâ; sed huic crimini affinem se esse, aut Ecclesiam suam, penitùs pernegat: *Non enim fugimus,* aiebat ejus Majestas, *sed fugamur.*

CHAPTER VIII.

THE CHURCH OF ENGLAND HAS NEVER SEPARATED FROM THE CATHOLIC CHURCH.

Q. You say that the Church of England did not separate herself from that of Rome; but did she not separate herself from the *Universal Church?* and (as S. Augustin says against the Donatist Schismatics) *Ecclesia quæ non communicat cum omnibus gentibus, non est Ecclesia*[1].

A. The Church of England never separated herself from *any* Catholic Church, much less from *the* Catholic Church: on the contrary, she *reformed* herself, in order to become again *more* truly[2] and soundly *Catholic,* both in doctrine and discipline; and so far from not *communicating* with the Catholic Church, she declares, that

Athanasian Creed.
Art. xx.

'except a man believe faithfully the Catholic faith, he cannot be saved:' she acknowledges the authority of the Catholic Church, she prays daily for its 'good estate:' she believes nothing that the Catholic Church has rejected, and rejects nothing that it believes: she is United in faith, hope, and charity, with every member of it, under Christ the Head of the Church[3]; and she admits the Baptism and Holy Orders of the Church of *Rome*, and thus communicates with her[4]: and as for the comparison with the *Donatists*, the example of the Donatists is closely imitated by Rome, which limits the Catholic Church exclusively to its own body, and[5] iterates the Sacrament of Baptism, and repeats Holy Orders, as the Donatists did; and separates herself from the Catholic Church, by making *new Articles of Faith*, thus *in fact excommunicating herself*, while in *words* she excommunicates others[6].

CHAP. VIII.

Above, p 3.

Above, p. 197.

Above, pp. 178—181.

---

[1] S. AUG. iii. p. 2511. ix. p. 549.

[2] Dr. HORN's Preface to his discourse at the Conference at Westminster Abbey, 1559; Strype, Annals, i. pp. 11—. 465; Cardwell's Conferences, p. 55; Bp. JEWELL, Apol. p. 170, 1591. Accessimus quantum maximè potuimus ad Ecclesiam Apostolorum . . . Nec tantum doctrinam nostram sed etiam precum publicarum formam ad illorum ritus direximus. See above, Pt. ii. ch. v.

On this subject see the important and authoritative statement made in the letter written, in the name of Henry VIII., by TUNSTALL, Bishop of Durham, to Cardinal Pole, July 13, 1536. (Bp. Burnet, Hist. of Reformation, vol. iii. pt. ii. Records, No. 52, p. 163, ed. Oxf. 1829) . . . . . Ye pre-suppose the King's grace to be *swerved* from the *unity* of Christ's Church: and that in taking upon him the title of supreme head of the Church of England, he intendeth *to separate his Church of England from the Unity of the whole body of Christendom*. . . . .

His full purpose and intent is, to see the laws of Almighty God purely and sincerely preached and taught, and Christ's faith, without blot, kept and observed in his realm; *and not to separate himself or his realm anywise from the unity of Christ's Catholic Church, but inviolably, at all times, to keep and observe the same;* and to *redeem* his Church of England out of all captivity of foreign powers heretofore *usurped* therein into the Christian state that all Churches of all realms were at the *beginning*, and

P

PART II. to abolish and clearly put away such *usurpations* as heretofore the Bishops of Rome have, by many undue means, increased to their great advantage. So that no man therein can justly find any fault at the King's so doinge, seeing he reduceth all things to that estate, that is comformable to those aunceint decrees of the Churche, which the Bishop of Rome (at his creation) solemnly doth profess to observe hymself. . . . .

By which (Councils) ye should have perceived that the Church of Rome had never of old such a monarchie, as of late it hath usurped. And if ye will say, that those places of the gospel, that ye do allege in your book, do prove it, then must ye grant also that the Council of Nice and others did erre, which ordained the contrary. And the Apostles also, in their Canons, did ordain, that all ordering of Priests, consecrating of Bishops, and all matters spirituall, shuld be finished within the Diocese, or at uttermost within the Province where the parties dwelle. . . . .

Now it is not like that the four first chief Councils General would have ordained so as they did, if the gospel, or the scripture, had been to the contrary. And where ye in your book much do stick to common custome of the Church, surely after Christ, above a thousand year, the custome was to the contrary, that now is used by the Bishop of Rome. . . . .

And to assure you of my mind what I do thinke; surely whosoever shall go about, by the primatie of Peter, which was in *preaching* the *word of God*, to establishe the *worldly authoritie* of the Bishop of Rome, which he now claimeth in diverse realms, in *worldly* things so perfect temporal, shall no more couple together than light and darkness. . .

Wherefore since the King's grace goeth about to reform his realm, and reduce the Church of England into that state, that both this realm and all others were in at *the beginning* of the faith, and many hundred years after; *if any prince or realm will not follow him, let them do as they list;* he doth nothing but stablisheth such laws as were in the beginning, and such as the Bishop of Rome professeth to observe. *Wherefore, neither the Bishop of Rome himself, nor any other prince, ought of reason to be miscontent therewith.*

[3] CASAUBONI Epistolæ, p. 491. Roterodami, 1709. Didicit Rex (he is speaking of King James I.) è lectione Sacræ Scripturæ (neque aliter Patres olim sentiebant ad unum omnes) veram et οὐσιώδη Ecclesiæ formam esse, ut audiant oves *Christi vocem* sui Pastoris, et ut *Sacramenta* administrentur ritè et legitimè, quomodo videlicet Apostoli præiverunt, et qui illos proximè sunt secuti. Quæ hâc ratione sunt institutæ Ecclesiæ, necesse est ipsas multiplici

communione inter se esse devinctas. *Uniuntur in capite Suo Christo*, qui est fons vitæ, in quo vivunt omnes, quos Pater elegit pretioso sanguine Ipsius redimendos, et vitâ æternâ gratis donandos. Uniuntur unitate *fidei et doctrinæ*, in iis utique capitibus, quæ sunt ad salutem necessaria; unica enim salutaris doctrina, unica in cœlos via. Uniuntur *conjunctione animorum et verâ charitate* charitatisque officiis, maximè autem precum mutuarum. Uniuntur denique *spei* ejusdem communione, et promissæ hæreditatis exspectatione.

⁴ Abp. BRAMHALL, ii. p. 35.

⁵ *Rebaptizare Catholicum, immanissimum scelus*, says S. Augustin, Ep. xxiii. The severe censures directed by the Church against *Iteration* of *Baptism*, and of *Holy Orders*, may be seen in BINGHAM, XII. v. XVI. 1. 4. XVII. v. 16. If it be alleged that the Iteration of Baptism specified in the text, is not, in all cases, strictly speaking, Iteration, as being in some cases accompanied with the use of the *conditional form*, '*Si non es baptizatus*,' &c., a reply may be brought to this allegation from the CATECHISMUS ROMANUS itself (ex Decreto Concil. Trid. Pii V P. M. jussu editus), P. ii. c. ii. Qu. p. 43. It will there be seen that the *conditional* form may *not* be used *except* in those cases where *diligent inquiry has* been made *whether* baptism has been administered or no,—Alexandri Papæ auctoritate in illis tantum permittitur, de quibus *re diligenter perquisitâ* dubium relinquitur, an Baptismum rite susceperint. Aliter verò *nunquam fas est*, etiam cum adjunctione (i. e. of the conditional form) Baptismum alicui administrare. Such are the words of the Trent Catechism. Now, by the Council of Trent, Sess. vii. de Bapt. iv. it is decreed, that if any one affirms "that *baptism* administered even by *heretics* in the name of the Trinity with the intention of doing what the Church does, is not true baptism, let him be anathema." And *yet* (as is affirmed in the evidence of Archbp. MAGEE, in Phelan's Digest, i. p. 291) "the Romanist Clergy in Ireland in *many cases* administer Baptism a *second* time to those who conform from Protestantism to their communion;" and the following precept is given to the Clergy of France by the Vicar-General of one of the Bishops, (Dieulin, Guide des Curés, Lyon, 1844, p. 624, 3rd edition,) Le Protestantisme de nos jours ayant dégénéré en pur rationalisme, au point que la plupart de ses ministres ne croient ni à la Trinité ni à la divinité de Jésus Christ, on est fondé à craindre que, mettant leurs doctrines en pratique, ils n'altèrent la forme du Sacrement, et ne baptisent au nom du Père, du Fils et du Saint-Esprit; *c'est pourquoi il est généralement prudent* de *réitérer* le Sacrement

de *baptême* aux hérétiques qui rentrent dans le sein de l'Eglise. The doctrine of the Council of Trent (Sess. vii.), that the *intention* of the Minister is of the *essence* of the Sacrament, appears to render its iteration necessary in the Church of Rome. See the perplexities of the Tridentine Divines on this subject, stated by Sarpi, lib. ii.

CASAUBON, ibid. p. 494, col. 2. Et vetus quidem Ecclesia, ut refractarios *Donatistas* ad suam communionem revocaret, etiam, commodis temporalibus Episcoporum resipiscentium, et aliorum quoque, admirabili charitate prospicere solita. *Romana* verò Ecclesia, ut gratiam cum Anglicanâ redintegraret, fulmina primò bullarum, deinde vim, modò apertam, modò occultam adhibuit; proditores nefarios suscepti hic parricidii manifestos gremio suo excepit, et nunc cùm maximè fovet; sententiam ex eâdem caussâ passos martyribus adscribit, et eorum innocentiam contra divina omnia humanaque jura quotidie propugnat. Ipse CARDINALIS BELLARMINUS nuper, ut REGEM serenissimum alliceret, istud miræ efficaciæ ad persuadendum argumentum adhibuit, '*Angliæ regnum ad Papam pertinere; et Regem Angliæ Romani Pontificis* etiam in *temporalibus* esse *subditum*, atque *feudatarium*.' Omitto alias et Regis et Ecclesiæ Anglicanæ, quà veteres, quà novas querelas, minimè hoc loco commemorandas. For a further parallel between Romanism and Donatism, see BRAMHALL, ii. p. 106.

⁶ FIRMILIAN (in S. Cyprian, Ep. p. 228), Bishop of Cæsarea in Cappadocia, to Pope Stephanus, when he had excommunicated the Asiatic and African Churches. Lites quantas parasti per Ecclesias mundi! Peccatum quàm magnum tibi exaggerâsti quando te à tot gregibus scidisti! Excidisti enim te ipsum. Noli te fallere. Siquidem ille est verè schismaticus, qui se à communione Ecclesiasticæ unitatis Apostatam fecerit.

Q. But can it be said that the Church of England communicates with the whole world, which was the test of a true Church, cited from S. Augustin? is *she* not an *isolated* Church? and is not such universal communion to be found in the Church of *Rome*, rather than in any other?

A. As was before stated, the Church of England communicates in *faith* and *prayers* with the whole world. If she does *not* perform all those *practical* offices of communion with other Churches, which one Church was enabled to discharge to another in the time of S. Augustin, we must bear in mind that the difficulties of *actual* communion are now much greater than at *that* period, when almost all Christendom was under one Imperial Government, and the members of European, Asiatic, and African Churches, were *fellow-citizens* as well as *fellow-Christians*, speaking one or two languages only; whereas now that the Roman Empire has been broken up, there are thirty different kingdoms and states in Europe alone, with nearly as many languages as countries[1].

Further, we must remember, that the most *Catholic* of all things is TRUTH[2]; and if the Church of England holds fast *the Truth*, she is united to the Catholic Church. "If we *walk* in the *light*, we have *fellowship* one with another."

We must also consider, that *true Catholic* communion is communion with the *past*, as well as with the *present*; and the Church of England communicates in doctrine, orders, and sacraments, with the Catholic Church from *the beginning*; and thus *she* communicates with the *primitive* and *apostolic* Church of *Rome*[3]; whereas the *present* Romish Church, by her corrupt and novel doctrines and practices, and by making those doctrines and practices to be terms of communion, has put herself out of communion with the *Truth*, has fallen away from the *Catholic Church*, and from *her former Catholic self*. She is in these respects a branch cut off from the *True Vine*; a limb severed from the mystical Body of our Blessed Lord and Saviour JESUS CHRIST, Who is "The WAY, The TRUTH, and The LIFE."

1 Tim. iii. 15.
Above, pp. 5, 6.
1 John i. 7.

John xv. 1—6.

John xiv. 6.

[1] CASAUBON, Epist. pp. 492-3, col. 1. Distractionem Imperii distractio Ecclesiæ Catholicæ est secuta; et illa omnia paullatim cessarunt, quæ modò dicebamus conservandæ unioni, et communioni exteriori corporis Catholici apprime serviisse. See also CASAUBON, Exerc. Bar. xvi. p. 637.

[2] S. AUG. Quæst. in S. Matth. xi. *Boni Catholici* sunt qui et *fidem integram* servant et bonos mores.

[3] Sir R. TWISDEN, p. 126. Upon the whole, it is so

PART II. absolutely false, that the Church of England made a departure from *the Church*, which is "the *Pillar and Ground of the* TRUTH," that I am persuaded it is impossible to prove that she did make the separation from the *Roman* itself; but that, having declared *in a lawful Synod* certain opinions held by some in her communion to be no articles of faith; and having, according to the precedent of former times, and the power which God had placed in her, redressed particular *abuses* crept into her, the Pope and his adherents would needs interpret this a departing from the *Faith!* But as S. Augustin said in a dispute with a Donatist, (c. lit. Petil. ii. 85,) *utrum schismatici nos simus, an vos, non ego, nec tu, sed* CHRISTUS *interrogetur.* See also BRAMHALL, i. p. 257. ii. pp. 61—63. 143.

CHAPTER IX.

THE BISHOP OF ROME HAS NO SUPREMACY, SPIRITUAL OR TEMPORAL, IN THESE REALMS.

Q. ALTHOUGH the Church of England is united in origin, doctrine, and discipline with the Catholic Church, yet is not the Bishop of Rome the *successor of St. Peter?* and did not our Lord give him *universal* supremacy over His Church? and has not, therefore, the Bishop of Rome authority over the Church of England *as* a part of the *Catholic Church?*

A. St. Peter was Bishop of Antioch [1], but it is *doubtful* whether he was Bishop of Rome [2]; and even if he was, it is also very *doubtful* whether the Bishop of Rome inherits by *office* what was given *personally* to St. Peter.

And it is *certain* that Christ gave *no* such pre-eminent power to St. Peter over his brother Apostles, as is now claimed by the Bishop of Rome [3]; but that *all* [4] the Apostles were *equal* in the *quality of* their *mission, commission, power, and honour.*

[1] GIESELER, Hist. Eccl. § 70, note 6.

² S. IREN. ap. Euseb. H. E. v. c. 6. Θεμελιώσαντες καὶ οἰκοδομήσαντες οἱ μακάριοι Ἀπόστολοι (St. Peter and St. Paul) τὴν ἐκκλησίαν (of Rome) Λίνῳ τὴν τῆς ἐπισκοπῆς λειτουργίαν ἐνεχείρισαν.

Bp. BEVERIDGE, p. 389 (Art. xxxvii.), brings strong proofs to show that St. Peter was never at Rome *as Bishop* of that particular Church, but he was there in the same manner *as* St. Paul was at Rome, viz., an *Apostle*. See also GIESELER, Eccl. Hist. § 68, and § 58, note 4 and 5, § 70, note 4 and 5.

³ Abp. BRAMHALL, ii. p. 160.

The *Secular* Claims have been mentioned above, pp. 200-3; the *Spiritual* Claims of the Popedom are thus stated by CARDINAL BELLARMIN de ROM. PONTIFICE: —Lib. ii. c. 2. Episcopus Romanus in Monarchiâ Ecclesiasticâ Petro succedit: c. 18, habet potestatem constituendi et confirmandi *Episcopos* per *totum Orbem;* item *deponendi* omnes Episcopos, et injustè depositos restituendi per totum Orbem; c. 18, habet potestatem ferendi *leges* et dispensandi per *universam Ecclesiam;* c. 20, illi *competit jus* mittendi *legatos* ad alias Ecclesias, qui in ipsius nomine omnia administrent; c. 21, ex *quâvis Christiani Orbis parte* legitimè ad ipsum *provocari* potest; ab ejus verò auctoritate *nulla conceditur appellatio;* c. 31, est CAPUT et SPONSUS Ecclesiæ. Lib. iv. c. 16, habet potestatem *ferendi leges* quæ *conscientias* obligent; c. 24, Omnis ordinaria Episcoporum potestas ab eo descendit.

⁴ S. CYPRIAN de Unit. Ecclesiæ, p. 107. Hoc erant cæteri Apostoli quod fuit Petrus; pari consortio prœditi et honoris et potestatis. CASAUBON, Exerc. Bar. p. 662.

BARROW, Pope's Supremacy, i. p. 57. Abp. BRAMHALL, i. p. 153. Whether a new Apostle was to be ordained (Acts i.), or the office of Deaconship to be erected (Acts vi.), or fit persons to be delegated for the ordering of the Church, as Peter and John, Judas and Silas (Acts viii. and xv.), or informations to be heard, against Peter himself (Acts xi.), or weightier questions, of the calling of the Gentiles, circumcision, and the law of Moses, to be determined, we find the *supremacy* in the *College of the Apostles*.

Bp. TAYLOR, x. p. 178. Bp. BULL, ii. p. 295.

Q. But does not St. Peter appear in Holy Scripture as taking the *lead* of the Apostles, and speaking in their behalf? and is he not designated by titles of special dignity in the writings of the early Fathers of the Church?

A. Yes, doubtless he is; as are some of the

other Apostles, especially St. Paul[1], who "had the care of *all the Churches.*" But we must not confound *primacy* with *supremacy.* St. Peter often appears as *first in order* among his brethren, but never as *higher in place* than the rest of the Apostles; as *Primus inter pares*, not as *summus supra inferiores*[2].

Part II.
2 Cor. xi. 28.

[1] Thus S. Aug. iii. p. 2313, Ipse *Caput* et *Princeps* Apostolorum, speaking not of St. Peter, but of St. *Paul.* Again, he says, x. p. 256, (Paulus) tanti Apostolatûs meruit *principatum.* So S. Ambrose de Spir. Sanct. ii. p. 13. *Nec Paulus Inferior Petro ;*—cum primo quoque facilè conferendus et *nulli secundus;* nam qui se imparem nescit, facit æqualem. Cf. Theodoret in Gal. ii. pp. 6—14. Noesselt. Corollar. ad Præf. ed. Halle, t. iii. So Petrus Cluniacus, (A.D. 1147,) contr. Petrobus. Bibl. Patr. Colon. xiii. pp. 221-2, calls St. Paul "*Summus post* Christum Ecclesiæ *Magister:*" and thus both St. Peter and St. Paul are called Κορυφαῖοι in the same sentence by Euthym. Zyg. Præf. ad S. Luc. Λουκᾶς Παύλῳ τῷ Κορυφαίῳ συναρμοσθεὶς καὶ συνέκδημος, καθάπερ δὴ καὶ Πέτρου τοῦ Κορυφαίου Μάρκος· and *all* the Apostles are called Κορυφαῖοι by Theophylact, in S. Luc. x. εὑρήσομεν τὰς δώδεκα πηγὰς, τοὺς κορυφαίους λέγω τοὺς δώδεκα Ἀποστόλους. See also Casaubon, Exerc. Baron. xv. pp. 327-8, and xvi. p. 658.

[2] Abp. Potter on the Church, ch. iii. p. 80, note. Barrow, Pope's Supremacy, p. 35, on the question, What St. Peter's primacy was?

Matt. xvi. 18.

Q. What, then, are we to say to the words of Christ to St. Peter, "*Verily I say unto thee, Thou art Peter, and on this rock I will build My Church?*"

A. Christ addressed these words to St. Peter, who had confessed Him, "the Son of Man," to be also the "Son of the living God." He calls him blessed for this good confession, which is as true as that he, Simon, is *Bar-Jona*, or *son of Jonas.* And He calls him Peter, *Petros*, or Stone, i. e. a genuine derivative from the divine *Petra*, or Rock, i. e. Himself[1]. And He says that He will build His Church on this *Petra*,

NO SUPREMACY IN THESE REALMS. 217

viz. on HIMSELF, confessed to be Son of Man and Son of God. CHRIST, God and Man, is the foundation of the Church. Faith in His Divinity and Humanity is its charter; and whosoever holds this faith is a true *Petros*, built on the Eternal PETRA. But without it there is no salvation; for "*other foundation can no man lay than that is laid* (or *lieth*, κεῖται), JESUS CHRIST," "Who gave (not *one* Apostle but) Apostles, for the edifying (or building) of His Church," which is not built on *one* Apostle, but "*on the foundation of the Apostles and Prophets,* JESUS CHRIST *Himself being the chief Corner-stone.*" Unity in the true Faith is the solidity of the Church; and the Rock on which the Church is built is CHRIST.

CHAP. IX.

1 Cor. iii. 11.
Eph. ii. 20.
iv. 8. 11.

Rev. xxi. 14.

[1] S. JEROME, Epist. ad Principiam, ii. p. 689. Super Petram Christum fundata est Catholica Ecclesia.

S. AUGUSTIN, Retractat. I. xxi. thus speaks of the interpretation of this passage: Dixi in quodam loco de Apostolo Petro, quod in *illo* tanquam in petrâ fundata sit Ecclesia; sed scio me postea sæpissimè sic exposuisse ut super Hunc intelligeretur Quem confessus est Petrus dicens, *Tu es filius Dei vivi:* ac sic Petrus ab hâc Petrâ appellatus *personam Ecclesiæ figuraret,* quæ super hanc Petram ædificatur, et accepit claves regni cœlorum. Non enim dictum est illi, Tu . es *Petra,* sed, Tu es *Petrus.* Petra autem erat CHRISTUS, quem confessus Petrus, sicut tota Ecclesia confitetur, dictus est Petrus. So he says, Sermon ccxliv. (interpreting Matt. xvi. 16), Petra erat ipse Christus, ille autem à Petrâ Petrus. Ideo surrexerat Petra ut firmaret Petrum; nam perierat Petrus nisi viveret Petra. Other interpreters understand *Petra* of the *faith* or *confession* of Peter, as, for instance, S. AMBROSE de Incarn. Dom. i. v. *Fides* Ecclesiæ est fundamentum; non enim de *carne* Petri sed de *fide* dictum est quia "portæ mortis ei non prævalebunt." See also Abp. LAUD against Fisher, sect. 33, § iv.

Other proofs that the *Petra,* or Rock, is CHRIST, may be seen in the Author's edition of the Greek Testament on Matt. xvi. 18.

Q. But is not St. Peter called by our Lord the *Rock* of His Church in the words just cited?

A. No. St. Peter was Πέτρος, *a stone*[1]; and John i. 42.

PART II.
Rev. xxi. 14.
θεμέλιοι
λίθοι.

1 Cor. iii. 10.

Isa. li. 1.
xxviii. 16.
xxxiii. 16.

hence he and the other Apostles with him are called in Scripture the *Twelve* Foundation *Stones* of the Church; hence St. Paul speaks of himself as "having laid the foundation, as a wise masterbuilder," of "God's building." CHRIST was ἡ Πέτρα, *the Rock*², *out* of which St. Peter and they were *hewn*, and *on* which they were *built*. *Tu es Petrus, quia* EGO PETRA, as S. Augustin explains the words, *neque enim*, he says, *à Petro Petra, sed à Petrâ Petrus;* and again, *Petrus ædificatur super Petram, non Petra super Petrum*².

¹ CASAUB. Exerc. Baron. pp. 233. 341. 349. Si vocum proprietatem respiciamus, probavimus aliud esse Πέτρον aliud Πέτραν. ELMSL. Œd. Col. p. 1590. BLOMF. Æsch. Pers. p. 466.

² S. AUGUST. Serm. cclxx. *Non* supra *Petrum* sed supra *Petram* quam confessus est ædificatur Ecclesia.—Serm. lxxvi. Tu es Petrus quia Ego Petra, neque enim à Petro Petra, sed à Petrâ Petrus. In Evang. S. Joann. 124, § 5. Non à Petro Petra, sed Petrus à Petrâ, sicut Christianus à Christo. SUICER, Lex. v. πέτρα. Forbes, Instruct. xv. p. 8. Bp. ANDREWES, Tortura Torti, p. 234. CRAKANTHORPE, Def. Eccl. Angl. p. 113. NEANDER, Ch. Hist. vol. iii. p. 224.

Rome herself has recognized the distinction, in the celebrated line "PETRA dedit *Petro; Petrus* diadema Radulpho;" and even Hildebrand says, "beatus Petrus à PETRÂ venerabile nomen *habens*," in Ussher's Sylloge, Epist. Hibern. xxix.

See the Author's note on Matt. xvi. 18.

It is to be regretted that the French word *Pierre* is applied both to the *person* and the *thing*, and thus gives rise to confusion between them.

Q. But did not our Lord use (not the Greek, but) the Syro-Chaldaic language in His speech to St. Peter, in which there is no such difference of *genders* as between *Petrus* and *Petra?*

A. Perhaps He did; but this objection, from the character of the Syriac tongue, as has been shown, has no weight¹; and it must be remembered, that St. Matthew's *Greek* account of

NO SUPREMACY IN THESE REALMS.   219

our Lord's speech is *divinely inspired*, and must   CHAP. IX.
be understood in its literal and grammatical
sense; we may not desert the inspired Greek of
the Holy Ghost for some imaginary Syro-Chaldaic
of our own. Besides, the Holy Spirit has declared
in *what* sense Simon was called *Cephas* by our
Lord: for, having recorded that Simon was called
Cephas, He adds, "which is by interpretation *a
Stone*." (John i. 42.)

¹ RAINOLDS' Conf. with Hart, pp. 23, 24. CASAUBON, Exerc. Baron. pp. 341, 342. LIGHTFOOT on John i. 42, p. 531 (Harmony), Matt. xvi. 18. Bp. BEVERIDGE on xxxviith Article, vol. ii. p. 396, ed. Oxf.

Q. But what do you say to the words which follow; "*And I will give unto thee the keys of* Matt. xvi. *the kingdom of heaven, and whatsoever thou shalt* 19. *bind on earth shall be bound in heaven, and whatsoever thou shalt loose on earth shall be loosed in heaven?*" Was not the *Power of the Keys*, as it is called, (see above, p. 107,) here given by Christ to Peter? and in him to his successors, the Bishops of Rome?

A. Doubtless these words were a prophetic announcement and an authoritative commission from Christ to St. Peter specially; and they were fulfilled, when, by the keys of Preaching and Baptism, St. Peter opened the kingdom of heaven to the Jewish and Gentile world—to the former on the day of Pentecost, and to the latter in the person of Cornelius.

But Christ gave the power of the Keys to *all* Bishops and Priests of the Church, as well as to the Apostle St. Peter. Christ gave that power to the *Church*, when He said, "Tell it to Matt. xviii. *the Church;* but if he neglect to hear *the Church*, 17, 18. let him be unto thee as an heathen;" and having p. 107. said these words, He proceeded to declare by *whom* this power was to be exercised, viz. by *all* His Apostles, and their successors 'even to the end of the world.' "Verily I say unto you, Whatsoever *ye* shall bind on earth shall be bound in Heaven, and whatsoever *ye* shall loose on earth shall be loosed in Heaven:" and again, after His Resurrection, "He breathed on them, and saith unto them, Receive *ye* the Holy Ghost; whose soever sins *ye* remit, they are remitted; and whose soever sins *ye* retain, they are retained." It would be a contradiction of these words, to say that the Power of the Keys was given *exclusively* to St. *Peter* and his *successors;* and it is the concurrent language [1] of all Christian Antiquity that he received that power as a figure of the *Church* in her *Unity*, as all the Apostles did in her *Universality*. It was not one *man* in the Church, but *the Church* of Christ which received the keys; and our Lord's words were addressed *to Peter*, as representing by his Faith, by his Office, and by his Acts, *all the Apostles and their Successors*, as one of the Bishops of Rome, Leo the Great [2], says; and S. Ambrose [3], *In beato Petro claves has regni cœlorum cuncti suscepimus sacerdotes.*

[1] TERTULLIAN, Scorpiac. p. 10. Memento claves hic Dominum Petro et per illum *Ecclesiæ* reliquisse. S. CYPRIAN de Unit. Eccles. p. 107. Apostolis *omnibus* post resurrectionem suam parem potestatem tribuit.—p. 108. Ecclesia una est, in quâ Episcopatus unus est cujus à singulis in solidum pars tenetur. S. HIERON, c. Jovinian. lib. i. At dicis, super Petrum fundatur Ecclesia; licet id ipsum in alio loco super *omnes* Apostolos fiat, et *cuncti* claves regni cœlorum accipiant, et *ex æquo* super eos Ecclesiæ fortitudo solidetur. HIERON, in Amos, vi. p. 12, Petra Christus est; Qui donavit Apostolis suis ut ipsi quoque petræ vocentur. S. BASIL, Const. Monast. p. 22, πᾶσι τοῖς ἐφεξῆς ποιμέσι καὶ διδασκάλοις παρέχει ἴσην ἐξουσίαν καὶ τούτου σημεῖον τὸ δεσμεῖν ἅπαντας καὶ λύειν ὥσπερ ἐκεῖνος. S. AMBROSE in Psalm xxxviii. Quod Petro dicitur, cæteris Apostolis dicitur. S. AUGUST. Serm. cxlix. Nunquid istas claves accepit Petrus, et Paulus non accepit? Petrus accepit, et Joannes et Jacobus non accepit et cæteri Apostoli? Aut non sunt istæ in Ecclesiâ claves ubi peccata quotidie dimittuntur? Serm.

ccxcv. Has claves non *homo unus* sed *unitas* accepit *Ecclesiæ*. Vide et iii. p. 2470. ANSELM in loc. Potestas clavium non solum Petro data est, sed, sicut Petrus unus pro omnibus respondit, sic Christus in Petro *omnibus* dedit. CASAUBON, Exerc. Baron. pp. 344—347. Bp. ANDREWES, Tortura Torti, p. 42. Petro promissæ claves non tamen ut Petro huic homini, quin Petro Ecclesiæ personam gerenti. Vide et pp. 62—64. BARROW, Pot. Clav. p. 47. Promissum commune est, et ad Ecclesiam totam ejusque rectores pertinet: nec enim *occasio* promissi Petrum unicè spectabat; neque *causa* propter quam promitteretur; nec alligabatur uni Petro promissi *materia,* nec in Petrum solum derivatus est ejus *effectus*.

[2] S. LEO, A.D. 450, Serm. iii. p. 53, ed. 1700. Transivit in *alios Apostolos* jus potestatis illius, et ad *omnes* Ecclesiæ Principes decreti hujus constitutio commeavit. Sed non frustra uni commendatur, quod omnibus intimetur. Serm. de Nativ. Hæc clavium potestas ad *omnes* etiam Apostolos et Ecclesiæ Præsules est translata. Quod autem sigillatim Petro sit commendata, ideo factum est quod Petri exemplum omnibus Ecclesiæ Pastoribus fuit propositum. See also vol. i. p. 217; the notes, vol. ii. p. 434, ed. 1700.

[3] S. AMBROSE, Ep. lxiii. quoted by Barrow de Pot. Clav. p. 49.

Q. But did not Christ give *supreme* power to St. *Peter* when He said to him, *Feed My sheep?* John xxi. 15, 16.

A. No; these words were not so much *verba ordinandi,* as *verba hortandi*[1]; and did not affect the *general* commission before given by Christ to all His Apostles in a solemn act of consecration. Whence St. Paul says to the presbyters at Ephesus, "Take heed to the *flock* over which the Holy Ghost has made *you* overseers, *to feed the* Church of God, which He hath purchased with His own blood;" and St. Peter, "The elders I exhort, who am also an elder, *Feed the flock of God* which is among you, taking the oversight thereof, not by constraint, but willingly." Wherefore, as S. Augustin says, *quum Petro dicitur, ad omnes dicitur,* "*Pasce oves Meas*[2]."

John xx. 21, 22.

Acts xx. 28.

1 Pet. v. 1, 2.

[1] CASAUBON, Exerc. Baron. pp. 344—347.
[2] S. AUG. de Agone Christiano, c. 30. Tract. in Joann. xlvii. Christus, quod pastor est, dedit et membris suis. Nam et Petrus pastor, et Paulus pastor, et cæteri Apostoli

PART II. pastores, et boni Episcopi pastores. See also v. pp. 345. 969, col. 3, 1763. See S. LEO in note to preceding question. Bp. FELL's note on S. Cyprian de Un. Eccl. p. 106. HAMMOND's Works, i. p. 516. BARROW, Pope's Supremacy, p. 68, pp. 37. 39.

Q. Since, as has been before said (pp. 87. 89), the best commentary on a law is contemporary and successive *practice*, what conclusion do we derive from *it* with respect to the alleged supremacy of St. Peter?

A. It is certain *à priori*, that St. Peter *could not have* supremacy over the other Apostles, from the fact that Christ did not authorize, but did plainly *prohibit* such a supremacy, when He told His Apostles, "*that the kings of the Gentiles exercise lordship over them (the Gentiles), but it should not be so with*" them; and again, "*whosoever will be great among you, let him be your minister;*" and "*he that is greatest among you shall be your servant;*" and that they had "*One Master, Jesus Christ, and that they were brethren;*" and again, He spake to them of *twelve* thrones, and not *one* throne, thus placing them on an *equality;* and the wall of the Church in the Revelation has "*twelve* foundations, and in them the names of the *twelve* Apostles."

Matt. xx. 25.
Matt. xxiii. 11.
Luke xxii. 25.
Matt. xx. 26.
Mark x. 43.
Matt. xxiii. 8. 10.
Matt. xix. 28.
Luke xxii. 30.
Rev. xxi. 14.

It is also clear, *à posteriori*, that St. James[1], who took the lead at a Council, that of Jerusalem, at which St. Peter was present, and in which St. Peter took part as one of the speakers, knew nothing of such a supremacy in St. Peter; that St. Paul knew nothing of it, who said that "*he himself is not a whit behind the very chiefest Apostles;*" and that he had "*the care of all the Churches,*" and who says accordingly, "*so I ordain in all the Churches;*" who classes Peter with James and John, who withstood St. Peter and rebuked him to his face, and who reproves certain of the Corinthians for saying, "I am of *Cephas;*" and that St. Peter himself knew nothing

Acts xv. 13.

2 Cor. xi. 5. 28.
xii. 11.

1 Cor. vii. 17.
Gal. ii. 9. 14.

1 Cor. i. 12.

of it, since he was *sent* by the Apostles to Samaria; and he speaks of "*us the Apostles*," as his *compeers*, not *inferiors;* and of CHRIST, "the living Stone;" and he writes on terms of *equality*, and not of *superiority*, as "a *brother-Elder*" to Elders. And, to descend to St. Peter's *successors*, it is certain also that S. Polycarp[2], Bishop of Smyrna, knew nothing of such a supremacy in Pope Anicetus; that Polycrates[3], Bishop of Ephesus, and the Synod of Asiatic Bishops, and S. Irenæus, Bishop of Lyons, and the Council assembled in that city, knew nothing of any such supremacy in Pope Victor[4]; that S. Cyprian, Bishop of Carthage, and the African Bishops, knew nothing of it in Pope Stephanus[5]; that S. Augustin and the Bishops of Africa knew nothing of it in Popes Zosimus and Boniface[6]; and that the *Bishops of Rome themselves*, for six hundred years, were so far from knowing any thing of such supremacy as residing in themselves or in any one else, that Pope Gregory the First[7] denounced the title of *Universal Bishop* as proud, wicked, insane, schismatical, blasphemous, and anti-Christian; "*Quisquis se universalem sacerdotem vocat*," says he, "*Anti-Christum præcurrit*." (Lib. vii. Epist. xxxiii.)

Acts viii. 14.
2 Pet. iii. 2.
1 Pet. ii. 5.
v. 1.

[1] HESYCH. presbyt. Hieros. ap. Phot. cod. p. 275. Πέτρος δημηγορεῖ, ἀλλ' Ἰάκωβος νομοθετεῖ.

[2] EUSEB. H. E. v. p. 23.

[3] ROUTH, Rel. Sac. i. pp. 370—387.
Bp. BILSON, Christian Subjection, p. 49. Peter, as you say the first Bishop of Rome, was resisted by Paul the teacher of the Gentiles; Anicetus by Polycarpus, St. John's own scholar; Victor by Polycrates, Irenæus, and all the brethren of Asia; Stephen by Cyprian; Damasus, Syricius, and Anastasius, by Flavianus, and all the Churches of the east of Asia, Pontus, Thracia, and Illyricum; Innocentius by Cyril; Zosimus and Bonifacius by Augustin and two hundred and sixteen Bishops of Africa.

[4] ROUTH, i. pp. 391—419.

[5] ROUTH, iii. p. 90. Compare, on these cases, Euseb. H. E. v. p. 14. GRABE ad Iren. ii. c. 3, p. 201. See above,

PART II. pp. 150, 151. Bp. PEARSON, Annales Cyprianici, pp. 48. 56, ed. Fell.

S. CYPRIAN in Concil. Carthag. vii. Routh, Reliquiæ Sacræ, iii. p. 91. Neque enim quisquam nostrûm *Episcopum se Episcoporum* constituit, aut tyrannico terrore ad obsequendi necessitatem collegas suos adigit, quando habeat *omnis Episcopus* pro licentiâ libertatis et potestatis suæ arbitrium proprium.

CONC. CARTH. iii. p. 28.   CONC. HIPPON. i. p. 27. CABASSUT. Notit. Concil. cap. xlix.   BINGHAM, IX. I. 11.

HOOKER, VII. XVI. 7. Whereby it appears that among the African Bishops *none* did use such authority over *any* as the Bishop of Rome did afterwards claim over *all*, forcing upon them opinions by main and absolute power.

⁶ GREGORII MAGNI, Pontificis Romani, Epistolæ, v. p. 43, ed. Paris, 1705, tom. ii. pp. 771—773. Nullus unquam decessorum meorum hoc tam *profano* vocabulo uti consensit; quia videlicet si unus Patriarcha Universalis dicitur, Patriarcharum nomen cæteris derogatur. Sed absit hoc, absit à Christiani mente, id sibi velle quempiam arripere, unde fratrum suorum honorem imminuere ex quantulâcunque parte videatur! Propterea Sanctitas vestra neminem unquam Universalem nominet. Si enim hoc dici licenter permittitur, honor Patriarcharum omnium negatur. Ep. v. 20, p. 748. Quis est iste qui contra statuta evangelica, contra canonum decreta, novum sibi usurpare nomen præsumit? Utinam sine aliorum imminutione unus sit qui vocari appetit Universalis! Sed absit à cordibus Christianis nomen illud *blasphemiæ* in quo omnium sacerdotum honor adimitur, dum ab uno sibi *dementer* arrogatur! Ep. vii. 27, p. 873. De eodem *superstitioso* et *superbo* vocabulo eum admonere studui, dicens, quia pacem nobiscum habere non posset, elationem prædicti verbi corrigeret, quam primus *Apostata* invenit. Ep. vii. 33, p. 881. Ego fidenter dico, quia quisquis se universalem sacerdotem vocat vel vocari desiderat in elatione suâ, *Anti-Christum* præcurrit, quia superbiendo se cæteris præponit. Nec dispari superbiâ ad errorem ducitur, quia, sicut perversus ille, Deus videri vult super omnes homines; ita quisquis iste est, qui solus sacerdos appellari appetit, super reliquos sacerdotes se extollit.—See also iv. p. 32. v. p. 29. vii. pp. 31. 34. ix. p. 68.

⁷ HOOKER, VII. VIII. 9. What the Bishop of Constantinople (i. e. after the Council of Trullo or Quini-Sextum) challenged, and was therein as then refused by the Bishop of Rome (i. e. the title of Universal Bishop), the same the Bishop of Rome, in process of time, obtained for himself; and having gotten it by bad means, hath both upheld and

augmented it, and upholdeth it by acts and practices much worse.—See VIII. III. 5. CHAP. IX.

Archbp. LAUD against Fisher, sect. 25. Mauricius being deposed and murdered by Phocas, Phocas conferred on Boniface III. that honour which two of his predecessors (Pelagius and Gregory) had declaimed against as monstrous and blasphemous, if not Anti-Christian. BARROW, Pope's Supremacy, p. 122. Boniface eagerly solicited it. See Bp. ANDREWES c. Bellarm. c. 12, p. 277. Gregory *refused* the title of Universal Bishop, ad. Eulog. viii. 30. Bp. OVERALL, Convocation Book, p. 285. Bp. BEVERIDGE on the xxxviith Article. CASAUBON, Exerc. Baron. pp. 315—388. GIESELER, Eccl. Hist. § 94, note 72. Gregory was mistaken in supposing that at the Council of Chalcedon the name " Universalis Episcopus " was given to the Bishop of Rome.

Q. Has then the Bishop of Rome no peculiar jurisdiction which does not belong to another Bishop?

A. Every Bishop possesses the highest spiritual authority in his own diocese, with respect to the ordinary affairs of his own Church; and all Bishops, *as Bishops*, are *equal*[1], whatever their dioceses may be. As S. Jerome[2], the secretary of a Pope (Damasus), says,— *Ubicunque est Episcopus, sive Romæ, sive Eugubii, ejusdem est meriti, ejusdem sacerdotii : potentia divitiarum et paupertatis humilitas sublimiorem vel inferiorem Episcopum non facit*[2]. On account of the civil eminence of Rome, the Bishop of Rome, as has been before stated (p. 103), anciently enjoyed *precedence* among Bishops, by the Canons of the Catholic Church ; but his jurisdiction as Bishop, Metropolitan, and Patriarch, was and is limited to his own Diocese, Province, and Patriarchate, in the same manner as that of every other Bishop, Metropolitan, and Patriarch[3].

---

[1] S. CYPRIAN, Ep. ad Antonian. p. 177. Manente concordiæ vinculo, et perseverante Ecclesiæ Catholicæ individuo Sacramento, actum suum disponit et dirigit *unusquisque Episcopus*, rationem propositi sui Domino redditurus.—Ep. ad Papian. p. 66. Quis longè est ab humi-

PART II. litate, an ego, an tu qui te Episcopum Episcopi et Judicem Judicis constituis?—Against *appeals* to extra-diocesan authority, Epist. 55. Cùm statutum sit ab omnibus nobis, et æquum sit pariter ac justum, ut cujusque causa *illic* audiatur ubi est crimen admissum, et cum singulis pastoribus portio gregis sit adscripta, quam regat unusquisque et gubernet, rationem sui actûs Deo redditurus, oportet utique eos *non circumcursare, &c.* See below, Pt. iii. ch. vii.

S. CYPRIAN, Ep. 54, p. 112, Fell. Una Ecclesia, item Episcopatus unus, Episcoporum multorum concordi numerositate diffusus. De Unit. Eccles. p. 108. Episcopatus unus est cujus à singulis *in solidum* pars tenetur (i. e. ita ut singuli omnem pleno jure possideant. Fell.). It is to be observed, that *in solidum* is a term of civil law, expressing that every one of the holders has a right to his share without acknowledgment to any one. See above, p. 18.

Archbp. LAUD, Conference with Fisher, p. 166.

Bp. BILSON, Christian Subjection, p. 60. The Bishop of Rome was *before* the rest in honour and dignity, but not *over* the rest in power and authority. His place was first when the patriarchs met; but his voice was not negative; he was subject both to the decrees of Councils and to the laws of Christian emperors, even in causes ecclesiastical.

BARROW, Pope's Sup. p. 149. The ancients did assert to each Bishop a free, absolute, independent authority, accountable to none on earth in the administration of affairs properly concerning his particular Church.—p. 151. The ancients did hold all Bishops, as to their office (originally according to Divine Institution, or abstracting from human sanctions framed to preserve order and peace), to be *equal;* for that all are successors of the Apostles, all derive their commission and power in the same tenour from God.

One Bishop may exceed another in splendour, wealth, extent of jurisdiction, as one King may surpass another in amplitude of territory; but as all Kings, so all Bishops are equal in office and essentials of power derived from God.

[2] S. HIERON. ad Evagr. Ep. p. 85. S. August. ii. p. 310.

[3] CRAKANTHORPE, Def. Eccl. Angl. p. 176. Romanus Episcopus ad *parœciam* suam Romanam, quâ est *Episcopus,* ad *provinciam* suam Romanam, quâ est *Metropolitanus,* ad *diœcesin* suam Romanam quâ est *Patriarcha,* æquè constringitur ac quivis in toto orbe Episcopus, Metropolitanus, aut Patriarcha, seu patriarchalis Primas; et illius censuræ, excommunicationes, judicia, decreta, omnes-

que omnino episcopales actus, quos extra aut ultra istos limites præstare tentat aut exercere, irriti plane sunt, et pro nullis habendi.

Q. But it being granted that the Bishop of Rome cannot claim supreme jurisdiction over the Universal Church as a matter of Right, still is it not expedient for the maintenance of *Unity* in the Church, that it should have One *Supreme Visible Head?*

A. Christ, the Universal Lord of the Church, and the lover of Unity, never instituted one. Let all the States of the earth be placed under One Civil Ruler, and then let the trial be made. If such a *personal supremacy* was not thought expedient by the Church when the greater part of the civilized world *was* under One Temporal Governor (the Emperor of Rome), it cannot be thought so now, when, as was before said (p. 218), there are about thirty different States and Kingdoms in Europe alone. If it was not desirable at a time when the range of Christendom and of the known world was comparatively narrow, it cannot be so, when the limits of both have been enlarged to a vast extent, and are becoming more and more intricate and comprehensive; and if it was even *condemned* as *anti-Christian, before* its effects had been seen, it cannot be reasonable to desire it *now*, when the world has had bitter *experience* of its tendency to engender *strife* instead of promoting *peace*, both in spiritual and secular affairs.

Q. In what respects has this tendency shown itself?

A. The claim of universal *spiritual* headship naturally leads to that of *secular* supremacy, which is indeed essential to render the former reasonable: and the *fact has* been, and *is*, that, in defiance of Reason and of Scripture, the Bishop of Rome, on the ground, in the first

Above, pp. 16. 21.

1 Pet. ii. 13, 14. v. 3.

PART II.
Below,
Pt. iii. chaps. iv. and v.
Above,
pp. 200—203.
1 Pet. ii. 13.

place, of *spiritual*, and then of *temporal*, *supremacy*, claims a right to *depose*[1] princes, to *dispose* of their dominions, and to *impose* Oaths on their subjects inconsistent with, and contrary to their duty to, their lawful sovereign[2]; and thus does all in his power to annul the obligations of civil allegiance, and to dissolve the bonds of civil society[2].

[1] Card. BELLARMIN de Rom. Pontif. v. p. 7. Omnium consensu hæretici Principes possunt et debent privari suo dominio.

In the words of the bull by which Gregory VII. deposed Henry IV., the Pope claims the right "in terrâ Imperia, Regna, Principatus, et omnium hominum possessiones pro meritis tollere unicuique et concedere." Of the *political* consequences of these principles, see Bp. BARLOW on Papal Power dangerous to Protestant Princes, pp. 82—109; and his Brutum Fulmen, pp. 9—12, p. 174.

GREGORY VII., Hildebrand, was canonized, and on his festival he is thus lauded in the Lesson for the Day, for deposing Henry IV. "Contra Henrici Imperatoris impios conatus fortis per omnia athleta impavidus permansit, seque pro muro domui Israel ponere non timuit; eundem Henricum fidelium communione *regnoque* privavit." This service was authorized by Pope Benedict XIII. Sept. 25, 1728, and is to be seen in the Paris Breviary of 1842, p. 676.

[2] PHELAN's and O'SULLIVAN's Digest of Evidence on Ireland, pt. ii. p. 21. *Roman Catholic Bishops* are *Peers* of the creation of the Sovereign Pontiff, who claims to be Supreme *Feudal Lord* wherever he has a hierarchy of Bishops or Vicars Apostolic.

Archbp. MAGEE, Digest of Evidence on Ireland, 1826, p. 12, says, "I am not able to explain to myself how the heads of the Roman Catholic Church, under a Protestant King, can consistently preserve the oath of allegiance to the sovereign. *I find myself unable to reconcile the most solemn oath that is taken upon the appointment of a Roman Catholic Bishop, with his allegiance to his sovereign.* It appears to me, that there is an *obligation as deep as that which can grow out of the feeling of Christianity at war with the civil obligation.* I can find in this oath no reservation or circumscription whatsoever.— p. 13. If this disturbing influence exerted on the *Bishop* be carried down through the *Priest*, either from the nature of his Oath, or any other way, it must be unnecessary to say, from the close and influential contact into CHAP. IX. which every officiating Priest is brought with the Roman Catholic population of the country, what the effect must be as to the general loyalty."—The Editors of the Digest say, p. 16: "As the preceding clauses of the oath were so many successive aggressions upon the honour of the Crown and the liberty of the subject, so the last sentence straitens, instead of relaxing, the obligations they impose. It virtually recapitulates the previous pledges; it declares that all things therein contained, the *feudal vassalage* of the Bishop, the *Regal Supremacy of his Lord*, and the duty of extending indefinitely the dominion of the Papacy, shall be maintained more inviolably than ever; and it concludes by making the party abjure all right in his local Prince to infringe on those prerogatives of the Universal Sovereign." Upon the whole, then, we may ask, with Dr. O'Connor, Columbanus, iii. p. 160, "How can the Bishop's oath be reconciled with the oath of civil allegiance, which excludes all indirect temporal power of the Pope in this realm?"

See also BARROW, Pope's Supr. p. 23. Bp. GIBSON, Codex, p. 117, and above, p. 207.

Q. You have spoken of the secular evils of the Papal headship; what are the *spiritual* ones?

A. It *destroys*[1] Unity in the Church on the plea of *preserving* it. It pretends to be a *Centre of Unity*, but is a *Source of Confusion* to all Christendom. It rejects the wisdom, revokes the judgments, and annihilates the authority of the Universal Church, as represented in General *Councils*[2], by its claim to negative and rescind their decrees; it claims infallibility, but not only has it erred grievously[3], but it would reduce the Church to a perpetual *necessity* of *erring* by subjecting it to the uncontrolled will of *one man*; it destroys the Order and Jurisdiction of *Bishops*[4], by resolving all into its own power; and so dishonours CHRIST, from Whom they derive their power, and it deprives the Apostles of their legitimate posterity and succession; thus perverting the character of the Church from Apostolic into Papal, and degrading Bishops into its own Vassals, as is evident from the Oath now imposed upon Bishops by the Pope of Rome, which fully

Gal. i. 1.
ii. 7.
2 Cor. xi. 28.

PART II. confirms the prophetic speech of Pope Gregory the First to the Bishops of Greece, "*Si unus universalis* est, restat ut *vos Episcopi non* sitis." (Epist. lib. v. 68, tom. ii. p. 984.)

¹ Archbp. LAUD, Sermons, p. 122, London, ed. 1651. While they seeke to tye all Christians to Rome by a divine precept, their ambition of soveraignty is *one* and *maine* cause that Jerusalem, even the whole Church of Christ, is *not at Unity* in itselfe this day.—Ibid. p. 258. The Pope, which Bellarmine hath put into the definition of the Church that there might be one ministerial Head to keepe all in Unity, is *as great as any*, if not *the greatest*, cause *of divided* Christianity.

² Card. BELLARM. de Pontifice, iv. c. 3. Tota firmitas Conciliorum est à Pontifice. By the bull *In Cœnâ Domini*, all who dare appeal from the Pope to a Council are under sentence of excommunication.

³ Pope GREGOR. I., ii. p. 771. Cùm fortasse *is in* errore perit, qui *Universalis* dicitur, *nullus jam Episcopus* remansisse in statu Veritatis invenitur. For an enumeration of errors and heretical opinions maintained by Bishops of Rome from time to time, see GERHARD, v. p. 407. E Papis, Zephyrinus fuit Montanista, Marcellinus idololatra, Liberius et Felix Ariani. Anastasius communicavit cum Photino, Vigilius fuit Eutychianus, Honorius Monothelita. Compare also BARROW, Pope's Supr. p. 266. BINGHAM, XVI. I. 14. ROUTH, Script. Eccles. ii. pp. 512—516; and even BOSSUET in his *Défense de la Déclaration;* and Hist. Eccl. Paris, 1768, i. p. 342. L'illustre M. BOSSUET donne à ce scandale du Pape Zosime le nom de *chûte terrible* (casus gravis), de même qu'à celui qu'avoit auparavant causé le Pape Libère. On the case of Pope Liberius who subscribed two semi-Arian formulas, A.D. 358, see GIESELER, Eccl. Hist. § 83, note 6. Popes Zephyrinus and Callistus are charged with promoting the Noëtian Heresy by the Author of the recently discovered Philosophumena, Lib. ix. See the Author's "S. HIPPOLYTUS and the Church of Rome," 1853.

⁴ Archbp. BRAMHALL, i. p. 252. Though the Popes do not abolish the order of Bishops or Episcopacy in the abstract, yet they limit the power of Bishops in the concrete at their pleasure by exemptions and reservations, holding themselves to be the Bishops of every particular see in the world, during the vacancy of it, and making all Episcopal jurisdiction to flow from them, and to be founded in the Pope's laws, because it was but delegated to the rest of the Apostles for a term of life, but resided solely in St. Peter

as an Ordinary to descend from him to his successors the Bishops of Rome, and to be imparted by them to other Bishops as their Vicars or Coadjutors, assumed by them into some part of their charge. (Bellarmin de Rom. Pontif. i. ii. iv. pp. 23—25.) By this account the Pope must be the Universal or Only Bishop of the world; the Keys must be his gift, not Christ's; and all the Apostles, except St. Peter, must want their successors in Episcopal jurisdiction. What is this but to trample upon Episcopacy, to dissolve the primitive bands of primitive Unity, to overthrow the discipline instituted by Christ, and to take away the line of Apostolical succession? See also BRAMHALL, i. p. 189. CASAUBON, Exerc. Baron. xiv. pp. 280, 281. BELLARMIN de Pontif. IV. xxiv. BARROW in Christian Inst. iv. p. 93. KEBLE, Preface to HOOKER, I. LX. Add to this what the Papacy had done and was daily doing to weaken all notions of independent authority in Bishops, of which proceedings the *full development* may be seen in the proceeding of the Italian party at Trent.

That all Power of Order is resolved by the Papacy into itself, is clear from the PONTIFICALE ROM. p. 87, ed. Rom. 1818. Antequam obtinuerit quis *Pallium*, licet sit consecratus, non sortitur nomen Patriarchæ aut Primatis aut Archiepiscopi, et non licet ei *Episcopos consecrare*, nec convocare concilium, nec Chrisma conficere, neque Ecclesias dedicare, *nec Clericos ordinare.*

CHAP. IX.

Q. But how, then, *is* the Unity of the Church to be preserved, since it *cannot* be by the claims of the Pope?

A. St. Paul informs us. "*There is one Body, and one Spirit, and one Hope of our calling; one Lord, one Faith, one Baptism; one God and Father of us all*[1]." He does not add, "*One Visible Head.*" Let all the members of the Catholic Church be "joined together in the same mind and in the same judgment;" let them "walk by the same rule, and mind the same thing;" let them be united in the *same Faith*, in the same *Sacraments*, and in the same *Apostolic Discipline* and *Government*; let them communicate with one another[2] by means of their lawful *Bishops*, in National and in General *Councils*, according to the institution of Christ, and to universal primitive practice; let them all, *each in*

Eph. iv. 4—6.

1 Cor. i. 10.
Eph. iv. 13.
Above, pp. 8. 19.

Matt. xviii. 17. 20.
Acts xv. 2. 28. xvi. 4.

PART II. *his own sphere*, "endeavour to maintain the unity of the Spirit in the bond of peace;" and they will then enjoy the blessing of *primitive Christian Unity*. But they can never attain this Unity by subjection to *one supreme visible Head*, of which the Primitive Church knew nothing; and especially they cannot acquire it by subjection to *such* a supreme visible Head as subverts the Ancient Faith by a New Creed, mutilates the Sacraments, destroys Apostolic government, and sets at nought the authority of the Church in her Synods; and having thus dissolved the bands of Unity, proceeds to exact an implicit subjection to all these Innovations and Infractions, as an essential condition of Communion with itself, and as a test of Church Membership, and as necessary to eternal salvation[2].

[1] S. AUG. in Epist. S. Joann. vi. In uno corpore sumus; Unum Caput habemus in Cœlo. TERTULLIAN de Præscript. c. 10. Communicatio pacis, appellatio fraternitatis, contesseratio hospitalitatis. See the Prayer for UNITY, in the Form of Prayer and Service for the QUEEN's Accession.

[2] RAINOLDS' Conf. with Hart, p. 206, 1598. The wisdom of God hath committed that chieftie of judgment, not to the sovereign power of One, but to the common care of many. For when there was a controversie in the Church of Antioch about the observation of the law of Moses (Acts xv. 2), they ordained that Paul and Barnabas, and certain other of them, should go up to Jerusalem to the Apostles and Elders about that question. So by their common decree the controversie was ended, the truth of faith kept, and peace maintained in the Church. After which example the Bishops who succeeded the Apostles made the like assemblies on like occasions. (Euseb. H. E. v. pp. 14. 21, 22. vii. pp. 26. 28, &c.) So did Apostles and Apostolic men provide against schisms. Their wisedome reached not to the policie of one Chief Judge. See also Bp. BILSON, Christian Subjection, p. 305. HOOKER, I. x. 14. IV. XIII. 8. VIII. III. 6.

Bp. CARLETON de Ecclesiâ, pp. 234—242. Multi Episcopi *unum* Episcopatum constituunt. Archbp. BRAMHALL, ii. pp. 320. 615, on Councils as means of Unity. BARROW on Unity of the Church, vi. pp. 534—548.

Bp. PATRICK, Sermon on St. Peter's Day, 1687, p. 69.

CHAP. IX.

The Holy Ghost hath told us that there is but one God the Father, of Whom are all things, and we in Him; and one Lord Jesus Christ, by Whom are all things, and we by Him (1 Cor. viii. 6); and one God and one Mediator between God and men, the man Christ Jesus, so that to use any other, is to fall into a Schism, and break the communion of the Church of Christ, as they of the Church of Rome have done, both by this and by changing the ancient Government, Discipline, and Faith of the Church; they *have separated themselves* from the rest of the Christian world, by usurping universal jurisdiction, as well as by many other things, and so *broken that charity* which gives the greatest efficacy to our prayers.

LESLIE, Rev. Charles, Case Stated, &c. p. 208, ed. 1714. This Universal Supremacy is merely imaginary; it was never named by Christ, and never was in fact. And so far is it from being the *Centre of Unity*, that the pretence to it has been the *great breach of Unity* among Christian Churches, and is at this day: for this is it which stops the Bishops in the communion of Rome from exercising that authority which Christ has given them over their own flocks, and which was freely exercised by the Bishops in the primitive Church; and which, if restored, would open the way to that Catholic Communion wherein the true Unity of the Church doth consist.

BINGHAM, XVI. I. 14. The unity of the Church was sufficiently provided for by the agreement of all Churches in the same Faith, and the obligation that lay upon the whole College of Bishops, as equal sharers in one Episcopacy, to give mutual assistance to each other in all things that were necessary to defend the faith, or preserve the unity of the Church entire in all respects, when any assault was made upon it. It was by this means, and *not* by any necessary recourse to any Single, Visible, Standing Head, that anciently the Unity of the Church was preserved.

[3] CONCIL. LATERAN. sub Leone X. sess. 10. *De necessitate salutis est* omnes Christi fideles *Romano Pontifici subesse*, prout Divinæ Scripturæ et Sanctorum Patrum testimonio edocemur, et Constitutione Bonifacii Papæ VIII. quæ incipit *Unam Sanctam* (quam) sacro præsenti Concilio approbante innovamus et *approbamus*.

Archbp. BRAMHALL, ii. p. 201. Pius the IVth did not only enjoin all ecclesiastics, seculars and regulars, to swear to his new Creed, but he imposed it upon *all Christians* as "veram fidem Catholicam, *extra quam nemo salvus esse potest*." (Bulla Pii IV. in Act. Concil. Trident. Labbè, Concil. xiv. p. 946. B.) See also above on this subject, Pt. i. ch. ii. and Pt. i. ch. ix. at end.

PART III.

The Church of England in its Civil Relations.

CHAPTER I.

DEFINITION OF CHURCH AND STATE.

PART III.

Q. What do you mean by the words "Church" and "State?"

A. In the case of a *Christian* nation, the term Church describes the Community in its *religious* capacity, the State describes it in its *civil*. Church and State are *duæ formaliter, sed una materialiter;* they are *different names* of the *same body politic*[1], as Christian and Citizen are different names of one human body.—And as an individual's Christianity does not depend on his citizenship, though his happiness as a Christian greatly depends on his conduct as a Citizen; so the existence of the Community as a Church does not depend on its constitution as a State, though its efficiency and prosperity as a Church is greatly affected by its civil acts as a State.

[1] HOOKER, VIII. I. 5. The Church and Commonwealth are names which import things really different, but those

things are accidents, and such accidents as may and should always dwell lovingly together in one subject, HOOKER, VIII. III. 6, in a free Christian state or kingdom, where one and the selfsame people are the Church and the Commonwealth. See further below here, chap. iii.

Archbp. LAUD, Sermons, 1651. Sermon i. on Ps. cxxii. 6, 7. When you sit down to consult, you must not forget the Church; and when we kneel down to pray, we must not forget the State: both are but *One Jerusalem.*—p. 9. Both Commonwealth and Church are collective bodies, made up of many into one; and both so near that *the same men which in a temporal respect make the Commonwealth, do in a spiritual make the Church*: so one name of the mother city serves both, that are joined up into one; and p. 35, The *same men* which, in respect of one allegiance, make the *Commonwealth* do, in respect of one Faith, make the *Church*.

SARAVIA de Honore Præsulibus debito, p. 71. Sunt qui Ecclesiam in Republicâ esse putant tanquam ejus sit quædam pars, et quod *Ipsa tota Respublica* non *sit Ecclesia*. Verùm hæc distinctio in Christiano populo locum non habet. Ubi totus aliquis populus nomen dedit Christo, et nemo illic sit qui Christi Baptismo non sit tinctus, Ecclesia est Respublica, et Respublica est externa et visibilis quædam Ecclesia.

CASAUBON de Lib. Eccles. ii. Epist. p. 176. Ex eo tempore quando Christianismi professio vulgò fuit suscepta, *qui Rempublicam* constituebat *populus idem* etiam *Ecclesia* fuit.

G. I. VOSSIUS de Jure Magistratûs in Rebus Ecclesiasticis, p. 863, ed. 1701. Potestas eorum qui publicâ sunt vocatione instructi vel *civilis* est vel *Ecclesiastica*. Civilis procurat humanum bonum uti εὐδαιμονίαν πολιτικήν. Atque hoc respectu Societas hominum non *Ecclesia* sed *Respublica* vocatur. Potestas verò Ecclesiastica procurat Spirituale bonum uti beatitudinem cœlestem; atque eo respectu hæc ipsa *Societas* non jam *Reipublicæ* sed *Ecclesiæ* nomen obtinet.

BURKE, vol. x. p. 43. An *alliance* between Church and State in a Christian Commonwealth is, in my opinion, an idle and a fanciful speculation. An *alliance* is between *two* things that are in their nature distinct and independent, such as between two sovereign states. But in a Christian Commonwealth the *Church and State are one and the same thing*. The Church has been always divided into two parts, the *clergy* and the laity; of which the *laity* is as much an essential integral part, and has as much its *duties* and *privileges* as the clerical member, and in the rule, order, and government of the Church has its share.

PART III.

Q. You say that Church and State are two different names of the same thing; and that the *same men* who in *spiritual* respects make the *Church* do in *temporal* make the *State;* can you explain by what *process* this came to be so?

A. Let us suppose, for example, the condition of the Roman Empire when Christianity was first preached. The State was then heathen, and its citizens were Pagans. The Gospel prevailed; many Roman citizens became Christians, and at length the Emperor of Rome professed the faith of Christ. Now, the citizens did not *lose* any of their *civil* rights, nor the Emperor[1] his *imperial*, by embracing Christianity; but both brought with them their secular privileges and functions into their new religious condition. And thus the Roman *State* became a Christian *Church;* and so it continued long to be. And when the Roman Empire was broken up into several nations, each Nation became not only an independent State, but also a National Church. And every heathen Nation which now embraces Christianity becomes a Church in the same manner as the Roman State did. And thus every Christian Nation is both a Church and a State, according to the relations in which it is viewed; not, however, that it is in any case a *perfect* Church (for there is *no* perfect Church on *earth*) any more than it is a *perfect* State, but one Church varies greatly from another in soundness, and from itself at various times.

[1] On the other hand, the Emperor gained *new rights* and was called to *new duties,* as Governor of the Community, not only as a State, but as a Church; or as Bp. ANDREWES expresses it, Tortura Torti, p. 377, Cæsari, si Christianus fit, ut Constantino, idem juris in Ecclesiam est in Novo Testamento quod in Vetere Josiæ fuit. Tum Reges Ecclesiæ gubernacula capessant cùm conversi ad fidem fuerint. *Reddenda* enim *Cæsari quæ Cæsaris* sunt. Cæsaris sunt quæ Cæsari debentur. Debentur autem Cæsari *Christiano* quæcunque olim à Populo Dei sub

Veteri Lege Regibus suis officia vel debita vel persoluta sunt—non in *Regni* rebus solùm, sed etiam *Ecclesiæ*.

Q. But may not a Nation divest itself of its religious character, and exist only in its civil one?

A. No doubt it may *de facto*, by apostatizing from Christianity, and lapsing into heathenism or infidelity; but no Community[1] can *prosper* without religion, any more than an Individual can; *non aliunde beata Civitas, aliunde homo*, as S. Augustin says, and *malè vivitur, ubi non de Deo benè creditur*.

Prov. xiv. 34.
Ps. xxxiii. 12.
Ps. cxxvii. 1.
Jer. xi. 8.
xii. 17.

[1] Archbp. LAUD, Sermons, vi. p. 176. Unity is a binder up; and Unity of Spirit (which is Religion's Unity) is the fastest binder that is. And lest it should not bind fast enough, it calls in the bond of peace; so that no man can exhort unto, and endeavour for the Unity of the *Church*, but at the same time he labours for the good of the *State*. . . . . Unity not kept in the Church is less kept in the State. And the schisms and divisions of the one are both mothers and nurses of all disobedience and disjointing in the other. So the Apostle's exhortation (Eph. iv. 3) goes on directly to the Church, and by consequent to the State.

Q. But did not ancient Republics flourish without religion?

A. No; as far as they did flourish, they flourished *by* religion[1].

[1] See the copious citations by Bp. Taylor on this subject, Rule of Conscience, iii. iii. Rule iv.

Q. But how could they flourish by *idolatry?*

A. They did not flourish by idolatry, *as idolatry;* but they flourished by *Religion*, as opposed to Atheism or *no Religion*.

HOOKER, V. XII. 6. V. LXXVI. 6.

Q. Are, then, civil communities bound to maintain religion?

A. Yes; and Christian men united together in that Society which is called a *Body Politic*,

Deut. xxviii. 1.

PART III.
1 Sam. xii. 14.
Isa. iii. 10.
Below, ch. iv.

are bound to maintain the *Christian* Religion in soundness and purity, as their *most important concern*[1].

[1] HOOKER, V. I. 2. Pure and *unstained* Religion ought to be the *highest of all cares* appertaining to public regiment; as well in regard of the aid and protection which they who serve God confess that they receive at His merciful hands, as also for the force which Religion hath to qualify all sorts of men, and to make them in public affairs the more serviceable; Governors the apter to rule with conscience; Inferiors for conscience sake the willinger to obey. Bp. ANDREWES, Tortura Torti, p. 381. Religionis cura non est *regia* tantum, sed in regiis *prima*.

BURKE, vol. x. p. 43. Religion is so far, in my opinion, from being out of the province or the duty of a Christian magistrate, that it is, and it ought to be, *not only his* care, but the *principal thing* in his care; because it is one of the great bonds of human society; and its object, the supreme good, the ultimate end and object of man himself.

Q. By what law are they so bound?

Prov. xiv. 34.

A. By the will of ALMIGHTY GOD, Who has made man a social being, and Whose work human Society is[1], which He wills not only *to exist*, but to exist in the most *perfect condition* of which it is capable; and since "Righteousness exalteth a Nation," and "Religion is the root of every virtue[2]," and the *Christian religion* is the foundation of all *Christian virtue;* therefore a civil Community is bound to promote by all means in its power the *public* and *private* exercise and well-being of the Christian Religion.

[1] BURKE, vol. vi. p. 326. God wills the State.
[2] HOOKER, V. I.

Q. Its duty, then, to itself, as well as to God, prescribes the same thing?

Ps. cxxvii. 1. cxliv. 15.
Judith v. 17—21.
vi. 10.

A. Yes, certainly, "happy and blessed are the People who have the Lord for their God;" "all things religiously taken in hand are prosperously ended[1];" and what the heathen poet said to his own country, may be said to all States and Kingdoms,

> "*Dis te minorem quod geris, imperas:*
> *Huc omne principium, huc refer exitum;*
> *Di multa neglecti dederunt*
>   *Hesperiæ mala luctuosæ.*"
>   (HOR. Carm. iii. 6. 5—8.)

[1] HOOKER, V. I. 2. S. AUGUST. Civ. Dei, v. c. 24. Lord Ch. J. COKE, Litt. 95. Nunquam res humanæ succedunt, ubi negliguntur divinæ. HOOKER, V. I. 4. When the Kings of Israel, to better their worldly estates (as they thought), left their own and their people's ghostly condition uncared for, by woful experience they both did learn that to forsake the true God of heaven is to fall into all such evils upon the face of the earth, as men either destitute of divine grace may commit, or unprotected from above may endure.

These words of HOOKER may be a warning to ENGLAND.

CHAPTER II.

ON THE DUTY OF KINGDOMS AND STATES TO PROFESS AND TO PROMOTE THE TRUE FAITH.

Q. BUT, it is asked by some, if a State provides for the interests of Religion, does it not intrude upon God's office?

A. God graciously vouchsafes to Kings and States the privilege of advancing His glory. This is the greatest honour they can enjoy, and the forfeiture of it is their severest punishment. It would be sin and folly on their part to ask Him *why* He gives them this privilege; and would be very unreasonable if they, who derive all their power from God and are most indebted to Him and dependent on Him, should not also be foremost to make acknowledgments to Him of this their obligation and of their dependence, by profession of His truth, by faithfulness in His service, and by zeal for His glory.

Q. You say that Kings and States *derive* their power from *God;* can then a power, which is sometimes tyrannically abused, be said to be divinely derived?

240 THE DUTY OF KINGDOMS AND STATES

PART III.   *A.* God is the *only* source of power; but He is the source of none of its *abuses*. He *permits* in this world much that He does not *approve*. And in His wisdom He often *uses bad Governors* to chastise *bad subjects*, and to prove and try good ones [1], and to train them by wholesome discipline to higher degrees of goodness, and thus to prepare them for greater fruition of glory.

[1] S. IREN. v. 29. Quidam Regum ad correctionem et utilitatem subditorum dantur à Deo, quidam ad timorem et pœnam. S. CHRYSOSTOM ad Rom. xiii. S. AUGUSTIN de Civ. Dei, v. c. 21. Qui dedit imperium Constantino Christiano, Ipse etiam Apostatæ Juliano. Qui Mario imperium dedit, etiam Caio Cæsari; qui Augusto, Ipse et Neroni. S. AUG. Epist. ad Vincent. Terror temporalium potestatum, quando veritatem oppugnant, justis et fortibus gloriosa probatio est, infirmis periculosa tentatio.

Q. You say that *God* is the source of all power,
1 Pet. ii. 13. but does not St. Peter call the Civil Magistrate an Ordinance or Creation (κτίσις) of *Man?*

A. Yes. The *form* of Government, and the choice of *persons* to administer it, are frequently from *man;* but the *authority* of civil Government when constituted, is from *God* [1]. The ordinance of the Civil Magistrate is *per* populum, who is its *mediate* and *instrumental* cause, but it is *à* Deo, who is its *principal* and *efficient* cause [2]. And therefore St. Peter says, "Submit yourself to every *ordinance of man*, for the *Lord's*
Rom. xiii. 1. *sake;"* and St. Paul, "Let every soul be subject to the higher powers or *authorities* (ἐξουσίαις), for there is no power *but from God* (ἀπὸ Θεοῦ): the powers that be, are ordained of God (ὑπὸ Θεοῦ); and he that resisteth the power, resisteth the *ordinance of God.*"

[1] Bp. ANDREWES, Private Devotions, p. 48, ed. 1830. All the kingdoms and governments of the whole earth are Thy ordinance (Rom. xiii. 2), albeit an institution of man (1 Pet. ii. 13). Bp. SANDERSON, Præl. vii. 15. BRAMHALL and HORSLEY in Christian Institutes, iii. 39. Abp.

LEIGHTON in 1 Pet. ii. 13. HOOKER, viii. 11. 6. Unto Kings by human right, honour by very divine right is due.

² Col. i. 16, ἐν αὐτῷ (Χριστῷ) ἐκτίσθη τὰ πάντα.. εἴτε θρόνοι, εἴτε κυριότητες, εἴτε ἀρχαί, εἴτε ἐξουσίαι, τὰ πάντα δι' αὐτοῦ καὶ εἰς αὐτὸν ἔκτισται.

Q. Kings and States derive their authority from God; but did not Christ disclaim all civil power, and renounce all exercise of it in His behalf, when He said to Pilate, *My kingdom is not of this world* (ἐκ τοῦ κόσμου τούτου)? *John xviii. 36.*

A. The Jews thought that the Messiah would be an *earthly* Potentate; and Christ, when He spake these words, was standing before the Roman Governor, being accused by the Jews of usurping Cæsar's authority; *this* is what He disclaimed; and it is to be observed that He does not say, My kingdom is not *in* this world (ἐν τῷ κόσμῳ τούτῳ), but, it is not *from* hence (ἐντεῦθεν), that is, not *derived from* this world (ἐκ τοῦ κόσμου τούτου¹), an expression which He used in the same sense on two other occasions. Nor is it to be advanced by worldly *force*, for then, as He says, His servants would have *fought* for Him. Jesus Christ expressly declared that to Himself "*all power* in heaven and earth is given;" He is "the Prince of the Kings of the earth;" He Himself is the source of all Power; and He did not come to make Himself an earthly King, but He *did* come to make Kings members and ministers of His kingdom. And it is clear from Holy Scripture, that though Christ did not come into the world to exercise earthly power in His own person, yet that all they who have earthly power, are His servants and ministers, and bound to exercise it for the promotion of His glory. *John xix. 12.* *John viii. 23. xv. 19.* *Matt. xxviii 18. Rev. i. 5.* *Wisd. vi. 4.*

¹ THEOPHYLACT in Joann. c. 18, p. 743. εἶπε, ὅτι ἡ βασιλεία μου οὐκ ἔστιν ἐκ τοῦ κόσμου τούτου· καὶ αὖθις, ὅτι οὐκ ἔστιν ἐντεῦθεν· οὐ γὰρ εἶπεν, οὐκ ἔστιν ἐν τῷ κόσμῳ, οὐδέ ἐστιν ἐνταῦθα· βασιλεύει μὲν γὰρ (ὁ Χρισ-

PART III. τὸs) ἐν τῷ κόσμῳ καὶ προνοεῖται τούτου, καὶ, ὡς βούλεται, περιάγει τὰ πάντα· οὐκ ἔστι δὲ ἐκ τοῦ κόσμου ἡ βασιλεία αὐτοῦ, ἀλλ' ἄνωθεν καὶ προαιώνιος—ἔπειτα πῶς ἂν νοηθείη τὸ εἰς τὰ ἴδια ἦλθεν, εἰ μὴ ἦν ὁ κόσμος ἴδιος αὐτοῦ;

S. AUG. Tract. in S. Joann. cxv. Non ait, 'Regnum meum non est *hic*,' sed 'non est *hinc*:' *Hic* enim *est* Regnum Ejus, usque in finem sæculi. On this text see also HOOKER, VII. xv. 11.

Q. How does this duty of Kings to maintain and promote the true Faith appear from Scripture?

Rom. xiii. 1. 4. 6.
Col. i. 16.
ἔκτισται...
ἐκτίσθη... in the original.
Dan. ii. 21. iv. 25.
1 Tim. vi. 15.
Prov. viii. 15.
Isa. xlix. 23. lx. 16.
Acts iv. 25 —27.

A. As has been before stated, Kings[1] are there represented as God's Vicegerents and "Ministers for good" to men (διάκονοι, λειτουργοί). They derive their power[2] from CHRIST, by Whom "all things were *created*, whether they be Thrones, or Dominions, or Principalities, or Powers;" and "Who is *the only Potentate*, the King of kings, and Lord of lords;" "by Whom kings reign and princes decree justice;" and God has promised that "Kings shall be the nursing-fathers, and Queens the nursing-mothers," of His Church. And the second Psalm, which prophesies of this very event, which has just been mentioned, I mean of Christ standing before Pilate, when, it is also to be observed, our Lord spake of Pilate's official power as derived *from above* (ἄνωθεν) (i. e. from *Himself*[3]), concludes with an exhortation from the Royal Psalmist to Kings and all

Ps. ii. 12.

in authority, to be *wise and serve the Lord with fear*, and to *kiss the Son*, i. e. to reverence Christ,

Ps. cxlviii. 11.

as their subjects reverence *them*. "Praise the Lord," he says again, "ye Kings of the earth, and all People, Princes, and all Judges of the

Rev. iv. 10.

World." And, in the Revelation, the *twenty-four elders cast their crowns before His throne;* and

Rev. xi. 15.
Rev. xix. 16.
xxi. 24.

the voices in heaven say, "*The kingdom of this world is become the kingdom of the Lord, and of His* CHRIST." *That* cannot be otherwise than glorious for Kings and Nations to *do*, which, *when done*, will be sung of by Angels in heaven, as redounding to the glory of Christ.

[1] S. IREN. v. 20. Cujus jussu nascuntur homines, Hujus jussu et reges constituuntur. TERTULLIAN, Apolog. 30. Ideo magnus est imperator, quia cœlo minor est; inde est imperator unde et homo; inde potestas illi unde et spiritus. Ad Scap. 2. Imperator homo à Deo secundus, quicquid est à Deo consecutus; et solo Deo minor, omnibus major, dum solo Deo minor. S. AUGUST. iv. 722. 1141. Jam in fronte Regum Crux illa fixa est, &c.

[2] HOOKER, VIII. IV. 6. No power (saith the Apostle) Rom. xiii. 1. but from God, nor doth any thing come from God but by the hands of our Lord Jesus Christ.—All authority of man is derived from God through Christ, and must by Christian men be acknowledged to be *no* otherwise held than *of* and *under* Him. See Bp. OVERALL, Convocation Book, Book i. c. 2, xxxv. xxxvi. CASAUBON de Lib. Eccles. c. 11, iv.

[3] S. AUG. in Psalm xxix. and xxxii. tom. iv. pp. 195 and 287.

Q. But if a National Community is obliged to promote religion, must it not profess *some one form* of religion, and one at variance with that of many of its members, where they *differ* in their religious opinions?

A. The Community consists of persons who are bound to profess the *true faith*, which is *one*[1]. Eph. v 5.

[1] S. HIERON. in Esai. xix. Unum altare dicitur, sicut *una fides*, et *unum baptisma*, et *una Ecclesia*. See above, pp. 28—31. See further below, Pt. iii. ch. iii.

Q. But when they *differ* in their belief, how can this be done? is it not very difficult to be attained?

A. All *good* things *are difficult;* and *Unity* is one of the *best*. It is too great a good to be acquired except by a hearty combination of *desire, resolution,* and *earnest endeavour* ($\sigma\pi o\upsilon\delta\acute{\eta}$[1]). But we cannot suppose it to be unattainable, for if it were, Scripture would not have required us to endeavour to *keep* it. They who differ ought to *consider the grounds* of their *differences;* they ought to reflect on the *sinfulness* of *strife*, and

Ps. cxxxiii.
2 Cor. xiii. 11.
Phil. i. 27.

1 Cor. iii. 3.
Gal. v. 20.

PART III.
Ps. cxxxiii. 1.
Eph. iv. 2.
1 Cor. i 10.

the *blessings of unity;* and they ought to endeavour therefore to *put an end* to their *differences,* according to the advice of the Apostle, "*endeavouring* earnestly (σπουδάζοντες) *to keep the Unity of the Spirit in the bond of peace;*" "*I beseech you, brethren, by the name of our Lord Jesus Christ, that ye* all speak the same thing, *and that there be no divisions among you, but that ye be* perfectly joined together *in the* same mind *and in the* same judgment" (νοὶ καὶ γνώμῃ); "doing *nothing* through *strife,* but being *of one accord,* earnestly following after the things which make for peace, and wherewith one may edify another."

[1] Archbp. LAUD, Sermons, vi. On Unity. Keep then the unity of the Spirit; but know withal (and it follows in the text, Eph. iv. 3) that if you will keep it you must *endeavour* to keep it. For it is not so *easy* a thing to keep Unity in great bodies as it is thought; there goes much *labour* and *endeavour* to it. The word is σπουδάζοντες; *study,* be careful to keep it. S. Augustin reads it, *satagentes, do enough* to keep it: and he that doth enough, gives not over till it be kept. Nay, the Apostle comes so home, that he uses two words, and both of singular *care* for Unity: for he does not simply say, *Keep it;* nor simply, *Endeavour it;* but, *Study, endeavour* to *keep it.* Now no man can *keep,* that is not careful; and no man will *endeavour,* that is not studious. "Neither is it" (says S. Chrysostom) "every man's sufficiency to be able to keep unity." And the word implies *such an endeavour as makes haste to keep:* and indeed no time is to be lost at this work.

Q. But if they, who differ, are *sincere* in their differences, are they responsible for their opinions, if they are *erroneous?*

A. Certainly they are. God has not only given us *Conscience,* but He has also given us His *Law* to *regulate* it. It is not indeed to be supposed that any man is *guilty because* he is *sincere,* or could be *innocent, without sincerity;* but sincerity in *error* may, and generally does, proceed from *bad moral* habits; it is often the result of want of consideration of God's Law, and of resistance to His grace, i. e. it proceeds from such a temper and practice as are forbidden and condemned by God, and as can produce no *good fruits;* and therefore it is not *conscience* or *good intention* alone which can give us any well-grounded assurance of acquittal and acceptance with God.

CHAP. II.
John xvi. 2.
Acts xxvi. 9.
Phil. iii. 6.

Q. You mean, then, that we ought to derive no assurance from our conscience, simply *as conscience,* and that we have no right to presume that its persuasions are not punishable, merely because they are *sincere?*

A. Yes[1]. The Jews, even when they put our Blessed Lord to death, *thought* that they were doing God service. "All the ways of a man" (says Solomon) "are clean in his own eyes; but the Lord weigheth the spirits;" and "There is a way which *seemeth* right unto a man; but the end thereof are the ways of *death.*"

Prov. xvi. 2.
xiv. 12.

[1] XXXIX ARTICLES, Art. xviii. They are to be had accursed, that presume to say that every man shall be saved by the law or sect that he professeth, so that he be diligent to frame his life according to that law and the light of nature. See also Art. xiii., and W. LAW, Letters to Bp. Hoadly, pp. 331—334, and p. 570, in Scholar Armed, vol. i. Of Sincerity and Private Judgment.

Q. In what cases, then, *may* our conscience *be pleaded by* us as justifying our practice?

A. When our conscience is *right,* i. e. when it is regulated by God's Law; or, in other words, when we have used all the means in our power to *reform* our conscience where it is *erroneous,* to *inform* it where it is *ignorant,* and to *conform* it to God's Will and Word, where it is refractory[1].

Acts xxiv. 16.
1 Tim. i. 5.
19. iii. 9.
iv. 2.

[1] CANONS, 1603, Canon lvii. We require and charge every person seduced as aforesaid to *reform* their *wilfulness,* and submit to the order of the Church; and if any will not be moved to *reform* their *error* and *unlawful course,* &c.

PART III.   HOOKER, Preface, VI. 6; and compare IV. x. 1. The most effectual medicine to heal their grief is not the *taking away* of the things whereat they are grieved, but the *altering* of *their own persuasion* concerning them. See also Bp. SANDERSON, Sermons, iv. § 24. 29. Notes in Christian Institutes, iv. 417 511—513. 607—609. See below, Pt. iv. chap. ii.

Q. But, if the endeavour for Unity fails, must still *some one form* of religion be professed?

A. There is, as has been shown (pp. 22—32), *one true faith*, and *one only*; and it is not less necessary for *Communities* to receive, nor less important for them to profess, this *one true faith*, than it is for *Individuals* to do so[1]. "How long *halt ye* between *two* opinions?" was not addressed by God's prophet to *Individuals*, but to a *State*. And a *mixture* of Religions in a State was denounced by God as a national sin in the case of the Cuthites, Avites, and Sepharvites, and other inhabitants of Samaritan cities. "He that sacrificeth unto any god, save unto the Lord, shall be destroyed." GOD declares that He will cut off all who "make *many* altars to sin," and "worship and swear by the *Lord*, and that swear by *Malcham*;" i. e. who *combine* false religions with the truth. He has revealed Himself as "a *jealous* God[2]," i. e. as one who will bear no rival in the worship due to Him; and that He is to be "worshipped in *truth*;" and that He will not spare those who join error and corruption with His pure faith and worship.

Rev. iii. 15.
1 Kings xviii. 21.
2 Kings xvii. 24—41.
Zeph. i. 5.
Lev. xix. 19.
Hos. viii. 11.
Deut. xxii. 9.
Exod. xxii. 20.
xxiii. 13.
xxiv. 14.
Jud. vi. 10.
1 Cor. v. 9.
2 Cor. vi. 14.

Religious *divisions*, and religious *indifference*, are sinful; and they cannot be remedied except by an earnest desire on the part of all the members of the community to join the stedfast and zealous profession of the *One true Faith*; and it is the duty of a Nation, and especially of its Rulers, as they hope to escape God's wrath and to receive His blessing, to aid and encourage all desires and endeavours for the performance of

His Will and advancement of His Glory, by maintaining and promoting NATIONAL UNITY in true religion, and to abstain from all that is of a contrary tendency.

CHAP. II.

[1] Bp. BILSON on Christian Subjection, p. 29. I reckon it cannot stand with a Prince's dutie to reverse the heavenly decree, "Thou shalt worship the Lord thy God, and Him only shalt thou serve," (Matt. iv. 10,) by establishing *two Religions* in *one* Realme.

[2] Lord BACON de Unitate Ecclesiæ, iii. Inter attributa Veri Dei ponitur, quod sit *Deus zelotypus*, (Exod. xx. 5. xxii. 20. xxiv. 14,) itaque cultus ejus non fert *mixturam*. Bp. ANDREWES on the Decalogue, p. 101. See S. AUGUSTIN's Sermon x. on the Judgment of Solomon (1 Kings iii. 16—28).

Q. But is it not unjust to levy taxes for the support of a national religious establishment, on those who *dissent* from it?

A. Almighty God did not so judge, when He commanded that a regular maintenance should be provided throughout Israel, (where there were many worshippers of Jeroboam's calves and of Baal,) for the maintenance of the Priests and the Temple. If every man were to be taxed only for what he *approved*, there would be *no State Revenue*. Many persons (e. g. Quakers, &c.) have religious scruples against *war*: is it therefore unjust that they should be taxed for the maintenance of the Army and Navy? No. *Salus populi suprema Lex*. So a Nation is not to suffer loss of or weakness in its *spiritual* army and navy, the Church, because many do *not approve* of its doctrines.

Exod. xxx. 16.
Deut. xii. 19. xiv. 29.
2 Chron. xxxi. 4.
Mal. iii. 10.

Q. How does this appear from the nature of *Taxes?*

A. Taxes are paid by subjects, in token of subjection to the civil Power, and to afford it the means of protecting their persons and property, and as a remuneration for its service in doing so; but Taxes do not oblige the civil Power to pro-

PART III. pagate the opinions of those who pay them, or not to propagate those which they disapprove. Christ ordered the Jews to pay tribute to Tiberius, who certainly did not propagate Judaism, but heathenism: and St. Paul ordered Christians Rom. xiii. 6. to pay tribute to Nero, who *persecuted Christianity;* and the reason he gives, is that the imperial power was God's minister attending on the preservation of peace. Since also *unity* of Religion is the great preservative of public and private peace, the civil Power acts unjustly to those who pay taxes, and inconsistently with its duty to them, if it encourages diversity of religions, and does *not* maintain *unity* in the truth.

Besides, Dissenters are Christians, and, as such, must desire the maintenance and extension of Christianity; and they cannot suppose, or at least can never prove, that a Nation can hope for Prosperity, without promoting Religion. All property is from God, and is God's, and ought to be consecrated to Him.

The individual Dissenter may prefer his own form of worship to that of the Church, yet since he *agrees* in many, perhaps in most, doctrines of Christianity with the Church, and since he *differs* as much from other Dissenters of other Denominations as he does from the Church, and since the Church is established, he ought for the sake of peace and unity to desire its prosperity. He may wish that those particular tenets, in which he *differs* from the Church, *were* not held and taught by the Church; but how can he desire that those tenets in which he *agrees* with it, and by virtue of his agreement in which he is so far a member of the Church, were not maintained in the Church, or that division were endowed instead of unity?

Q. But may not the State rightly promote *different* forms of Religion?

A. And where is it to *stop*, when it once begins

to do so? "*ullusne excludet jurgia finis?*" Besides, by endowing *various forms* of Religion, it would virtually endow *none*. It would deprive itself of its only sound support, that of Religion. It would not promote Religion, but *Indifference to Religion*. It would produce in the mind of the people the dangerous opinion that *all Religions are equally* true, and that there is no one true Faith; and thus would propagate Infidelity, and so hasten its own dissolution. But no: the duty of a State is to discern and maintain the *true* form of Religion; and if it endeavours to do this, religious differences, which arise from the *neglect* of this duty, will with God's blessing disappear.

Q. Have we any Scripture Rules for such cases as these, where religious differences prevail?

A. During the ministry of Jesus Christ and His Apostles, no State or Governing Power had become Christian; but St. Paul writing to Christian Communities, sundry members of which differed from each other in religious opinions, does not teach them that on this account they are to maintain *no* form, or *different* forms, of religious belief; but, on the contrary, he exhorts them all *to stand fast in the one true faith*, not to be *corrupted from the simplicity* or *singleness* (ἁπλότητος) *that is in Christ*, and *by speaking the truth in love* to confirm themselves and others in the true faith. [1 Cor. xvi. 13. Phil. i. 27. 2 Cor. xi. 3. Eph. iv. 15.]

Q. But may not the Community *err* in its religious belief?

A. It may, as an Individual may; but the possibility of its making a mistake in its belief will never excuse a State, any more than an Individual, for professing no belief at all; but it ought to make it careful to prove the truth and to hold it fast; to "buy the truth" at any cost, and not to "sell it" at any price. [1 Thess. v. 21. Prov. xxiii. 23.]

Q. Ought not this possibility of error to make

250 THE DUTY OF KINGDOMS AND STATES

PART III.

Luke xiv. 23.
Rev. iii. 9.
2 Cor. i. 24
Rom. xvi. 17.
1 Tim. vi. 3—5.
2 John 10.

a Community charitable to those who hold different opinions in religion?

A. Certainly; and therefore it ought to abstain from enforcing religious opinions [1] with the civil sword; but it has a duty to be done to God and to itself [2], by *promoting*, and *encouraging* what is *true*, and by *abstaining* from giving aid or patronage to what is *false*.

[1] TERTULLIAN. ad Scapulam, 2. Religionis non est religionem cogere. S. AUGUST. ii. 403, 404. (Epist. c.) LACTANT. Div. Inst. v. 20. Defendenda religio est non occidendo sed moriendo. Religio *cogi* non potest. Verbis potius quàm verberibus res agenda est.

[2] HOOKER, V. LXVIII. 7.

Q. Is there any exception to this rule of *Toleration?*

Dan. iii. 29.
2 Pet. ii. 10.
Exod. xxii. 28.

A. When opinions, *calling themselves religious*, lead to practices which tend to public scandal, to the subversion of order, the destruction of loyalty, and to the dissolution of the Community, there those practices may properly be made the object of civil restraints and penalties [1].

[1] Bp. BARLOW, Case of a Toleration, p. 30, ed. 1692.

Q. But if the Community, acting as a *State*, touches religious matters, is there not a danger that it may intrude into some concerns which ought to be treated by it as a *Church*, and not as a State?

Ezek. xxii. 26. xliv. 23.
Matt. xxii. 21.
Mark xii. 17.
Luke xx. 25.

A. This may happen; but there is a check upon such a deviation, in the fact that the Clergy are members of the Community as a State [1]: and that the Clergy are commanded by God to teach the difference between the holy and the profane; and the civil Rulers of the State are to consider well the sin and danger of profanely intermeddling with holy things. But although such results *may* happen, it would be unpatriotic, unloyal, and unchristian, to desire, on that account, that the State should be without the power of exercising the noblest of her functions, that of *promoting the glory* of GOD and the welfare of the People by religious acts; and although in Christian *prudence* and *charity*, *individuals* ought to *forego* the *use* of *indifferent* things, *not publicly ordered*, when there is a great probability of their *abuse*, and when this abuse is *hard*[2] to *rectify*; yet in the case of a *positive public good*, it would be *unwise* and *uncharitable* to allow that danger of its *abuse* should make us forget and forfeit the great *legitimate uses* of the public maintenance of Christianity by a State; rather, we ought to endeavour to *remove* the *abuse*, and thus to *confirm* and extend the *use*.

CHAP II.

Below,
pt. iv. ch. ii.
2 Kings
xviii. 3. 4.
Rom. xii. 21.
Col. iv. 5.

[1] Bp. GIBSON, Codex, pp. 1—20.
[2] HOOKER, V. LXV. 12—17.

Q. What are the uses in the present case?

A. The State, by professing publicly the true Christian Faith in its national acts; by mixing Prayers, and religious Services, and Sacraments, with the discharge of its civil duties; by supporting the moral and religious Discipline of the Church, as relates to Clergy and Laity; by giving additional vigour to ecclesiastical laws; by an adequate increase of the Episcopate of the country, according to the needs of the population; so that the Parochial Clergy may be stimulated to catechize their people, and to prepare them for Confirmation, and for the Holy Communion; and so that Confirmations may be duly administered in the Parish Churches of the country; and by providing for the erection, repair, and endowment of Churches and Schools[1]; by guarding the use of a sound and uniform Liturgy, and of Scriptural instruction, in the Churches and Chapels of the land; by securing a competent maintenance to the Clergy; by assigning to Bishops a place in Courts and Parliaments[2]; by preferring pious, learned, and faithful Clergymen;

Zech. iv. 2, 3.

1 Cor. ix. 7—11.
1 Tim. v. 18

PART III. confers great benefits, both spiritual and temporal, on all classes of society. It animates the
Deut. xxxii. whole body with religious life, and maintains it
28—31. in peace and unity; it preserves the Nation from
Matt. xi. 5.
Luke iv. 14. Fanaticism on one side and from Infidelity on
vii. 22. the other; by giving external dignity to religion,
James ii. 3. it preserves the rich from the danger of despising
Micah iv.13. it; by endowing it, it provides for the regular,
sober, and unreserved preaching of the Word and
due administration of the Sacraments, and for
pastoral superintendence and religious consola-
tion to both rich and poor; in fine, it consecrates[3]
itself to Almighty God, and brings down a
blessing from Him on all its undertakings.

[1] See S. HIERON. in Zech. viii. on the erection of Churches, "*expensis reipublicæ.*" GERHARD de Magistratu Politico, vi. 592. *Scholæ sunt* seminaria ac plantaria Ecclesiæ. Quemadmodum in corpore humano est suavissima venarum et arteriarum συζυγία, sive combinatio, ita in corpore Christi mystico, Ecclesiæ et Scholæ pulcherrimâ quâdam harmoniâ sibi invicem sunt conjunctæ. De scholis igitur rectè instituendis Magistratus solicitus sit vel maximè.

[2] HOOKER, VII. xv. 8. Let not envy so far prevail as to make us account that a blemish, which, if there be in us any spark of sound judgment or of religious conscience, we must, of necessity, acknowledge to be one of the chiefest ornaments unto this land, by the ancient laws whereof the Clergy being held for the chief of those Three Estates, which together make up the entire body of this Commonwealth, under one supreme Head and Governor, it hath all this time ever borne a sway proportionable in the weighty affairs of the land: wise and virtuous kings condescending most willingly thereunto, even of reverence to the Most High; with the flame of whose sanctified inheritance, as it were with a kind of divine presence, unless their chiefest civil assemblies were so far forth beautified, as might be without any notable impediment unto their heavenly functions, they could not satisfy themselves as having showed towards God an affection most dutiful.

Archbp. LAUD, Answer to the Lord Say's Speech against the Bishops, (Remains, vol. ii. pt. 2, fol. 1700,) pp. 1—21. The Bishops of England have ever sat all of them in Parliament, the highest Court of Judicature, ever since

Parliaments were in England. See Bp. GIBSON, Codex, p. 125, note *w*, and p. 128. Christ. Inst. iv. p. 661.

BURKE, Reflections on the Revolution in France, v. 195. While we provide first for the poor, and with a parental solicitude, we have not relegated Religion, like something we were ashamed to show, to obscure Municipalities or rustic Villages. No; we will have her exalt her mitred front in Courts and Parliaments; we will have her mixed throughout the whole mass of life, and blended with all the classes of society.

³ Archbp. LAUD, Sermon i. The commonwealth can have no blessed and happy being but by the Church.

LORD CHANCELLOR ELDON (Letter to Rev. M. Surtees, Feb. 1825). My opinion is, that the Establishment is framed not for the sake of making the Church political, but for the purpose of making the State religious; that an Establishment with an enlightened toleration is as necessary to the peace of the State as to the maintenance of Religion; without which the State can have no solid Peace.

DECLARATION of the ENGLISH LAITY, A.D. 1833. We find ourselves called upon by the events which are daily passing around us, to declare our firm conviction that the consecration of the State by the public maintenance of the Christian Religion is the first and paramount duty of a Christian People; and that the Church Established in these Realms, by carrying its sacred and beneficial influences through all orders and degrees, and into every corner of the land, has for many ages been the great and distinguishing blessing of this country; and not less the means, under Divine Providence, of National Prosperity, than of individual Piety.

Q. And what do you hence conclude with regard to the duty of *Individuals?*

A. It is their part to cherish a spirit of religious concord, and to abstain from religious divisions, which may embarrass their Rulers in the discharge of this high and holy duty of maintaining Religious Unity; and dutifully and thankfully to assist their Governors, by earnest prayer for them and by loyal co-operation with them in all their endeavours to maintain it.

CHAPTER III.

ON THE CHURCH OF ENGLAND AS THE SPIRITUAL MOTHER OF CHRISTIANS IN THIS COUNTRY.

Above, p. 234.

Q. You have said that a Christian community bears the name either of a State or of a Church, according to the functions which it exercises.

A. Yes[1].

[1] Archbp. BRAMHALL, Reply to Bishop of Chalcedon, Disc. iii. p. 182. The English Church and the English Kingdom are one and the same society of men, differing, not really, but rationally, from one another in respect of some distinct relations. See above, p. 234, 5.

Q. But however true this theory might have been in England in *former* times, e. g. the fifteenth, sixteenth, and seventeenth centuries, is it not inconsistent to speak *now* of the Church and State, as two names for the *same* community, when a great number of persons, even in the Imperial Legislature, no longer *belong to the Church*, but are *separated from* it, and *opposed to* it?

See above, pp. 23—25.

Above, pt. ii. ch. i. —ix.

Above, pt. i. ch. iv.

A. All men are either Christians or not Christians; and all Christians appertain to the Visible Church. *No one does not belong to the Church except* Atheists, Jews, Infidels, and Apostates[1]. If those persons, of whom you speak, are *Christians*, and if the Church of England is what she has been shown to be, a true branch of the Universal Church, it follows that she is their spiritual Mother. She is the Mother of *all* Christians in *this country*. In the words of Scripture, *she* is to *them all* "the House of God," "the Body of Christ," "the Mother of all living:" and she is appointed by Christ to be the dispenser of His grace *to them all;* and they cannot rightly receive any sacramental grace[2], except by her[3]. She is the Spouse of Christ, and these spiritual gifts are *dos Ecclesiæ*, her dowry, and ners alone. As *Christians*, then, Schismatics are Members, though *unsound* members, of the Church, and must be objects of her regard, as she *ought* to be an object of reverence to them; they are *children* of the Church, though *not obedient* ones; and as long as she is a Church, and as long as they are Christians, neither can she forget her maternal love to them, nor can they cast off their filial duty to her.

CHAP. III.

Above, pp. 12. 16. 45—47.

[1] HOOKER, III. I. 7. V. LXVIII. 6.
[2] S. CYPRIAN, Ep. 55. p. 112. Fell. Christianus non est qui in Christi Ecclesiâ non est.
[3] S. AUG. de Bapt. c. Don. i. c. 23. Ecclesia *omnes* per Baptismum parit, sive *apud* se sive *extra* se; *Ecclesiæ jure* quod est in Baptismo, nascuntur quicunque nascuntur. Ibid. c. 18. Baptizantur *extra* Ecclesiæ communionem, sed tamen baptismate ECCLESIÆ, quod, ubicunque est, sanctum est per se ipsum, et ideo non est eorum qui se separant. *Neque enim* (c. 14) *separatio* eorum *generat* (in baptismo), sed *quod* cum Ecclesiâ tenuerunt.—S. AUG. in Ps. xxxii. Velint nolint schismatici, *fratres* nostri sunt. —S. AUG. c. Crescon. ii. 16, compares the sacramental graces of the Church, when diffused in schismatic congregations, to the rivers of Eden flowing *out* of Eden: these graces are then waters *of* Paradise, but not *in* Paradise. In what respect Schismatics may be said to belong to the Church, and in what to be separated from it, see above, part i. ch. ii. and ch. v., and BINGHAM, XVI. I. 17. BRAMHALL, ii. 81.

Q. But has not this opinion of Hooker, Casaubon, Vossius, Laud, Saravia, Bramhall, Burke, and others, who asserted the *coincidence* of Church and State, in a Christian country, become inapplicable in England, through the prevalence and growth of religious dissent in this country, and from the fact that Nonconformists are now admissible to Parliament, and may take part in framing the Laws?

Above, p. 235.

A. When Hooker and others said that in a

Christian Nation the State coincides with the Church, they never imagined that *all* men in the *State* would be *sound* members of the *Church*, or even profess all the articles of the Christian Faith: e. g. Hooker says, " Such *politic societies* as do embrace the true religion have the name of *Church* given unto them. We here mean true religion in the *gross*, and *not according to every particular*, for they which in some *particular points* of religion do swerve from the truth, may nevertheless most truly (if we compare them with men of an heathenish religion) be said to hold that religion which is true." (viii. 1. 2.)

Besides, this opinion of which you speak, is not only the opinion of Hooker, &c. but of the English Divines who *preceded* them [1], and of the early Christian Fathers; or rather, as we have seen, it is the doctrine of JESUS CHRIST Himself. "*The Field*" of the Church, says our Lord, "*is the World.*" There will always be *tares* in the Field, (i. e. in the *universal* Church,) and in every portion of it, (i. e. in all *national Churches*,) even to the Harvest: but the world does not *cease* to be the Field, although it may be nearly overgrown with Tares.

There was abundance of Tares (i. e. of scoffers, and sacrilegious persons, as well as schismatics) in the *national field* of England in the age of Hooker and of Laud, (as is notorious from their writings and sufferings [2],) and tares abounded in the field, and had the principal place in the Field, in the antecedent times of Popery; but yet, as we have seen, the English *Nation*, as it was then, was by them affirmed to be the English Church; just as the *State* of Israel and of Judah was the *Church* of God, even in the wilderness, (Acts vii. 38,) when the people rebelled against God, and in the times of Ahab, of Manasseh, and of the Pharisees. It is true, indeed, that where tares *abound* in it, a Nation is a Church in a corrupt and *unsound state*.

 The fallacy of those who would thence argue that it is not then a Church, proceeds from the same source as the error of those who affirmed that *heretics* and *schismatics* are³ *wholly severed* from the Church, and that therefore Baptism administered by them is no sacrament. It is this same error as that of those who think that because Rome is a very *corrupt* Church, therefore she is *no* Church at all. It arises from not observing the nature of the difference, first, between the Church Visible and Invisible, and then between the Church Visible in a sound, and the same Church in an *unsound* state⁴.

CHAP. III.

Above, p. 73. 4

---

¹ Bp. GARDINER, in his important treatise de Verâ Obedientiâ, (ed. Hamburg, 1536,) p. 806. Tom. ii. of Browne's Fasciculus Rerum expetendarum et fugiendarum. Quatenus in Angliâ commoratur, de *regno* est; quatenus verò Christianus est, in Angliâ etiam commorans, de *Ecclesiâ Anglicanâ* esse censetur. Caput, inquiunt, Princeps est Regni, non Ecclesiæ: cùm tamen Ecclesia Anglicana nihil aliud sit quàm virorum et mulierum, clericorum et laicorum in regno Angliæ commorantium in *Christianâ professione* unita congregatio.

² There were Puritans and Papists then in Parliament. "It is notorious," says a Romanist writer (Dr. O'Conor, Hist. Address, ii. 302), "that the Oath of Supremacy did not exclude the Catholic members from the Irish Parliaments of 1615, 1639, 1640, 1641." See ibid. p. 431. HUME's Hist. c. xlvi. A.D. 1604, Gunpowder Plot. . . . Some of the conspirators were startled by the reflection that many *Roman Catholics* must be present, as attendants on the king, or as having *seats in the house of Peers*. See also Mr. C. BUTLER's Memoirs of English (R.) Catholics, ii. p. 43. By the Test Act, 25 Car. ii. c. 2, and by 30 Car. ii. c. 1, Roman Catholics were excluded from Parliament.

 Some persons who had only received Presbyterian orders were allowed to officiate and hold benefices in the Church, in the age of Richard Hooker. See Nichols, 25; e. g. Whittingham, Dean of Durham; and Travers, Preacher at the Temple, London, and made Provost of Trinity Coll. Dublin. See Hooker's Works by Keble, vol. iii. p. 554. iv. 690, and Hooker's forebodings, Pref. i. 1, and V. LXXIX.

PART III. 6. Lord Bacon iii. 14. The principles of Leicester, Knollys, and Walsingham are well known.

³ Whereas the true doctrine is, that "men remain in the *visible Church* till they *utterly renounce* the profession of Christianity." HOOKER, III. I. 8, 9, 10. "Where *professed unbelief* is there can be no visible Church; there may be, where sound belief wanteth."

⁴ Against which error HOOKER carefully warns his readers (see above, p. 16) in his *Third* Book (III. I. 9), without which the *Eighth* cannot be rightly understood.

Q. But if, as you have said, the Church regards Dissenters as belonging to her, does she not thereby encourage Schism?

A. No. The Church is charitable to schismatics, and she knows that it is a work of *charity* to *schismatics* to warn them that *wilful schism* is mortal sin; for such *God* declares it to be. And in all this, she remembers that many schismatics are not such either wilfully or willingly, but only by the circumstances of birth or education, or by neglect on the part of Ministers of the Church; and even they, who *are* so, are still men and Christians, and as such, they profess to obey the voice of God and of Christ. Therefore she cannot reject them; she cannot despair of them. Though they are *tares* or *bad*¹ *wheat* (ζιζάνια), still they are in *her field*, and by God's converting power they may become *good* wheat. They are now *chaff*, but they are on her *floor*, and they may become *good grain*². And though *they* are schismatical, yet she is Universal: and she therefore regards them as still hers, though their *schism* is not hers. *Odit errores, sed amat errantes*³, she loves the *erring*, but not their *errors*; and *because* she loves the *erring*, therefore she loves not their *errors*, but desires that they may be exchanged for *truth*; whereas *if* she despaired of them, and renounced them, she would be acting in a spirit of hatred to the erring, and of love to their errors.

Above, p. 38.

Above, p. 11—15.

¹ It is to be observed, that ζιζάνια does not here properly

signify *tares*, but a bad *kind* of *wheat*, (*resembling* it, S. AUG. iv. 9. 11,) which *may become good,* as the *good may become bad.* (See *Lightfoot* and *Scultet.* in Matt. xiii. 25.) Hence S. Chrysostom in loc. αὐτῶν τῶν ζιζανίων πολλοὺς εἰκὸς μεταβαλέσθαι, καὶ γίγνεσθαι σῖτον. See also S. AUG. in Ps. lxiv. 12.—TERTULLIAN, Præscr. Hær. 31, renders ζιζάνια by *avenæ.*

² S. AUG. v. 1519. Homo heri fuit *palea,* hodie fit *frumentum.*

³ S. AUG. de Baptismo c. Donat. i. 12.

Q. But if, as you seem to imply, schismatics may receive some graces, which are the dowry of the Church, are they, as far as these graces are concerned, in a worse state than if they were not schismatics?

A. Yes, certainly they are. It is one thing to *have* a thing, and another to have it *profitably*[1]; one thing to *possess,* another to *use* and *enjoy* it. It is one thing to belong to the Church, and another to appertain to its *Unity.* Schismatics belong to the Church, but not to its *Unity;* and the graces which they may have "*insunt* iis, (says S. Augustin,) sed non iis *prosunt,* verum etiam *obsunt,*" they are *in* them[2], but not *for* them, but they are even *against* them, *as long as they remain wilfully separated* from the *Unity* of the *Church,* i. e. as long as they *continue* wilful schismatics; and it is only *when* they *return* to the *Unity* of the Church, that these graces then "*incipiunt* prodesse in *unitate,* quæ in *schismate* prodesse non poterant[3]," begin to profit them in their *Unity* with the Church, which could not profit them in their *separation* from it.

[1] S. AUG. c. Donat. iv. 24. Salus extra Ecclesiam non est, et ideo quæcunque ipsius Ecclesiæ habentur extra Ecclesiam (i.e. in schismate) non valent ad salutem; aliud est habere, aliud utiliter habere. See also ii. p. 332, Ep. 89, and de Bapt. c. Donat. i. 8. Non ideo se putent sanos quia eos dicimus habere aliquid sanum. Cf. iv. p. 1621, on the case of Simon Magus.

[2] S. AUG. in S. Joann. vi. In *bonis* sancta insunt ad *salutem,* in *malis* ad judicium.—Contra Gaudentium, ii. 11.

PART III. [3] S. Aug. c. Donat. i. 18. c. Crescon. ii. 12. c. Petil. c. 15. Tractat. in S. Joann. vi. Rem Columbæ sed præter Columbam habes; veni igitur ad Columbam, ut prodesse tibi incipiat, quod habes.

Q. But if grace does not profit in separation from the Unity of the Church, how then did it happen, that when the Apostles forbad one who Mark ix. 38. cast out devils in Christ's name, because he did Luke ix. 49. not follow them, Christ said, "Forbid him not?"

A. It does not appear that the person spoken of separated himself from Christ, though he did not follow *in person* in the company of the Apostles; on the contrary, he worked miracles, not in his *own name*, but in Christ's. But even supposing him to have been separated from Christ, then Christ approved *His own power*, even when exercised by one separated from Him; but He did *not* approve the *separation* of him who exercised it, any more than God approved the *sins* of Balaam, Saul, Caiaphas, or Judas, when He prophesied and preached by their mouths; Christ says that the man is on our side (i.e. His works conduce to our good), but he does not say that Luke xi. 23. he is with us, and He says, "He that is not with Matt. xii. 30. Me is against Me; and he that gathereth not with Me scattereth."

Num. xi. 28. *Q.* But do we not read in the book of Numbers that when Eldad and Medad prophesied in the *Camp*, and not in the *Tabernacle* with the other Elders, and Joshua said, "My Lord Moses, forbid them," Moses replied, "Enviest thou for my sake? Would God that *all* the Lord's People were Prophets, and that the Lord would put His Spirit upon them?" And does not this justify the act of Preaching in Separation?

Num. xi. 16, 17. 24—26. *A.* No. Eldad and Medad had been *visibly called* and *sent* by *God*, and *ordained* by *Moses*; and while they prophesied, "the Spirit rested upon them." Moses, too, it is to be observed, approves their *prophesying*, but does not approve their prophesying in a *different place* from the other Elders. A Prophet may be in error and in sin, while his prophesying is true and holy. Their case shows indeed that the Spirit of God is not *restricted* to a particular *place*[1]; but their example in no respect justifies any one in preaching *without* a due *call* and mission, for *they were* duly called and sent; nor does it justify any one, even *if* duly called and sent, in preaching in *Separation*.

[1] Bp. BEVERIDGE, Sermons, i. 33, and see the present Author's notes on these passages, in his edition of the Holy Bible and of the Greek Testament.

℞. But if preaching in schism be sinful, how is it that St. Paul declares, that when some preached Christ even of envy, *strife, and contention* (ἐρίθεια), yet *every way*, whether in pretence, or truth, Christ was preached, therein he rejoiced, yea, and would rejoice? *Phil. i. 15—18.*

℟. It may be well doubted whether St. Paul is there speaking of *ministerial preaching* at all, for he says that the *majority* of the brethren (οἱ πλείονες) were bold to speak the word, and it cannot be supposed that the majority were *Preachers*. But supposing him to speak of *ministerial* preaching, then we say that St. Paul approved the *preaching* of the Gospel, but not[1] the *preaching* of it *in envy and strife;* for he teaches us that envy and strife are carnal; and in the very next chapter of this same Epistle to the Philippians, he says, using the *same word* as here for *strife* (ἐρίθεια), "Let *nothing* be done through *strife;*" and St. James says, using again the same word (ἐρίθεια), that "where there is *strife*, there is *every evil work;*" and "if ye have bitter envying and *strife* (ἐρίθεια) in your hearts, this wisdom is earthly, sensual, devilish." St. Paul again says, that *strife* (ἐρίθεια) is a carnal *1 Cor. iii. 3. Phil. ii. 3. James iii. 14. 16.*

262 THE CHURCH OF ENGLAND THE SPIRITUAL.

PART III.
Gal. v. 20.
1 Cor. xii. 2.

work, and excludes from heaven. *Schism* is against *Charity;* and the same Apostle says, "Though I have the gift of prophecy, and understand all mysteries, and all knowledge; and though I have all Faith, so that I could remove mountains, and have not *Charity*, it profiteth me nothing [2]: and those have not *Charity*, who love not the *Unity* of the Church, "Non habent Dei charitatem, qui non diligunt *Ecclesiæ unitatem* [3]."

[1] ZONAR. in Canon. Apostol. 66, p. 34. Τὰ καλὰ καλῶς γινέσθω. Οὐ καλὸν τὸ καλὸν ὅταν μὴ καλῶς γένηται.—καλὰ μὲν ἐδίδασκον, οὐ καλῶς δέ, (*bona* quidem, sed non *benè*,) says Theodoret in locum; and see S. Chrysostom's Sermon on this text, v. p. 416, ὑγιὲς ἦν τὸ δόγμα, ἑαυτοὺς δὲ ἀπολλύουσιν ἐκεῖνοι ἐξ ἀπεχθείας κηρύττοντες.

S. AUGUST., Tractat. in Joann. xlvi. Quod *fecit malè*, non prædicat de cathedrâ Christi; inde lædit, unde mala facit, non unde bona dicit; cùm audis bona dicentem, ne imiteris mala facientem. Tom. iii. 1735, 1836, 1837.

HOOKER, V. LXII. 5. Whatsoever we do without religious affection is hateful in God's sight, who is therefore said to respect *adverbs* more than *verbs*,—and the mind approves itself to God, not by *doing*, but by *doing well*.

[2] S. AUGUST. in Joann. Evang. Tract. xiv. Omnia illa, quæ laudantur in Ecclesiâ, *nihil illis prosunt*, quia *conscindunt unitatem*, id est, tunicam illam *charitatis*. Quid faciunt? Diserti sunt multi inter illos, magnæ linguæ, flumina linguarum. Numquid Angelicè loquuntur? Audiant amicum sponsi zelantem sponso, non sibi: *Si linguis hominum loquar et Angelorum, charitatem autem non habeam, factus sum ut æramentum sonans, aut cymbalum tinniens.*

[3] S. AUGUST. c. Don. iii. 21.

Q. What, therefore, would you infer from the doctrines of this chapter, respecting the practical duties of individual members of the Church toward the State?

A. If we love our Country, it is our duty to pray and labour above all things that it may be purely and soundly Christian. If it has fallen into an unsound condition in this respect, we shall not give it over as incorrigible and incurable; but we shall labour that it may be *restored to health;* we shall never, therefore, consider *one* national sin as a reason or excuse for *more*, (as if men's sins could rescind God's laws!) but as a call for exertions on our part in the work of *recovery;* remembering always the blessings promised by God to those who "build the old waste places, and raise up the foundations of many generations, and are called the *repairers* of the breach, the *restorers* of paths to dwell in."

Chap. III.

Isa. lviii. 12.

"*Righteousness,*" and Righteousness alone, "*exalteth* a *Nation.*" And all Nations are bound to worship Christ. And if the STATE would discharge its duty in this respect (which no change of time or circumstances can ever alter), if, depending on the bounty of Almighty God for all its blessings, and grateful to Him for them, it would endeavour that additional Bishops, Clergy, and Churches should be provided, in proportion to the increased and increasing Population, then there is good ground for hope that our strifes, dissensions, and animosities, would be greatly abated; and that individuals, families, and districts, would return into the bosom of the Church in entire and happy communion, and would dwell together in Unity, like brethren, and dear children of God, and that, with the increase of private and national piety, the public Peace and Prosperity would be greatly promoted. And the SOVEREIGN, Statesmen, and Individuals who may effect, or aid in effecting, this great work, will be the truest Benefactors of their country, and will be blessed by God in Eternity [1].

Prov. xiii. 34.

Prov. xiv. 34.
Ps. ii. 10, 11.
Dan. xii. 3.

[1] HOOKER, V. LXXVI. 8. We confess with S. Augustin, (de Civ. Dei, v. 24,) that the chiefest happiness for which we have some Kings in so great admiration above the rest, is not because of their long reign, but the reason wherefore we most extol their felicity is, if so be they have virtuously reigned; if the exercise of their power hath been service and attendance upon the Majesty of the Most High; if they have feared Him as their own subjects have feared them; and thus heavenly and earthly happiness are wreathed into

PART III. one Crown, as to the worthiest of Christian Princes it hath by the Providence of Almighty God hitherto befallen.

The ENGLISH TRANSLATORS of the HOLY BIBLE, in their Preface to the Authorized Version, A.D. 1611. It doth certainly belong unto Kings, yea, it doth *specially belong* unto them, to have care of religion, yea, to know it aright, yea, to profess it zealously, yea, to *promote it to the uttermost of their power. This is* their glory before all nations which mean well; and this will bring unto them a far more excellent weight of glory in the day of the Lord Jesus. See below, pt. iii. chap. iv.

Q. What also would you infer to be the duties of members of the Church to their dissenting brethren?

A. That they owe them the charitable offices of counsel, exhortation, assistance, and prayer, in order that they may be induced to reconsider the grounds of their dissent, and examine the true principles of the Church, as instituted by Christ, and to meditate on the sin and danger of schism, and on the blessings of Unity, and on the Divine promises to those who promote it.

CHAPTER IV.

ON THE ECCLESIASTICAL SUPREMACY OF CHRISTIAN RULERS.

Q. Not to speak here of *other* forms of Civil Government,—in cases where the form of Civil Government, as in England, is a *Monarchy*, what is the relation of the Sovereign Power to the Church?

A. In *Christian* Kingdoms the Sovereign Power is ordinarily the "Supreme Governor over all Persons, in all causes," in the community as a Church[1] as well as a State.

[1] CASAUBON de Lib. Eccles. c. v. Quin suprema auc-

toritas in Republicâ Christianâ ad principes jure pertineat, ne dubitandum quidem videtur.

Bps. CARLETON, BILSON, ANDREWES, and WARD, cited by Archdeacon Pott on the Rights of Sovereignty in Christian States, p. 31. 33, 34. 143. 227. HOOKER, Preface, ch. vii. 6. See below, pt. iii. ch. v. See also Abp. WAKE, Authority of Christian Princes, 1697, and PALMER on the Church, ii. p. 340.

Q. But how is this ecclesiastical supremacy of Princes consistent with CHRIST'S Headship of the Church?

A. Christ's Headship differs from that of Kings in *objects*, in *order*, in *measure*, and in *kind*[1]. It differs in *objects*,—for Christ is the Head over all *things* to the *Universal* Church; Kings are Heads over all *persons* in the Churches of *their own Kingdoms*. It differs in *order*,— for Christ ruleth over Kings; they rule under Him. In *measure*,—for His power is universal and absolute; theirs is special and restrained. In *kind*,—for He is the One Invisible source of *inward* life to His Body, the Church; Kings exercise an *external* rule over those visible members of it who live in their times and realms. Kings are Christ's servants, for the promotion of His Glory, and the advancement of His Kingdom. The ecclesiastical Headship of Kings is, therefore, far from being inconsistent with that of Christ; on the contrary, it is subordinate and ministerial to it.

[1] HOOKER, VIII. IV. 1—8. BRAMHALL, ii. 218. See below, pt. iii. ch. v.

Q. On what grounds does the *Ecclesiastical* supremacy of Kings rest?

A. On those of Reason, Scripture, and Authority.

Q. How of Reason?

A. For the maintenance of order in a civil community, there must be *degrees;* and where

PART III. there are degrees, there must be some one *highest* of all: and this highest degree is best assigned to *one* person. And in the case of a *Monarchy*, as England, where it *is* so assigned, it is most fit that this supreme power should reside in the temporal Monarch, for otherwise there would be two supreme heads; and no one "*can serve two masters.*" And this supremacy of Kings is warranted also by express precepts and examples of Holy Writ.

Matt. vi. 24.
Luke xvi. 13.

Q. How does this appear?

A. Kings are there shown to us as God's Vicegerents upon earth, and, as such, claiming subjection from *all* persons in their dominions without distinction; and it would be degrading to them as His Ministers, and to Him whose Ministers they are, to suppose that they have no concern but with the *bodies*[1] of their subjects; and moreover by His ordinance *spiritual* things *are to be* their *special* care; and if their *regal duty* extends to these things, they must have *regal authority* in them, for God never *commands* to do any thing without also authorizing the proper *means* of doing it.

Rom. xiii. 1
1 Tim. ii. 2.

---

[1] Bp. BILSON, Christian Subjection, p. 339. If Princes were first ordained of God for those things only which are needful to maintain this *temporall life*, the power and charge of princes would consist in meats, drinkes, and apparell; and princes would have no further care of their people than they have of their hounds and horses, to see them well fed and smooth kept; which is a very wicked and brutish opinion. Praiers must be made for kings, and for all that are in authority, in order that they may discharge their duties according to God's ordinance, which is, that their subjects, by their help and means, may lead an *honest, godly,* and *quiet* life; *godliness and honesty* being the *chiefest ends of our praiers and effects of their powers.*

1 Tim. ii. 2.

P. 343. If their *dutie* stretch so far, *their authority* must stretch *as* far. Their charge ceaseth where their power endeth. God never requireth princes to do what He permitteth them not to do. If, then, godliness and honestie be the chiefest part of their charge, *ergo* they be likewise the chiefest end of their power.

CHAP. IV.

HOOKER, VIII. III. 2. A gross error it is to think that regal power ought to serve for the good of the body and not of the soul, for men's temporal peace, and not for their eternal safety; as if God had ordained kings for no other end and purpose but only to fat up men like hogs, and to see that they have their mast.—Cp. V. LXXVI. 4. VIII. VI. 11. See Bp. ANDREWES, below, pt. iii. ch. vii.

CASAUBON, Dedicat. Exerc. Baron. Utinam considerare principes vellent, aliud esse sacerdotem agere, ex ambone Scripturas interpretari, Sacramenta administrare, in nomine Christi ligare et solvere; aliud auctoritate suâ prospicere ut quæ sunt sacerdotis agat sacerdos. *Has* partes in Ecclesiâ Dei pii principes sibi semper vindicârunt. *Nova, infanda, execranda* theologia est, quæ docet curam subditorum pertinere ad principem tantùm quatenus *homines* sunt, non quatenus *Christiani.* See also SARAVIA de Imperandi Auctoritate et Christianâ Obedientiâ, ii. c. 52. iii. c. 35.

Q. But you spoke of Scripture Examples, as authorizing the Ecclesiastical supremacy of Kings?

A. Yes. The Leaders and Kings of God's own people of Israel had this authority. They were appointed by God to be *custodes utriusque tabulæ*, i. e. guardians of the *first* table of His Law as well as of the *second.* His Law was never "to depart out of their mouth;" and they were "to read therein all the days of their life," and "to meditate therein day and night:" and "to turn from it neither to the right hand nor to the left." And therefore the Kings, by God's command, as soon as they were *enthroned*[1], were to transcribe with their own hands the Law into a book, from that of the Priests and Levites; and they who exercised this authority well and faithfully were spiritually and temporally blessed by God in themselves and in their people, and are commemorated in Scripture with special commendation by the Holy Spirit. This power was their trial, and the manner in which they exercised it was the very essence of their character[2].

See below, p. 295.

Josh. i. 7, 8. Deut. xvii. 18.

1 Kings xv. 3, 4. 11—15. 2 Chron. xvii. 6. xix. 4. xxiv. 4. xxix. 3. xxxiv. 2.

[1] Bp. BILSON, Christian Subjection, p. 178—180. Therefore this touched not the king's private conversation as a man, but his princely function as a *magistrate*. Bp. BEVERIDGE on XXXIX Articles, Art. xxxvii. vol. ii. p. 368.

[2] S. AUGUST. Epist. ad Bonifac. 50. (al. 185.) Omnes Reges qui in populo Dei non prohibuerunt nec everterunt quæ contra Dei præcepta fuerant instituta, culpantur; qui prohibuerunt et everterunt, super aliorum merita probantur.

[1] Bp. BILSON, p. 262—271. HOOKER, VIII. I.

Q. This is true; but we hear of nothing done for the Church of *Christ* by sovereign Princes in the *New Testament*, nor of any power exercised by them in ecclesiastical affairs.

A. No. Kings had not yet become Christians; but they *were* to *become so*. As S. Augustin says[1], from the second Psalm, which is prophetic of the glories and triumphs of Christianity, "*Nondum implebatur illa prophetia* (of that Psalm), *Et nunc Reges, intelligite; erudimini qui judicatis terram; servite Domino in timore;*" but *now*, he adds, that this prophecy of the Royal Psalmist *has been* fulfilled, and they *have* become Christians, "*Serviant Reges terræ Christo, legem ferentes pro Christo:*" and again, "*Rex, quia* homo *est, servit Deo, vivendo fideliter; quia vero etiam* Rex *est, servit, leges justa præcipientes et contraria prohibentes convenienti vigore sanciendo.*"

[1] S. AUGUSTIN. ii. p. 349, 350. 357. 446. 448. 594. 970. 976, 977. 983. 1143. 1161. iii. 1813. iv. 388. 783. 917. ed Paris, 1836.

Q. Does he support this by any Scripture authority?

A. Yes. Hezekiah and Josiah (he adds[1]) served God by destroying the groves and high places and idolatrous temples; even the king of the Ninevites served Him by reducing his people to repentance and holiness of life; Darius served

Him, by punishing the enemies of the prophet Daniel; even Nebuchadnezzar served Him by a severe law (*terribili lege*) against blasphemy. Who, therefore, (he asks,) after the completion of the prophecies which foretold that *adorabunt Eum omnes Reges, omnes Gentes servient Illi,* " all Kings shall fall down before Him (Christ), and all Nations shall do Him service," " Who now in his sober senses will venture to say to *Christian* princes, Take *no* care, who attacks and who maintains the Church of Christ; take no thought, who among your subjects is religious, and who guilty of sacrilege? No, (he adds,) this cannot be; Kings serve God² when they order what is good, and prohibit what is bad, not only in secular matters but in *spiritual*. They *then* serve Him *as Kings,* when they do for Him what they *could not do, unless they were Kings;* and let them bethink themselves, *if* they *fail* so to do, what account will they be able to render hereafter to Almighty God? This then (he concludes) is their duty,—*to maintain the peace of the Church,* whose *spiritual children they are.*"

Ps. lxxii. 11.

¹ S. Aug. Epist. ad Bonifacium, ii. 977. Quis mente sobrius Regibus dicat, Nolite curare in regno vestro à quo teneatur vel oppugnetur Ecclesia Domini vestri; non ad vos pertinet in regno vestro quis velit esse religiosus sive sacrilegus?

² S. Aug. c. Crescon. iii. 51. Tractat. in Joann. xi. Quomodo (aliter) redderent rationem de imperio suo Deo? Pertinet hoc ad reges sæculi Christianos, ut pacatam velint matrem suam Ecclesiam unde spiritualiter nati sunt.

Bp. Bilson, Perpetual Government of Christ's Church, chap. x. p. 206, ed. Oxf. 1842.

Q. These are indeed the words of S. Augustin; but were the same sentiments generally entertained by Christians after the empire became Christian?

A. Yes, universally; and he who would raise objections to the supreme power, both of *right*

PART III. and *duty* as exercised in spiritual matters by the sovereigns of England, would be undermining the foundations of Reason, on which all Christian Monarchy rests; he would be contravening the examples of the Old Testament [1], and the precepts of the New; he would be not only condemning the practice of Constantine, Theodosius, Justinian [2], and all the great Christian Emperors and Kings, and especially those of England [3]; but impugning the judgment of all the wisest and most pious Fathers of the Church.

[1] BOOK OF WISDOM, chap. vi. ver. 1—6. Hear, therefore, O ye Kings, and understand; learn, ye that be Judges of the ends of the earth. Give ear, ye that rule the people, and glory in the multitude of nations. For power is given you of the Lord, and sovereignty from the Highest, Who shall try your works, and search out your counsels. Because, being Ministers of His Kingdom, ye have not judged aright, nor kept the law, nor walked after the counsel of God; horribly and speedily shall He come upon you: for a sharp judgment shall be to them that be in high places. For mercy will soon pardon the meanest: but mighty men shall be mightily tormented.

Deut. xvii. 18.
Ps. ii. 10, 11.
Isa. xlix. 23.
Rom. xiii. 4.
Luke xiv. 23.

Bp. BILSON, Christian Subjection, pp. 179. 183. If you deny that this is the prince's charge, to see the law of God fully executed, His Son rightly served, His spouse safely nursed, His house timely filled, His enemies duly punished, you must countervail that which Moses prescribed, David required, Esay prophesied, Paul witnessed, and Christ commanded, with some better and sounder authority than theirs is.

[2] Bp. BILSON, Christian Subjection, p. 189. 273. 280.
CONSTANTINE, Epist. ad Ecclesias post Synod. Nicæn.—Euseb. Vit. Const. iii. THEODOSIUS (says St. Ambrose) morti vicinus potiorem Ecclesiæ quàm imperii curam egit JUSTINIAN, Novell. 3. Ea quæ sanctis Ecclesiis conducunt non minori nobis curæ sunt *quàm ipsa anima.* Codex Tit. i. De Summâ Trinitate. Decere arbitramur nostrum imperium subditos nostros de religione commonefacere; ita enim et pleniorem acquiri Dei ac Salvatoris Nostri Jesu Christi benignitatem possibile esse existimamus, si quando et nos pro viribus Ipsi placere studuerimus, et nostros subditos ad eam rem instituerimus.

S. LEO, Epistola xxi., ad Theodosium juniorem, A.D. 449. Præter imperiales curas piissimam solicitudinem

Christianæ religionis habetis, ne in populo Dei schismata aut hæreses aut ulla scandala convalescant, quia tunc est optimus regni vestri status, quando Sempiternæ Trinitati servitur gloriosissimè.

See also the answer of S. OPTATUS, iii. 3, to the question of the Donatists, "Quid est Imperatori cum Ecclesiâ?"

CASAUBON, Ded. Exerc. Baron. Religionis aut neglectæ aut restitutæ decus dedecusve divina eloquia regibus non adscriberent, si ad illorum officium ejus rei cura non pertineret. Constantinus M., Theodosius, Justinianus, et omnes pii imperatores, negotiis religionis quàm diligenter se immiscuerint, quis ignorat?

Ample evidence will be found of this fact in the authorities cited by HOOKER, VII. XVIII. 2. BARROW, Pope's Supremacy, p. 227–234; GROT. de Potestate, 215. 244. 263. 269, 270; BINGHAM, XVI. VI. 6. Archbp. WAKE, Authority of Christian Princes, p. 10.

[3] See Sir R. TWISDEN on Schism, p. 97—100, for examples of exercise of regal power in matters ecclesiastical in England from the earliest time—and further, ibid. p. 208—210.

PALMER on the Church, ii. 335.

Q. How did the diversity of God's dealings with the Church in its relation to Kings at *different* times conduce to *one* and the *same* end?

A. In the *first* ages of Christianity, to show the divine power of His Gospel, God maintained His Church, not only in *independence* of the aid of Kings, but even in *opposition* to their furious attacks; and He did *this* in such a glorious manner as to win Kings to His Church, for her and for themselves; but *when* He had so done, He completed the grand work, and consummated the sacred evidence of the divine truth and power of Christianity, by enlisting Kings in His service, and by making them Defenders of the Faith and Champions of the Church [1].

Matt. xi. 25.
1 Cor. i. 25—27. ii. 8.
Ps. lxviii. 12.

[1] S. CYRIL. Hierosol. Cat. xviii. Ἡ καθολικὴ ἐκκλησία διὰ τῶν ὅπλων τῆς δικαιοσύνης τῶν δεξιῶν καὶ ἀριστερῶν, διὰ δόξης καὶ ἀτιμίας, πρότερον μὲν ἐν διωγμοῖς καὶ θλίψεσι, τοὺς ἁγίους μάρτυρας τοῖς τῆς ὑπομονῆς ποικίλοις καὶ πολυανθέσιν ἔστεψε στεφάνοις, νυνὶ δὲ ἐν καιροῖς εἰρήνης Θεοῦ χάριτι τὰ τῆς ὀφειλομένης ἔχει τιμῆς ὑπὸ βασιλέων καὶ τῶν

PART III. ἐν ὑπεροχαῖς ὄντων καὶ παντὸς ἀνθρώπων εἴδους τε καὶ γένους.

S. AMBROSE, Epist. xvii. to the Emperor Valentinian. Cùm omnes homines, qui sub ditione Romanâ sunt, Vobis militent Imperatoribus terrarum atque Principibus, tum Ipsi Vos Omnipotenti Deo et sacræ Fidei militatis.

S. LEO M. Serm. xxxv. 96. Tantùm contulit fidei impugnatio persequentium, ut nihil magis Regium ornet principatum quàm quod domini mundi membra sunt Christi, nec tam gloriantur quod in Imperio geniti, quàm gaudent quod in Baptismate sunt renati.

HESYCHIUS ad S. Augustin. (August. Opp. ii. p. 1112.) Ex quo clementissimi Imperatores Christiani esse cœperunt, quanquam paulatim fides, causâ persecutionis, crescebat in sæculo, *factis regibus Christianis, ubique in parvo tempore Christi Evangelium penetravit.*

CASAUBON de Lib. Eccl. ii. v. Epist. p. 189.

CHAPTER V.

THE ROYAL SUPREMACY IN THE CHURCH OF ENGLAND.

Q. WHAT is the title which describes the English Sovereign's relation to the Church of England?

A. The Sovereign of England is styled "supreme Governor over all persons, in all causes, ecclesiastical as well as civil," in all his dominions [1], wherever the Church is *established* as the national form of Religion [2].

[1] XXXIX ARTICLES, Art. xxxvii. The Queen's Majesty hath the chief power in this realm of *England* and *other her dominions,* unto whom the chief Government of all estates of this realm, whether they be ecclesiastical or civil, in all causes doth appertain, and is not, nor ought to be, subject to any foreign jurisdiction.

CANONS, 1603. Canons, 1, 2. 36. King CHARLES I. Declaration before XXXIX Articles.

[2] The Churches in the British *Colonies,* where the Church is *not established,* are in the condition in which

Christian Churches were *before* the Empire became Christian; and are regulated by the primitive Common Law of the Church of Christ.

Q. Therefore *no foreign power*, such as that of the Bishop of Rome, has any ecclesiastical jurisdiction in this kingdom?

A. None[1].

[1] See above, Part ii. ch. iv. HOOKER VIII. II. 3. CANONS, 1603. Can. xxxvi. And see the clear statement of the grounds and limits of the Royal Supremacy in Art. xxxvii.

Q. And the Sovereign is supreme *over all spiritual persons*, as well as secular?

A. Yes; St. Paul teaches us that "*every* soul is to be subject to the higher powers" ($\dot{\epsilon}\xi o \upsilon \sigma i \alpha \iota \varsigma$)[1]; St. Peter that we are to "submit to the King as *Supreme*;" and *spiritual* persons, being enjoined in Scripture to put others "in mind to be subject to principalities and powers," and "to obey magistrates," are specially bound to practise the obedience which they are enjoined to preach.

Rom. xiii. 1.
1 Pet. ii. 3.
Above, p. 240.

Tit. iii. 1.

[1] Bp. BILSON, Christian Subjection, p. 174. He that speaketh to *all* exempteth *none: Let every soul be subject to the higher powers* (Rom. xiii. 1). In these words clergiemen be not excepted, *ergo* comprised.—P. 176. Christ Himself was a priest and a prophet, yet He not only submitted Himself to the Roman Governor, but confessed the President's power over Him to be from Heaven. S. Paul appealed unto Cæsar, and appeared before Cæsar as his lawful Governor. S. Jude detested them for false prophets that despised Governments, or spake evil of Rulers. It is *no religion*, it is *rebellion* against God, for clergiemen to exempt themselves from the Prince's power. The command is general: Let *every* soul be subject. The punishment is eternal: Whosoever resisteth the power resisteth the ordinance of God, and they that resist shall receive to themselves damnation.—P. 177. Of the Clergy and the Laity, the Clergy must rather obey, that they may be teachers of obedience; not in words only, but in deeds also: they must not hinder their doctrine by their doings. HOOKER V. LXII. 9.

Q. Do then *spiritual* persons *derive their spiritual power* from Kings?

Part III.

A. No; they do not derive it from any *human* source. The Sovereign is supreme over all persons, but not over all causes[1]. Spiritual persons derive their spiritual power from CHRIST *alone;* but the authority to *exercise*[2] it *actually* and *legally* upon particular *persons*, and in particular *places*,—as *dioceses and parishes*,—*this* they derive from laws, ecclesiastical and civil, and from the Sovereign, who, by his royal assent, is the *efficient* cause of law[3].

[1] Bp. BILSON, Christian Subjection, p. 173. We confess princes to be supreme *governors* of their realms and dominions; *in* all spiritual things and causes, but not *of* the things themselves, but of all their subjects.
See above, pt. i. ch. xii., and below, chap. vii.

[2] Archbp. LAUD, Speech at the censure of Bastwick. (Remains, vol. ii. pt. 2, p. 68.) Our being Bishops *jure divino* takes nothing from the King's right or power over us. For though our *office* be from God and Christ immediately, yet may we not *exercise* that power, either of Order and Jurisdiction, but as God has *appointed* us; that is, not in His Majesty's or any Christian King's Kingdoms, but by and under the power of the King given us so to do.

[3] Bp. SANDERSON, Prælect. VII. c. v.—viii.

Q. May not then the Church of England be called a *State* Church?

A. No; not unless the Ancient Church might have been so called after the empire became Christian. It would be ingratitude and impiety to suppose that the Church of God is *injured* by the fulfilment of His promises to her, and that her spiritual constitution is impaired, because, according to His gracious prophecy, "Kings have become her nursing-fathers, and Queens her nursing-mothers;" and temporal laws have been made in her behalf[1].

Isa. xlix. 7. 23.

[1] HOOKER, VIII. VI. 10.

Q. You speak of the ancient Church; but is not what is called in England the Oath of Royal Supremacy of *modern* date?

A. The *principle* of the Royal Supremacy is CHAP. V. coeval with the English monarchy, and, indeed, with *all Christian monarchy*. And with respect to the *declaration* of this principle, it is found, not only in the Oath of Supremacy¹, but in the ancient Statutes² of the Realm; and it must be remembered that the *assertion* of the Royal Supremacy, in this Oath, being a *defensive protest*³ against papal usurpations, and being designed to *exclude* all other Supremacy, became more necessary in proportion as the usurpations, against which it was a safeguard, became more prevalent and dangerous.

¹ 25, 26, and 28 Henry VIII. c. 7, A.D. 1536. GIBSON's Codex, p. 22 – 24.

² As in 16 Richard II. c. 5, A.D. 1392 (GIBSON's Codex, p. 74). So the Crown of England, which hath been so free *at all times* that it hath been *in no earthly subjection*, but immediately subject to God, in all things touching the regality of the same crown, and to no other, should be submitted to the Popes, and the laws and statutes of the realm by him defeated and avoided at his will, in perpetual destruction of the sovereignty of the King our Lord, his crown, his regality, and of all his realm; which God defend!

³ HOOKER, VIII. II. 3. Supremacy is no otherwise intended or meant, than to *exclude* partly *foreign* powers, and partly the power which belongeth in several unto others contained as parts within that politic body over which those kings have supremacy. On the sense in which this oath is imposed, see PHELAN's Hist. 1543, Append. Note B. This Oath has been often taken by Roman Catholics, *ibid.* p. 251.

Q. To what usurpations do you refer?

A. On the one hand to those of the *Bishop of Rome*, who, if he had his will, would not allow Princes to do any thing in ecclesiastical matters in their own kingdoms unless he gave them leave¹; and on the other, to the principles of the *Puritanical Discipline*, which, in *this respect*, as in several others, agree with the *Popish*².

¹ HOOKER, VIII. II. 14. What persons devoted to the

PART III. *Papacy* yield that princes may do, it is with secret exception always understood, *if* the Bishop of Rome give leave. Our own *Reformers* (i. e. the maintainers of the *Puritan Discipline)* do the very like. See VIII. IV. 9, and VIII. VI. 12, and Bp. TAYLOR, below, pt. iii. ch. v.

² Archbp. BANCROFT, Survey of the Pretended Holy Discipline. 1593, p. 240—258. The *Puritans* take from Christian princes, and ascribe to their own pretended regiments, the supreme authority under Christ in causes ecclesiastical; and thus they join with the *Papist.*

Bp. SANDERSON on Episcopacy, xvi. p. 41. The rest [i. e. the other Religious Communities, *Popish and Puritanical*] (not by *remote* inferences, but) by *immediate* and *natural* deduction out of their own acknowledged principles, do someway or other deny the *King's supremacy* in matters Ecclesiastical; either claiming a power of jurisdiction over him, or pleading a privilege of exemption from under him. The *Papists* do it *both* ways; in their several doctrines of the Pope's Supremacy, and of the Exemption of the Clergy. The *Puritans* of both sorts who think they have sufficiently confuted every thing they have a mind to mislike, (if they have once pronounced it Popish and Anti-christian,) do *yet herein* (as in *very many other things,* and some of them of the most dangerous consequence) *symbolize with the Papists,* and after a sort divide that branch of Anti-christianism wholly between them: the *Presbyterians* claiming to their *Consistories* as full and absolute Spiritual Jurisdiction over Princes (with power even to excommunicate them, if they shall see cause for it) as the *Papists* challenge to belong to the *Pope:* and the *Independents exempting* their *Congregations* from all spiritual subjection to them, in as ample manner as the *Papists* do their Clergy.' Whereas the *English Protestant Bishops* and *Regular Clergy,* as becometh good Christians and good subjects, do neither pretend to any Jurisdiction over the Kings of *England,* nor withdraw their subjection from them; but acknowledge them to have Sovereign Power over them as well as over their other subjects. See also Archbp. WAKE'S Appeal, Pref. p. iii.

Q. But is not the Sovereign of England sometimes styled *Head of the Church?*

A. No; not by those who speak properly. That title was laid aside by Queen Elizabeth, and exchanged for that of "*Supreme Governor* over all persons, in all causes, ecclesiastical as well as civil," and it has not been borne by any English monarch since that time[1].

[1] HOOKER, VIII. IV. 8. Archbp. BRAMHALL. i. p. 29, and the notes of the learned Editor. Bp. GIBSON's Codex, p. 45, note.

CHAP. V.

Q. In what does this supremacy consist?

A. To speak *generally*, and reserving the *particular* modes of its exercise for future consideration (below, chap. vi.) the sovereign's office as " supreme Governor over all persons in all causes " in the Church, is " to maintain it in the unity of true religion [1];" not to suffer " any unnecessary questions to be raised;" " to have a princely care," that Churchmen may do the work which is proper to them; to " contain within their duty all estates and degrees committed to his charge by God;" and " to restrain the stubborn and evil-doers with the power of the civil sword."

[1] K. CHARLES I. Declaration prefixed to XXXIX Articles; and see Art. xxxvii. CANONS of 1603, Canons i. ii. CANONS of 1640, Canon i.

OFFICE for the QUEEN'S ACCESSION, Book of Common Prayer.—" Blessed Lord, Who hast called Christian princes to the defence of Thy Faith, and hast made it their duty to promote the spiritual welfare, together with the temporal interest of their people; We acknowledge with humble and thankful hearts Thy great goodness to us, in setting Thy servant our most gracious QUEEN over this Church and Nation; give her, we beseech Thee, all those heavenly graces that are requisite for so high a trust; let the work of Thee, her God, prosper in her hands; let her eyes behold the success of her designs for the service of Thy true religion established amongst us; and make her a blessed instrument of protecting and advancing Thy truth."

To show that the Principles here stated are consistent with the doctrine of other branches of the Catholic Church, it may be observed, that Archbp. PLATON, Metropolitan of Moscow, in his 'Ορθόδοξος Διδασκαλία, authorized by common use in the *Eastern Church*, (Koray's Greek version, Athens, 1836, p. 135,) thus speaks on this subject:— " Christian kings are the prime guardians and champions of the Church, and are *bound to provide* (χρεωστοῦσι νὰ φροντίζωσι) for the *welfare of the Church, as for* that of the *State*. The Christian Church demands of princes, first that they be learned in God's law (Deut. xvii. 18);

secondly, that they be examples of piety and virtue to all men; thirdly, that they take care that the Church be well governed (εὐτάκτως), and that they encourage faithful ministers and governors; fourthly, that they repress schism, and defend the Church from persecutors and scoffers; fifthly, that they propagate true religion, and provide suitable maintenance for its teachers. Hence every one may see clearly how closely the body politic is united with the Church (βλέπει πᾶς ἕνας πόσον εἶναι σφικτὰ ἡνωμέναι ἡ πολιτικὴ κοινωνία καὶ 'Εκκλησία). And since the sovereign of a Christian state *has no superior upon earth*, and no one in this world can recompense him for these his labours, he lives on the faithful assurance of attaining hereafter an unfailing and inestimable reward."

To this may be added the following testimony of the Greek presbyter, CONSTANTINUS ŒCONOMUS, περὶ τῶν τριῶν τῆς ἐκκλησίας βαθμῶν: Nauplia, 1835, p. 318. We honour princes as pastors of their people, according to God's ordinance; we honour the king; we make prayers for all men, for kings and all in authority. To the CHURCH OF ENGLAND, and all other Churches in which the sovereign is reverenced as the supreme governor, we say, Let this your custom prevail, as seems to you good; and may all your Christian people be blessed by God, and your sovereign reign and prosper for evermore!

Among Roman Catholic writers also one of the most learned, the Abbé FLEURY, Disc. sur l'Hist. Ecclés., Dissert. ix., says: "Le titre de *chef de l'Eglise* que les Anglicans ont donné à leur Roi, ne doit pas être pris à la rigueur. En lui donnant cette qualité, ils ne pretendent point qu'il puisse exercer les fonctions Ecclésiastiques, donner la mission aux Evêques et aux Prêtres, administrer les sacremens, en un mot, qu'il soit le principe de la puissance spirituelle. Il ne lui donne point d'autre autorité dans les matières de la Réligion, que celle de faire des Lois pour maintenir le bon ordre de l'Eglise, de soutenir et appuyer celles qui sont faites par les Evêques, d'assembler des conciles, de contenir les Ecclésiastiques comme les Laïques dans la soumission due au Prince, à l'exclusion de toute puissance étrangère."

Q. But does not the ascription of these powers in Ecclesiastical matters to the Civil Magistrate lead to what is termed *Erastianism?*

A. *Erastianism* (so called from *Erastus*, a physician of Heidelberg, whose work on Church government appeared in 1589, after the author's death) appears to have owed its rise and influence to the domineering claims¹ of the Genevan Ecclesiastical Regimen in the infliction of Church censures². The promoters of that Regimen, seeing³ no other mode of overthrowing Episcopacy, (and perceiving that *this* mode might probably be successful,) enlisted the *Laity* on its side by associating *Lay* Elders with *Presbyters* in the exercise of spiritual discipline, *contrary to all former practice in the Church*⁴. But by so doing it led the way to its own destruction; for it thus lent its countenance to the *principle* of *Erastianism*, which being exasperated by the spiritual pride and tyranny of the Genevan discipline, turned the Calvinistic weapon of the *Lay-eldership*, by which Presbyterianism had overthrown Episcopacy, *against Presbyterianism itself*, and proceeded to transfer the power of Excommunication *entirely* to *Lay* hands, and to vest it in the *Civil Tribunals*.

CHAP. V.

¹ See ZURICH LETTERS, Second series, Epist. c. p. 154.
² Bp. TAYLOR, xiii. 471. The Presbytery pretends mightily to the Sceptre of Christ, as the Pope does to the Keys of St. Peter; and they will have all Kings submit to that.
³ HOOKER, VI. I. 2, with Mr. Keble's Note.
⁴ Archbp. BANCROFT, Survey of the Pretended Holy Discipline, Lond. 1593, p. 23. By reason of the great authority that the *Preachers* had intituled the *Civil Magistrates* to, for the banishment of their *Bishop*, Calvin very wisely considered with Farellus and Viretus, that, if they took that course, (of making his Ecclesiastical Senate consist *solely* of *Ministers*,) he should find *unresistible opposition*. And their device therefore was, that their Ecclesiastical Senate should consist of *Twelve Citizens*, to be *chosen yearly*, and but of *Six Ministers*, who were to *continue* for their *lives*. And this was the *first time*, for aught I find, that the *Consistorian Discipline ever drew breath*.

Q. But did Erastianism limit itself to the question of the power of excommunication?

A. No; its partisans in England, about the year 1645, went on still further to maintain that

PART III. the authority of the Church consisted only in *persuasion*[1]; that *no* Church government is of *divine right*, but is merely of *human* constitution, depending wholly on the will of the civil magistrate. The Erastians, then, having made a league with the Independents, overthrew the Presbyterian power in England. But the asserters of Erastian opinions were powerful not so much by *their own arguments*[2], as by the *errors* of their *adversaries*, the Presbyterians; and if they had enjoyed[3] such a form of government as that of the English Constitution in Church and State, where the *spiritual power is vested, by divine right, in spiritual persons*, and where the Civil magistrate has a general *external* authority " over all *persons in all causes*," Erastianism would either never have existed at all, or would never have gained the influence which it did[4].

[1] BUDDEI Isagoge, i. p. 828. Censebant Erastiani Ecclesiæ nullum regimen, *nullam potestatem*, per *censuras, excommunicationem* inprimis, applicandi à verbo Dei datam esse; potestatem clavium in *solo verbi præconio* consistere; et Ecclesiam Magistratui Christiano subjectam omnem auctoritatem ex merâ Magistratûs delegatione usurpare.

RUTHERFORD, Divine Right of Church Government, London, 1646, p. 537. GILLESPIE, Aaron's Rod, Lond. 1646, p. 161. BAILLIE's Letters, ii. p. 149, ed. 1775. HUGHES, Pref. ad S. Chrysost. de Sacerdotio, p. cxx. HEY on the xxxviith Article. KEBLE, Pref. to Hooker's Works, 2nd ed. p. lviii.

[2] HAMMOND on the Power of the Keys, i. p. 429, folio. In taking up his opinion and maintaining it, Erastus had more to impute to Beza and the Genevans' *errours*, innovations, and excesses, than to *his own arguments*. See HOOKER, Preface, § 2.

Bp. SANDERSON, Prælect. vii. 29, p. 208, gives a very clear and concise summary of the *Papal, Puritan*, and *Erastian* theories of Church Government.

[3] HAMMOND, ibid. p. 247. With respect to the quarrel of Erastus against Excommunication, I shall give you no other account of it than what from himself I have received; certain it is that the fabric of the Church of

England would never have provoked him to this enmity, if he had lived here under the best, or perhaps the worst, days of our Episcopacy.

" Archdeacon POTT, in his work entitled the Rights of Sovereignty in Christian States defended, &c., a charge to the Clergy of the Archdeaconry of London, 1828, has shown, with great learning, how the Doctrine of the xxxviith Article (in illustration of which he cites Hooker, Bp. Sanderson, Bp. Andrewes, and Bp. Bilson) is an effectual safeguard against Erastianism on one side, and Popery and Puritanism on the other. " In a word, (says he, p. 24,) the personal union of the Church and Commonwealth, where the same individuals compose both, cannot be denied: but this does not destroy the natural distinction of societies, or cancel those rights which belong essentially to each. The *spiritual Pastor* retains his privilege, of which he cannot be divested; and the *sovereign Power* keeps its supremacy within those limits which the word of God and the known ends of government must always put. It is impossible to deny that this supremacy may be exercised in things relating to religion by the sovereign power in Christian states, unless we will take one of these opinions, either that the Christian character itself (1) *excludes* all such dominion; or (2) *restrains* it to a fancied reign of *Christ* on earth, distinct from His universal rule; or (3) confines it to His *Ministers* alone; or (4) vests it in some supposed *Vicegerent*, to whom it is thought to be derived. All these notions have had their turn in the world, and are most opposite to Scripture, Reason, and the Judgment (conformable to both) upon which the model of our own happy and well-settled Government in Church and State hath been established.

" By defending the capacity and privileges of sovereign powers to bear sway in all causes that are left free to discretion, and by showing at the same time the perpetual exceptions to things determined and provided by Divine authority, Mr. Hooker has for ever overthrown both the wild suggestions of *Erastian* theorists, and the groundless claim of a perpetual *Empire in the Church*, independent, even in Christian countries, on the sovereign power."

Q. You ascribe to the Crown authority in ecclesiastical matters. Do you attribute, then, to the Sovereign of England a *sacred* as well as a civil character?

A. Certainly, as the laws of the land do, which give to the King the title of Sacred Majesty.

Q. And does the *Church of England* recognize

PART III. this *sacred* character in the Kings and Queens of England?

𝔄. Yes; and therefore the Sovereigns of England, at their Coronation, having taken the Coronation Oath, are first anointed with holy oil, and are blessed and "consecrated Kings over the people, whom the Lord their God has given them to rule and govern [1];" they then receive the sword from God's Holy Table, to be used by them as ministers of God, "for the punishment of evil-doers, and the *protection of the holy Church of God;*" they then receive the "orb set under the cross," that they may remember that "the whole world is subject to the power and empire of Christ their Redeemer, Who is the Prince of the kings of the earth, King of kings, and Lord of lords; so that no man can reign happily who derives not his authority from Him, and directs not all his actions by His laws:" and when they afterwards receive the Ring, "the ensign of kingly dignity, *and of defence of the Catholic Faith,*" and the Sceptre and the Crown, the badges of kingly power and justice, and the Rod of equity and mercy, they "in lowly devotion bow the head to God," and acknowledge that they rule by Him, and, when enthroned, that they sit in *judgment* under Him, which that they may the better discharge, they receive the Holy Bible from the Altar of God.

---

[1] OFFICE for the CORONATION of the Kings and Queens of England. See also the Prayer for the High Court of Parliament, in which the designation *'most religious'* is applied to the Sovereign as an *official attribute.*

HOOKER, VIII. II. 14. Crowned we see our kings are and enthroned and anointed: the crown a sign of military, the throne of sedentary or judicial, the oil of *religious* or *sacred* power.

Archbp. LAUD'S Sermons, vi. p. 151. And the eye of nature could see *aliquid divinum* (Arist. Ethic. i. 2), somewhat that was divine in the governors and orderers of Commonwealths. In their very office: Inasmuch as they are singled out to be the ministers of Divine Providence upon earth, and are expressly called the officers of God's Kingdom, Sap. 6. And therefore the School concludes that any the least irreverence of a King *sacrilegium dicitur,* is justly extended to be called Sacrilege. And since all *sacrilege* is a violation of some thing that is *holy,* it is evident that the office and person of the King is *sacred,* and therefore cannot be violated by the Hand, Tongue, or Heart, of any man, that is, by deed, word, or thought; but 'tis God's cause, and He is violated in him. And here kings may learn that those men which are sacrilegious against God and His Church, are for the very neighbourhood of the sin the likeliest men to offer violence to the *Honour* of *Princes* first, and their *Persons* after.— (This last sentence, written in the year 1628, was *prophetic.*)

Q. You speak of the Sovereign having a *sacred* character, but you do not mean, I suppose, that the Sovereign, as supreme governor, claims any power of performing any *sacred function* in the Church; such as the Ministry of the Word and Sacraments, the exercise of the power of the Keys, or in propounding articles of Faith, or in conferring Holy Orders?

A. Certainly not. The Kings of England challenge *no such authority in the Church;* on the contrary, they have always *protested against*[1] any such ascription, whenever it has been imputed to them: Their office is *not to minister* in their own persons, but to *exercise royal care* that they who *are appointed to minister* in the Church *do* that which by *God* they are *appointed to do.* But we are not like *Urijah the Priest,* who *did all that King Ahaz commanded him,* so as even to make an idolatrous altar, and to offer sacrifice upon it. The Power of Princes in matters Ecclesiastical is what is called a δύναμις οἰκονομικὴ, or ἀρχιτεκτονικὴ, i. e. a power to distribute and regulate; a power, *not to build,* but to *rule the builders.* Herein, *imperantis est, non imperata facere, sed imperando facere ut fiant*[2]; the commander *effects not* what is commanded,

2 Kings xvi. 10—16.

PART III.

Below, ch. vi. & vii.

but *by commanding, he effects* that it *may be effected*. And this power is to be exercised by them, *not* in any *new* or *arbitrary* manner, but *according to the received laws* of the Church; for "Rex est sub Deo et Lege," and "Rex *nihil potest* nisi quod *jure potest*[3]."

[1] XXXIX ARTICLES, Art. xxxvii. Where we attribute to the Queen's Majesty the chief government, by which titles we understand the minds of some slanderous folks to be offended, we give not to our princes the ministering either of God's Word, or of the Sacraments, the which thing the injunctions also lately set forth by *Elizabeth* our Queen do most plainly testify; but that only prerogative, which we see to have been given always to all godly princes in Holy Scriptures by God Himself; that is, that they should rule all states and degrees committed to their charge by God, whether they be ecclesiastical or temporal, and restrain with the civil sword the stubborn and evil-doers.

QUEEN ELIZABETH's Admonition, in Bp. Gibson's Codex, p. 54, note. Her Majesty forbiddeth all manner her subjects to give ear or credit to such perverse and malicious persons, which most sinisterly and maliciously labour to notify to her loving subjects, how by the words of the Oath of Supremacy it may be collected that the Kings or Queens of this realm may challenge authority and power of Ministry of Divine Service in the Church; whereby her said subjects are much abused by such evil-disposed persons. Her Majesty neither doth nor ever will challenge any authority than that which is and was of *ancient time* due to the imperial crown of this realm; that is, *under God* to have the sovereignty and rule over all manner of *persons* born within her realms, of what estate, either ecclesiastical or temporal, soever they be, so as no other *foreign power* shall or ought to have any superiority over them.

HOOKER, VIII. III. 4. VIII. VIII. 1. CASAUBON de Libert. Eccles. ii. v. Epist. p. 187. Sir R. TWISDEN on Schism, p. 94. Abp. BRAMHALL, ii. 219, 220. Bp. STILLINGFLEET, Eccles. Cases, on Jurisdict. ii. 97.

[2] GROTIUS de Imperio Potestatum summarum circa Sacra, pp. 240. 245.

[3] HOOKER, VIII. II. 3, 13, and 17. *For* the received laws and liberty of the Church the King hath *supreme* authority, but *against* them *none*.

The following note is from Bp. ANDREWES. It contains the most comprehensive, concise, and perspicuous statement extant concerning the nature of the Royal Supremacy, both with respect to what it *is*, and to what it *is not*. It derives additional importance from the fact of its having been authorized by King James I. (Dudley Carleton's Letters, p. 223, ed. 1780.) These are its words;

Bp. ANDREWES, Tortura Torti, p. 380. Primò, sub *Primatûs* nomine Papatum novum Rex non invehit in Ecclesiam; sic enim statuit, ut non *Aaroni Pontifici*, ita nec *Jeroboamo Regi* jus ullum esse, conflatum à se Vitulum populo proponendi, ut adoret; id est, non vel *fidei novos articulos* vel *cultûs Divini novas formulas* procudendi.

Exod. xxxii. 4.
1 Reg. xii. 28.

Neque verò id agit Rex, ne patitur quidem, ut sibi potestas sit, vel *incensum adolendi* cum *Oziâ*, vel *Arcam attrectandi* cum *Ozâ*.

2 Chron. xxvi. 16.
2 Sam. vi. 6.

Docendi munus, vel dubia Legis explicandi, non assumit, non vel *Conciones* habendi, vel *Rei Sacræ* præeundi, vel *Sacramenta* celebrandi; non vel personas *sacrandi*, vel res; non vel *clavium* jus, vel *censuræ*. Verbo dicam; nihil ille sibi, nihil nos illi fas putamus attingere, quæ ad *Sacerdotale munus* spectant, seu *potestatem Ordinis* consequuntur. Procul hæc habet Rex; procul à se abdicat.

Atqui in his quæ *Exterioris* Politiæ sunt, ut præcipiat, suo sibi jure vendicat; nosque adeò illi lubentes meritò deferimus. *Religionis* enim *curam* rem *Regiam* esse, non modo Pontificiam, et IN REGIIS PRIMAM, quamque ille non solùm *foris* ab externâ vi, sed et *domi* ab incuriâ hominum asserere teneatur.

Nam cùm Lege Ipsâ Dei custos sit et vindex, non *secundæ* modò *tabulæ*, sed et *primæ*, primæ quoque ad se curam pertinere putat, et *primam primæ*. *Et cùm omnis anima ei subjici jubetur, animæ* etiam consultum vult, magis autem id quàm *corpori*.

Deut. xvii. 18.
Jos. i. 8.
Rom. xiii. 1.

Vis illa dicam sigillatim quæ sint? Quodcunque in rebus Religionis Reges *Israel* fecerunt, nec sine laude fecerunt, id ut *ei* faciendi jus sit ac potestas. Leges auctoritate Regiâ ferendi ne blasphemetur Deus, non negabitis, fecit *Rex Babel;* ut jejunio placetur Deus, fecit *Rex Ninive;* ut festo honoretur, fecit *Ester* cùm Purim, *Machabæus* cùm Encænia promulgaret. Denique iis omnibus de rebus, de quibus in *Codice*, in *Authenticis*, in *Capitularibus* à *Constantino, Theodosio, Justiniano, Carolo Magno*, Leges latæ leguntur.

Dan. iii. 29.
Jonah iii. 7.
Est. ix. 26.
1 Mac. iv. 56. 59.

Tum, delegandi qui de Lege sic latâ judicent, quod *Josaphat*. Tum subditos, ne sic latam violent, juramento obstringendi, quod et *Asa* et *Josias*.

2 Chron. xix. 8.
xv. 14.

Quod siqui in Leges ita latas committant, etsi Religionis ea causa sit, sive *Pseudoprophetæ* crimen est, sive *Idololatræ*, sive *Blasphemi*, sive *Sacra polluentis*, in eos auctoritate Regiâ animadvertendi.

xxxiv. 32.
Deut. xiii. 5. 10.

PART III.

Lev. xxiv. 23.
Num. xv. 35.
1 Chron. xiii. 2.
2 Chron. xix. 4.
1 Reg. viii. 64.
2 Chron. xxiv. 4.
xxix. 5.
Deut. xvii. 19.
Jos. i. 8.
Num. xxvii. 21.
Mal. ii. 7.
? Chron. xix. 11.
1 Sam. xv. 17.
Deut. xvii. 12.
. Reg. ii. 27.
Exod. xxxii. 20.
2 Reg. xviii. 4.

2 Chron. xxiv. 12.

Conventus auctoritate suâ indicendi, etiam de Arcâ reducendâ, et figendâ loco suo, quod fecit *David*: etiam de populo ad Dei cultum revocando, quod *Josophat*: etiam de Templo dedicando, quod *Salomon*: collapso instaurando. quod *Joas*: pollúto purificando, quod *Ezekias*.

Quamquam verò non frustrà sibi præceptum putat à Deo, *ut describat sibi Legis exemplar, secum habeat semper, legat sedulò, dies noctesque meditetur*, condiscat inde cultum Dei vel ad ipsas usque Ceremonias; nec hoc illi dictum, ut totus ab alieno ore pendeat, ipseque à se nihil planè dijudicet: in his tamen *Os Eleazari* non invitus *consulit, et requirit legem ab iis, quorum labia scientiam custodiunt*: adhibebit in sacris legibus ferendis, quos adhibere par est, quosque ratio suadet rerum illarum consultissimos, deque iis optimò respondere posse. Et in his, quæ ad Deum pertinent, *Amariam Sacerdotem*, non *Zabadiam Ducem* jubebit præsidere.

Quoad *Personas*, omnibus omnium Ordinum jus dicendi: qui sit (dicam stilo Scripturæ) *Caput Tribûs* Levi, non minùs quàm cæterarum, nec minùs Clericorum quàm Laicorum Rex: contra *Abiathar siquis superbierit, decreto* suo compescendi: etiam *Abiathar* ipsum, si ita meritus, pontificatu *abdicandi*.

Quoad *Res*, excelsa diruendi; id est, peregrinum cultum abolendi; nec modò *Vitulum aureum* ab Aarone conflatum, quod *Moses*, sed et *Serpentem æneum* à Mose erectum confringendi, quod *Ezechias*; et sive in idololatriam abeat *Vitulus aureus*, sive in superstitionem *Serpens æneus*, utrumque comminuendi.

Nam de rebus, quæ ad decorem Domûs Dei spectant, quæ dici solent *Adiaphora* statuendi, quod *Joas*; et quæ materia schismatis esse assolent, futiles et inutiles quæstiones, auctoritate suâ compescendi, quod *Constantinus*; ne vos quidem ipsi negatis jus esse.

Postremò; si de Christianis exemplum malitis, id postulat, ut Episcopus sit τῶν ἐκτὸς, quod *Constantinus*: ut *Rector Religionis*, quod non modo *Carolus Magnus*, sed et *Ludovicus Pius*.

Hæc Primatûs apud nos jura sunt, ex jure Divino.

CHAPTER VI.

ON THE ROYAL SUPREMACY IN THE CHURCH OF ENGLAND.

In Ecclesiastical Synods.

Q. In what *manner* is the supreme power exercised by the Sovereign in the Church of England?

A. In four ways, *viz.*
1. *Citatio;* or the convoking and dissolving Ecclesiastical Councils or Synods.
2. *Assensio;* or the right of assenting to the decrees of those Synods before they become law.
3. *Promotio;* or, "the advancement of principal Church governors to their places of prelacy [1]."
4. *Judicatio;* or, "higher judicial authority than others are capable of [1]."

[1] HOOKER, VIII. II. 1.

Q. Have Christian Princes always possessed the power of convoking Ecclesiastical Synods?

A. Yes. Before the Empire became Christian, the Church had no General Synod; and, in ancient times, no General Council was ever regarded as legal, unless convened with the consent of the Ruler of the country where it was held [1].

[1] See the note at the end of this Chapter.
XXXIX ARTICLES, Art. xxi. General Councils may not be gathered together without the commandment and will of Princes; and Bp. BEVERIDGE on Art. xxxvii. p. 373.
CANONS of 1603, Preface; Canon cxxxix. HOOKER, V. I. 2. Archbp. BRAMHALL, i. 30. 171.
BARROW, Pope's Supremacy, 185. Nothing can be more evident than that the Emperors at their will and by

PART III. their authority did *congregate* all the first General Synods.—186. 188. 191. 193. It inseparably doth belong to Sovereigns in the General Assemblies of their states to *preside* and moderate affairs; proposing, stopping, controuling (in person or by proxy, p. 194—203).

Parliamentary Report on Roman Catholic Regulations in Foreign States, 1816, p. 159. Note in Christian Institutes, iii. p. 254.

Q. And Councils therefore were *not* summoned by the *Bishops of Rome?*

A. No: there is *no* instance of any Council, claiming to be General, convoked by the Bishop of Rome for *more than a thousand years after Christ*[1].

[1] CARDINAL CUSANUS de Concord. Eccles. ii. cap. 25. Ex illo tempore quo Imperatores Christiani esse cœperunt, ex illorum nutu pendere visa sunt negotia Ecclesiæ, atque adeo maxima Concilia ex eorum sententiâ convocabantur, ut ex Eusebio, Socrate, Sozomeno, Nicephoro patet. *Octo prima Generalia Concilia* ab Imperatoribus erant collecta, et *Pontifex Romanus,* ad instar *aliorum Patriarcharum,* divales (h. e. imperatorias) sacras jussiones pro veniendo aut mittendo ad Concilia recepit. CASAUBON de Lib. Eccles. iii. 11. Epist. p. 192

Bp. ANDREWES on the Right and Power of calling Assemblies, 4to, 1606, p. 45, vol. v. 141—168. Thus farre the trumpet giveth a certaine sound. Now after this there is a great silence in the volumes of the Councils in a manner for the space of 200 yeres, until the yere 1180 or thereabout, when the Council of Lateran was; and then indeed the case was altered. By that time had the Bishop of Rome got one of the trumpets away, and carried with him to Rome, so leaving princes but one. *But so long they held it.*

The student will find a clear account of the practice used in the convocation of Church Synods, in Father SARPI's History of the Council of Trent, Book ii. ad ann. 1545. See also the note at the end of this Chapter.

Q. What is the Synod of the English Church called?

A. The Convocation[1].

[1] The Convocation of England and Wales consists of two Assemblies, also called Convocations, one for the

Province of Canterbury, the other for that of York. That of Canterbury is divided into two houses: the Upper House, in which the 21 Bishops of the Province sit; and the Lower House, in which the Deans sit, and the Archdeacons and the Proctors of the Chapters and from the Parochial Clergy; amounting to 145 members. In the Province of York the Bishops and Clergy sit in one House.

The Convocation of the Irish Church dates from the beginning of the 17th century, and still subsists; see the works of the Right Hon. JOSEPH NAPIER, and the Rev. ALFRED T. LEE, 1865, on this subject.

Q. Is the Convocation—taken in its general acceptation—a Representative assembly?

A. Yes; in the words of the Canon Law of England, "The sacred Synod of this nation, assembled in the name of Christ, and by the King's authority, is the true Church of England by Representation [1]."

[1] CANONS of 1603. Canon 139. CARDWELL, Synodalia, Preface, x—xxiii. BURN. ii. 17—30.

Q. If then, as that Canon Law declares [1], "the Convocation be the representation of the Church," "both Clergy and Laity," "absent and present," can it be said that "the Canons of the Church do not bind the Laity?"

A. Canons Ecclesiastical have no authority against Statute or Common Law, or against the Royal Prerogative; but, as Chief Justice Coke says, "when the Convocation makes Canons concerning matters which properly appertain to them, and the Sovereign has confirmed them, they are binding on the whole realm [2]." And whether these Canons may have coactive force or no *in foro exteriore*, yet they cannot but have weight with true members of the Church *in foro conscientiæ* [3].

[1] CANONS of 1603. Canons 139, 140. 25th HENRY VIII. 18.
[2] Lord Chief Justice COKE, in GIBSON'S Codex, p. xxix. Vaughan, 327, ibid. p. xxviii. "A lawful Canon is the law of the kingdom, as well as an Act of Parliament. Whatever is the law of the kingdom is as much the law as any

PART III. thing else that is so." Bp. STILLINGFLEET, Eccl. Cases, i. 252. 260.

³ CARDWELL, Synodalia Præf. p. xxv.

Q. You say, "when the Sovereign has confirmed them;" is then the Regal Power exerted in *making* laws for the Church?

A. No; it is not concerned in the *framing* of those laws, (for the Convocation itself "decrees and ordains¹,") but in their *ratification*, and in *preventing* the enactment of such laws as may not be conducive to the welfare of the community ².

¹ CANONS of 1603. Canon 1.
² KING CHARLES I., Declaration, prefixed to the XXXIX Articles (penned by Abp. LAUD; see Bp. Pearson, Minor Works, ii. 171). Out of our Princely care that the Churchmen may do the work which is proper unto them, the Bishops and Clergy from time to time in Convocation, upon their humble desire, shall have licence under our Broad Seal to *deliberate* of and *to do* all such things as, being *made plain* by them, and *assented* to by us, shall concern the *settled continuance* of the Doctrine and Discipline of the Church of England now established.

CASAUBON de Lib. Eccles. ii. v. Imperatores Pii, quæ Patres in Ecclesiâ decreverant, ea ut reciperentur à *populo universo* sanciebant. See ibid. ii. iii.

BARROW, Pope's Supr. 206. The effectual confirmation of Synods, which gave them the force of laws, depended on the Imperial sanction.—p. 207. By long prescription, commencing with the first General Synod, did the Emperor enjoy this prerogative.

HOOKER, VIII. VI. Touching the supremacy which our kings have in this case of making laws, it resteth principally in the *strength of a negative voice*. GROTIUS de Potestate, p. 262. Abp. BRAMHALL, i. 146. 272. Bp. ANDREWES, Tortura Torti, ed. 1629, p. 165, thus states the ancient and uniform practice of Christendom with respect to the *summoning* of Ecclesiastical Synods, and the *ratification* of their decrees by the Imperial power:—

Refero jam *verba, loca* etiam *cito,* Conciliorum *Quatuor Generalium* è quibus illa constet Imperatorum *authoritate convocata.* NICÆNUM I. *Constantini* authoritate, ex *Concilii* ipsius *Synodicâ Epistolâ; Convocata est* (hæc Synodus) Dei *amantissimo Rege Constantino congregante nos ex variis urbibus et provinciis.* CONSTANTINOPOLITANUM PRIMUM, *Theodosii* Senioris, ex *Concilii ipsius Epistolâ; Convenientes secundùm rescriptum Pietatis tuæ;* et ibidem, *literis vocationis tuæ Ecclesiam honorâsti.* EPHESINUM, *Theodosii* Junioris et *Valentiniani.* Nam et Imperatores jubent, suo *Oraculo cogi;* et Concilium *septem Epistolis septies* fatetur se, *nutu auctoritatis vestræ coactum,* et aliis multis *secundùm oraculum, mandatum, rescriptum, toties,* verbis tam disertis, ut nihil *Ephesino* clarius, nihil planius. CHALCEDONENSE, *Valentiniani* et *Martiani.* Quod, præterquam frons ipsa loquitur, facta est *Synodus ex decreto piissimorum et fidelissimorum Imperatorum Valentiniani et Martiani,* Concilium quoque ipsum Epistolâ suâ fatetur; *Sancta et magna Synodus, secundùm Dei gratiam et sanctionem vestræ Pietatis congregata.* Tum et *in definitione ipsâ* expressè idem habetur, et ab illis denique *missionem petunt,* ut et *Ephesini.*

Possent et *quatuor* alia hic *Generalia* subjungi, nisi tu hoc non postulâsses; pòst, ubi postulas, faxo ut illa habeas. (Vide ibid. p. 346.)

Submisisse autem *sese* Imperatori, ab eoque *confirmationem* suam habuisse, *profero* tibi *verba, cito loca.* NICÆNUM à *Constantino; et Synodi decreta confirmans consignavit.* CONSTANTINOPOLITANUM à *Theodosio;* ex ipsâ Concilii ad eum Epistolâ. *Necessariò quæ facta sunt in Sacrâ Synodo ad Pietatem tuam referimus. Petimus autem, ut Clementiæ tuæ scripto confirmetur Synodi sententia, et quemadmodum honorâsti nos literis tuis cùm huc convocares, ita et eorum quæ decreta sunt clausulam velis etiam obsignare.* EPHESINUM à *Theodosio et Valentiniano,* ex Concilii ipsius Epistolâ. *Unde confugimus omnes ad auctoritatem Pietatis vestræ, petentes, ut quæ contra Nestorium acta sunt, eosque qui cum eo decipiunt, habeant vim suam atque robur; quæ verò ab illis qui Nestorium vindicant vacua sint atque irrita.* CHALCEDONENSE à *Martiano: Sacro nostro Serenitatis Edicto venerandam Synodum confirmantes.* En tibi *loca;* en *verba.*

Fateris autem *jussu Imperatoris congregata Concilia,* sed addis *interdum.* Dele verò *interdum,* vel designa nobis GENERALE UNUM ALIQUOD de primis illis *octo,* et doce *absque illius jussu* convocatum. Sed nec *interdum* etiam vis factum hoc fuisse ab Imperatore, *nisi in executione mandati summi Pontificis,* ubi, quid tu *summum Pontificem* crepas, vel *mandatum* ejus, vel *Executorem mandati Pontificii Cæsarem?* Nullum tum quidem *Pontificis mandatum,* quin submissa supplicatio; nec *Pontifex* tum *mandavit,* sed *Cæsar;* nec *Cæsar* executus est, sed *Pontifex.* Quin nullus tum *Pontifex summus;* Episcopus tantùm *Romanus:* parvus ad *Romanum tum habebatur respectus:* alii Episcopi illum tum *fratrem et cöepiscopum* nominabant.

PART III.

Q. Are there no other Synods in England besides the *Provincial Convocations?*

A. Yes; the Annual Visitations held by the Bishop and Archdeacons in each Diocese are, properly, *Diocesan Synods;* and ought (it is humbly suggested) to be restored, as speedily as may be, to practical efficiency as such.

CHAPTER VII.

ON THE ROYAL SUPREMACY IN THE CHURCH OF ENGLAND.

In Ecclesiastical Promotions and Judicature.

Q. To pass to the third mode in which the Regal Supremacy is exercised; are the Bishops of the Church of England *made* by the Sovereign?

A. No; no *earthly* power can *make* a Bishop. "Kings do not *make*[1], but only do *place*, Bishops[2]." *Consecration makes* a Bishop; the *Royal grant places* him. His *beneficium* is *à Rege*, but his *officium* is *à Deo*. His *commission* is from CHRIST, his *permission* to *exercise* it in special *places*, and over special *persons*, is from the supreme power.

[1] The English *Ordinal* is entitled, "The Form and Manner of *Making*, &c. of *Bishops*," &c.
[2] HOOKER, VIII. VII. 1.

Q. Can you explain this more fully?

A. A Bishop's power consists in two things: 1. in *Order;* and 2. in *Jurisdiction*[1]. His power of *Order* is either *Episcopal*, and consists in Ordaining Priests and Deacons, in Confirmation, and other Apostolical acts; or it is *Sacerdotal*, and is exercised in the Preaching of the Word, and in the administration of the Sacraments; and this power of *Order* he receives wholly and

Above, pp. 273, 274.

exclusively from GOD, the Sacerdotal at his Ordination as Priest, the Episcopal at his Consecration as Bishop, and not before.

His *Jurisdiction* is partly of divine, partly of human origin.

[1] HOOKER, VI. II. 1. When the Apostle doth speak of ruling the Church of God, his words have evident reference to the power of *jurisdiction*: our Saviour's words to the power of *order*, when He giveth His disciples charge, saying, "Preach—Baptize—Do this in remembrance of Me."

Bp. BILSON, Christian Subjection. Bishops have their authority to preach and minister the Sacraments, *not* from the *Prince*, but from *Christ* Himself; only the Prince giveth them publicke liberty, without let or disturbance, to do that which Christ commandeth.

Bp. SANDERSON, Episcopacy not prejudicial to Royal Power, p. 32, § ii. 12. All power, to the exercise whereof our Bishops have pretended, cometh under one of the two heads, of *Order*, or of *Jurisdiction*. The power of *Order* consisteth partly in preaching the word and other offices of public worship, common to them with their fellow-ministers; partly in ordaining Priests and Deacons, admitting them to their particular cures, and other things, of like nature, peculiar to them alone. The power of *Jurisdiction* is either internal, in retaining and remitting sins *in foro conscientiæ*, common to them also (for the substance of the authority, though with some difference of degree) with other *Ministers;* or external, for the outward government of the Church in some parts thereof peculiar to them alone. For that *external power* is either *Directive*, in prescribing rules and orders to those under their jurisdictions, and making Canons and constitutions to be observed by the Church, wherein the inferior clergy, by their representatives in Convocation, have their votes as well as the *Bishops;* and both dependently upon the *King* (for they cannot either meet without his Writ, or treat without his Commission, or establish without his Royal Assent): or *Judiciary* and *Coercive*, in giving sentence *in foro exteriore*, in matters of ecclesiastical cognizance,—excommunicating, fining, imprisoning offenders, and the like. Of these powers, some branches, not only in the exercise thereof, but even in the very substance of the power itself, (as namely that of external jurisdiction coercive,) are by the laws declared, and by the Clergy acknowledged to be wholly and entirely derived from the King, as the sole fountain of all authority of external jurisdiction.

PART III. whether spiritual or temporal, within the realm, and consequently not of Divine Right.

Q. In what respects?

A. It is *divine* as far as it consists in the use of the Keys, and in the *spiritual* superintendence of those under his care, *in foro conscientiæ*. But the authority which he may possess over them *in foro exteriore*, (that is, by means of *civil* censures, or *secular* punishment in the *Exterior* Court [1],) is of *human* origin. St. Peter [2] *received* the *Keys* from Christ, but was ordered by Him to *put up* the *sword*, when he drew it without any authority or commission to do so.

Above, pp. 273, 274.

Matt. xvi. 19. xxvi. 52.

[1] Archbp. BRAMHALL, i. 272. We do not draw or derive any *spiritual* jurisdiction from the Crown; but either liberty and power to exercise *actually* and *lawfully* upon the subjects of the Crown that *habitual* jurisdiction which we received at our ordination, or the *enlargement* of our jurisdiction *objectively* by the prince's referring more causes to the Church than it formerly had; or, lastly, the increasing it subjectively, by their giving to ecclesiastical judges an external coercive power.—p. 129. We must distinguish between the interior and exterior court. The power which is exercised in the court of Conscience for binding and loosing is solely from *Ordination*. It is not the power of the Keys, or any part thereof, in the exercise of ecclesiastical jurisdiction, even in the exterior court, which is from the Crown; but it is the application of the matter, the regulating the exercise of actual ecclesiastical jurisdiction in the outer court, to prevent oppression of their subjects, and to provide for the tranquillity of the commonwealth, which belongs to sovereign Princes.

See Bp. GIBSON's Codex, p. 114, where it will be seen that no *temporal* power is possessed by a Bishop till his *Election* has been *confirmed* by the Metropolitan.

[2] Bp. BILSON, Christian Subjection, p. 174. The word *Governor* doth sever the magistrate from the minister. Bishops be no governors of countries; Princes be. Bishops bear not the sword to reward and revenge; Princes do. This appeareth by the words of our Saviour, expressly forbidding His Apostles to be rulers over countries, and leaving it to princes. The princes of the Gentiles exercise dominion over them; and they that exercise authority over them are called Benefactors; but ye shall not be so.—p. 175. Peter was sharply rebuked by Christ for using the sword; and a Bishop must be no striker.

Matt. xx. 25.
Luke xxii. 25.
Matt. xxvi. 52.
1 Tim. iii. 3.
Tit. i. 7.

Q. But you said that in England a Bishop is placed in his See by the *Crown?*

A. Yes; the right of designation, nomination, and presentation for confirmation of his election, for investiture, and for consecration [1], of the person whom they may judge most fit to hold the *temporalities* and to discharge the *duties of any particular see*, has, from time immemorial, been vested in the Kings of England.

[1] Bp. GIBSON, Codex, p. 110. STATUTE OF PROVISORS, 25 Edward III. A.D. 1350. GIBSON's Codex, pp. 65, 66. Bp. STILLINGFLEET, Eccl. Cases, i. pp. 161. 313. Notes to "Christian Institutes," IV. 472, ed. 1837.

Q. Whence does it arise, that the Crown of England is entitled to *place* English Bishops?

A. From the nature of the office of *Christian* Kings, as God's Ministers for the general welfare of His People, and for the guardianship [1] of His Law, and from the ancient practice of the Catholic Church generally, and of the Church of England in particular; and because their sees were founded and endowed with their temporalities by Sovereigns of England. These Sees being of the King's foundation, he is patron of them [2].

But this does not apply to those British Colonies, where the Church is not established by Law, and where Episcopal Sees have not received their endowments from the State.

[1] Bp. ANDREWES, Catechet. Doct. p. 301. It is the duty of Princes, who are *custodes utriusque tabulæ*, keepers of both tables, seeing they cannot perform the work of sanctification themselves, to take care that fit persons be provided and encouraged in this work. Seeing that the care of the Church is committed to the Sovereign ruler, and that the *soul is the principal part*, therefore it is his duty to see that fit and able persons be provided for this work, such as may be *doctores gentium*, teachers of the Nations.

[2] HOOKER, VIII. III. 3. GROTIUS de Summâ Potestate, pp. 263. 267. Archbp. BRAMHALL, ii. pp. 401—408. Bp.

PART III. GIBSON's Codex, p. 104, note. See also VAN ESPEN, Jus Eccles. 1. Tit. XIII. III. iv.

Q. But since it was enacted by the English Legislature, that "*if any Archbishop or Bishop refuse to consecrate the person elected or nominated within twenty days after such election is signified to him by the King's letters patent, he shall incur the pains and penalties of the statute and provision of Præmunire,*" may it not be asked,—on the principle *si vis scire an velim, effice ut possim nolle,*—are not bishops virtually *made* as well as *placed* by the Crown? and is not, therefore, their mission human, and not *divine?*

A. No. First of all,— on the sound principle of the English Law, *Distingue tempora et concordabis Leges* (2 Inst. 256)—the *time* and *circumstances* of this statute [1] are to be considered. It was made A.D. 1533, for the *recovery* of the ancient and undoubted rights of the Crown and realm of England from the usurpation of the See and Court of *Rome*, which had then strong and active partisans in England. It was directed, not against *English Bishops*, acting in the discharge of a sacred *duty*, but, as its Preamble plainly declares, against the adherents and supporters of *the Pope's spiritual* and *secular usurpation and rapacity* [2].

And there are other important considerations connected with this statute.

---

[1] Act of *Præmunire*, 25 Henry VIII. cap. 20. A.D. 1533. GIBSON's Codex, p. 107.

[2] See the Preamble. Where sithens the beginning of this Parliament for the repress of the exaction of *Annates* and first-fruits of Archbishopricks and Bishopricks of the realme wrongfully taken by the *Bishop of Rome*, it is ordained that the payment of *Annates*, &c. or for any *Bulls*, &c. should *cease*. The statute (23 Henry VIII.) referred to in the Preamble recites that "great and inestimable sums of money have been daily conveyed out of this realme to the impoverishment of the same, and especially such sums of money as the Pope's holiness, his predecessors, and the

Court of Rome by long time have taken of all those spiritual persons which have been named, elected, presented, or postulated to be Archbishops or Bishops within the realme of England under the title of *Annates*, &c.—which they have been compelled to pay before they might receive any fruits of the said Archbishoprick or Bishoprick whereunto they were named—which *Annates* were first suffered to be taken within this realme for the only defence of Christian people against the infidels, and now they be claimed as mere duty, only for lucre, against all right and conscience."

Q. What are these considerations?

A. First of all, Kings are bound by their Oaths at their Coronation to "maintain the laws of God and the true profession of the Gospel; and to maintain and preserve inviolably the Doctrine, Worship, Discipline, and Government of the Church;" and their power is given them for the edification, and not for the destruction, of the Church; and Bishops are solemnly warned by God not to be guilty of haste in laying on of hands[1]; and by the Law of the Church Universal, no consecration of a Bishop can take place against the voice of the majority of the Bishops of the Province (CONC. NICÆN. Can. iv. CONC. ANTIOCH. Can. xix. BINGHAM, Bk. II. cap. xi. § 4).

1 Tim. v. 22.

A penal statute of this kind cannot oblige the conscience to violate the law of God and the Church[2].

Next it is to be observed, that in the case supposed, the choice is controlled by *spiritual* and *ecclesiastical* restraints.

---

[1] HOOKER, VIII. VII. 7.
[2] Bp. SANDERSON, Prælect. viii. p. 228.
King Henry VIII. himself, four years *after* the Statute of *Præmunire*, declared that *Bishops ought to reject* a person presented by the *Crown*, if the said person were proved morally or doctrinally incompetent. For in the "Institution of a Christian Man," sanctioned and promulgated by the King (A.D. 1536), the following doctrine is laid down:—
"Bishops and Priests are to reject and repel from the said room (i.e. the ministry of the Word and Sacraments) such as they *shall judge to be* unmeet therefor. . ."

PART III. Within this realm the presentation and nomination of the *Bishopricks* appertaineth unto the kings of this realm. And unto the Priests and Bishops belongeth by the authority of the Gospel to *approve and confirm* the person which shall be by the King's Highness nominated, . . . or else to *reject* him from the same for his demerits and unworthiness."

Q. What are these?

A. The person[1] nominated by the Crown must be above a stated age; he must have received the Holy Orders, first of Deacon and then of Priest (ordinarily after a year's probation as Deacon), from the Bishop; and, *before* his ordination to the Priesthood, must have brought to the Bishop a testimonial signed by three or more Ministers of religion; and have subscribed certain Articles of doctrine and discipline; he must have taken certain oaths, and "have taken some Academic degree;" or "at *the least* be able to render an account of his faith in the Latin tongue;" he must have been examined, tried, and approved in learning and godliness by the spiritual authority; and "if any Bishop shall have admitted any to Holy Orders who is not so qualified and examined," he is to be suspended from ordaining for two years[2]; so that we see the *foundation* of all his power is *spiritual;* and, further, it is justly observed, that this very statute of *Præmunire* affords a clear proof that the essence of the episcopal power in England is regarded by this statute as *spiritual;* for by the very mention of *coercion* in the case supposed, it declares that *consecration* is *necessary* to constitute that power[3].

[1] 13 Eliz. c. 12. XXXIX ARTICLES. CANONS of 1603, Canon xxxiv. Preface to Ordinal, in Book of Common Prayer. 3 Articles of Canon xxxvi. Oath of Supremacy and Allegiance, and of Canonical Obedience.
F. MASON, in Christian Institutes, iv. p. 475.
[2] CANON xxxv.
[3] PLOWDEN on the Constitution, p. 251.

Q. These considerations are important. But, in the present condition of affairs in this country, is it not true that the nomination to Bishoprics, &c. has passed from the hands of the Crown into those of the First Minister, who is liable to be swayed by political considerations, and depends for the maintenance of his power on Parliamentary majorities; and thus has not the Supremacy of the Crown been virtually annulled, and become in fact the Supremacy of the Minister for the time being; or, indeed, the Supremacy of a Parliamentary Majority?

A. Parliaments and Ministers of the Crown are responsible to Almighty God. They owe it to Him not to usurp the Royal Prerogative in matters Ecclesiastical, and not to use it *against* the Crown and *against* the Church, but to protect and strengthen the Crown in the maintenance of its just rights, and in the exercise of its religious duty as Defender of the Faith.

Their hearts are in God's hands, and, if men pray for them, as they ought to do, He will rule and guide them to the promotion of His glory.

Besides this, the Sovereigns of England have it in their power to protect their Prerogatives by such ancient, constitutional means as their Predecessors employed ever since the Reformation; and, to maintain their Ecclesiastical Supremacy by the instrumentality of such a Commission [1] or Standing Council, to advise them in Ecclesiastical promotions, as would command the confidence of the Nation, and would defend the rights and liberties of the Crown, and would aid it in discharging its duty and maintaining its safety by upholding the Doctrine and Discipline of the Church.

[1] As was done by King Charles II., and by King William III. See His Majesty's Commission to Thomas, Lord Archbishop of Canterbury, &c., A.D. 1699.

"WILLIAM III., by the Grace of God, King, &c. &c., to

PART III. the Most Reverend Father in God, our right trusty and right entirely-beloved counsellor, Thomas, Lord Archbishop of Canterbury, Primate of all England and Metropolitan; and to the Most Reverend Father in God, John, Lord Archbishop of York, Primate of England and Metropolitan; and to the Right Rev. Fathers in God, Gilbert, Lord Bishop of Sarum; William, Lord Bishop of Worcester; Simon, Lord Bishop of Ely; and John, Lord Bishop of Norwich, greeting. We, *being sensible that nothing can conduce more to the glory of God, our own honour, and the welfare of the Church, than our promoting to preferment therein the most worthy and deserving men according to their merits;* and conceiving you, the said Thomas, Lord Archbishop of Canterbury; John, Lord Archbishop of York; Gilbert, Lord Bishop of Sarum; William, Lord Bishop of Worcester; Simon, Lord Bishop of Ely; and John, Lord Bishop of Norwich, to be proper and competent judges in such cases; *Know ye, therefore, that we, reposing special trust and confidence in your approved wisdoms, fidelities, and circumspections, have nominated, constituted, ordained, and appointed, and by these presents do nominate, constitute, ordain, and appoint you,* the said Thomas, Lord Archbishop of Canterbury; John, Lord Archbishop of York; Gilbert, Lord Bishop of Sarum; William, Lord Bishop of Worcester; Simon, Lord Bishop of Ely; and John, Lord Bishop of Norwich, *to be our commissioners for the purposes hereinafter mentioned.* And we do hereby give and grant unto you, our said commissioners, or any three or more of you, (whereof we will that you, the said Thomas, Lord Archbishop of Canterbury, to be always one; and, where any preferment or place to be disposed of lies within the province of York, you, the said John, Lord Archbishop of York, to be also one,) full power and authority to meet at such convenient times and places as you, the said Thomas, Lord Archbishop of Canterbury, shall, by your summons of the rest of our said commissioners, from time to time appoint, for the putting the powers hereby granted in execution, in such manner as is hereby appointed. And we do hereby declare our will and pleasure to be, that when our royal person shall be resident within our kingdom of England, you do, at such meetings, consider of one or more person or persons proper to be recommended to us to succeed to any bishopric in England, or any other ecclesiastical preferments in England above the tax or real value of twenty pounds in our books which are in our gift or disposal from time to time as they shall respectively become vacant during our residence within our said kingdom of England. And that you, or a sufficient number of you, empowered as aforesaid, do signify, under

your hands, your recommendation of such person or persons as you in your wisdoms shall think most fit to be appointed by us to succeed to any such vacant preferments, to the end that the names of such person or persons may be presented to us by one of our principal Secretaries of State, that our royal pleasure may be further known therein. . . .
. . . . . And further, we do hereby declare our pleasure to be, *that neither of our principal Secretaries of State do, at any time,* either when we shall be resident in England or in parts beyond the seas, move us in behalf of any person whatsoever for any place or preferment which we have hereby left to the recommendation or disposal of our said commissioners, as aforesaid, without having first communicated both the person and the thing by him desired to you, our said commissioners, or so many of you as are hereby empowered to act; and without having your opinion and recommendation in such manner as hereinbefore is directed. And if at any time we be moved in like manner by any other person whatsoever, our pleasure is, and we do hereby declare, that neither of our principal Secretaries of State shall present any warrant to us for any royal signature in such a case, until you, our said commissioners, or so many of you as are hereby empowered to act, have been acquainted therewith, and have given your opinion and recommendation as aforesaid. And, further, our will and pleasure is, that this our commission, and the powers hereby granted, shall continue in force until we shall declare our pleasure to the contrary, notwithstanding the same commission be not continued by adjournment. And, lastly, we have revoked and determined, and by these presents do revoke and determine certain letters patents under our great seal of England, bearing date the sixth day of April, in the seventh year of our reign, whereby we constituted and appointed you, the said Thomas, Lord Archbishop of Canterbury; John, Lord Archbishop of York; William, Lord Bishop of Coventry and Lichfield; Gilbert, Lord Bishop of Sarum; and Simon, Lord Bishop of Ely, together with the then Right Reverend Father in God, Edward, Lord Bishop of Worcester, lately deceased, to be our commissioners for the purposes above mentioned, and every clause, article, and thing therein contained. In witness whereof, we have caused these our letters to be made patents. Witness ourself at Westminster, the ninth day of May, in the twelfth year of our reign.

" Per Breve de Privato Sigillo,

" CHUTE."

See Cardwell's Documentary Annals, ii. p. 353, and Neve's Lives of the Archbishops, p. 247. See also King

PART III. Charles II. Commission to the same effect, A.D. 1681, Wilkins' Concilia, iv. p. 607.

Q. You said that one of the modes in which the Kings of England exercise their supreme authority over all persons in the Church is by *judicature* in causes ecclesiastical : of what kind is this administration of justice?

A. It is partly *forensic*, and partly *synodical*.

Q. How is it *forensic?*

A. In trying ecclesiastical causes, not *in foro conscientiæ*, but *in foro exteriore*, and inflicting civil punishments in pursuance of spiritual censures.

Q. How is it *synodical?*

A. In determining controversies after consideration had and report made of them by the Convocation of the Church; where the *judicium directivum* is in the Church, the *imperativum in Rege*.

Q. Has, then, the Crown the power of pronouncing on religious dogmas? and may it declare one doctrine to be orthodox, and another heretical, as it thinks fit?

A. No. By the laws of England [1], "*nothing is to be adjudged heresy, but that which heretofore has been so adjudged by the authority of the* canonical Scriptures, *or the* first four General Councils, *or some other* General Council, *wherein the same hath been declared heresy by the express word of Scripture; or such as shall be termed heresy by the High Court of Parliament with the assent of the Clergy in Convocation.*" The Sovereign therefore pronounces, in all religious questions, not according to any *new principles*, but according to the *received religious laws* of the Church [2]. He has *supreme* power *according* to the laws, but *against* them, *none*. 'He can do nothing *against* the truth, but *for* the truth.' Accordingly at their Coronation the Sovereigns

2 Cor. xiii. 8.

of England promise[1] to "*maintain* the Laws of God, the true profession of the Gospel, and the Protestant Reformed Religion established by Law, and to *maintain* and *preserve inviolably* the *settlement* of the United Church of England and Ireland, and the *Doctrine, Worship, Discipline, and Government* thereof."

Hence it is clear that the Sovereign has *no* power to *alter* a single tittle or iota in the doctrine, worship, discipline, or government of the Church.

---

[1] 1 Eliz. cap. 1. A.D. 1558. Bp. GIBSON's Codex, pp. 48. 351. On the reception of the first four General Councils in England, see ROUTH, Rel. Sacr. III. p. iv. note.

[2] HOOKER VIII. VIII. 3. The King judges not *of*, but *after* (i. e. *according to*) the Laws. JENK. Cent. 9. Rex non debet judicare sed *secundum Legem*. And by the ACT OF SUBMISSION, 25 Hen. 8. c. 19, all ancient Canons, &c. not contrary to God's law or the law of the land, remain in force.

Bp. BILSON, Christian Subjection, p. 327 (dedicated to Queen Elizabeth, A.D. 1586, and authorized by her). We give Princes *no* power to devise or *invent new religions*, to alter or change sacraments, *to decide or debate doubts of faith*, to disturb or infringe the canons of the Church.—p. 332. We *never* said that Princes had any spirituall power, and the sword which they beare we never called but externall and temporall; for the true spirituall and eternal sword is the Word of God.

Bp. BILSON, Christian Subjection, p. 297. That princes may prescribe what faith they list, what service of God they please, what form of administering the Sacraments they think best, is *no* part of *our doctrine;* and yet that princes may by their laws prescribe the *Christian* Faith to be preached, the *right* service of God to be used, the Sacraments to be ministered according to the *Lord's* institution, this is no absurdity in *us* to *defend*.

Parliamentary Report on Rom. Cath. Subjects, pp. 129, 130. 1816.

Lord CLARENDON on Religion and Polity, p. 1. It is the duty of Sovereign Princes to preserve and provide for the advancement of religion, and for the due exercise of it, and devout reverence for it in their dominions. As *they cannot prescribe what laws they please, contrary to the*

PART III. *laws of nature or of God*, so *they cannot impose what religion they please*, contrary to what He has enjoined.

[3] Coronation Oath; in the Form and Office of Coronation of Her Majesty Queen Victoria, 1838, p. 27.

Q. How is this power exercised?

A. The judicial power of the Crown was formerly exercised in the Court of Delegates, from which it was transferred (by 2 and 3 Will. 4. c. 92, and 3 and 4 Will. 4. c. 41) to the Judicial Committee of the Privy Council [1]. By 3 and 4 Vict. c. 86, every English Archbishop and Bishop who is a Privy Councillor, was a Member of this Committee for hearing of Ecclesiastical causes. But that English Final Court of Appeal [2], to which some exceptions were taken, has now been somewhat modified by more recent legislation (1873). *Any* Bishop of the Church of England may now be chosen an assessor, and the other Judges will be the same in all causes.

As in *civil causes* the Sovereign administers Justice by *civil Judges*, so in *spiritual* matters [3], Justice ought to be administered by Judges *spiritual* [4].

It is certain, that by the Ancient common Law of the Christian Church, the causes of Bishops and Clerks accused of false doctrine were tried by the Metropolitan of the Province with his Suffragans, and that from their sentence there was no appeal [5].

[1] See BURN's Eccl. Law, 1. p. 64, ed. Phillimore: and JOYCE, Rev. J. W., Ecclesia Vindicata, p. 73, and FULLER, Rev. M. J., on "the Court of Final Appeal," Oxf. 1865.

[2] See the Debate in the House of Lords, June 4, 1850; and the resolution of the Lower House of Convocation of Canterbury, May 19, 1865.

[3] Bp. GIBSON's Codex, pp. 351. 353. Upon the abrogation of all the ancient statutes made against heretics (see 29 Car. 2. cap. 9, for taking away the writ *de hæretico comburendo*), "The cognizance of Heresy and punishment of Heretics returned into its ancient channels, and now belongs to the Archbishop as Metropolitan of the Province,

and to every Bishop within his own proper Diocese, who are to punish only by *Ecclesiastical* censures. And so, saith my Lord Coke, *it hath been put in ure in all Queen Elizabeth's reign, and so it was resolved by the Chief Justice, Chief Baron, and two of the Justices upon Consultation, 9 Jac.* 1. *in the case of Legate.*—How far the *Convocation* of each province, which had once an undoubted right to convict and punish Heretics in a Synodical manner, doth still retain, or not retain, that right, I shall not presume to say, till the learned Judges be clear and final in their opinions." See their opinions in Cardwell, Synod. A.D. 1710, ii. p. 761.

⁴ 24 Hen. 8. c. 12. GIBSON'S Codex, i. p. 83. CAWDREY'S Case, pp. xxvi. xxviii. xxxvi. lxxvii. COKE'S Institutes, vol. vi. pt. iv. ch. 74. HOOKER, VIII. VIII. "It hath been taken *as if we* did hold that Kings may prescribe what themselves think good to be done in the Service of God, how the Word may be taught, how Sacraments administered; that Kings may personally sit in the Consistory *where Bishops* do, *hearing* and determining what causes soever do appertain unto those courts; that Kings and Queens in their own proper persons are by judicial sentence to decide the questions which rise about matters of Faith and Christian Religion. Which opinion *we account as absurd* as they who have fathered it upon us. . . . Our laws do evermore refer the ordinary judgment of spiritual causes unto spiritual persons." VIII. VIII. 9. "If the cause be spiritual, Secular Courts do not meddle with it." See above, p. 286, Bp. ANDREWES: "Rex in his quæ ad *Deum* pertinent Amariam sacerdotem, non Zabadiam ducem, jubebit præsidere." So CASAUBON concerning King JAMES, Exc. Baron. ded. p. 7, "Partem tibi debitam quæ ad *temporalia* spectat intrepidè tibi vindicas, partem alteram curæ quæ spiritualia attingit *Episcopis* tuis relinquis:" and King JAMES himself, Apol. for Oath of Allegiance, p. 269, "I never did nor will presume to create any Articles of Faith, or *to be judge* thereof; but to submit my exemplary obedience unto them (the Spiritual Rulers) in as great humility as the meanest of the land."

The following important statements on this subject are from Bp. GIBSON's Codex, Introductory Discourse, p. xviii. 2nd edition, 1761:—We will now proceed to consider the Administration of *Ecclesiastical* matters (under the Prince as Supreme Head of the Church) as it stands distinguished by the Law and Constitution of England from the Administration of *Temporal* Matters (under the same Prince, as Supreme Sovereign in the State), and how these two Administrations flow from the same Fountain, and each is

PART III. designed by the Constitution for its own proper end and limited to its own proper channel.

These things cannot be described better than in the words of a known Statute, made in the Twenty-fourth year of King Henry the Eighth, and commonly called the *Statute of Appeals*, where by divers sundry old, authentick Histories, and Chronicles, it is manifestly declared and expressed that "this Realm of England is an Empire, and so hath been accepted in the world, governed by one Supreme Head and King, having the Dignity and Royal Estate of the Imperial Crown of the same; Unto whom a Body Politick, compact of all sorts and degrees of people, divided in terms and by names of Spiritualty and Temporalty, been bounden and owen to bear, next to God, a natural and Humble Obedience; He being also institute and furnished, by the goodness and sufferance of Almighty God, with plenary, whole, and entire power, pre-eminence, authority, prerogative, and jurisdiction, to render and yield justice, and final determination to all manner of folk, resiants or subjects within this his Realm, in all causes, matters, debates, and contentions, happening to occur, insurge, or begin within the limits thereof, without restraint or provocation to any forain Princes or Potentates of the World; The *body Spiritual* whereof having power, when any cause of the *Law Divine* happened to come in question, or of spiritual learning, that it was declared, interpreted, and shewed, by that part of the said Body Politick, called the Spiritualty, now being usually called the English Church, which always hath been reputed, and also found of that sort, that both for knowledge, integrity, and sufficiency of number, it hath been always thought, and is also at this hour, sufficient and meet of itself, without the intermedling of any exterior person or persons, to declare and determine all such doubts, and to administer all such offices and duties, as to their rooms spiritual doth appertain: For the due administration whereof, and to keep them from corruption, and sinister affection, the King's most Noble Progenitors, and the Antecessors of the Nobles of this Realm, have sufficiently endowed the said Church, both with Honour and Possessions: And the Law Temporal, for trial of Property of Lands and Goods, and for the Conservation of the People of this Realm in Unity and Peace, without Rapine or Spoil, was, and yet is, administered, adjudged, and executed, by sundry Judges and Ministers of the other part of the said Body Politick, called the Temporalty: And both their Authorities and Jurisdictions do conjoyn together in the due Administration of Justice, the one to help the other."

Here (says Bp. GIBSON) we see the respective Business

committed by our Constitution to the *Spiritual* and the Temporal Courts, distinctly laid out; with a Declaration that it is the Duty of each to *help* (and not to destroy) *the other*. And, that it is of the utmost importance to the peace and happiness of the whole Community, that both these keep themselves *within their own proper bounds;* we need no better authority, than that excellent Remark of my Lord Coke, with reference to this very Statute: *Certain it is* (says he) *that this Kingdom hath been best governed, and Peace and Quiet preserved, when both Parties, that is, when the Justices of the* TEMPORAL *Courts, and the* ECCLESIASTICAL *Judges, have kept themselves within their proper jurisdiction, without encroaching or usurping upon one another.*

Ibid. p. xxi. iv. The said limitation which the Statute makes of Spiritual Causes to Spiritual Persons, together with the Ground of that Limitation, viz. their Knowledge and Experience in Spiritual Matters, seems in reason to be as applicable to the Court commonly called the Court of Delegates, as to the Inferior Courts. It will not be denied, that the last Resort of all Ecclesiastical Causes (which by the 24 Hen. 8. is to the Archbishops) was by 25 Hen. 8. c. 19, given to the King upon the single consideration of his being Supreme Head of the Church; the Recognition of which, in a general Oath to be taken by all his subjects, was enacted by that very Parliament. It is also plain, that the Matters carried by the Spiritual Judges into that Court, are not only of an Ecclesiastical nature (having first passed through the Ecclesiastical Courts, as such), but are more *merely* and undeniably so, than the others, being purged from all Temporal Matter, before they arrive there, by Prohibitions prayed on one side or the other, upon any the least pretence or colour of such mixtures. Add to this, that as the *first* Statute *of Appeals*, 24 Hen. 8, expressly limits the cognizance of Spiritual Matters to Spiritual Persons; so this second Statute, which entitles the King to the ultimate cognizance by Commission, doth not *limit* him to any *other* persons, but leaves him wholly to his own choice. But though at the Reformation, when the Bishops and Clergy were generally *suspected* of a secret affection to the Papal authority, it might be advisable to leave the King a *Power* of appointing Commissioners out of the Temporalty if he pleased (however contrary to the *natural reason* of the thing, and the general tenor of our Constitution, as laid out in the *Statute* of *Appeals*); yet, in fact*, there are no footsteps of any of

---

* Reg. Offic. Cur. Delegat.

PART III. the *Nobility, or Common Law Judges,* in Commission, till the year 1604 (i. e. for seventy years after the erecting of the Court): nor from 1604 are they found in above one Commission in forty, till the year 1639; from whence (i. e. from the downfall of Bishops and their jurisdiction, which ensued) we may date the present Rule of Mixtures in that Court. I shall add no more upon this head, but that in the Reign of Edward the Sixth, the method for Trial of all causes which should come by appeal from the Courts of the Archbishops, was fixed in the following

Reformatio Legum : *de Appellationibus.*

manner: Quò cùm fuerit causa devoluta (i. e. to the King) eam vel *Concilio Provinciali* definiri volumus, si gravis sit causa, vel à tribus quatuorve Episcopis à nobis ad id constituendis.

⁵ See DE MARCA, Concordia Sacerdotii et Imperii, lib. vii. p. 318. VAN ESPEN, Jus Eccl. Univ., pp. 111, 112, pars i. tit. xix. cap. iii. BINGHAM, Book ii. chap. xvi. TILLEMONT, Mémoires, &c., Vie de S. Augustin, tom. xiii. pp. 861—3, p. 1031, ed. Paris, 1703. DUPIN de Ant. Eccl. Disc., sect. xii. p. 56, and the present writer's remarks 'On the Judicial Functions of Metropolitans,' Lond. 1865.

On this important subject, which concerns the well-being of all our *Colonial Churches,* the following statements may be cited from that publication, pp. 9—15.

"Among the difficulties," says De Marca (p. 318), " which we have to encounter in explaining the ancient discipline of the Church, none has been treated with less accuracy than that which concerns the deposition of Bishops. Ordinations of Bishops were performed, and judicial sentences upon them in Ecclesiastical causes were pronounced, by the *Synod* of each Province, with the authority of the *Metropolitan;* and from this sentence *there was no appeal.*"

De Marca thus writes—"An illustrious example of the usage just described is displayed in S. Cyprian, who was Bishop of Carthage, and Chief of the African Province. When he, with the sentence of his Council, had excommunicated certain clerks, and also an heretical false Bishop, he remonstrated vehemently with Cornelius, then Bishop of Rome, because when these persons had fled to Rome, Cornelius had hesitated for a little while whether he might not admit them to communion. On this account Cyprian boldly proclaimed the rights of the Bishops of each Province to take cognizance of causes in their own Province, in the sight of God, Who would require them to render an account to Him of their doings; and to decide those causes finally, *without appeal to Rome,* or *to any other place.*"

The Epistle of Cyprian is still extant, in which this CHAP. VII. principle is asserted. He thus speaks (Ep. lv. p. 207, ed. Venet. 1758):—

"Inasmuch as it was decreed by us all, and inasmuch as it is equitable and just, that every one's cause should be heard *there* where the crime was committed; and inasmuch as each Pastor has his own portion of the flock committed to his trust, and must render an account himself to God, it is not right that those persons, over whom we are set, should *rove to any other quarter*, and disturb the harmony of Bishops united together, but that they should plead their own cause where accusers and witnesses may easily be had."

Another precedent of the same kind may be seen in S. Cyprian's Epistles, Ep. lxviii. p. 287. A Spanish Bishop, Basilides, had been deprived by the Metropolitan and Bishops of his Province; and another Bishop, Sabinus, had been consecrated by them in his room, and S. Cyprian, and the African Bishops with him, affirmed in an Epistle to the Clergy and Laity in Spain, that from that judgment there was no appeal; and that the Clergy and Laity ought to communicate with Sabinus and not with Basilides.

Let us now pass on to the age of the Emperor Constantine.

In the Council of Nicæa, held in A.D. 325, the first General Council of the Christian Church, the principles, which had been previously stated by S. Cyprian in the Epistles just cited, were received and confirmed.

In the words of De Marca, "That custom of the Church, which assigns to the Councils of each Province the authority to ordain and to depose Bishops, was committed to writing, and was enacted by the fifth canon of the Nicene Council.". . . .

Accordingly, an African council, which was held *after* the Council of Nicæa, thus speaks in a synodical epistle to Celestine, Bishop of Rome (circ. A.D. 426, when S. Augustin was guiding the counsels of the African Church): "*Decreta Nicæna* sive inferioris gradûs clericos, sive ipsos Episcopos, suis Metropolitanis apertissimè commiserunt. Prudentissimè enim justissimèque viderunt, quæcunque negotia in suis locis, ubi orta sunt, finienda." The following is the testimony of Dr. Isaac Barrow in his work on the Pope's Supremacy:—"When the diocesan administration was introduced, the last resort was decreed to the synods of them, or to the Primates in them, all *other appeals* being prohibited (Concil. Constantinop., can. 6), to which canon the *Emperor Justinian* referred :—' It is

PART III. decreed by our ancestors that against the sentence of these prelates there should be no appeal' (Cod. Lib. i. tit. 4, c. 29). The Council of Milevis says:—'Let them appeal only to African Councils, or to the Primates of the provinces; and he who shall think of *appealing beyond sea*, let him be admitted into communion by *none in Africk*' (Con. Milev. cap. 22; Conc. Afr. can. 72)."—*Barrow*, Pope's Supremacy, p. 420, vol. vi. ed. Oxf. 1818.

Another authority to which we may refer is that of the celebrated civilian and canonist, VAN ESPEN. He thus writes:—"It is indubitable, that in Africa the Primates or Metropolitans exercised judicial authority over the bishops." Jus Ecclesiasticum Universum: Col. Agrippin. 1748, fol. pp. 111, 112, pars i. tit. xix. cap. iii.

"The canonists declare, with one consent, that by common law the Metropolitan is the ordinary judge of his Suffragans, and that he may proceed against them 'per solam querelam,' and that he may do this *without appeal*."

The following principles are laid down in the Canon Law (Decret. Secund. Pars. Caus. vi. Quæst. iii. et Quæst. iv. p. 482):—

"Judicium Archiepiscopi *alterius* Provinciæ expetere non licet. Non aliorum, sed Primatis judicio, quisque se subjiciat Episcopus."

"If the judgments of the comprovincial Bishops are unanimous, there is no appeal from the sentence of the Metropolitan; but if they are divided, then the Metropolitan of the next adjoining province is to be taken into counsel with them."

The learned canonist and historian, DUPIN, in his work on the Ancient Discipline of the Church, thus speaks, sect. xii. p. 56:—

"The Metropolitan is the judge of the Bishops and of his province, *not however alone*, but with the *Synod* of his province, as may be seen in the decrees of the Council of Chalcedon, c. 9, c. 17. Concil. Carthag. iii. c. 6, 7. Concil. Tolet. iii. c. 20. Concil. Aurel. v. c. 17. Concil. Matiscon. ii. c. 2. There are," he adds, "*innumerable instances* of the deprivation of *Bishops* by their *Metropolitans* in provincial *Synods*." See also BINGHAM, Antiquities of the Christian Church, book ii. chap. xvi.

If, therefore, it should be urged that there may be tyranny in Metropolitans, the answer is easy. The Metropolitan does not judge except in a *Synod*. Let the organization of the Colonial Churches be improved. Let the number of Suffragan Bishops in each of the provinces of the Colonial Churches be increased, so that each Province may have its Synod of Bishops. Let the Colonial Churches, planted by England in every quarter of the globe, be developed with that spiritual organization, and be animated with that inner life, which gave dignity, beauty, and efficiency to the ancient Churches of Christendom in the days of Cyprian and Augustin.

PART IV.

Rites and Ceremonies of the Church of England.

CHAPTER I.

ON THE RITES AND CEREMONIES OF THE CHURCH OF ENGLAND.

PART IV.

Q. What is meant by *Rites* and *Ceremonies?*

A. By Rites are meant religious observances, ordained by competent Authority.

Q. Why are they called *Rites?*

A. Because they are ῥητοί, i. e. *prescribed* or *ordered*.

Q. What do you mean by *Ceremonies?*

A. Solemn and sacred observances [1].

[1] Vossius, Etymol. Lat. p. 89, in v. Verisimilius longè Josephus Scaliger, qui censet *cerimonias* dici ab antiquo *cerus*, id est *sanctus*, unde in Saliari carmine *cerus, manus*, id est, *sanctus bonusque*. Ita à *cerus* erit *cerimonia*, ut à *sanctus sanctimonia*, à *castus castimonia*. Sunt et ejusdem generis *alimonia* et *querimonia*.

Q. In the terms Rites and Ceremonies, as here used, do you include the two Christian *Sacraments?*

RITES AND CEREMONIES.   313

A. No. These two Sacraments were "ordained by CHRIST Himself;" but by Rites and Ceremonies, I here mean sacred and solemn observances appointed by lawful *human* authority. {CHAP. I.}

Q. What rules are to be observed by those persons who prescribe Rites and Ceremonies?

A. That they appoint nothing inconsistent with the Apostolic injunctions, *Let all things be done decently and in order;* and, *Let all things be done to edifying*, and for the promotion of *the glory of God*. Hence they must take care that the Rites, which they ordain, be reasonable and decorous, and, as much as may be, in conformity with the ancient practice of the Universal Church; and that Ceremonies, which are *commandments of men*, be not taught for *doctrines*, and enjoined as necessary to salvation [1]. {1 Cor. xiv. 40. 26. Rom. xiv. 19. 1 Cor. x. 31. Matt. xv. 9.}

[1] HOOKER, III. VII. 1. IV. I. 3. V. VI. 2. V. xxx. 2. F. MASON, in Christian Institutes, iv. pp. 433—460.

Q. Whence do we ascertain the Rites and Ceremonies of the CHURCH OF ENGLAND?

A. From the Tables and Rules prefixed to the Book of Common Prayer, and from the *Rubrics* of the same.

Q. What is meant by a *Rubric?*

A. Properly, a law written in red letters (*rubris litteris*), as the titles of the Old Roman laws, and the ritual directions in the Prayer Book formerly were.

Q. When were these Rubrics drawn up?

A. At the times of the promulgation of the BOOK OF COMMON PRAYER: in the reign of Edward VI. in 1549, 1550, 1552; in that of Queen Elizabeth in 1560; of King James I. in 1604; and at the Restoration of King Charles II. in 1661.

Q. By whom were these Rubrics framed?

A. By Bishops and Presbyters of the Church.

Q. Do you think yourself bound in conscience

PART IV. to observe them, where competent authority or the necessity of the case does not exempt you from the observance [1]?

A. Certainly.

[1] See the grounds of exemption stated by Bp. STILLINGFLEET, Eccl. Cases, i. 264, 265.

Q. On what grounds?

A. Because they are laws made by the Community, both as a Church and a State, and were approved by the two Houses of Parliament, and ratified by Royal authority.

Q. How were they made by it as a Church

A. In Convocation [1].

[1] PREFACE to the Book of COMMON PRAYER. "Yet we have good hope, that what is here presented, and hath been by the *Convocations of both Provinces* with great diligence examined and approved, will be also well accepted and approved by all sober, peaceable, and truly conscientious sons of the Church of England." See also the preamble of the Act of Uniformity, 1662, sect. 1. "Upon mature and full deliberation the said Presidents (of the Convocations of the two Provinces of Canterbury and York), Bishops and Clergy of both Provinces, have reviewed the said Books (of Common Prayer, and of the Form and Manner of the Making and the Consecrating of Bishops, Priests, and Deacons)," &c.

Q. How were they made by it as a State?

A. In the High Court of Parliament.

Q. In what Statutes?

A. In the Acts of Uniformity passed in the reigns of Edward VI., Queen Elizabeth, and Charles II.[1]

[1] A.D. 1548, 1551, 1558, 1661. Bp. GIBSON's Codex, pp. 259. 265. 267. 275.

Q. Is the force of the Spiritual enactment strengthened by this *Civil* sanction?

A. Yes; *Lex humana, jubendo quod jubet lex divina, novam superaddit obligationem*[1]. Therefore, when we obey the Rubric, we obey not only as *Christians*, but as *Citizens;* and he who *disobeys*, when God commands by the voice both of the State and of the Church, is doubly guilty; *apud homines pœnas luit, et apud Deum frontem non habebit*².

CHAP. I.
Jer. xxvii.
6. 8.

¹ Bp. SANDERSON, Prælect. v. 10.
GROTIUS de Sum. Potest. pp. 214. 244.
² S. AUG. cited by Grotius, 214, and de Vera Relig. c. xxvi.
BARROW, iii. 288. It is a great mistake to think that the civil law doth anywise derogate from the ecclesiastical: their concurrence yieldeth an accession of weight and strength to each. Now that spiritual laws are backed by civil sanctions, the knot of our obligation is tied faster; and by disobedience to them we incur a double guilt, and offend God two ways, both as Supreme Governor of the world, and as King of the Church.

Q. You have specified the authority by which these Rites are ordered; but *in addition* to such Ceremonies, may not Ministers and members of a Church adopt Ceremonies from *ancient* or *foreign* Churches; such Ceremonies having been appointed by those Churches, as edifying and decorous?

A. No; *no private person*¹, lay or clerical, is at liberty to introduce any thing into a Church on his own authority: it is not his province, but it is exclusively the office of the Church to which he belongs, to decree the Ceremonies to be observed by its Members; and whether such additional Ceremonies, as you have mentioned, be derived from ancient or from modern practice, they are equally innovations and usurpations of the authority of the Church, and their introduction is equally schismatical and presumptuous. It is not less an act of pride and disobedience in an *individual* to *introduce* into a Church what is *not* ordered by lawful Authority, than it is to *despise* what *is* prescribed by that Authority².

PART IV.

¹ BOOK OF COMMON PRAYER. Of Ceremonies. Although the keeping or omitting of a ceremony, in itself considered, is but a small thing, yet the wilful and contemptuous transgression and breaking of common order and discipline is no small offence before God. "Let all things be done among you," saith St. Paul, "in a seemly and due order;" the *appointment* of the which order pertaineth not *to private men;* therefore *no man* ought to take in hand nor *presume to appoint or alter* any public or common order in Christ's Church, except he be lawfully called and authorized thereto. See also CANON xiv. The clergy make an express promise of conformity, see Can. xxxvi.

² S. AUG. Regula ad Servos Dei, 3 (i. p. 1273). Nolite cantare nisi quod *legitis* esse cantandum; quod autem ita scriptum est ut non cantetur, *non cantetur.*

HOOKER, V. LXXI. 7. We had rather glorify and bless God for the fruit we daily behold reaped by such ordinances as His gracious Spirit enableth the ripe wisdom of this *National Church* to bring forth, than vainly boast of *our own peculiar and private inventions,* as if the skill of profitable regiment had left her *public habitation* to dwell in retired manner with some few men of our liking. We make not our childish appeals sometimes from our own to *foreign* Churches, sometimes from both unto Churches *ancienter* than both are; in effect always from all others to *our own selves.* But, as becometh them that follow with all humility the ways of peace, we honour, reverence, and obey in the very next degree unto God the voice of the Church of God *wherein we live.*

Q. What "ornaments of the Church and of its Ministers, at the times of their ministration," are allowed by the Church of England?

A. Those ornaments which were in the "Church of England, by the Authority of Parliament in the second year of King Edward¹."

¹ Rubric in the Book of Common Prayer, before the Order of Morning Prayer: cp. Canons of 1603, Canon 24.

Q. What are these?

A. Such as are specified in the First Book of Common Prayer¹ put forth in the reign of King Edward VI., and authorized by legislative sanction in the Act of Uniformity passed at that time; and as have not since been abrogated.

[1] A.D. 1549. See WHEATLY on the Common Prayer, chap. ii. sect. iv., and on the subject of this chapter, see NICHOLS on the Book of Common Prayer, folio, 1712. PALMER, Rev. W., Origines Liturgicæ. CARDWELL, Conferences on the Book of Common Prayer, 1840. CLAY, Rev. W. K., on the Book of Common Prayer, 1841. PROCTER, Rev. F., History of the Book of Common Prayer, 1855.

CHAPTER II.

OBJECTIONS CONSIDERED.

Q. BUT may it not be said, that—as these Rites and Ceremonies are *indifferent* things [1], and may vary in different Churches, and very reasonably and advantageously so [2], and may be changed from time to time in the same Church [3] —it is of little importance whether we conform to them or no?

A. No: for if this were so, there would be an end of all human authority [4]. Things *indifferent* are properly those concerning which Almighty God *has not spoken* by any law, either *for* them or *against*: and *indifference* (ἀδιαφορία) is the special character of the legitimate objects of *human* law, as distinguished from *divine*: τὸ νομικὸν δίκαιον is that ὃ ἐξ ἀρχῆς οὐδὲν διαφέρει, ὅταν δὲ θῶνται, διαφέρει [5]. 'In *mediis* rebus Lex posita est Obedientiæ.' Even *natural Reason* tells us that certain states of the body are appropriate accompaniments and exponents of certain affections of the mind [6], and tend to general edification [7]; and for the recommendation of certain attitudes in devotion we have the authority of *Scripture Example;* and in the Public Worship of a Church, discrepancy is to be deprecated, and *Uniformity* is greatly to be desired, as tending to promote *Unity;* and although, indeed, this or *that particular* ceremony may be

Luke xxii. 41.
Acts vii. 60.
Phil. ii. 10.
iii. 14.

a matter of little moment, yet that *some* ceremonies there should be, is essential to the maintenance of Religion; and *when* laws *have* been made by Authority prescribing certain ceremonies, we are *no longer* free to use or omit them, as we please.

Obedience to lawful *Authority* is not a matter of *Indifference*[8], and nothing is more destructive to a Community, and nothing more displeasing to God, Who is the Author not of confusion but of peace, than disobedience.

Besides, if these things be matters of indifference, nothing can be more frivolous than wranglings concerning them. In a word, the fruits of *disputing*, instead of *obeying*, are contempt of lawful authority, loss of time and labour, forfeiture of peace and charity, and the neglect of the "weightier matters of the law [9]."

Marginal references: Exod. xxii. 28. Acts xxiii. 3. 5. 2 Pet. ii. 10. Jude 8. 1 Tim. i. 4. vi. 4. 20. 2 Tim. ii. 16. 23. 1 Cor. xiv. 33. Tit. i. 10. Matt. xxiii. 23. Luke xi. 42.

---

[1] S. AUGUST. ii. 186. 188. 291. (Epist. liv. lxxxii.) BARROW in Christian Institutes, iii. 157. F. MASON, ibid. iv. 463. 487. Bp. SANDERSON, ibid. iv. 574. BINGHAM, XVI. I. 15.

[2] S. IREN. ap. Euseb. v. 24. The διαφωνία in ceremonies in different Churches τὴν ὁμόνοιαν τῆς πίστεως συνίστησιν. S. GREG. MAG. Ep. i. 43. In unâ fide nihil officit Ecclesiæ *consuetudo diversa.* HOOKER, IV. XIII. 3.

[3] XXXIX ARTICLES, Art. xxxiv. Of the Traditions of the Church. It is not necessary that Traditions and Ceremonies be in all places one, or utterly like; for at all times they have been divers, and may be changed according to the diversity of countries, times, and men's manners, so that nothing be ordained against God's Word. Every particular or National Church hath authority to ordain, change, and abolish Ceremonies or Rites of the Church, ordained only by man's authority, so that all things be done to edifying.

[4] PREFACE to BOOK OF COMMON PRAYER. XXXIX. ARTICLES, Art. xxxiv.

[5] ARISTOT. Ethic. v. 10. S. BERNARD, Ep. vii. CANONS of 1603. Can. xxx. Things of themselves indifferent do in some sort alter their natures, when they are either commanded or forbidden by a lawful magistrate, and may not be omitted at every man's pleasure, contrary to the

law, when they be commanded, nor used when they are prohibited.

HOOKER, V. VIII. 2. Matters ritual are the just province of authority.

⁶ HOOKER, V. XXX. 2. When we make profession of our faith, we *stand*; when we acknowledge our sins, we *fall down*, because the gesture of constancy becometh us best on the one; in the other the behaviour of humility. —V. LXVIII. 3. Our kneeling at Communion is a gesture of piety: what doth better beseem our bodies than to be sensible witnesses of minds unfeignedly humble?

⁷ HOOKER, VI. I. 3.

⁸ XXXIX ARTICLES, Art. xxxiv. F. MASON in Christian Institutes, iv. 436, and notes. Bp. SANDERSON, ibid. pp. 557. 623, and W. WALL, ibid. p. 464.

⁹ HOOKER, V. XXXI. 1. By them which trouble us with these doubts, (i. e. concerning the propriety of wearing the *surplice*, and such like matters,) we would more willingly be resolved of a greater doubt, whether it be not a kind of taking God's name in vain, to debase religion with such frivolous disputes, a sin to bestow time and labour upon them. Things of so mean regard and quality, although *necessary* to be *ordered*, are *notwithstanding* very unsavoury when they come to be *disputed* of.

HOOKER, III. IX. 3. Unto laws made and received by a whole Church, they which live within the bosom of that Church must *not* think it a matter *indifferent* either to yield or not to yield obedience. Is it a small offence to despise the Church of God? "My son, keep thy father's commandment," saith Solomon, "and forget not thy *mother's* instruction; bind them both always about thy heart." It doth not stand with the duty which we owe to our heavenly Father, that to the ordinances of our Mother the Church we should show ourselves disobedient. Let us not say we keep the commandments of the *one* when we break the law of the *other*; for unless we observe *both*, we obey *neither*.

1 Cor. xi. 22.
Prov. vi. 20

Q. You say we must obey these laws; and you acknowledge that these laws are *human*; do then *human laws* bind the *conscience*?

A. Not *as human laws* ¹: nothing but the law of *God* can do so; but human laws, which are not contrary to God's law, bind the conscience *indirectly*, by virtue of the Divine law, which *commands us to obey* those who *have rule over us*. Thus, in the case supposed, we are bound to

James iv. 11, 12.

1 Pet. ii. 13—19.

320 OBJECTIONS CONSIDERED

PART IV.
Eph. vi. 5, 6.
Col. iii. 23.
Tit. iii. 1.
Rom. xiii. 1—5.

conform to the Rubric, because God says in His Word, "Submit yourselves to every ordinance of man for the Lord's sake." For example, we are not bound in conscience to *kneel on account of any special virtue in the act itself*: but we are bound in conscience to *obey the lawful authority which enjoins us to do so*[2]. Thus, in obeying the Rubrics of the Church, we do in fact obey GOD; *Cùm, Christo jubente, servis homini, non homini servis, sed Illi Qui jussit,* i. e. *Deo*[3]; and in disobeying them, we do in fact despise GOD[4].

---

[1] Bp. SANDERSON's Prælections and Sermons, i. 302. ii. 177. iii. 10. Note in Christian Institutes, iii. p. 4.

[2] XXXIX ARTICLES, Art. xx. The Church hath power to decree Rites or Ceremonies.

[3] S. AUGUST. iv. 2018. 1028. 1056. v. 418.

[4] HOOKER, V. VIII. 4. Suppose we that the *Sacred Word* of *God* can at their hands receive due honour by whose incitement the *holy ordinances of the Church* endure open contempt? No; it is not possible that they should observe as they ought the one, who from the other withdraw unnecessarily their own or their brethren's obedience.

Exod. i. 16, 17.
Dan. iii. 18. vi. 9.
1 Macc. i. 45. ii. 34.
2 Chron. xv. 16.
Luke ii. 49.
Acts v. 29.

Q. It is not meant, I suppose, that we should obey *every* human ordinance, without reference to the nature of the thing commanded?

A. No; we are not to obey a human ordinance, if it be plainly *against* the *Divine* law: we *are* to obey *man* for the sake of God, but we *are not* to disobey GOD for the sake of man.

Q. But these Ceremonies of the Church are *not* enjoined *in Holy Scripture;* and does not,

Art. vi.

in the language of the Church, "Holy Scripture contain *all* things necessary to salvation?"

A. Yes. Scripture contains all things necessary to salvation; and of these necessary things

Rom. xiii. 2.
Matt. xvii. 27. xxii. 21. xxiii. 2, 3.
Luke iv. 16. xvii. 14.

one of the *very first* is obedience to lawful authority in all things not unlawful[1], *that is, in all things not contrary to the general laws of Nature and Reason, and to the positive ones of Holy*

OBJECTIONS CONSIDERED. 321

Scripture. And both the precept and example of our blessed Lord, Who was "obedient to the law for man," is conclusive on this point[2].

CHAP. II.
John x. 22.
Acts ii. 15.
iii. 1.

[1] S. AUGUSTIN, Ep. 36, tom. ii. p. 101. In his rebus, de quibus nihil certi statuit Scriptura divina, mos populi Dei vel instituta majorum pro lege tenenda sunt.
S. HIERON. Ep. xxviii. ad Lucinium Bæticum. Ego illud te breviter admonendum puto, traditiones Ecclesiasticas (præsertim quæ fidei non officiant) ita observandas, ut à majoribus traditæ sunt: nec aliorum consuetudinem aliorum contrario more subverti. Sed unaquæque provincia abundet in suo sensu, et *præcepta majorum leges Apostolicas arbitretur.*
[2] HOOKER, II. VIII. 6, 7. III. VI. and III. VII. 2—4. III. XI. 14. V. LXX. 6. V. LXXI. 7.
Bp. ANDREWES on the Decalogue, pp. 209. 271.

Q. But if I have a *scruple* of *conscience* as to the lawfulness of a ceremony, ought I to conform to it?

A. It is true, certainly, that our conscience *obliges* us; even when it *errs;* but then it does not exempt us from the *guilt* and *punishment* of error. Hence we must take all the care in our power, that our conscience *may not err,* but be rightly instructed and informed. And with this view we must consider, that lawful Authority has *pronounced* a public judgment in *favour* of the Ceremony, by *ordering* it; and in Christian charity, humility, and discretion, we shall not be disposed to doubt that this *public judgment* is *worth* more than our own *private opinion.* Our *private conscience* must remember that the *public conscience* is better than itself[1]; and it ought, therefore, to endeavour to bring itself into *conformity* with it. Next, we must bear in mind, that the thing is *established,* and for the sake of peace ought not to be stirred by private persons, without urgent necessity; that the order, which enjoins the observance, is the judgment of the competent authority, to which, by God's Word, we owe *obedience* in all things *not* clearly unlaw-

Above.
p. 244.

Y

ful, "not only for wrath but also for *conscience* sake;" that the *command* is *clear*, but our *exemption* is *not* so; (and 'in *dubiis* rebus *tutior* pars est eligenda;') and lastly, that there are many things which it may not be expedient for *others* to *command*, in which, notwithstanding, when they *are* commanded, it is necessary for *us* to obey[2].

Part IV.
Rom. xiii. 5.
Jer. xxxv. 16.
1 Pet. ii. 13—20.

[1] HOOKER, IV. I. 12. Their sentences will not be greatly regarded, when they oppose their *me-thinketh* to the *Orders* of the Church of England.

[2] S. AUG. c. Faust. Man. xxii. 75. Reum facit superiorem iniquitas imperandi, innocentem subditum ordo serviendi.

Bp. ANDREWES on the Decalogue, p. 340.

Rom. xiv. 5. 23.

Q. But does not St. Paul say, "Let every one be *fully persuaded in his own mind*;" and, "Whatsoever is not of *faith* is sin?"

A. St. Paul is there speaking of indifferent matters, that is, of matters not prescribed or forbidden by God, and on which the *lawful public Authority* had *not* pronounced any *judgment*, and in which, therefore, every one was at liberty to do what in his own conscience he thought best[1]. But where such public Authority *has* pronounced its judgment, (as *is* the case with the Rites and Ceremonies of the Church,) he condemns those who resist it in the following words, "If any man *thinks fit* (δοκεῖ) to be contentious, we have no such custom, neither the Churches of God:" and, "Whosoever resisteth the Power, resisteth the ordinance of *God*."

1 Cor. xi. 16.

Rom. xiii. 2.

[1] HOOKER, IV. XII. 6, 7.

Q. But if I *give scandal*, or *offence*, to others by compliance with those ceremonies, am not I guilty of want of *charity;* since St. Paul says, "If meat make my brother to offend, I will eat no flesh while the world standeth;" and, "It

1 Cor. viii. 13.
Rom. xiv. 21.

is good to do nothing whereby thy brother stumbleth, or is offended, or is made weak?"

A. St. Paul is speaking of things, by abstinence from which he *sacrificed* his *own appetite*, and did not disobey *authority*. The former is right, but not the latter. And, with respect to *giving scandal*, it is not possible to give *greater scandal* to the weak, than by teaching them disobedience to Authority by an *example* of *resistance* to it; and *this* too in a matter of *religion*. *This is* indeed to *make our brother to offend*. And this is to give scandal not only to our *weak* brethren, but to the *strong*, both among our equals, and inferiors, and our governors; and our *governors* are more than *brethren*, they are *fathers;* and *obedience* is *charity* too, and something more; and, lastly, it is to offend *our own consciences*, and to disobey God [1].

---

[1] XXXIX Articles, Art. xxxiv. Of the Traditions of the Church. Whosoever through his private judgment willingly and purposely doth openly break the Traditions and Ceremonies of the Church, which be not repugnant to the Word of God, and be ordained and approved by common authority, ought to be rebuked openly, as he that offendeth against the common order of the Church, *hurteth the authority of the magistrate*, and *woundeth the consciences of the weak brethren*.

Hooker III. ix. 3. The laws thus made, God doth Himself in such sort authorize, that to despise *them* is to despise *Him*.

Bp. Taylor on Scandal, Life of Christ, § xiii. 7.

Q. But may Scandal be never lawfully given?

A. No. Scandal *can never* be lawfully *given*, but it *is not seldom* unlawfully *taken*. A scandal means a stumbling-block; and Christ Himself was a stumbling-block to the Jews. The Pharisees were *offended* ($\dot{\epsilon}\sigma\kappa\alpha\nu\delta\alpha\lambda\dot{\iota}\sigma\theta\eta\sigma\alpha\nu$) by His words; yet He did not desist from preaching [1]. St. Paul speaks of the *offence* of the cross, yet it was not to *cease;* and he says, "God forbid that

Luke ii. 34.
1 Cor. i. 23.
1 Pet. ii. 8.
Matt. xiii. 57. xv. 12.
Rom. ix. 33.
Gal. v. 11. vi. 14.

PART IV. I should *glory, save* in the *cross* of our Lord Jesus Christ." Offence may be *taken,* where none is *given;* and offence *not justly* taken hurteth no one but the taker.

[1] THEOPHYL. in S. Luc. xiii. Οὐ τοῦτο ἐσκόπησεν ὁ Χριστὸς, ὅπως μὴ σκανδαλίσῃ αὐτοὺς, ἀλλ' ὅπως εὐεργετήσῃ τὸν θεραπείας δεόμενον· δεῖ γὰρ ἡμᾶς, ἔνθα ὠφέλεια ἀνακύπτει πολλὴ, μὴ φροντίζειν τῶν ἀνοήτως σκανδαλιζομένων.

TERTULLIAN de Vel. Virg. 3. *Bonæ res* neminem scandalizant nisi *malam mentem.*

HOOKER, IV. XII.

INDEX I.

OF MATTERS.

AARON, his ordination, 71, 72
ABSOLUTION, 112—120, requisites for, and power of, 114—119
ABUSE, takes not away the lawful use, 186
ACTS OF PARLIAMENT (*see Index II.*)
ADVENT, the Second, 33, 34
AERIUS, his heresy, 88
AIDAN of Lindisfarn, 157
ALBAN, S., 136
ALEXANDRIA, Patriarch of, 103
ANGELS OF CHURCHES, 86
ANICETUS, Pope, 149
ANTIOCH, Patriarch of, 101. 103
APOCRYPHAL BOOKS, 50, 51
APOSTLES, meaning of the term, 73, 74; their offices, ordinary and extraordinary, 90, 91 (*see Bishops, Episcopacy, Apostolic Succession*); equality of, 214—217. 221
APOSTOLIC SUCCESSION (*see Succession*) in the Church of England, 187
APPEAL, FINAL, in matters of Doctrine, Court of, 302—311
APPEALS TO ROME, 143—145; restrained, 163
ARK, the, 9. 24
ARMINIAN testimonies to Episcopacy, 93, 94
ARTICLES, THIRTY-NINE, their character, 177—181
ARTICULI CLERI, 164
AUGUSTIN, S., of Canterbury, 135—157

BAPTISM, Sacrament of admission into the Church, 8. 66, 67; of regeneration and remission of original sin, 107. 117; of Infants, 117; against iteration of, 209—212; conditional form of administering, 211; schismatical, 211. 257
BENEDICTION, episcopal and sacerdotal, 120—131
BERTHA, Queen, 146. 156
BISHOPS (*see Episcopacy*), meaning of the term, 76; successors and representatives of the Apostles, 77—90; functions of, 16. 90—94; as Diocesans, Metropolitans, and Patriarchs, 95—106; not more than one in a city, 98; benediction by, 126, 127; the centres of unity in their respective Dioceses, 130; their equality as Bishops, 214, 215. 225—227; Bishops and Clerks, accused of false doctrine, tried by the Metropolitan of the Province with his Suffragans, 304; on the deposition of Bishops, 308—311
———— of England (*see Church of England*), number of at the Saxon Invasion greater than at this day, 138. see also 154, 155; as Peers of Parliament, 251, 252, derive their *office from* God; how far its *exercise* is *by man* (*see Jurisdiction*); *placed*, not *made*, by the Crown, 151. 292—311
———— of the Church of Rome, their Oath to the Pope (*see Oath*); are feudal vassals of the Papacy,

326 INDEX I.

and Peers of the Pope's creation, 227
BONIFACE III., Pope, 158. 203. 225; VIII., 203
BRITISH CHURCH, 138—157
BULLS, PAPAL, *Unam Sanctam*, 202; and *in Cœnâ Domini*, 207
——— of Excommunication, 206, 207

CAERLEON, Bishop of, 137
CALVINISTIC testimonies in favour of Episcopacy, 93, 94
CANON LAW (*see Councils, Decretals*), statement of, with respect to Papal Power, 198—203
——————— of England, 289 (*see Convocation*)
CANON of 1571, concerning Preachers, 185
CANON, the, and CANONICAL BOOKS of Scripture, 43—45. 49
CANONS of 1603, their regard for antiquity, 179; their rules for preaching, 185, 186
CANTERBURY, the *Patriarchal* See of England, 156. 166
CATALOGUES of Church Governors, 88
CATECHIZING, 54, 55
CATHEDRAL CHURCH the Parish Church of the Diocese, 130, 131
CATHOLIC, 5, 6. 256—258
—————— COMMUNION, what, 212, 213
CATHOLICS, who, 6. 213
CEREMONIES (*see Rites*)
CHRIST (*see* JESUS CHRIST)
CHURCH, etymology, 1. 139; names for, 1, 2; definition of, 22, 23; her constitution, 2—4. 7. 16, 17; how one or united, 3; her unity, how maintained, 3, 4 (*see Unity*); how Holy, 4; Catholic, 5. 256, 257; Apostolic, 7; Visible and Militant, 8—20. 256, 257; types of, 9. 24; Parables concerning, 10; notes of, 13. 106; Invisible, 14; has no One Visible Head, 15, 16. 214—233; her dignity and glory, 20, 21; salvation only in, 23—30; one only, 26, 27; prefigured by Eve, 27; the Spouse and Body of Christ, 20. 26, 27;

on errors in, 32—42. 65; Catholic, cannot fail, 32; waxes and wanes, 32. 33; likened to a Sea, 133, 134; keeper and witness of Holy Writ, 43—51; interpreter of Scripture, 52—64; Discipline (*see Power of Keys*); the depository of grace, and the house of discipline, 118, 119. 254—256; communion and unity, 128. 208—213. 231—233; the duty of kings and states to the Church, 239—311 (*see Kings*); her state in persecution and in peace, 273
CHURCH OF ENGLAND, her catholicity, 133, 134; her origin, 134—140; her Bishops in unbroken succession from the time of the Apostles, 135 and following; independent of Rome, 135—169; her reformation, *restorative* character of, 170—195; her primitive character, 171—173; her continuity, 174—208; how Protestant, 176, 177; her regard for antiquity, 170—181. 185; her Scriptural character, 178, 179. 185; how far she admits private judgment, 184; the Apostolic succession of her Bishops, 187—196; her priesthood and sacrifice, 194, 195; her ordinations, 187—196; her visibility from the Apostolic age, 171—176. 196—208; did not separate herself from the Church of Rome, 196—208; a true branch of the Catholic Church, 134—140. 208—213; why she recognizes Roman Catholic orders, 193—208; her conduct towards reformed communions, 193; Church and State of England, *two names* for one community, 234—237; the Church the spiritual mother of all Christians in England, 254—264; supremacy of Kings (*see Kings*)
——— and STATE, 250—264
——— OF ROME (*see Rome*)
CHURCHES, who is their real owner, 191; Consecration of, 191; endowment of, 247—253
———, SUBURBICARIAN (*see Suburbicarian*)

INDEX I.

CLERGY, their authority in matters of doctrine, 55, 56; origin of name, 68, 69; *necessity* of, 69—71; lawful call, 71; and mission, 72; grace received by at ordination, 74; three orders, 75—78; in England, 136. 187; number, conforming at Reformation, 193; their duty to the Sovereign, 105. 272—281 (see *Priest, Ministry, Orders*)

COLUTHUS, case of, 92

COMMITTEE, the JUDICIAL, of Privy Council, 304; does not possess the confidence of the Church, 304

COMMON PRAYER, 128, 129; set forms of, benefit of, 132, 133; Book of (see *Index II.*); Paul IV. and Pius IV. offered to confirm, 198; its history, 313

COMMUNION of Churches, 212. 231 (see *Unity*)

CONFIRMATION, 126; benediction in, 126, 127

CONSCIENCE, an erroneous, no excuse *as conscience*, 244; is to be *reformed*, 245

CONSECRATION, words of, 126

CONSTANTINOPLE, Patriarch of, 103

CONSTITUTIONS of Clarendon, 164

CONVOCATION, of Church of England, its nature, power, and duties, 288

CORONATION of English Sovereigns, 282

COUNCILS, General, use of, 17. 34; authority, 34, 35. 65; right of calling, and of presidency in, belongs to Sovereign Princes, and not to the Bishop of Rome, 287—291; the first four, reverence of Gregory the First for, 147; by whom called, 287; their authority recognized by English Parliament, 302 (see *Index II.*)

COUNCIL of Arles, 137
———— Chalcedon, 177
———— Constantinople, 177
———— Ephesus, 147, 148. 177. 197
———— Nice, 141. 170. 176
———— Sardica, 137. 143—145
———— Trent, not a General Council, its illegality, 180, 181; its creed, 178—181; its anathema, 205

COUNCIL of Trullo, 148

COVENANT, Solemn League and, abjuration of, 162

CYPRUS, case of Church of, 147—149

DAVID'S, St., Bishops of, 140. 166

DEACONS, 75; their name and office, 77

DECRETALS of Dionysius Exiguus, Isidorus, and Gratian, 199; others, 200

DELEGATES, Court of, 304

DINOTH, Abbot of Bangor, 148

DIOCESAN EPISCOPACY, 95—106

DIOCESE, meaning of the word, 97

DISCIPLINE OF CHURCH, 13, 14; its institution, aims, ends, and obligations, 106—118

DISSENTERS, 38—40. 42; duties to, 247—264

DONATISTS, 192. 209. 212

EASTER, time of keeping, 139. 150

ECCLESIA, its meaning, 2; of Athens, 2
———— permixta (see *Church Visible*)
———— IN EPISCOPO, the maxim illustrated, 136, 137 (see *Succession*)

ECCLESIASTICAL BOOKS of Scripture, 49, 50

ELDAD and MEDAD, case of, 260

ELIZABETH, Queen, excommunicated, 198. 205, 206; on the limits of the royal supremacy, 284

EMPIRE, ROMAN, its divisions how *preparatory* to the Polity of the Church, 96—101; how it became a *Church*, 236

ENDOWMENTS, RELIGIOUS, 247—253

ENGLAND (see *Church, Church and State*, and *Kings*)

EPISCOPACY (see *Bishops*), Divine Institution of, 72—95; Lutheran, Arminian, and Calvinistic testimonies in favour of, 93, 94
———— Diocesan, 95—106

EPISCOPUS, 80. 87

ERASTIANISM, 279—281
ETHELBERT, King, 136—155
EVE, a figure of the Church, 27
EVIDENCE, internal and external, of Scripture, 46, 47
EVIL men in the Church, 9—14
EXPOSITORS of Scripture, 55—64

FAITH, the one true, 242—246
FATHERS OF THE CHURCH, Authority of, 60—63
FIDELES, 71

GENERAL COUNCILS (see Councils)
GRACE, gratis datur, 149
GREGORY I., Pope, 135—158; his declarations irreconcilable with later claims of the Papacy, 224 (see Index II.)
GREGORY VII., 160. 198; his Dictatus Papæ, 202, 203; canonized, and lauded by the Church of Rome for deposing Henry IV., 228

HEAD OF THE CHURCH (see Jesus Christ, Church, and Kings)
HEATHEN, condition of, and duties of Christians to, 30, 31
HENRY II., his concessions to the Pope, 167
—— VIII., his acts in Ecclesiastical matters, 164. 168; his character, 168; excommunicated by the Pope, 206
HERESY, what is, 36; guilt of, 37; how differs from schism, 38; uses of, 63 (see Schism); causes of, where to be heard, 302—308
HERETICS, how far in the Visible Church, 40, 41; duties towards, 42; formerly agreed on one point, 88
HILDEBRAND (see Gregory VII.)
HOLY GHOST, the Author of Episcopacy, 89; His office in Ordination, 74, 75
HOMILIES, 178, 179
HUMAN LAWS, how they bind the conscience, 319
—— TEACHING, 56, 57

INDIFFERENCE, RELIGIOUS, 246
INDIFFERENT THINGS, 31

IN SOLIDUM, 18, 19. 226
INTENTION, GOOD (see Conscience)
INTERCESSION, 120—130
INTERPRETATION (see Scripture)
INVESTITURE of Bishops, 153
INVOCATION and CONSECRATION, words of, 126
ISCHYRAS, case of, 92
ITALY, Diocese of, distinct from that of Rome, 100

JAMES I., 179
JEROBOAM, an example of Schism and Heresy, 39
JERUSALEM, CHURCH of, the Mother of all Churches, 139. 146
JESUS CHRIST, how He governs the world, 17—19; the object of the Faith of the Church both before and after His coming, 30, 31; the Church His house, 21; His body, 20. 25. 28; His Spouse, 14, 15; the second Adam, 28; the Great Apostle, 73, 74. 86; and Founder of Apostolic and Episcopal Office, 86; His Office in Absolution, 115; in Intercession, 123; Benediction, 125; His commission to St. Peter, and in him to all Bishops and Pastors, 214—221; His language when He stood before Pilate, 241, 242; all Human Power is derived through Him, 241—243; the rock on which the Church is built, 216—219; His Headship of the Church distinguished from that of Kings, 265
JEWS, the Librarii of Christians, 43
JOHN THE BAPTIST, his baptism, 193, 194
—— King of England, his concessions to the Pope, 167, 168
JUDAS, 87; baptism by, 191. 193
JUDGE, no one living infallible in controverted causes, 64—66
JURISDICTION, spiritual source of, 273. 283. 293 (see Keys)
JUS CYPRIUM of the Church of England, 147—150

KEYS, Power of, 107—120; given to all Presbyters, 107. 219—221;

of divine, not human, origin, 274. 283—294.
KINGS and QUEENS, Christian Deputies and Vicegerents of Almighty God, 105; derive their power from Him, 239; through Jesus Christ, 18. 241—243; Ecclesiastical Supremacy of Christian Princes in their own Realms, 18. 19. 104, 105. 151. 166. 236; Founders of Episcopal Sees, 295, 296; in what their true happiness consists, 238. 239. 262—286; their religious duty, 238—264

——— OF ENGLAND, their Ecclesiastical Supremacy, its *nature and limits*, 264—311; their headship distinguished from Christ's, 265; their *sacred* character, 282

KORAH and his company, examples of Schism, 40, 41
Κυριακὸς, 1

LAITY, 68 (*see Fideles*)
LAY ELDERS, the novelty of their office, 279
LAZARUS, 116; sister of, 48
LITERÆ FORMATÆ, 102
LITURGY (*see Prayer, Common Prayer*)
LIUDHARD, Bp., 146
LONDON, 137. 153, 154
LUTHERAN testimonies to Episcopacy, 93, 94

MARY, St., the VIRGIN, at Cana, 48
MASORA, the, 44
MATTHIAS, St., 85. 87
METROPOLITANS (*see Bishops*), 98. 102
MINISTERS, unworthiness of, hinders not the effect of the ordinances which they minister, 190, 191
MINISTRY, LAWFUL, what constitutes a, 68—90 (*see Clergy, Priest, Ordination*)

NADAB and ABIHU, examples of heresy, 40
NAG'S HEAD FABLE, 189

OATH, qualifications of a good, 161

OATH of Supremacy, its history and nature, 272—275
——— of Roman Catholic Bishops to the Pope, 160, 161. 228; *persequi Hæreticos*, 207; and obligation of vassalage, 228; inconsistent with civil allegiance, 228. 229
ORDERS, THE THREE, of Christian Ministers, 75. 78. 187 (*see Clergy*)
ORDINAL, English, 187—189 (*see Church of England*)
ORDINATION, requisites to a lawful one, 71—75. 91; the Office of the Holy Ghost in, 74; grace of, 75. 149. 190, 191 (*see Clergy* and *Priests*)
ORIGINAL SIN, punishment of, remitted in baptism, 116, 117
ORNAMENTS of the Church and of its Ministers allowed by the Church of England, 316

PALLIUM, its origin, use, and abuse, 158—163. 229
PARABLES, Scripture, concerning the Church, 10—15
PARISHES, 97
PARKER, Abp., his consecration, 189
PARLIAMENT, Bishops of England in, 251, 252
PATRIARCHAL DISPENSATION, Priesthood of, 121, 122
PATRIARCHATE of England (*see Canterbury*
PATRIARCHATES, modification and transfer of precedence of, 103—106; tenets of, by Nicene Canon, 99; and by Ephesine, 147, 148. 155, 156
PATRIARCHS (*see Bishops*), 99—106
PAUL, St., his primacy, 216
PETER, St., his primacy, faith, confession, keys, pastoral office, 107—109. 214—233
PETRA and PETRUS, 216—219
PHOCAS, 225
PICTS and SCOTS, Church among, 138
PIUS IV., 198; his creed, 180, 181
——— V., his bull against Queen Elizabeth, 198. 206
POPE OF ROME, his claim to be the Head of the Visible Church, 15

—18. 19. 214—233; his claim to be an infallible Judge in controverted causes, 64—66; ancient precedence and extent of his Patriarchate, 99; has no jurisdiction in England, 138. 214—233 (*see Church of England*); Oath imposed by him on Ecclesiastics, 158—162. 207; protests against his usurpations in that country, 164, 165; his secular claims, 199—203. 228; form of coronation, 202; his spiritual claims, 203—207. 215; destructive of Church Unity, 229; his treatment of Councils and Bishops, 203. 229—231; examples of resistance to encroachments of, 164—170. 220, 221; errors and heresies of various Popes, 230 (*see Visible Head*)
POPISH and PURITANICAL Principles of Polity, the similarity of, 276. 279
POWER, the true source of, 239—241
PRACTICE, the best interpreter of laws, 87
PRÆMUNIRE, Statute of, 164—170. 296—299
PRAYER, Public (*see Common Prayer*)
PREACHING, 55—59; Canons of the Church of England concerning, 184, 185; Schismatical Preaching, 258—262
PRESBYTERS (*see Priest* and *Bishops*)
PRIEST (*see Clergy*), meaning of term, 76; how far *Presbyter* and *Episcopus* commutable, 79, 80; *Presbyters* cannot ordain, 92, 93; power in Absolution (*see Absolution*); in Intercession and Benediction (*see Intercession*); Priesthood of Patriarchal Dispensation, 121; of Christian Church, 194; Priests as *Angeli Ecclesiæ*, 128, 129; Priesthood in the Church of England, 194
PRIESTHOOD, necessity of, 69—72 (*see Priest, Clergy*)
PRIVATE JUDGMENT defined, 184
PRIVY COUNCIL, Judicial Committee of, 304

PROMOTIONS, Episcopal, 295. 299
PROTESTANTISM, 176, 177
PROVINCES of the Church. 97—102
PROVISORS, Statute of, 164
PURITANS, in the Principles of their civil and ecclesiastical polity symbolize with the Papists, 276. 279.

QUARTODECIMANI, 150

RAHAB, house of, 24
REBAPTIZATION, 209
RECUSANCY, Romish, in England, date of its origin, 198
REFORMATION in England, not Innovating, but restorative, 170—196 (*see Church of England*)
REFORMATIONS in a Church, how to be made, 65, 66
REGALIA SANCTI PETRI, 160
REGENERATION, 116, 117
RELIGION, its political effects, 234—264
REPENTANCE, 116—119
RITES and CEREMONIES in the Church of England, origin of the terms, 312; their nature and obligation, 312—324
ROCHESTER, 153
ROME, Bishop of (*see Pope*)
———, Church of, not *the* Catholic Church, 6, 7; when founded, 138; its novel, unscriptural, and antiscriptural dogmas and practices, 178—183. 192; violent obtrusion of them, 199. 203—208; anathemas, 206, 207; reiterates Ordination and Baptism, 209—212; Bishops of (*see Oath* and *Pope*); in what sense a true Church, 174—177. 196; its schism, 207
RUBRICS, history and authority of, 313—316
RULE OF FAITH, 59. 64

SACRAMENTS, the, from Christ on the Cross, 28; nature of, 66, 67; necessity of, 67; due administration of, by a lawful Ministry, 66—74
SACRIFICE, the Christian, 194
SAMARITAN WOMAN, 48

SCANDAL, on giving and taking, 322
SCHISM, its nature and sin, 39—41. 197. 258; its political effects, 237. 246
SCHISMATICAL Assemblies and Preaching, 257—262
SCHISMATICS, how far in the Visible Church, 41; duties to, 42. 258—262; formerly agreed in one point, 88
SCHOOLS, their connexion with the Church, 251
SCOTCH CHURCH, 138, 139. 185
SCRIBES and PHARISEES, why and how far to be heard, 58. 174
SCRIPTURE, HOLY (*see Canonical, Ecclesiastical, Apocryphal*), committed to the keeping of the Church, 43; its integrity, 39. 45; genuineness, 46; authority and Inspiration, 46, 47; evidence, internal and external, of, 47, 48
——————, Custody and Interpretation of, 43—65
——————, Supremacy and sufficiency of, 64. 178. 181—183
——————, Versions of, 51, 52
SINCERITY (*see Conscience*)
STATE ENDOWMENTS of different Creeds, 247
STATES and PRINCES, religious duty of, 239—253 (*see Kings*)
STATESMEN, duties of, 69. 246. 250. 263
STATUTE of Provisors, 164
STEPHEN, King, his concessions to Rome, 167
STRIFE, preaching in, 258—262
SUBURBICARIAN CHURCHES, 99—101. 141. 152

SUCCESSION, Apostolic (*see Apostolic*), 187—194
SUFFRAGAN Bishops, 102
SUPREMACY (*see Oath, Kings*)
σωζόμενοι, σῶμα, 25

TABLES of the Law in the Ark, 43
TARES and WHEAT, 10—12 258
TAXES for Religion, 247—259
TOLERATION. 247
TRENT, Council of (*see Councils*)
——————, Creed, 178—180

UNITY of the Church, in what it consists, and how to be maintained, 3 17—19. 128, 129. 208, 209. 229—233. 243—264; advantage and duty of maintaining both religious and civil, 243—251 (*see Church*)
UNIVERSAL BISHOP (*see Church*)
UNIVERSITIES of England, their part in the Reformation, 171. 173; Subscription at, 187
URBAN VIII., Pope, 206

VICTOR, Pope, 149—151
VISIBLE HEAD, no one, of the Church, 15. 19. 64

WILFRID, 164
WILLIAM III., King, his Commission for Episcopal Promotions, &c. 299—301
WORD OF GOD (*see Scripture*)

YORK, 135. 154

ζιζάνια, 10—12. 258

INDEX II.

OF AUTHORS AND PLACES CITED.

ACTS OF PARLIAMENT, (*Bp. Gibson's Codex Juris Eccles. Anglican.* 2nd ed. *Oxford*, 1761, *folio.* See also Index I.) Of uniformity, 188; abjuration of covenant, 162; statute of provisors, 164; of præmunire, 164; for restraint of appeals to Rome, 164; to restore to the Crown its style and jurisdiction, and against annates, Peter-pence, &c., 165; on the royal supremacy, 165; on heresy, its definition, 302; on the first four general councils, 302; of submission of clergy, 303

AMBROSE, S. (*ex ed. Bened. Paris*, 1836. *IV Voll. 8vo*) on the *oneness* of the Church, 26; Eve a figure of the Church, as Adam of Christ, 28; on salvation only in the Church, 29, 30; on the Church as Uxor and Virgo, 38; visible Church subject to increase and decrease, 33; on the power of absolution, 114—116. 120; given to all Presbyters, 221; on the Church compared to a sea, 134; on *St. Paul's* primacy, 216; on St. Peter's confession, 217. 221; on the religious duty of Christian kings, 272

ANDREWES, Bp. (*Pattern of Catechistical Doctrine, Lond.* 1650, *fol. Sermons, Oxford*, 1841. *V Voll. 8vo*) salvation only in the Church, 30; on catechizing, 55; on sacerdotal intercession and benediction, 121, 122; on priests as *Angeli Ecclesiæ*, 128; on the English Reformation, 179; on the unworthiness of ministers not affecting the validity of the ordinance which they minister, 191; on the Christian Sacrifice, 196; on the beginning of Popish recusancy, 199; on St. Peter's confession, primacy, and name, 218. 225; on the religious duties of princes, 236. 297; on the nature and limits of the royal supremacy, 238. 267. 284—286; on the right of calling synods, 288. 290; on the right of *placing* bishops, 295

ANSELM on St. Peter's primacy, 221; the keys given to *all* the Apostles, 221

ARTICLES, THIRTY-NINE, *enact nothing new*, 178; on the visible Church, 13; on the only way of salvation, 30. 32; councils may err, 34; on the canon of Scripture, 45. 49; on the power and authority of the Church, 54; on a lawful call to the ministry, 72; on lawful oaths, 162; on royal supremacy, 166. 169; its *limits*, 284; Rome a Church, 176; on general councils, 181; on the unworthiness of ministers, 190; on an *erring* conscience not a safe conscience, 245; on summoning of councils, 287; on the authority of the Church in decreeing rites and ceremonies, 318—320

ATHANASIUS, S., on Scripture paramount to Councils, 35

AUGSBURGH, Confession of, on episcopacy, 93 (*Libri Symbol. Eccles. Evangelicæ, Huse. Lipsiæ,* 1837)

INDEX II.

AUGUSTIN, S. (*ed. Benedict. Paris*, 1836—1838. *XI Voll.* 8vo) on the Catholicity of the Church, 6; on Baptism profitably received, 8; on the types of the visible Church, 9; the ark, 11; St. Peter's sheet, 11; field of wheat and tares, 12; threshing-floor, 12; net, 12; on the body and soul of the Church, 13; difference between a visible and invisible Church, 15. 42. 255; on the salvation of man before the Incarnation, 30; on the invisible Church, 15; on the prophecies respecting the Church, 20; on the oneness of the Church, 26; analogy between Adam and Eve and Christ and the Church, 28; remission of sins only in the Church, 29; visible Church may be more or less clear at different times, 33; councils may err, 33; on the latter days, 34; on heresy and schism, 37; on the Church as *Virgo et Mater*, 38; on difference of heresy and schism, 39; heretics and schismatics, how far in the Church, 42; on the Jews as the librarii of the Christians, 44; on the Church as a witness of Holy Writ, 45, 46. 48; on the Scripture proving the Church, 49; on canonical books, 45; on the Hebrew and Greek originals, on versions, 51; on human teaching, 56, 57; on authorized teachers, 59; on the authority of the doctors of the Church, 61; on the paramount authority of Scripture, 61. 64. 182, 183; on the good educed from the evil of heresy, 63; on the sacraments, 67. 128; on Christians as Priests, 69; on a due mission, 73; on Episcopacy, 76; whatever is held by the whole Church is Apostolical, 84; on the heterodoxy of Aerius, 89; on regeneration, 117; on benediction and intercession, 123, 124; on the angels of Churches, 86; on Church discipline, 110, 111; on the power of absolution in the Church, 113; the Church the house of discipline, 119; on efficacy of public prayer, 128; on Apostolic succession, 188; on *unworthy ministers*, but *valid ministrations*, 193; on the transfer of Donatist endowments, 193; on true Catholicity, 213; on St. Paul's primacy, 216; on St. Peter's, *in typo unicæ ecclesiæ*, 217. 220; on St. Peter's *name*, 218; the *keys* were given to *all* the Apostles, who were *all* Pastors, 107, 108. 220, 221; on the true Head of the Church, 232; on the source of all power, 240. 242; its uses, 240; *totus mundus Ecclesia*, 255; on the graces of the Church in schismatical congregations, 255. 259, 260; on true charity, and its opposites, 262; on religious rights, power, and duty of Princes, 268, 269; on obedience to rubrics, 316

BACON, Lord, (*Works, Lond.* 1778. *V Voll.* 4to) the Church the keeper of Holy Writ, 43; on *mixtures* in religion, 247

BANCROFT, Archbp. (*Survey of the Pretended Holy Discipline, Lond.* 1593. *Dangerous Positions, &c. under Pretence of Reformation, Lond. S. A.*) on the identity of Popish and Puritan principles of polity against sovereigns, 276; on Lay Elders, 279

BARLOW, Bp. (*Remains, Lond.* 1693. *Cases of Conscience, Lond.* 1692. *Popery dangerous to Protestant Kings, Lond.* 1679) 228; on the necessity of a lawful call to the ministry, 72; on Toleration, 250

BARNES, J., Catholico-Romano Pacificus, on the *Jus Cyprium* of England, 149

BARONIUS, Cardinal, on necessity of submission to the Pope, 202, 203

BARROW, Dr. Isaac, (*Works, Lond.* 1683. *IV Voll. folio*) on the Visible Church, 21; on salvability of heathen, 31; on authorized preaching, and obedience to our spiritual guides, 58; on the apostolic institution, and universality of episcopacy, 89; on *diocesan* episcopacy, 89, 90; on modifications in the precedence and extent of patriarchates, 104; on the power of the keys, 109; on the right of investiture, 152; on changes in the oath of Roman Catholic Bishops to the Pope, 161; on the novelties of the Trent Creed, 180; on St. Peter's primacy, 215. 222; on Councils, 216; on the parity of Bishops, 226; on calling and presidency of Church synods, 287; and ratification, 287. 290; on obedience to rubrics, 318, cumulative force of civil sanction of Church laws, 315. 318; no appeals from the sentences of Primates and their Synods, 309

BASIL, S. (*Opera, Paris*, 1618. *III Voll. folio*) on the Sacraments, 67; on St. Peter's commission, 220

BAXTER, Richard, on priestly intercession, 124

BEDA, Ven., on the British Episcopate, 139; on the erection of sees in England, 153; on S. Gregory, S. Augustin of Canterbury, King Ethelbert, and Queen Bertha, 146—153, *passim*

BELLARMIN, Cardinal, on the *secular* claims of the Papacy, 202. 212; on its *spiritual* claims, 215. 230; on the deposition of heretical Princes, 228; on the Pope's superiority to Councils, 230

BENTLEY, Richard, D.D. (*Works*, ed. *Dyce, Lond.* 1838. *III Voll. 8vo*) on versions of Scripture, 52; on Bishops, successors of the Apostles, and on the difference of episcopi and presbyteri, 81, 82

BERNARD, S. (*ed. Benedict. VI Voll. Paris*, 1839) on the supremacy of Kings over ecclesiastical persons, and the obedience due from the latter, 106

BETHELL, Bp., General View of the Doctrine of Regeneration in Baptism, Lond. *fifth* edition, 1850, 117

BEVERIDGE, Bp. (*Sermons, Oxford*, 1842. *On XXXIX Articles, Oxford*, 1840. *II Voll. 8vo*) on the word *Church*, 1; the Church the keeper of Holy Writ, 51; on *diocesan* episcopacy, 96; on the independence of the British Church, 137; on the *Canon de Concionatoribus*, 185; on apostolic succession, 188; how St. Peter was at Rome, 215; on the royal supremacy, 19; on general councils, 287

BEZA, Theodore, on episcopacy, 94

BILSON, Bp. (*Perpetual Government of Christ's Church, Oxford*, 1842. *On Christian Subjection, Lond.* 1586) on the words *Clergy, Laity*, and *Priest*, 69; on the grace given by the Holy Spirit in ordination, 74; on episcopacy, 85. 87; on the priesthood of the patriarchal dispensation, 169; on the mission of S. Augustin, 154; on resistance to encroachments of Bishops of Rome, 223; on parity of Bishops, 226; the Pope has no jurisdiction in England, 169; nor out of his own diocese, 226; nor over other Bishops, 226; the duty and power of Kings not *limited* to *temporals*, 266. 268; on the duty of ecclesiastics to their sovereign, 273; on the source of episcopal powers, 293; *exterior* and *interior*, 294. 303; on the *limits* of the royal supremacy, 273. 293, 294

BINGHAM, Rev. J. (*Orig. Eccl. Lond.* 1834. *VIII Voll. 8vo*) on apocryphal books, 50; on the three orders, 76; on priests, 76; on priestly intercession, 123; on functions of Bishops, 91; on modification of sees, 104; on Church Assemblies, 130; on Bishops as centres of unity, 130; on the number of Bishops in England, 138; on the Bishop of Rome's jurisdiction, 143; on the *Jus Cyprium* of England, and on the British episcopacy, 148; on iteration of Baptism, 211; on the true means of Church unity, 233

BOSSUET, Bp. (*History of the Variations of Protestant Churches*, English Translation, Dublin, 1829. II Voll. 8vo) 175; his testimony to the Apostolic Succession of the Church of England, 189

BRAMHALL, Archbp. (*Works*, Oxford, 1842—1844) on the difference between particular Churches and the Universal one, 33; on schism, 38; on the British Church, 138; on S. Augustin's mission, 146. 148. 154. 158; on the Pallium, 159; on the inalienableness of the Regale, 167; on the Trent Creed, 181; on Apostolic Succession, 188, 189; on the title of Universal Bishop, 158; on the transfer of patriarchates, 105. 163. 166; on Henry VIIIth's character as affecting that of the Reformation, 169; on the oath of Roman Catholic Bishops to the Pope, 161; on the Reformation, 173; on the *primitive* character and *continuity* of the Church of England, 173; how Rome a *true* Church, 174; on English ordination, 189; on the Christian sacrifice, 196; the Church of England not liable to the charge of *schism*, 197; origin of Roman Catholic recusancy in England, 198; on Roman errors and novelties, 197; on the *parity* of the Apostles, 214; on the Pope's conduct toward the Apostles and their successors, and to Councils, 230; on the Trent Creed, 233; on Church and State, two names for one community, 254; on the royal supremacy, and on the title Head of the Church, 277; on the source of episcopal powers, 294

BREREWOOD, E., on British episcopacy, 137

BROWN, Fasciculus Rerum Expetendarum, 149

BROWNE, Thomas, B.D., on English Orders, 189

————, Bishop E. H. (*Exposition of Thirty-Nine Articles*, II Voll. 1853, *passim*)

BUDDEUS (*Isagoge*, Lips. 1727. II Voll. 4to) on the forged decretals, 199; on Erastianism, 280

BULL, Bp. (*Works, Oxford*, 1827. VI Voll. 8vo) on the Catholic Church, 6; no one visible head of the Church, 16; on the authority of the Primitive Church, as a standard for other Churches, 53; the Church of Jerusalem the mother of all Churches, 140; on the true foundation and *continuity* of the Church of England, 173; the orthodoxy of the Church of England acknowledged by Popes and Romanists generally in practice, 198; on the Nag's Head fable, 189; on Roman errors and corruptions, 173; on the parity of the Apostles, 215

BULLS, Papal, 206

BURKE, Rt. Hon. E. (*Lond.* 1826, 1827. XVI Voll. 8vo) on the *Protestantism* of the Church of England, 177; on Church and State, *two names for one thing*, 235; on the Religious duties of a State, 238; on the *cause* of a State, 238; on Bishops as Peers of Parliament, 253; on Church and State, 255

CABASSUTIUS (*Notitia Conciliorum Sanctæ Ecclesiæ*, Lovani, 1776) on lawful Ordination, 92; on diocesan episcopacy, 99

CALVIN, John, on episcopacy, 93, 94; Rome a *true* Church, 176

CANONICUM Jus Romanum (*Corpus, J. C. L. Richter, Lipsiæ*, 1839,) [*see Index I.*] claims of Papacy, 201. 203

CANONS of the Church of England, of 1603 (*see Cardwell, and Index I.*); Rome a Church, 176; on Preaching, 185; on *abuse* not taking away *lawful use*, 186; the Church of England not liable to a charge of *schism*, 197; their regard for antiquity, 179; on royal supremacy, 272, 273. 277; on right of calling Councils, 287. 289; on the English Convocation, 289; on an *erring* conscience to be *reformed*, 245

CARDWELL, E., D.D. (*Synodalia, from* 1547 *to* 1717, *Oxford. II Voll.* 1842) (*see Canons*)
CARLETON, Bp., on the divine institution of episcopacy, 91; on episcopal ordination, 91; on the royal supremacy, 265
CASAUBON, Isaac, (*Exercit. in Baronii Annales, Genev.* 1654. *Epistolæ, Roter.* 1709, *folio*) on the word Church, 1; on its Catholicity, 7; on the only way of Salvation, 31; is Rome a true Church? 175; on episcopacy, 136; on the English Reformation, 170. 172. 179; on Anglican orders, 189; on the scriptural and apostolical character of the English Church, 189; vindication from the charge of schism, 197; on Church unity and communion, 210. 213; on the treatment of the Church of England by Rome, 212; on Πέτρα and Πέτρος, 218; on St. Peter's confession, 221; on Church and State, two names for one thing, 235; on the royal supremacy, 264; the duty and power of Princes not restricted to *temporals*, 264. 271; on Church Synods, 290
CATECHISM, of King Edward VI., 1553. on Discipline as a note of the Church, 13
CATECHISMUS ROMANUS, on iteration of baptism, 211
CHARLES I., King, (*Works, Lond.* 1687, *folio*) on the Church as an interpreter of Holy Writ, 53; on the functions of Bishops, 91; on Common Prayer, 133; on the royal supremacy, 290
CHILLINGWORTH, W. (*Works, Lond.* 1674, *folio*) on episcopacy, 90; on the power of absolution, 118
CHRYSOSTOM, S. (*ed. Savil. Etonæ,* 1612, 1613. *VIII Voll. folio*) on translations of Scripture, 46; on the word κλῆρος, 68; on the three Orders, 71; on episcopal ordination, 91; on the supremacy of Kings over spiritual persons, 105. 240; on Church discipline, 110, 111; on the power of the keys, 115; on Christianity in Britain, 136; on sacerdotal intercession and benediction, 125; on efficacy of public prayer, 131; on wheat and tares, 259

CHURTON, Rev. Edward, *History of Early English Church,* 136
CLARENDON, Lord, on the inalienability of Regalia, 167; on the *limits* of the royal supremacy, 303
CLEMENS Alexandrinus, S. (*ed. Lips.* 1831. *VIII Voll.* 8vo) on the *oneness* of the Church, 27
CLEMENS Romanus, S. (*Patres Apostolici, ed. Jacobson, Oxon.* 1838. *II Voll.* 8vo) on the difference of Clergy and Laity, 68; on the three Orders, 75; on apostolic ordination, 74; on the apostleship of Christ, and on the three Orders, 74
COKE, Lord Chief Justice, on *practice* as the interpreter of *law,* 87; on impunity, 110; on the Acts of the Reformation, 165; on the political uses of religion, 239; on the authority of the canons, 289
COLBERT, Bp., on English ordinations, 189
COMBER, Thomas, D.D. (*Companion to the Temple, Oxford,* 1841. *VII Voll.* 8vo) on confirmation, 127
COMMON PRAYER, Book of (*see Index I.*), Church figured by the ark, 9; office of Baptism, 117; ordinal, 71; on *necessity* of the Priesthood, 71; and its qualification, 71. 292; on the three Orders, 78; on lawful ordination, 179. 188; gift of the Holy Spirit in, 107; on Church discipline, 110; on regeneration, 117; its regard for antiquity, 178. 179; on the religious duties of Kings, 277 (*see Articles*); on *making* Bishops, 292; on rites and ceremonies, 314. 317; absolution, 107; commination, 110; confirmation, 117; preface to, 314; on ceremonies, 312—319
CORONATION Office, 282

COSIN, Bp. (*Scholastic History of the Canon of Holy Scripture*, *Lond.* 1672) on the Canon of Scripture, 44; on the *Canon de Concionatoribus*, 185

COTELERIUS on sacerdotal intercession, 123

COUNCILS. [see *Index I.*] (*ed. Labbe. Paris*, 1641. 1672. *XVII Voll. folio*) of Laodicea on Canon of SS., 45; Nicene on the three Orders, 78; on the Roman Patriarchate, 141; Chalcedon on Episcopacy, 89; Antioch and others on diocesan episcopacy, 96 —106 *passim*; on the difference of Bishops and Presbyters, 89. 92; of Nice, 177; Arles, 137. 143; Sardica, 137. 144; of Ephesus on Metropolitan Jurisdiction, 147; on professions of faith, 197; of Mayence, &c., 205; of Constantinople, 177

COURAYER, P. F. Le, on English ordinations, 189

COURTENAY, Archbp., on the regalia of England, 165

CRAKANTHORPE, Richard, D. D. (*Defensio Ecclesiæ Anglicanæ*, *Lond.* 1625) the Church has no one visible head, 16; on councils, 33; on heretics and schismatics, how far in the Church, 42; on patriarchs, metropolitans, and diocesans, 99—102; on the limits of the Roman Jurisdiction, 99; on the British Church, 136; on the *anteriority* of the English Church to that of Rome, 138; on the Sardican canons, 144; on novelties and corruptions of Rome, 204; on the Pope's authority, 226

CRANMER, Archbp. (*Works edited by Rev. H. Jenkyns, Oxford*, 1833. *IV Voll.* 8*vo*. *Catechism*, *set forth by him in* 1548, ed. *Oxford*, 1829) on the Catholic Church, 6; on the visible Church, 14; on the power of the keys, 112; on Church discipline, 112; on absolution, 118

CUSANUS, Cardinal, on the *imperial* (not *papal*) right of convening synods, 288

CYPRIAN, S. (*ed. Fell. Amst.* 1691) on the unity of the Church, 4; its discipline, 4; on the types of the visible Church, 11, 12; salvation only in the Church, 25. 29; on the *oneness* of the Church. 28; on graces of the Church, 30; on schism and heresy, 40; on the necessity of a lawful call to the ministry, 72; on Bishops the successors of the Apostles, 79; one Bishop only in a city, 98; on Peter as a figure of the Church, 107; on Church discipline, 110; on absolution, 113; on St. Peter as the figure of the Apostles, 215; on the necessity of episcopacy to a Church, 130; on Bishops as *centres* of *unity*, 131; on apostolic succession, 187; on the equality of the Apostles, 215. 220; and of Bishops, as such, 225; on the title *Episcopus Episcoporum*, 224; against appeal to Rome, 226; on the trial and deposition of Bishops, 309

CYRIL, S., of Jerusalem, (*ed. Benedict. Venet.* 1763, *folio*) on the catholicity of the Church, 5; on canonical and apocryphal books, 45; on the glory of the Church, both in persecution and peace, 271

DECLARATION of English laity, A.D. 1833; on the consecration of the State by the public maintenance of the Church, 253

DE MARCA, Archbp. (*De Concordiâ Sacerdotii et Imperii*, *Venet.* 1770. *Libri VIII. quibus accesserunt Dissertationes Ecclesiasticæ*) on the word *Clergy*, 68; on diocesan episcopacy, 95; on appeals to Rome, 144, 145; on the pallium, 159; on the Oath of Roman Catholic Bishops to the Pope, 160; ancient discipline of the Church as to deposition of Bishops, 308, 309.

DUPIN (*Dissertationes Ecclesiasticæ*) on diocesan episcopacy 97; on the limits of the Roman Patriarchate, 141; on appeals to Rome, 145;

Z

on the pallium, 159; Metropolitan, with Synod of his Province, judge of Bishops, 310

EDWARD THE CONFESSOR, Laws of, 166
ELIZABETH, Queen, on the royal supremacy, 284
EPIPHANIUS on Bishops successors of the Apostles, 79; on the heresy of Aerius, 89
ERSKINE, Cardinal, on the Bull *in Cœnâ Domini*, 207
EUSEBIUS (*Hist. Eccles. ed. Oxon.* 1843. *IV Voll.* 8vo) on episcopacy, 85; on the cases of Popes Anicetus and Victor, 223
EUTHYMIUS ZYGABENUS, 216
EVANS, Rev. Robert Wilson, on St. Polycarp and Anicetus, 150

FIELD, Richard, D.D. (*Of the Church, Oxf.* 1655, *folio*) on the Church as a witness of Scripture, 49
FIRMILIAN, S., on the *oneness* of the Church, 27; on the remission of sins, 108; to Pope Stephanus, 212
FLEURY, Abbé, (*Discours sur l'Histoire Ecclésiastique, Nismes*, 1785. *Histoire Ecclésiastique, Bruxelles*, 1713. *XXXVI Tomes*, 12mo) on ancient limits of Roman Patriarchate, 142. 163; on the forged decretals, 199; on the Bull *in Cœnâ Domini*, 207
FULGENTIUS on the Church as a threshing-floor, 11

GARDINER, Bp., on the Regale, 169. 257
GERHARD, Jo. (*Loci Theologici, Genev.* 1639. *X Voll. folio*) on the nature and limits of Jurisdiction, civil and ecclesiastical, 19; on the Church as witness and interpreter of Scripture, 49. 54; on errors of Popes, 230; on the inalienability of regalia, 167; on the connexion of schools with the Church, 252
GIBBON, Edward, on episcopacy, 84
GIBSON, Bp. (*Codex Juris Eccles.*

Anglican. Oxf. 1761; *see Acts of Parliament*) on cathedrals, 131; on the pallium, 159; on the Oath of Roman Catholic Bishops to the Pope, 161. 229; as Peers in Parliament, 251; on the Royal Supremacy, 275. 231, on source of Episcopal powers, 244; on right of *placing* Bishops, 295; on Præmunire, 296; on the cognizance of heresy, 304; on censures of heresy, 304—308
GILDAS on the planting of Christianity into England, 136
GILFRID on Augustin's arrival in England, 137
GILLESPIE on Erastianism, 280
GRABE, J. Ernest, on the Eucharistic sacrifice, 195
GREGORIUS MAGNUS, S. (*ed. Bened. Paris*, 1705. *IV Voll. folio*) on the authority of the first four general councils, 147; on his own elevation to the see of Rome, 152; on the royal supremacy and the right of investiture and ecclesiastical supremacy of the emperor, 153; on English sees, 154; on King Ethelbert's pious munificence, 157; against image-worship, 205; on the sufficiency of Scripture, 205; on one visible Head of the Church, 223, 224. 230
GROTIUS (*Opera, Lond.* 1679. *III Voll. folio*) on episcopacy, 88. 94; on the English Reformation as compared with others, 171; on the English Canon *de Concionatoribus*, 185; on the Eucharistic sacrifice, 195, 196; on the spiritual power and duty of Christian princes, 271

HAMMOND, Henry, D.D. (*Works, Lond.* 1684. *IV Voll. folio*) on confirmation, 126; on priests as *Angeli Ecclesiæ*, 129; on sacerdotal intercession, 129; on the efficacy of public prayer, 130, 131; on S. Augustin's mission, 148; on modification of patriarchates, 166; on equality of Apostles, 222; on the pallium, 159;

on the patriarchate of England, 166; on the inalienability of regalia, 166; on the primitive and Scriptural foundation and character of the Church of England, 170; on the title of Universal Bishop, 222; on Erastianism, 280; on English Church government, 280

HARSNETT, Bp., on the true principles of the English Reformation, 173

HERBERT, George, on episcopal and sacerdotal benediction, 126

HOMILIES (*appointed to be read in Churches in the time of Queen Elizabeth, ed. Oxf.* 1822) on discipline, a note of a Church, 106; on their regard for antiquity, 179; on the secular claims of Papacy, 202; on absolution, 118; on the qualifications of a good oath, 162

HOOKER, Richard, (*Works, edited by Rev. John Keble, Oxf.* 1836. *IV Voll.* 8vo) on the word Church, 1; the Church a permanent Society, 3; on Baptism the door of the Church, 8; on Baptism profitably received, 8; on the Invisible Church, 14; difference between, and Visible, 15. 22. 255, 256; on the means of Church unity, 19; on the definitions of the term *Church*, 22, 23; on salvation only in the Church, 25; Councils may err, 35; on catechizing, 55; on human teaching, 55; England must reform though Rome would not, 66; on the nature of the sacraments, 8; on the visible Church, 14. 22. 255; has no one visible head, 16; on the ark as a type of the Church, 25; on the necessity of submission in controverted points to the decisions of the Church, 35; on heretics and schismatics, how far in the Church, 41. 255; on the Church as a witness of Scripture, 47; on preaching, 55; on the sacraments, 67; on the *necessity* of clergy, 72; on the authority of the priesthood, 74; whence derived, 74. 290; grace in ordination, 74; on episcopacy, 84. 87. 89; on diocesan episcopacy, 96; on the power of absolution, 109. 117--120; on sacerdotal intercession and benediction, 121. 124. 127; on confirmation, 127; on set forms of Common Prayer, 132, 133; on the Church as a sea, 134; on the Reformation, 173; in what sense Rome a true Church, 175. 196. 205; on the sufficiency of Scripture, 183; on reordination, 190. 194; abusus non tollit usum, 186; vindication of English Church from charge of schism, 197; on consecration of Churches, 192; the Pope's usurped jurisdiction, 224; on the Church and State, two names for one thing, 234; on the civil fruits of true religion, 238; on the religious duty and true felicity of kings, 239. 263; on the source and channel of all power, 243; on the remedy for an *erring* conscience, 246; on Bishops as Peers of Parliament, 252; on schismatical teaching, 262; on the royal supremacy, 282; on the Headship of Christ, how distinct from that of kings, 265; their duty not restricted to *bodily* things, 267; the duty of the clergy to their sovereign, 273; on the Puritan principle of polity identified with the Popish, 275; on the *sacred* character of English sovereigns, 277; on the nature and limits of the Royal Supremacy, 274. 284; on the right of *placing* Bishops, 292; on the duty and authority of the Church in ordering rites, 316. 319; on obedience to it, 320

HORN, Dr., 209
HORNE, Bp., on Schism, 40
HUGHES on Erastianism, 280
HUGO on the Sacraments, 67

IGNATIUS, S. (*Patres Apostolici, ed. Jacobson, Oxon.* 1838. *II Voll.* 8vo) on Episcopacy, 7. 78; on sin of schism, 40; the three orders of ministers necessary to a

Church, 136. 147: on Church assemblies, 131; on sacramental grace dispensed only through the Church, 29

INETT, John, D.D., origin of English Church, 140

INSTITUTION of a Christian Man on Confirmation of Bishops Elect, 297

IRENÆUS, S. (*ed. Grabe, Oxon.* 1702, *folio*) on the unity of the Church, 4; its Catholicity, 6; on divine truth, grace, and salvation, dispensed only through the Church, 24, 25. 29 ; the true faith only in the Church, 29; on the sins of heresy and schism, the one the sin of Nadab and Abihu, the other that of Korah, 40; on lawful teachers and interpretation of Scripture, 56; on the necessity of Apostolic Succession, 56. 187; on the *indirect* use of power ill-employed, 240; on the source of all power, 243; on variety of rites, 318

JAMES I., King, on the Scriptural, primitive, and Catholic character of the Church of England, 179; *non fugimus, sed fugamur,* 207

JEROME, S. (*Victorii, Paris,* 1643. *XI Voll. folio,* and *ed. Benedictin. Paris,* 1699) on the Catholic Church and on that of Rome, 7 ; on the types of the visible Church, 9; on errors in the Church, 10; on Scripture paramount to Councils, 35; on the sufficiency of Scripture, 183; on the *one altar,* that of the Church, 27. 243; on the latter days, 34; Eve, figure of the Church, 28 ; on heresy, 36; on schism, 39; heretics how far in Church, 42; on the integrity of the text of the Old Testament, 44; on the Hebrew and Greek originals, 52; on ecclesiastical books, 52; on the word *clergy,* 68; on the three orders of ministers, 76; on the Bishops successors of the Apostles, 79. 83—85; his language concerning episcopacy, 83, 84; on the angels of the Churches, 111; on repentance, 117; on laying on of hands in confirmation and ordination, and reception of penitents, 126, 127 ; on the necessity of *priests* to a Church, 195; on the proper conditions of an oath, 162; on the equality of the Apostles, 220 ; and of Bishops, 226; on Arianism, 174; on Church extension, 252; on the observance of Church customs, 321

JEWELL, Bp., on absolution, 118; on the English Reformation, 208; *non tam discessimus quàm ejecti sumus,* 207; on the primitive character of the English Church, 173. 209

JOHNSON (*Codex Canonum, in the Clergyman's Vade Mecum, Lond.* 1709. *II Voll.* 12*mo*) on the diocesan episcopacy, 96

JUSTINIAN, his care for religion, 270

KEBLE, Rev. John, on lay elders and Erastianism, 279, 280

KETTLEWELL, Rev. John, (*On the Creed, Lond.* 1713) on the Church the depository of grace, 29

LACTANTIUS on religious toleration, 250

LAPPENBERG, Dr. J. M. (*History of England under the Anglo-Saxon Kings,* translated by *B. Thorpe, F.S.A. Lond.* 1845. *II Voll.*) 139

LAUD, Archbp. (*Sermons, ed. London,* 1651. *Conference with Fisher [Piersey] the Jesuit, ed. Cardwell, Oxford,* 1839. *Remains, Lond.* 1700, *folio*) the Church has no one visible head, 16 ; on councils, 34 ; is to be obeyed, 36 ; on the genuineness of Scripture, 48; on the Church as a witness of Scripture, 49; on Scripture the one infallible Judge, 64 ; on the course to be taken when general councils cannot be had, 66 ; England must reform though Rome would not, 66; on episcopacy, 88; on the patriarchate of England, 142; on the English Reformation, 172; in what sense Rome a true Church, 174; on the *Protestantism* of the Church of England, 177; on the novelties of the Trent creed, 180; on the uncatholic and illegal character of the Trent council, 181; on the Christian sacrifice in the Church of England, 195; on spiritual and secular claims of the Papacy, 206; on the *lawfulness* of the Reformation, 205; the Reformation not *schismatical*, 207; on the Pope's usurped jurisdiction, 225, 226; the Bishop of Rome not a centre of unity, but a cause of disunion, 230; on Church and State, two names for one thing, 235; on the fruits of Church unity, 237; on the necessity of σπουδή to secure it, 244; upon Bishops as Peers of Parliament, 252; on Church and State, 253; on the *sacredness* of Princes, 282; on the *office* of Bishops *whence* derived, and its *exercise how* regulated, 274

LAW, Rev. William, on benediction, intercession, and absolution, 131; on sincerity, 245

LEO MAGNUS, S. (*ed. Lugd.* 1700. *II Voll. folio*) on prayers for heathen, 32; Presbyters cannot ordain, 92; on the equality of the Apostles, 221; on the religious duties of kings, 270, 271

LESLIE, Rev. Charles. (*Case stated between Rome and England, Lond.* 1714) the Church has no one visible head, 16; on necessary qualifications for the priesthood, 72; on the Bull *in Cœná Domini*, 207; on the *true* means of unity, 233

LINGARD, Dr., on the Nag's Head fable, 189

LOWTH, Rev. William on the Prophecies respecting the Church, 20

LUTHER, Martin, Rome how a true Church, 176; traces his own ministerial commission through Rome, 191

MAGEE, Archbp., on the oath of Roman Catholic Bishops to the Pope, 228; on iteration of Baptism, 211

MASON, Francis (*Vindiciæ Ecclesiæ Anglicanæ, Lond.* 1625), on absolution, *dispositive, declaratory,* and *authoritative,* 113. 115. 117; on Augustin's mission, 150. 155. 158; on modification of patriarchates, 166; on the rights of the British Church, 150; on Apostolic succession in the Church, 189; on rites and ceremonies, 313. 319

MELANCHTHON on episcopacy, 93

MONTAGUE, Bp., on absolution, 118

NEALE, Daniel, (*History of the Puritans, Lond.* 1837. *III Voll.* 8*vo*) on Rome a true Church, 176; on the Nag's Head fable, 189; on the number of clergy conforming at the Reformation, 193

NECESSARY doctrine, &c. (A.D. 1543) on the Catholic Church, 7

NORRIS, Rev. J., on acts of toleration, 40

O'CONNOR, Dr., on the oath of Roman Catholic Bishops, 161

ŒCONOMUS on the royal supremacy, 278

OPTATUS, S. (*De Schismate Donatistarum, Oberthur, Wiceberg,* 1789 —1791. *II Voll.* 8*vo*) his appeal to Scripture, 64; on the three Orders of ministers, 71. 76; on the supremacy of Kings, 105

ORIGEN on the canon of Scripture, 46; on Christianity in Britain, 136

OVERALL, Bp. (*Convocation Book concerning the Government of God's Catholic Church, and the Kingdoms of the whole World, Lond.* 1790) the Church has no one visible Head, 16; on government, civil and ecclesiastical, 17; on national Churches, 17. 19; on the ecclesiastical supremacy of Christian princes, 19; on the source of power, 17

PACIAN, S., on the word Catholic, 7
PALMER, Rev. William, (*On the Church*, Lond. 1839. II *Voll.* 8vo) on the unity of the Church, 5; on the limits of the Roman patriarchate, 143; on English ordinations, 189; on the commencement of recusancy in England, 198; on Romish usurpations, 199; on the royal supremacy, 265
PANCIROLI, *Notitia*, on dioceses, 96
PARIS, Matthew, on king Rufus and Anselm, 162
PARLIAMENT (see *Acts*)
PARLIAMENTARY REPORT (*on Regulation of Roman Catholic Subjects in Foreign States*, 1816) 207
PATRICK, Bp., on Schismatical Acts of Rome, 232
PEARSON, Bp. (*Opera Postuma*, Lond. 1688. *Vindiciæ Epistolarum Ignatii*, Cantab. 1672. *On the Creed*, fol. Lond. 1715. *Minor Theological Works*, edited by Edward Churton, M.A. II *Voll*. Oxford, 1844) on the word *Church*, 1; on the word *Ecclesia*, 2; on the definition of a Church, 3; on the term Catholic, 5; on Baptism, the entrance of the Church, 8; on the Church visible and invisible, 15; on salvation only in the Church, 25—27; Bishops alone can ordain, 92; on ecclesiastical books, 51; on the spiritual grace given in ordination, 75; on deacons, 77; on episcopacy, 84, 92; on sacerdotal intercession and benediction, 123; on the Apostolic Succession, 188; on resistance to Papal encroachments, 224
PHELAN, W., D.D. (*History of Church of Rome in Ireland*, Dublin, 1827) on oath of supremacy, 275; and O'SULLIVAN, (*Digest of Evidence on the State of Ireland*, 1824, 1825, Lond. 1826. II *Voll.* 8vo) on oath of Roman Catholic Bishops to the Pope, 228
PLATON, Archbp., on the Royal supremacy, 277

PONTIFICAL, Roman, oath of Roman Bishops, 207; on the dependence of all Bishops on the Pope, 231
POTT, Joseph Holden, M.A., Archdeacon (*Rights of Sovereignty in Christian States Defended*, Lond. 1821) 265; on different theories of Church government in reference to the State, 281
POTTER, Archbp. (*On Church Government*, London, 1724, 8vo) on the Catholic Church, 6; on authorized teaching, 58; on the case of Ischyras, 92; on sacerdotal intercession and benediction, 121
PRIDEAUX, Humphrey, Dean, on the matter and form of English orders, 189
PROSPER Aquitanus, S. (*Opera*, ed. Venet. 1782. II *Voll.* 4to) benediction only in the Church, 29; on virginitas animæ, 38
PULLER, Timothy, D.D., on sacerdotal intercession and benediction, 127
PÜTTER, Professor, on the forged decretals, 199

QUESNEL on limits of Roman patriarchate, 142; on appeals to Rome, 144

RAINOLDS, John, D.D., on authorized preaching, 60; on the authority of the Scribes and Pharisees, 59; on St. Peter's confession and primacy, 219; on Church unity, and the means of maintaining it, 232
REFORMATIO LEGUM ECCLES. on the Hebrew and Greek originals, 52
ROUTH, Martin Joseph, D.D. (*Reliquiæ Sacræ*, Oxon. 1814—1818. IV *Voll.* 8vo. *Scriptorum Ecclesiasticorum Opuscula*, Oxon. 1832. II *Voll.* 8vo), on the canon of Scripture, 45; on the title *Episcopus Episcoporum*, 223; on the sufficiency of Scripture, 182; on resistance to Papal encroachments, 223
RUFFINUS on the canon of Scripture and apocryphal books, 46.

49; on the limits of the Roman patriarchate, 141

RUTHERFORD on Erastianism, 280

SANDERSON, Bp. (*Sermons*, Lond. 1674, *folio. Prælectiones VII de Juramenti Obligatione*, Lond. 1710. *De Obligatione Conscientiæ*, Lond. 1710. *Episcopacy not prejudicial to Regal Power*, Lond. 1673) on the authority of the universal Church, 53; on episcopacy, 87; on unlawful oaths, 162; how Rome a true Church, 175; on the Church of Rome guilty of Schism, 205; on the remedy for an erring conscience, 246; on the Source of Power, 240; on the sovereign the *efficacious cause* of law, 274; on the identity of Popish and Puritanical principles of polity, 276; on the source of episcopal powers, 293

SARAVIA, Hadrian, D.D., on the Angels of Churches, 86; on the English Reformation, 170. 193; on Church and State, two names for one thing, 235

SCULTETUS on the Patriarchal Priesthood, 122

SOAVE, Pietro, (i. e. *Sarpi* Paolo *Historia del Concilio Tridentino*; *sine loci notâ*. 1629) on the original text of Scripture, 52; on Paul IVth's conduct to Queen Elizabeth, 207; on Church Synods, 288

SPARROW, Bp., on absolution, 118

SPELMAN, Sir H., on Augustin's Mission, 150

STILLINGFLEET, Bp. (*Eccles. Cases. II Voll. 8vo.* Lond. 1702—1704, *Origines Britannicæ*, Lond. 1837) on the Episcopatus unus cujus à singulis Episcopis *in solidum* pars tenetur, 17; on the British Church, 154; on the Sardican decrees, 144; on protests against Papal usurpations, 164; on the royal supremacy, 284

STREITWOLF (*Libri Symbolici Ecclesiæ Catholicæ*, Gott. 1831. *II Tom. 8vo*) on lawful Ordinations, 93; on the Bull *in Cœnâ Domini*, 207

SUICERUS (*Thesaurus Eccles. ed. Amst.* 1682. *II Voll. folio*) on the word *Diæcesis*, 143

TAYLOR, Bp. Jer. (*Works edited by Bp. Heber*, Lond. 1828. *XV Voll. 8vo*) on the visible Church, 14; on the Church as the Spouse of Christ, 21; on salvation only in the Church, 26; on benediction, 125; on confirmation, 126; on set forms of public prayer, 133; on the cause of the prosperity of heathen states, 237; on the similarity of Popish and Puritan principles, 276. 279

TERTULLIAN (*Rigaltii*, Paris, 1641, *folio*) on the unity of the Church, 4; on Episcopacy, 7; on the Rule of Faith, 37. 88. 182; on the Canonical Scriptures, 46; on lawful teachers, 56; on the paramount authority of Scripture, 60; on Bishops the successors of the Apostles, 78; on the power of the Keys, 110; on heresy, 36; on authority of the primitive apostolical Churches, 53; on the ministers of the Sacraments, 70; on supremacy of Kings, 105; on apostolical succession, 135. 187; on Christianity in England, 136; on sufficiency of Scripture, 182; on parity of the Apostles, 220; on Church unity, 232; on the source of royal power, 243; on religious toleration, 250; on scandal, 324

THEODORET (*ed. Schulze*, Halæ, 1769. *V Voll. 8vo*) on Bishops, successors and representatives of the Apostles, 79, 80; on the *evil* of schism, though *good* may *indirectly* come out of the evil, 262

THEOPHILUS, Ant. S., on the Church compared to a sea, 134

THEOPHYLACT (*ed. Benedict. Venet.* 1754. *IV Voll. folio*) on the Catholic Church, 7; no one visible head, 15; on the necessity of a due mission for the ministry, 73; on the universal dominion of Christ, 241; on giving scandal, 324

TOWNSON, T., D.D., on the Pope's coronation, 202

TRANSLATORS, English, of the Bible, on the religious duty of Princes, 264

TUNSTALL, Bp., on the primitive and Catholic character of the Church of England, 209, 210

TWISDEN, Sir Roger, (*Historical Vindication of the Church of England in point of Schism, as it stands separated from the Roman, Lond.* 1675) on origin of the Church of England, 140; on the English Patriarchate, 156; on the English Reformation, 213; on the pallium, 159; on the independence of the English Church, 163; on appeals to Rome, 164; on the religious acts of English Kings, 271

USHER, Archbp., on diocesan episcopacy, 95

VAN ESPEN (*Jus Ecclesiasticum Universum, Coloniæ Agripp.* 1748, *folio*) on the oath to the Pope, 161; on the right of *placing* Bishops, 296; Primates or Metropolitans exercised judicial authority over Bishops, 310; no appeal from sentence, if unanimous, 310

VAN MILDERT, Bp., on the Christian sacrifice, 196

VOSSIUS on Church and State, 235; on the word Ceremonia, 312

WAKE, Archbp., on the use of Christian antiquity, 62; on the Reformation in England, 172

WALSH, Father, on the oath of Roman Catholic Bishops to the Pope, 160

WATERLAND, Daniel, D.D. (*Works, edited by Bp. Van Mildert, Oxford,* 1823. *XI Voll.* 8*vo*) on regeneration, 9. 118; on use and value of Christian antiquity, 62, 63; on Baptismal regeneration, 117; on priestly intercession, 123; on the Christian priesthood, 123; on the Christian sacrifice, 196

WHITGIFT, Archbp., on the royal supremacy, 268

WILKINS, David, (*Concilia Magn. Brit. et Hibern. ab A.D.* 446 *ad A.D.* 1717. *IV Voll. folio,* 1737) on the British episcopate, 137. 150; Dinoth's speech to Augustin, 140; the letter of the Roman legate to Pope Adrian, 140; on S. Augustin's intercourse with the British Bishops, 150

WORDSWORTH, Christopher, D.D., late Master of Trinity College, Cambridge, (*Christian Institutes, Lond.* 1837. *IV Voll.* 8*vo. Ecclesiastical Biography, Lond.* 1839. *IV Voll.* 8*vo*) (*see Inett*) on toleration, 40; on episcopacy, 90; on ordinary and extraordinary functions of Apostles, 91; on unepiscopal reformed communions, 94; on the Crown's inability to alienate its regalities, 167; on the primitive and Catholic character of the Church of England, 173; on the true and sole proprietor of Churches, 193; on the beginning of recusancy in England, 198; on an erroneous conscience, 246; on rites and ceremonies, 313. 319; on human laws, how they bind the conscience, 318; on General Councils, 288

WORDSWORTH, Charles, D.D., Bp. of St. Andrew's, (CATECHESIS, or *Christian Instruction preparatory to Confirmation and First Communion, Lond.* 1857) 127

ZONARAS. Let *good* be done *well*, 262

THE END.

Gilbert and Rivington, Ld., St. John's House, Clerkenwell Road, London.

Works by the late Chr. Wordsworth, D.D.

BISHOP OF LINCOLN.

THE HOLY BIBLE,

With Introductions and Notes, by CHR. WORDSWORTH, D.D., sometime Bishop of Lincoln.

THE OLD TESTAMENT,

In the Authorized Version, with Introductions, Notes, and Index.

PART	In Parts.	£	s.	d.	VOL.	In Volumes.	£	s.	d.
I.	Genesis and Exodus	0	14	0	I.	The Pentateuch	1	5	0
II.	Leviticus, Numbers, Deuteronomy	0	12	0					
III.	Joshua, Judges, Ruth	0	9	0	II.	Joshua to Samuel	0	15	0
IV.	Books of Samuel	0	7	0					
V.	Kings, Chronicles, Ezra, Nehemiah, Esther	0	15	0	III.	Kings to Esther	0	15	0
VI.	Book of Job	0	7	0					
VII.	Psalms	0	11	0	IV.	Job to Song of Solomon	1	5	0
VIII.	Proverbs, Ecclesiastes, Song of Solomon	0	9	0					
IX.	Isaiah	0	10	0	V.	Isaiah to Ezekiel	1	5	0
X.	Jeremiah, Lamentations, Ezekiel	0	16	0					
XI.	Daniel	0	5	0	VI.	Daniel, Minor Prophets, and Index	0	15	0
XII.	Minor Prophets	0	9	0					
	Index	0	2	0					
		£6	0	0			£6	0	0

Any Part or any Volume may be had separately.

THE GREEK TESTAMENT,

With Introductions, Notes, and Index.

PART	In Parts.	£	s.	d.	VOL.	In Volumes.	£	s.	d.
I.	Gospels*	0	16	0	I.	Gospels, and Acts of the Apostles	1	3	0
II.	Acts of the Apostles	0	8	0					
III.	St. Paul's Epistles*	1	3	0					
IV.	General Epistles, Apocalypse, Index	0	16	0	II.	Epistles, Apocalypse, and Index	1	17	0
		£3	3	0			£3	0	0

* With Corrections left by the Editor at his death.

Any Part or any Volume may be had separately.

LONDON: LONGMANS, GREEN & CO.

Works by the late Chr. Wordsworth, D.D.

BISHOP OF LINCOLN.

A Church History to A.D. 451. 4 vols., crown 8vo, cloth.
  Vol. 1.—To the Council of Nicæa, a.d. 325. 8s. 6d.
  Vol. 2.—From the Council of Nicæa to that of Constantinople. 6s.
  Vol. 3.—Continuation. 6s.
  Vol. 4.—Conclusion, to the Council of Chalcedon, a.d. 451. 6s.

Elements of Instruction on the Church. 16mo, cloth. 1s.; sewed, 6d.

Guides and Goads. An English Edition of "Ethica et Spiritualia." 32mo, cloth. 1s. 6d.

The Holy Year. Original Hymns. Sixth Edition. 16mo, cloth, 2s. 6d. and 1s.; limp, 6d.

Ditto, with Music. Square 8vo, cloth. 4s. 6d.

Lectures on Inspiration of the Bible. Small 8vo, cloth. 1s. 6d.; sewed, 1s.

Miscellanies, Literary and Religious. 3 vols., 8vo, cloth. 36s.

S. Hippolytus and the Church of Rome. Crown 8vo, cloth. 7s. 6d.

Theophilus Anglicanus. 12mo, cloth. 2s. 6d.

On Union with Rome. Small 8vo, cloth. 1s. 6d.

On the Intermediate State of the Soul after Death. New Edition. 32mo, cloth. 1s.

Christopher Wordsworth, Bishop of Lincoln, 1807—1885. By John Henry Overton, Canon of Lincoln, and Rector of Epworth; and Elizabeth Wordsworth, Principal of Lady Margaret Hall, Oxford. With Portraits. 8vo. Library Edition, 16s. New and Cheaper Edition, with Portraits. Crown. 7s. 6d.

CONTENTS.

Parentage and Childhood—School and College Life—Early Manhood and Early Travels—Harrow—Early Westminster Life—Westminster and Stanford-in-the-Vale—Convocation—The Episcopate: First Three Years—The Episcopate: Burning Questions—The Episcopate: Practical Work in the Diocese—Intercourse with Foreign Churches—Literary Work—Closing Days—Personal Reminiscences—Index.

LONDON: LONGMANS, GREEN & CO.

July 1895

A Selection of Works
IN
THEOLOGICAL LITERATURE
PUBLISHED BY
Messrs. LONGMANS, GREEN, & CO.
39 Paternoster Row, London, E.C.

Abbey and Overton.—THE ENGLISH CHURCH IN THE EIGHTEENTH CENTURY. By CHARLES J. ABBEY, M.A., Rector of Checkendon, Reading, and JOHN H. OVERTON, D.D., Canon of Lincoln and Rector of Epworth. *Crown 8vo. 7s. 6d.*

Adams.—SACRED ALLEGORIES. The Shadow of the Cross—The Distant Hills—The Old Man's Home—The King's Messengers. By the Rev. WILLIAM ADAMS, M.A. *Crown 8vo. 3s. 6d.*
    The four Allegories may be had separately, with Illustrations. *16mo. 1s. each.*

Aids to the Inner Life.
    Edited by the Rev. W. H. HUTCHINGS, M.A., Rector of Kirby Misperton, Yorkshire. *Five Vols. 32mo, cloth limp, 6d. each; or cloth extra, 1s. each.*
    With red borders, 2s. each. Sold separately.
    OF THE IMITATION OF CHRIST. By THOMAS À KEMPIS.
    THE CHRISTIAN YEAR.
    THE DEVOUT LIFE. By ST. FRANCIS DE SALES.
    THE HIDDEN LIFE OF THE SOUL.
    THE SPIRITUAL COMBAT. By LAURENCE SCUPOLI.

Barry.—SOME LIGHTS OF SCIENCE ON THE FAITH. Being the Bampton Lectures for 1892. By the Right Rev. ALFRED BARRY, D.D., Canon of Windsor, formerly Bishop of Sydney, Metropolitan of New South Wales, and Primate of Australia. *8vo. 12s. 6d.*

Bathe.—Works by the Rev. ANTHONY BATHE, M.A.
    A LENT WITH JESUS. A Plain Guide for Churchmen. Containing Readings for Lent and Easter Week, and on the Holy Eucharist. *32mo, 1s.; or in paper cover, 6d.*
    AN ADVENT WITH JESUS. *32mo, 1s.; or in paper cover, 6d.*
    WHAT I SHOULD BELIEVE. A Simple Manual of Self-Instruction for Church People. *Small 8vo, limp, 1s.; cloth gilt, 2s.*

Benson.—THE FINAL PASSOVER: A Series of Meditations upon the Passion of our Lord Jesus Christ. By the Rev. R. M. BENSON, M.A., Student of Christ Church, Oxford. *Small 8vo.*

Vol. I.—THE REJECTION. 5s.
Vol. II.—THE UPPER CHAMBER.
Part I. 5s.
Part II. 5s.
Vol. III.—THE DIVINE EXODUS. Parts I. and II. 5s. each.
Vol. IV.—THE LIFE BEYOND THE GRAVE. 5s.

Bickersteth.—YESTERDAY, TO-DAY, AND FOR EVER: a Poem in Twelve Books. By EDWARD HENRY BICKERSTETH, D.D., Bishop of Exeter. *One Shilling Edition*, 18mo. *With red borders*, 16mo, 2s. 6d.
The Crown 8vo Edition (5s.) *may still be had.*

Blunt.—Works by the Rev. JOHN HENRY BLUNT, D.D.

THE ANNOTATED BOOK OF COMMON PRAYER: Being an Historical, Ritual, and Theological Commentary on the Devotional System of the Church of England. *4to.* 21s.

THE COMPENDIOUS EDITION OF THE ANNOTATED BOOK OF COMMON PRAYER: Forming a concise Commentary on the Devotional System of the Church of England. *Crown 8vo.* 10s. 6d.

DICTIONARY OF DOCTRINAL AND HISTORICAL THEOLOGY. By various Writers. *Imperial 8vo.* 21s.

DICTIONARY OF SECTS, HERESIES, ECCLESIASTICAL PARTIES AND SCHOOLS OF RELIGIOUS THOUGHT. By various Writers. *Imperial 8vo.* 21s.

THE BOOK OF CHURCH LAW. Being an Exposition of the Legal Rights and Duties of the Parochial Clergy and the Laity of the Church of England. Revised by Sir WALTER G. F. PHILLIMORE, Bart., D.C.L., and G. EDWARDES JONES, Barrister-at-Law. *Crown 8vo.* 7s. 6d.

A COMPANION TO THE BIBLE: Being a Plain Commentary on Scripture History, to the end of the Apostolic Age. *Two Vols. small 8vo. Sold separately.*
THE OLD TESTAMENT. 3s. 6d. THE NEW TESTAMENT. 3s. 6d.

HOUSEHOLD THEOLOGY: a Handbook of Religious Information respecting the Holy Bible, the Prayer Book, the Church, etc., etc. *Paper cover*, 16mo. 1s. *Also the Larger Edition*, 3s. 6d.

Body.—Works by the Rev. GEORGE BODY, D.D., Canon of Durham.

THE LIFE OF LOVE. A Course of Lent Lectures. *Crown 8vo.* 4s. 6d.

THE SCHOOL OF CALVARY; or, Laws of Christian Life revealed from the Cross. 16mo. 2s. 6d.

THE LIFE OF JUSTIFICATION. 16mo. 2s. 6d.

THE LIFE OF TEMPTATION. 16mo. 2s. 6d.

Boultbee.—A COMMENTARY ON THE THIRTY-NINE ARTICLES OF THE CHURCH OF ENGLAND. By the Rev. T. P. BOULTBEE, formerly Principal of the London College of Divinity, St. John's Hall, Highbury. *Crown 8vo.* 6s.

Bright.—Works by WILLIAM BRIGHT, D.D., Canon of Christ Church, Oxford.
WAYMARKS IN CHURCH HISTORY. *Crown 8vo.* 7s. 6d.
MORALITY IN DOCTRINE. *Crown 8vo.* 7s. 6d.
LESSONS FROM THE LIVES OF THREE GREAT FATHERS: St. Athanasius, St. Chrysostom, and St. Augustine. *Crown 8vo.* 6s.
THE INCARNATION AS A MOTIVE POWER. *Crown 8vo.* 6s.

Bright and Medd.—LIBER PRECUM PUBLICARUM ECCLESIÆ ANGLICANÆ. A GULIELMO BRIGHT, S.T.P., et PETRO GOLDSMITH MEDD, A.M., Latine redditus. *Small 8vo.* 7s. 6d.

Browne.—AN EXPOSITION OF THE THIRTY-NINE ARTICLES, Historical and Doctrinal. By E. H. BROWNE, D.D., formerly Bishop of Winchester. 8vo. 16s.

Campion and Beamont.—THE PRAYER BOOK INTERLEAVED. With Historical Illustrations and Explanatory Notes arranged parallel to the Text. By W. M. CAMPION, D.D., and W. J. BEAMONT, M.A. *Small 8vo.* 7s. 6d.

Carter.—Works edited by the Rev. T. T. CARTER, M.A., Hon. Canon of Christ Church, Oxford.
THE TREASURY OF DEVOTION: A Manual of Prayer for General and Daily Use. Compiled by a Priest.
> 18mo. 2s. 6d.; *cloth limp*, 2s.
> Bound with the Book of Common Prayer, 3s. 6d.
> Red-Line Edition. *Cloth extra, gilt top.* 18mo, 2s. 6d. net.
> Large-Type Edition. *Crown 8vo.* 3s. 6d.

THE WAY OF LIFE: A Book of Prayers and Instruction for the Young at School, with a Preparation for Confirmation. Compiled by a Priest. 18mo. 1s. 6d.

THE PATH OF HOLINESS: a First Book of Prayers, with the Service of the Holy Communion, for the Young. Compiled by a Priest. With Illustrations. 16mo. 1s. 6d.; *cloth limp*, 1s.

THE GUIDE TO HEAVEN: a Book of Prayers for every Want. (For the Working Classes.) Compiled by a Priest. 18mo. 1s. 6d.; *cloth limp*, 1s. Large-Type Edition. *Crown 8vo.* 1s. 6d.; *cloth limp*, 1s.

[continued.

Carter.—Works edited by the Rev. T. T. CARTER, M.A., Hon. Canon of Christ Church, Oxford—*continued.*

SELF-RENUNCIATION. 16mo. 2s. 6d.

THE STAR OF CHILDHOOD: a First Book of Prayers and Instruction for Children. Compiled by a Priest. With Illustrations. 16mo. 2s. 6d.

NICHOLAS FERRAR: his Household and his Friends. With Portrait engraved after a Picture by CORNELIUS JANSSEN at Magdalene College, Cambridge. *Crown 8vo. 6s.*

Conybeare and Howson.—THE LIFE AND EPISTLES OF ST. PAUL. By the Rev. W. J. CONYBEARE, M.A., and the Very Rev. J. S. HOWSON, D.D. With numerous Maps and Illustrations.

LIBRARY EDITION. *Two Vols. 8vo. 21s.*
STUDENTS' EDITION. *One Vol. Crown 8vo. 6s.*
POPULAR EDITION. *One Vol. Crown 8vo. 3s. 6d.*

Creighton.—PERSECUTION AND TOLERANCE: being the Hulsean Lectures preached before the University of Cambridge in 1893-4. By M. CREIGHTON, D.D., Lord Bishop of Peterborough. *Crown 8vo. 4s. 6d.*

Devotional Series, 16mo, Red Borders. *Each 2s. 6d.*

BICKERSTETH'S YESTERDAY, TO-DAY, AND FOR EVER.
CHILCOT'S TREATISE ON EVIL THOUGHTS.
THE CHRISTIAN YEAR.
FRANCIS DE SALES' (ST.) THE DEVOUT LIFE.
HERBERT'S POEMS AND PROVERBS.
KEMPIS' (À) OF THE IMITATION OF CHRIST.
WILSON'S THE LORD'S SUPPER. *Large type*
*TAYLOR'S (JEREMY) HOLY LIVING.
*——— ——— HOLY DYING.

* *These two in one Volume. 5s.*

Devotional Series, 18mo, without Red Borders. *Each 1s.*

BICKERSTETH'S YESTERDAY, TO-DAY, AND FOR EVER.
THE CHRISTIAN YEAR
FRANCIS DE SALES' (ST.) THE DEVOUT LIFE.
HERBERT'S POEMS AND PROVERBS.
KEMPIS À) OF THE IMITATION OF CHRIST.
WILSON'S THE LORD'S SUPPER, *Large type.*
*TAYLOR'S (JEREMY) HOLY LIVING.
*——— ——— HOLY DYING.

* *These two in one Volume. 2s. 6d.*

Diggle.—RELIGIOUS DOUBT: its Nature, Treatment, Causes, Difficulties, Consequences, and Dissolution. By the Rev. JOHN W. DIGGLE, M.A., Vicar of Mossley Hill and Hon. Canon of Liverpool, Author of 'Bishop Fraser's Lancashire Life.' *Crown 8vo. 7s. 6d.*

Edersheim.—Works by ALFRED EDERSHEIM, M.A., D.D., Ph.D., sometime Grinfield Lecturer on the Septuagint, Oxford.

THE LIFE AND TIMES OF JESUS THE MESSIAH. *Two Vols. 8vo. 24s.*

JESUS THE MESSIAH: being an Abridged Edition of 'The Life and Times of Jesus the Messiah.' *Crown 8vo. 7s. 6d.*

PROPHECY AND HISTORY IN RELATION TO THE MESSIAH: The Warburton Lectures, 1880-1884. *8vo. 12s.*

Ellicott.—Works by C. J. ELLICOTT, D.D., Bishop of Gloucester and Bristol.

A CRITICAL AND GRAMMATICAL COMMENTARY ON ST. PAUL'S EPISTLES. Greek Text, with a Critical and Grammatical Commentary, and a Revised English Translation. *8vo.*

1 CORINTHIANS. 16s.	PHILIPPIANS, COLOSSIANS, AND
GALATIANS. 8s. 6d.	PHILEMON. 10s. 6d.
EPHESIANS. 8s. 6d.	THESSALONIANS. 7s. 6d.
PASTORAL EPISTLES. 10s. 6d.	

HISTORICAL LECTURES ON THE LIFE OF OUR LORD JESUS CHRIST. *8vo. 12s.*

Epochs of Church History.—Edited by MANDELL CREIGHTON, D.D., LL.D., Bishop of Peterborough. *Fcap. 8vo. 2s. 6d. each.*

THE ENGLISH CHURCH IN OTHER LANDS. By the Rev. H. W. TUCKER, M.A.

THE HISTORY OF THE REFORMATION IN ENGLAND. By the Rev. GEO. G. PERRY, M.A.

THE CHURCH OF THE EARLY FATHERS. By the Rev. ALFRED PLUMMER, D.D.

THE EVANGELICAL REVIVAL IN THE EIGHTEENTH CENTURY. By the Rev. J. H. OVERTON, D.D.

THE UNIVERSITY OF OXFORD. By the Hon. G. C. BRODRICK, D.C.L.

THE UNIVERSITY OF CAMBRIDGE. By J. BASS MULLINGER, M.A.

THE ENGLISH CHURCH IN THE MIDDLE AGES. By the Rev. W. HUNT, M.A.

THE CHURCH AND THE EASTERN EMPIRE. By the Rev. H. F. TOZER, M.A.

THE CHURCH AND THE ROMAN EMPIRE. By the Rev. A. CARR, M.A.

THE CHURCH AND THE PURITANS, 1570-1660. By HENRY OFFLEY WAKEMAN, M.A.

HILDEBRAND AND HIS TIMES. By the Rev. W. R. W. STEPHENS, M.A.

THE POPES AND THE HOHENSTAUFEN. By UGO BALZANI.

THE COUNTER REFORMATION. By ADOLPHUS WILLIAM WARD, Litt. D.

WYCLIFFE AND MOVEMENTS FOR REFORM. By REGINALD L. POOLE, M.A.

THE ARIAN CONTROVERSY. By H. M. GWATKIN, M.A.

Fosbery.—Works edited by the Rev. THOMAS VINCENT FOSBERY, M.A., sometime Vicar of St. Giles's, Reading.

    VOICES OF COMFORT. *Cheap Edition. Small* 8*vo.* 3*s.* 6*d.*
        The Larger Edition (7*s.* 6*d.*) *may still be had.*

    HYMNS AND POEMS FOR THE SICK AND SUFFERING. In connection with the Service for the Visitation of the Sick. Selected from Various Authors. *Small* 8*vo.* 3*s.* 6*d.*

Fremantle. — THE WORLD AS THE SUBJECT OF REDEMPTION. Being an attempt to set forth the Functions of the Church as designed to embrace the whole Race of Mankind. (The Bampton Lectures, 1883.) By the Hon. and Rev. W. H. FREMANTLE, M.A., Dean of Ripon. New Edition, Revised, with New Preface. *Crown* 8*vo.* 7*s.* 6*d.*

Gore.—Works by the Rev. CHARLES GORE, M.A., Canon of Westminster.

    THE MINISTRY OF THE CHRISTIAN CHURCH. 8*vo.* 10*s.* 6*d.*
    ROMAN CATHOLIC CLAIMS. *Crown* 8*vo.* 3*s.* 6*d.*

Goulburn.—Works by EDWARD MEYRICK GOULBURN, D.D., D.C.L., sometime Dean of Norwich.

    THOUGHTS ON PERSONAL RELIGION. *Small* 8*vo.* 6*s.* 6*d.* *Cheap Edition,* 3*s.* 6*d.*; *Presentation Edition,* 2 *vols. small* 8*vo.* 10*s.* 6*d.*

    THE PURSUIT OF HOLINESS: a Sequel to 'Thoughts on Personal Religion.' *Small* 8*vo.* 5*s. Cheap Edition.* 3*s.* 6*d.*

    THE GOSPEL OF THE CHILDHOOD: a Practical and Devotional Commentary on the Single Incident of our Blessed Lord's Childhood (St. Luke ii. 41 to the end). *Crown* 8*vo.* 2*s.* 6*d.*

    THE COLLECTS OF THE DAY: an Exposition, Critical and Devotional, of the Collects appointed at the Communion. With Preliminary Essays on their Structure, Sources, etc. 2 *vols. Crown* 8*vo.* 8*s. each.*

    THOUGHTS UPON THE LITURGICAL GOSPELS for the Sundays, one for each day in the year. With an Introduction on their Origin, History, the modifications made in them by the Reformers and by the Revisers of the Prayer Book. 2 *vols. Crown* 8*vo.* 16*s.*

    MEDITATIONS UPON THE LITURGICAL GOSPELS for the Minor Festivals of Christ, the two first Week-days of the Easter and Whitsun Festivals, and the Red-letter Saints' Days. *Crown* 8*vo.* 8*s.* 6*d.*

    FAMILY PRAYERS, compiled from various sources (chiefly from Bishop Hamilton's Manual), and arranged on the Liturgical Principle. *Crown* 8*vo.* 3*s.* 6*d. Cheap Edition.* 16*mo.* 1*s.*

Harrison.—Works by the Rev. ALEXANDER J. HARRISON, B.D., Lecturer of the Christian Evidence Society.
> PROBLEMS OF CHRISTIANITY AND SCEPTICISM ; Lessons from Twenty Years' Experience in the Field of Christian Evidence. *Crown 8vo.* 7s. 6d.
> THE CHURCH IN RELATION TO SCEPTICS : a Conversational Guide to Evidential Work. *Crown 8vo.* 7s. 6d.
> THE REPOSE OF FAITH, IN VIEW OF PRESENT DAY DIFFICULTIES. *Crown 8vo.* 7s. 6d.

Holland.—Works by the Rev. HENRY SCOTT HOLLAND M.A., Canon and Precentor of St. Paul's.
> GOD'S CITY AND THE COMING OF THE KINGDOM : *Crown 8vo.* 7s. 6d.
> PLEAS AND CLAIMS FOR CHRIST. *Crown 8vo.* 3s. 6d.
> CREED AND CHARACTER : Sermons. *Crown 8vo.* 3s. 6d.
> ON BEHALF OF BELIEF. Sermons preached in St. Paul's Cathedral. *Crown 8vo.* 3s. 6d.
> CHRIST OR ECCLESIASTES. Sermons preached in St. Paul's Cathedral. *Crown 8vo.* 2s. 6d.
> LOGIC AND LIFE, with other Sermons. *Crown 8vo.* 3s. 6d.

Hutchings.—SERMON SKETCHES taken from some of the Sunday Lessons throughout the Church's Year. By the Rev. W. H. HUTCHINGS, M.A., Canon of York. *Crown 8vo.* 5s.

Ingram.—HAPPINESS IN THE SPIRITUAL LIFE; or, 'The Secret of the Lord.' By the Rev. W. C. INGRAM, D.D., Dean of Peterborough. *Crown 8vo.* 3s. 6d.

INHERITANCE OF THE SAINTS ; or, Thoughts on the Communion of Saints and the Life of the World to come. Collected chiefly from English Writers by L. P. With a Preface by the Rev. HENRY SCOTT HOLLAND, M.A. *Crown 8vo.* 7s. 6d.

Jameson.—Works by Mrs. JAMESON.
> SACRED AND LEGENDARY ART, containing Legends of the Angels and Archangels, the Evangelists, the Apostles. With 19 Etchings and 187 Woodcuts. 2 *vols.* 8vo. 20s. *net.*
> LEGENDS OF THE MONASTIC ORDERS, as represented in the Fine Arts. With 11 Etchings and 88 Woodcuts. 8vo. 10s. *net.*
> LEGENDS OF THE MADONNA, OR BLESSED VIRGIN MARY. With 27 Etchings and 165 Woodcuts. 8vo. 10s. *net.*
> THE HISTORY OF OUR LORD, as exemplified in Works of Art. Commenced by the late Mrs. JAMESON ; continued and completed by LADY EASTLAKE. With 31 Etchings and 281 Woodcuts. 2 *Vols.* 8vo. 20s. *net.*

Jennings.—ECCLESIA ANGLICANA. A History of the Church of Christ in England from the Earliest to the Present Times. By the Rev. ARTHUR CHARLES JENNINGS, M.A. *Crown 8vo.* 7s. 6d.

Jukes.—Works by ANDREW JUKES.

THE NEW MAN AND THE ETERNAL LIFE. Notes on the Reiterated Amens of the Son of God. *Crown 8vo.* 6s.

THE NAMES OF GOD IN HOLY SCRIPTURE: a Revelation of His Nature and Relationships. *Crown 8vo.* 4s. 6d.

THE TYPES OF GENESIS. *Crown 8vo.* 7s. 6d.

THE SECOND DEATH AND THE RESTITUTION OF ALL THINGS. *Crown 8vo.* 3s. 6d.

THE MYSTERY OF THE KINGDOM. *Crown 8vo.* 2s. 6d.

THE ORDER AND CONNEXION OF THE CHURCH'S TEACHING, as set forth in the arrangement of the Epistles and Gospels throughout the Year. *Crown 8vo.* 2s. 6d.

Knox Little.—Works by W. J. KNOX LITTLE, M.A., Canon Residentiary of Worcester, and Vicar of Hoar Cross.

SACERDOTALISM, WHEN RIGHTLY UNDERSTOOD, THE TEACHING OF THE CHURCH OF ENGLAND. *Crown 8vo.* 6s.

SKETCHES IN SUNSHINE AND STORM: a Collection of Miscellaneous Essays and Notes of Travel. *Crown 8vo.* 7s. 6d.

THE CHRISTIAN HOME. *Crown 8vo.* 3s. 6d.

THE HOPES AND DECISIONS OF THE PASSION OF OUR MOST HOLY REDEEMER. *Crown 8vo.* 2s. 6d.

CHARACTERISTICS AND MOTIVES OF THE CHRISTIAN LIFE. Ten Sermons preached in Manchester Cathedral, in Lent and Advent. *Crown 8vo.* 2s. 6d.

SERMONS PREACHED FOR THE MOST PART IN MANCHESTER. *Crown 8vo.* 3s. 6d.

THE MYSTERY OF THE PASSION OF OUR MOST HOLY REDEEMER. *Crown 8vo.* 2s. 6d.

THE WITNESS OF THE PASSION OF OUR MOST HOLY REDEEMER. *Crown 8vo.* 2s. 6d.

[continued.

Knox Little.—Works by W. J. KNOX LITTLE, M.A., Canon Residentiary of Worcester, and Vicar of Hoar Cross.—*continued.*

THE LIGHT OF LIFE. Sermons preached on Various Occasions. *Crown 8vo.* 3s. 6d.

SUNLIGHT AND SHADOW IN THE CHRISTIAN LIFE. Sermons preached for the most part in America. *Crown 8vo.* 3s. 6d.

Lear.—Works by, and Edited by, H. L. SIDNEY LEAR.

FOR DAYS AND YEARS. A book containing a Text, Short Reading, and Hymn for Every Day in the Church's Year. 16mo. 2s. 6d. *Also a Cheap Edition*, 32mo. 1s.; *or cloth gilt*, 1s. 6d.; *or with red borders*, 2s. 6d.

FIVE MINUTES. Daily Readings of Poetry. 16mo. 3s. 6d. *Also a Cheap Edition*, 32mo. 1s.; *or cloth gilt*, 1s. 6d.

WEARINESS. A Book for the Languid and Lonely. *Large Type. Small 8vo.* 5s.

THE LIGHT OF THE CONSCIENCE. 16mo. 2s. 6d. 32mo. 1s.; *cloth limp*, 6d.

CHRISTIAN BIOGRAPHIES. *Nine Vols. Crown 8vo.* 3s. 6d. *each.*

MADAME LOUISE DE FRANCE, Daughter of Louis XV., known also as the Mother Térèse de St. Augustin.	THE REVIVAL OF PRIESTLY LIFE IN THE SEVENTEENTH CENTURY IN FRANCE.
A DOMINICAN ARTIST: a Sketch of the Life of the Rev. Père Besson, of the Order of St. Dominic.	A CHRISTIAN PAINTER OF THE NINETEENTH CENTURY.
HENRI PERREYVE. By PÈRE GRATRY.	BOSSUET AND HIS CONTEMPORARIES.
ST. FRANCIS DE SALES, Bishop and Prince of Geneva.	FÉNELON, ARCHBISHOP OF CAMBRAI.
	HENRI DOMINIQUE LACORDAIRE.

DEVOTIONAL WORKS. Edited by H. L. SIDNEY LEAR. *New and Uniform Editions. Nine Vols.* 16mo. 2s. 6d. *each.*

FÉNELON'S SPIRITUAL LETTERS TO MEN.	THE HIDDEN LIFE OF THE SOUL.
FÉNELON'S SPIRITUAL LETTERS TO WOMEN.	THE LIGHT OF THE CONSCIENCE.
A SELECTION FROM THE SPIRITUAL LETTERS OF ST. FRANCIS DE SALES.	SELF-RENUNCIATION. From the French.
	ST. FRANCIS DE SALES OF THE LOVE OF GOD.
THE SPIRIT OF ST. FRANCIS DE SALES.	SELECTIONS FROM PASCAL'S 'THOUGHTS.'

Liddon.—Works by HENRY PARRY LIDDON, D.D., D.C.L., LL.D., late Canon Residentiary and Chancellor of St. Paul's.

LIFE OF EDWARD BOUVERIE PUSEY, D.D. By HENRY PARRY LIDDON, D.D., D.C.L., LL.D. Edited and prepared for publication by the Rev. J. O. JOHNSTON, M.A., Principal of the Theological College, and Vicar of Cuddesdon, Oxford; and the Rev. ROBERT J. WILSON, D.D., Warden of Keble College. *With Portraits and Illustrations. Four Vols.* 8vo. *Vols. I. and II.*, 36s. *Vol. III.*, 18s.

CLERICAL LIFE AND WORK: Sermons. *Crown 8vo.* 5s.

ESSAYS AND ADDRESSES: Lectures on Buddhism—Lectures on the Life of St. Paul—Papers on Dante. *Crown 8vo.* 5s.

EXPLANATORY ANALYSIS OF PAUL'S EPISTLE TO THE ROMANS. 8vo. 14s.

SERMONS ON OLD TESTAMENT SUBJECTS. *Crown 8vo.* 5s.

SERMONS ON SOME WORDS OF CHRIST. *Crown 8vo.* 5s.

THE DIVINITY OF OUR LORD AND SAVIOUR JESUS CHRIST. Being the Bampton Lectures for 1866. *Crown 8vo.* 5s.

ADVENT IN ST. PAUL'S. Sermons bearing chiefly on the Two Comings of our Lord. *Two Vols. Crown 8vo.* 3s. 6d. each. *Cheap Edition in one Volume. Crown 8vo.* 5s.

CHRISTMASTIDE IN ST. PAUL'S. Sermons bearing chiefly on the Birth of our Lord and the End of the Year. *Crown 8vo.* 5s.

PASSIONTIDE SERMONS. *Crown 8vo.* 5s.

EASTER IN ST. PAUL'S. Sermons bearing chiefly on the Resurrection of our Lord. *Two Vols. Crown 8vo.* 3s. 6d. each. *Cheap Edition in one Volume. Crown 8vo.* 5s.

SERMONS PREACHED BEFORE THE UNIVERSITY OF OXFORD. *Two Vols. Crown 8vo.* 3s. 6d. each. *Cheap Edition in one Volume. Crown 8vo.* 5s.

THE MAGNIFICAT. Sermons in St. Paul's. *Crown 8vo.* 2s. 6d.

SOME ELEMENTS OF RELIGION. Lent Lectures. *Small 8vo.* 2s. 6d.; *or in paper cover*, 1s. 6d.
The Crown 8vo Edition (5s.) *may still be had.*

SELECTIONS FROM THE WRITINGS OF H. P. LIDDON, D.D. *Crown 8vo.* 3s. 6d.

MAXIMS AND GLEANINGS FROM THE WRITINGS OF H. P. LIDDON, D.D. Selected and arranged by C. M. S. *Crown 16mo.* 1s.

DR. LIDDON'S TOUR IN EGYPT AND PALESTINE IN 1886. Being Letters descriptive of the Tour, written by his Sister, Mrs. KING *Crown 8vo.* 5s.

Luckock.—Works by HERBERT MORTIMER LUCKOCK, D.D., Dean of Lichfield.

THE HISTORY OF MARRIAGE, JEWISH AND CHRISTIAN, IN RELATION TO DIVORCE AND CERTAIN FORBIDDEN DEGREES. *Crown 8vo. 6s.*

AFTER DEATH. An Examination of the Testimony of Primitive Times respecting the State of the Faithful Dead, and their Relationship to the Living. *Crown 8vo. 6s.*

THE INTERMEDIATE STATE BETWEEN DEATH AND JUDGMENT. Being a Sequel to *After Death. Crown 8vo. 6s.*

FOOTPRINTS OF THE SON OF MAN, as traced by St. Mark. Being Eighty Portions for Private Study, Family Reading, and Instructions in Church. *Two Vols. Crown 8vo. 12s. Cheap Edition in one Vol. Crown 8vo. 5s.*

THE DIVINE LITURGY. Being the Order for Holy Communion, Historically, Doctrinally, and devotionally set forth, in Fifty Portions. *Crown 8vo. 6s.*

STUDIES IN THE HISTORY OF THE BOOK OF COMMON PRAYER. The Anglican Reform—The Puritan Innovations—The Elizabethan Reaction—The Caroline Settlement. With Appendices. *Crown 8vo. 6s.*

THE BISHOPS IN THE TOWER. A Record of Stirring Events affecting the Church and Nonconformists from the Restoration to the Revolution. *Crown 8vo. 6s.*

LYRA GERMANICA. Hymns translated from the German by CATHERINE WINKWORTH. *Small 8vo. 5s.*

MacColl.—Works by the Rev. MALCOLM MACCOLL, M.A., Canon Residentary of Ripon.

CHRISTIANITY IN RELATION TO SCIENCE AND MORALS. *Crown 8vo. 6s.*

LIFE HERE AND HEREAFTER: Sermons. *Crown 8vo. 7s. 6d.*

Mason.—Works by A. J. MASON, D.D., Hon. Canon of Canterbury and Examining Chaplain to the Archbishop of Canterbury.

THE FAITH OF THE GOSPEL. A Manual of Christian Doctrine. *Crown 8vo. 3s. 6d.*

THE RELATION OF CONFIRMATION TO BAPTISM. As taught in Holy Scripture and the Fathers. *Crown 8vo. 7s. 6d.*

Mercier.—OUR MOTHER CHURCH: Being Simple Talk on High Topics. By Mrs. JEROME MERCIER. *Small 8vo.* 3s. 6d.

Molesworth.—STORIES OF THE SAINTS FOR CHILDREN: The Black Letter Saints. By Mrs. MOLESWORTH, Author of 'The Palace in the Garden,' etc, etc. *With Illustrations. Royal 16mo.* 5s.

Mozley.—Works by J. B. MOZLEY, D.D., late Canon of Christ Church, and Regius Professor of Divinity at Oxford.

ESSAYS, HISTORICAL AND THEOLOGICAL. *Two Vols. 8vo.* 24s.

EIGHT LECTURES ON MIRACLES. Being the Bampton Lectures for 1865. *Crown 8vo.* 3s. 6d.

RULING IDEAS IN EARLY AGES AND THEIR RELATION TO OLD TESTAMENT FAITH. Lectures delivered to Graduates of the University of Oxford. *8vo.* 10s. 6d.

SERMONS PREACHED BEFORE THE UNIVERSITY OF OXFORD, and on Various Occasions. *Crown 8vo.* 3s. 6d.

SERMONS, PAROCHIAL AND OCCASIONAL. *Crown 8vo.* 3s. 6d.

A REVIEW OF THE BAPTISMAL CONTROVERSY. *Crown 8vo.* 3s. 6d.

Newbolt.—Works by the Rev. W. C. E. NEWBOLT, M.A., Canon and Chancellor of St. Paul's Cathedral, Select Preacher at Oxford, and Examining Chaplain to the Lord Bishop of Ely.

COUNSELS OF FAITH AND PRACTICE: being Sermons preached on various occasions. *New and Enlarged Edition. Crown 8vo.* 5s.

SPECULUM SACERDOTUM; or, the Divine Model of the Priestly Life. *Crown 8vo.* 7s. 6d.

THE FRUIT OF THE SPIRIT. Being Ten Addresses bearing on the Spiritual Life. *Crown 8vo.* 2s. 6d.

THE MAN OF GOD. Being Six Addresses delivered during Lent at the Primary Ordination of the Right Rev. the Lord Alwyne Compton, D.D., Bishop of Ely. *Small 8vo.* 1s. 6d.

THE PRAYER BOOK: Its Voice and Teaching. Being Spiritual Addresses bearing on the Book of Common Prayer. *Crown 8vo.* 2s. 6d.

Newman.—Works by JOHN HENRY NEWMAN, B.D., sometime Vicar of St. Mary's, Oxford.
> PAROCHIAL AND PLAIN SERMONS. *Eight Vols. Cabinet Edition. Crown 8vo.* 5s. *each. Cheaper Edition.* 3s. 6d. *each.*
> SELECTION, ADAPTED TO THE SEASONS OF THE ECCLESIASTICAL YEAR, from the 'Parochial and Plain Sermons,' *Cabinet Edition. Crown 8vo.* 5s. *Cheaper Edition.* 3s. 6d.
> FIFTEEN SERMONS PREACHED BEFORE THE UNIVERSITY OF OXFORD *Cabinet Edition. Crown 8vo.* 5s. *Cheaper Edition.* 3s. 6d.
> SERMONS BEARING UPON SUBJECTS OF THE DAY. *Cabinet Edition. Crown 8vo.* 5s. *Cheaper Edition. Crown 8vo.* 3s. 6d.
> LECTURES ON THE DOCTRINE OF JUSTIFICATION. *Cabinet Edition. Crown 8vo.* 5s. *Cheaper Edition.* 3s. 6d.
> *⁎⁎⁎ A Complete List of Cardinal Newman's Works can be had on Application.*

Norris.—RUDIMENTS OF THEOLOGY: a First Book for Students. By JOHN PILKINGTON NORRIS, D.D., late Archdeacon of Bristol, and Canon Residentiary of Bristol Cathedral. *Cr. 8vo.* 3s. 6d.

Osborne.—Works by EDWARD OSBORNE, Mission Priest of the Society of St. John the Evangelist, Cowley, Oxford.
> THE CHILDREN'S SAVIOUR. Instructions to Children on the Life of Our Lord and Saviour Jesus Christ. *Illustrated.* 16mo. 2s. 6d.
> THE SAVIOUR KING. Instructions to Children on Old Testament Types and Illustrations of the Life of Christ. *Illustrated.* 16mo. 2s. 6d.
> THE CHILDREN'S FAITH. Instructions to Children on the Apostles' Creed. *Illustrated.* 16mo. 2s. 6d.

Overton.—THE ENGLISH CHURCH IN THE NINETEENTH CENTURY, 1800-1833. By the Rev. JOHN H. OVERTON, D.D., Canon of Lincoln, Rector of Epworth, Doncaster, and Rural Dean of the Isle of Axholme. *8vo.* 14s.

Oxenden.—Works by the Right Rev. ASHTON OXENDEN, formerly Bishop of Montreal.
> PLAIN SERMONS, to which is prefixed a Memorial Portrait. *Crown 8vo.* 5s.
> THE HISTORY OF MY LIFE: An Autobiography. *Crown 8vo.* 5s.
> PEACE AND ITS HINDRANCES. *Crown 8vo.* 1s. *sewed*; 2s. *cloth.*
> THE PATHWAY OF SAFETY; or, Counsel to the Awakened. *Fcap. 8vo, large type.* 2s. 6d. *Cheap Edition. Small type, limp,* 1s.
> THE EARNEST COMMUNICANT. *New Red Rubric Edition.* 32mo, *cloth.* 2s. *Common Edition.* 32mo. 1s.
> OUR CHURCH AND HER SERVICES. *Fcap. 8vo.* 2s. 6d.

[continued.

Oxenden.—Works by the Right Rev. ASHTON OXENDEN formerly Bishop of Montreal—*continued.*
  FAMILY PRAYERS FOR FOUR WEEKS. First Series. *Fcap. 8vo.* 2s. 6d. Second Series. *Fcap. 8vo.* 2s. 6d.
    LARGE TYPE EDITION. Two Series in one Volume. *Crown 8vo.* 6s.
  COTTAGE SERMONS; or, Plain Words to the Poor. *Fcap. 8vo.* 2s. 6d.
  THOUGHTS FOR HOLY WEEK. 16mo, *cloth.* 1s. 6d.
  DECISION. 18mo. 1s. 6d.
  THE HOME BEYOND; or, A Happy Old Age. *Fcap. 8vo.* 1s. 6d.
  THE LABOURING MAN'S BOOK. 18mo, *large type, cloth.* 1s. 6d.

Paget.—Works by FRANCIS PAGET, D.D., Dean of Christ Church.
  STUDIES IN THE CHRISTIAN CHARACTER: Sermons. With an Introductory Essay. *Crown 8vo.* 6s. 6d.
  THE SPIRIT OF DISCIPLINE: Sermons. *Crown 8vo.* 6s. 6d.
  FACULTIES AND DIFFICULTIES FOR BELIEF AND DISBELIEF. *Crown 8vo.* 6s. 6d.
  THE HALLOWING OF WORK. Addresses given at Eton, January 16-18, 1888. *Small 8vo.* 2s.

PRACTICAL REFLECTIONS. By a CLERGYMAN. With Prefaces by H. P. LIDDON, D.D., D.C.L., and the BISHOP OF LINCOLN. *Crown 8vo.*
  THE BOOK OF GENESIS. 4s. 6d.
  THE PSALMS. 5s.
  ISAIAH. 4s. 6d.
  THE HOLY GOSPELS. 4s. 6d.
  ACTS TO REVELATIONS. 6s.

PRIEST (THE) TO THE ALTAR; or, Aids to the Devout Celebration of Holy Communion, chiefly after the Ancient English Use of Sarum. *Royal 8vo.* 12s.

Prynne.—THE TRUTH AND REALITY OF THE EUCHARISTIC SACRIFICE, Proved from Holy Scripture, the Teaching of the Primitive Church, and the Book of Common Prayer. By the Rev. GEORGE RUNDLE PRYNNE, M.A. *Crown 8vo.* 3s. 6d.

Puller.—THE PRIMITIVE SAINTS AND THE SEE OF ROME. By F. W. PULLER, M.A., Mission Priest of the Society of St. John Evangelist, Cowley, Oxford. *Crown 8vo.* 7s. 6d.

Pusey.—LIFE OF EDWARD BOUVERIE PUSEY, D.D. By HENRY PARRY LIDDON, D.D., D.C.L., LL.D. Edited and prepared for publication by the Rev. J. O. JOHNSTON, M.A., Principal of the Theological College, Vicar of Cuddesdon, Oxford, and the Rev. ROBERT J. WILSON, D.D., Warden of Keble College. *With Portraits and Illustrations. Four Vols.* 8vo. *Vols. I. and II.,* 36s. *Vol. III.,* 18s.

Pusey.—Works by the Rev. E. B. PUSEY, D.D.
  PRIVATE PRAYERS. With Preface by H. P. LIDDON, D.D. 32mo. 1s.
  SELECTIONS FROM THE WRITINGS OF EDWARD BOUVERIE PUSEY, D.D. *Crown 8vo.* 3s. 6d.

Sanday.—Works by W. SANDAY, D.D., Margaret Professor of Divinity, and Ireland Professor of Exegesis.

> INSPIRATION: Eight Lectures on the Early History and Origin of the Doctrine of Biblical Inspiration. Being the Bampton Lectures for 1893. 8vo. 16s.
>
> THE ORACLES OF GOD: Nine Lectures on the Nature and Extent of Biblical Inspiration and the Special Significance of the Old Testament Scriptures at the Present Time. *Crown 8vo.* 4s.
>
> TWO PRESENT-DAY QUESTIONS. I. Biblical Criticism. II. The Social Movement. Sermons preached before the University of Cambridge. *Crown 8vo.* 2s. 6d.

Seebohm.—THE OXFORD REFORMERS—JOHN COLET, ERASMUS, AND THOMAS MORE: A History of their Fellow-Work. By FREDERICK SEEBOHM. 8vo. 14s.

Williams.—Works by the Rev. ISAAC WILLIAMS, B.D.

> A DEVOTIONAL COMMENTARY ON THE GOSPEL NARRATIVE, *Eight Vols. Crown 8vo.* 5s. *each. Sold Separately.*

THOUGHTS ON THE STUDY OF THE HOLY GOSPELS.	OUR LORD'S MINISTRY (Third Year).
A HARMONY OF THE FOUR GOSPELS.	THE HOLY WEEK.
OUR LORD'S NATIVITY.	OUR LORD'S PASSION.
OUR LORD'S MINISTRY (Second Year).	OUR LORD'S RESURRECTION.

> FEMALE CHARACTERS OF HOLY SCRIPTURE. A Series of Sermons, *Crown 8vo.* 5s.
>
> THE CHARACTERS OF THE OLD TESTAMENT. *Crown 8vo.* 5s.
>
> THE APOCALYPSE. With Notes and Reflections. *Crown 8vo.* 5s.
>
> SERMONS ON THE EPISTLES AND GOSPELS FOR THE SUNDAYS AND HOLY DAYS. *Two Vols. Crown 8vo.* 5s. *each.*
>
> PLAIN SERMONS ON CATECHISM. *Two Vols. Cr. 8vo.* 5s. *each.*
>
> SELECTIONS FROM ISAAC WILLIAMS' WRITINGS. *Cr. 8vo.* 3s. 6d.
>
> THE AUTOBIOGRAPHY OF ISAAC WILLIAMS, B.D., Author of several of the 'Tracts for the Times.' Edited by the Venerable Sir GEORGE PREVOST, as throwing further light on the history of the Oxford Movement. *Crown 8vo.* 5s.

Wordsworth.—Works by the late CHRISTOPHER WORDSWORTH, D.D., Bishop of Lincoln.

THE HOLY BIBLE (the Old Testament). With Notes, Introductions, and Index. *Imperial 8vo.*
Vol. I. THE PENTATEUCH. 25s. Vol. II. JOSHUA TO SAMUEL. 15s. Vol. III. KINGS to ESTHER. 15s. Vol. IV. JOB TO SONG OF SOLOMON. 25s. Vol. V. ISAIAH TO EZEKIEL. 25s. Vol. VI. DANIEL, MINOR PROPHETS, and Index. 15s.
Also supplied in 12 Parts. Sold separately.

THE NEW TESTAMENT, in the Original Greek. With Notes, Introductions, and Indices. *Imperial 8vo.*
Vol. I. GOSPELS AND ACTS OF THE APOSTLES. 23s. Vol. II. EPISTLES, APOCALYPSE, and Indices. 37s.
Also supplied in 4 Parts. Sold separately.

LECTURES ON INSPIRATION OF THE BIBLE. *Small 8vo.* 1s. 6d. cloth. 1s. sewed.

A CHURCH HISTORY TO A.D. 451. *Four Vols. Crown 8vo.*
Vol. I. TO THE COUNCIL OF NICÆA, A.D. 325. 8s. 6d. Vol. II. FROM THE COUNCIL OF NICÆA TO THAT OF CONSTANTINOPLE. 6s. Vol. III. CONTINUATION. 6s. Vol. IV. CONCLUSION, TO THE COUNCIL OF CHALCEDON, A.D. 451. 6s.

THEOPHILUS ANGLICANUS: a Manual of Instruction on the Church and the Anglican Branch of it. *12mo.* 2s. 6d.

ELEMENTS OF INSTRUCTION ON THE CHURCH. *16mo.* 1s. cloth. 6d. sewed.

ST. HIPPOLYTUS AND THE CHURCH OF ROME. *Cr. 8vo.* 7s. 6d.

ON UNION WITH ROME. *Small 8vo.* 1s. 6d. *Sewed,* 1s.

THE HOLY YEAR: Original Hymns. *16mo.* 2s. 6d. *and* 1s. *Limp,* 6d.
" " With Music. Edited by W. H. MONK. *Square 8vo.* 4s. 6d

GUIDES AND GOADS. (An English Edition of 'Ethica et Spiritualia.' *32mo.* 1s. 6d.

MISCELLANIES, Literary and Religious. *Three Vols. 8vo.* 36s.

ON THE INTERMEDIATE STATE OF THE SOUL AFTER DEATH. *32mo.* 1s.

Younghusband.—Works by FRANCES YOUNGHUSBAND.

THE STORY OF OUR LORD, told in Simple Language for Children. With 25 Illustrations on Wood from Pictures by the Old Masters and numerous Ornamental Borders, Initial Letters, etc., from Longmans' New Testament. *Crown 8vo.* 2s. 6d.

THE STORY OF THE EXODUS, told in Simple Language for Children. With Map and 29 Illustrations. *Crown 8vo.* 2s. 6d.

www.ingramcontent.com/pod-product-compliance
Lightning Source LLC
Chambersburg PA
CBHW031421230426
43668CB00007B/387